Hands-On System Programming with C++

Build performant and concurrent Unix and Linux systems with C++17

Dr. Rian Quinn

BIRMINGHAM - MUMBAI

Hands-On System Programming with C++

Commissioning Editor: Richa Tripathi
Acquisition Editor: Shriram Shekhar
Content Development Editor: Tiksha Sarang
Technical Editor: Riddesh Dawne
Copy Editor: Safis Editing
Project Coordinator: Prajakta Naik
Proofreader: Safis Editing
Indexer: Tejal Daruwale Soni
Graphics: Jisha Chirayil
Production Coordinator: Arvindkumar Gupta

First published: December 2018

Production reference: 1211218

Published by Packt Publishing Ltd.
Livery Place
35 Livery Street
Birmingham
B3 2PB, UK.

ISBN 978-1-78913-788-0

www.packtpub.com

To my beautiful wife, Charmaine Quinn. Without her, this book would not have been possible.

– Dr. Rian Quinn

`mapt.io`

Mapt is an online digital library that gives you full access to over 5,000 books and videos, as well as industry leading tools to help you plan your personal development and advance your career. For more information, please visit our website.

Why subscribe?

- Spend less time learning and more time coding with practical ebooks and videos from over 4,000 industry professionals

- Improve your learning with skill plans designed especially for you

- Get a free eBook or video every month

- Mapt is fully searchable

- Copy and paste, print, and bookmark content

Packt.com

Did you know that Packt offers eBook versions of every book published, with PDF and ePub files available? You can upgrade to the eBook version at `www.packt.com` and, as a print book customer, you are entitled to a discount on the eBook copy. Get in touch with us at `customercare@packtpub.com` for more details.

At `www.packt.com`, you can also read a collection of free technical articles, sign up for a range of free newsletters, and receive exclusive discounts and offers on Packt books and eBooks.

Contributors

About the author

Dr. Rian Quinn is a Chief Technology Officer (CTO) in the Advanced Technologies Business Unit at Assured Information Security, Inc. focused on trusted computing, hypervisor related technologies, machine learning/artificial intelligence, and cyber security for more than 10 years and has 9 years of technical management and business development experience. He holds a Ph.D. in Computer Engineering, specializations in information assurance and computer architectures, from Binghamton University. He is the co-founder and lead developer of the Bareflank Hypervisor, and is an active member of several open source projects, including Microsoft's Guideline Support Library (GSL) and OpenXT.

About the reviewer

Will Brennan is a C++/Python software engineer based in London with experience of working on high-performance image processing and machine learning applications.

Packt is searching for authors like you

If you're interested in becoming an author for Packt, please visit `authors.packtpub.com` and apply today. We have worked with thousands of developers and tech professionals, just like you, to help them share their insight with the global tech community. You can make a general application, apply for a specific hot topic that we are recruiting an author for, or submit your own idea.

Table of Contents

Preface

With this book, we aim to provide you with an understanding of Linux/Unix system programming, a reference manual on Linux system calls, and an insider's guide to writing smarter, faster code using C++. The book will explain the differences between POSIX standard functions and special services offered by modern C++.

This book will also teach the reader about basic I/O operations, such as reading from, and writing to, files, advanced I/O interfaces, memory mappings, optimization techniques, thread concepts, multithreaded programming, POSIX threads, interfaces for allocating memory and optimizing memory access, basic and advanced signal interfaces, and their role on the system. This book will also explain clock management, including POSIX clocks and high-resolution timers. Finally, this book uses modern examples and references to provide up-to-date relevance to C++ and the wider community, including the Guideline Support Library and its role in system programming.

Who this book is for

This book is for beginner to advanced Linux and general UNIX programmers working with C++, or anyone looking for a general overview of Linux, C++17, and/or systems programming with POSIX, C, and C++. Although this book covers a lot of topics on modern C++, its focus is on system programming. It is expected that the reader already has a general familiarity with C and C++, as both will be leveraged throughout this book.

What this book covers

Chapter 1, *Getting Started with System Programming*, lays the foundation for the book, helping to define what system programming is by providing some basic examples and explaining the benefits of system programming with C++.

Chapter 2, *Learning the C, C++17, and POSIX Standards*, reviews the C, C++, and POSIX standards, providing an overview of the facilities provided by each standard with respect to system programming, as well as a general overview of the topics that will be discussed throughout this book.

Chapter 3, *System Types for C and C++*, provides a comprehensive overview of the system types that are provided by C and C++ and how they are used when carrying out system programming. This chapter will also discuss many of the pitfalls associated with the native types and how to overcome them.

Chapter 4, *C++, RAII, and the GSL Refresher*, provides a general overview of the additions provided by C++17. This chapter will also discuss the benefits of **Resource Acquisition Is Initialization** (**RAII**), and how to leverage it when carrying out system programming. This chapter will conclude with an overview of the Guideline Support Library, which is used throughout this book to help maintain C++ core guideline compliance.

Chapter 5, *Programming Linux/Unix Systems*, provides a comprehensive overview of programming on Linux /UNIX-based systems, including an overview of the System V specification, programming Linux processes, and Linux-based signals.

Chapter 6, *Learning to Program Console Input/Output*, provides a complete overview of how to leverage C++ to program console input and output, including `std::cout` and `std::cin`. More advanced topics, such as how to handle custom types, will also be discussed.

Chapter 7, *A Comprehensive Look at Memory Management*, provides a complete review of the memory management facilities provided by both C and C++. In this chapter, we will review the shortcomings of C and how modern C++ can be used to overcome many of these shortcomings.

Chapter 8, *Learning to Program File Input/Output*, reviews how to read and write to files using C++17 and compare these facilities to those provided by C. In addition, we will dive into the `std::filesystem` additions provided by C++17 for working with files and directories on disk.

Chapter 9, *A Hands-On Approach to Allocators*, covers C++ allocators and how they can be leveraged to perform system programming. Unlike most other attempts at describing C++ allocators, we will walk you through how to create multiple, real-world examples of stateful allocators, including a memory pool allocator, and demonstrate its potential performance benefits.

Chapter 10, *Programming POSIX Sockets Using C++*, provides an overview of how to program POSIX sockets (in other words, network programming) using C++ with a series of examples. In this chapter, we will also discuss some of the issues associated with POSIX sockets and how they can be overcome.

Chapter 11, *Time Interfaces in Unix*, provides a thorough overview of the time interfaces provided by both C and C++ and how they can be used together to deal with time while system programming, including how to use the interface for benchmarking.

Chapter 12, *Learning to Program POSIX and C++ Threads*, discusses the thread programming and synchronization facilities provided by both POSIX and C++ and how they interrelate. We will also provide a series of examples that demonstrate how to leverage these facilities.

Chapter 13, *Error - Handling with Exceptions*, covers both C and C++ error handling, including C and C++ exceptions. In this chapter, we will also walk through a series of examples that demonstrate the benefits of leveraging C++ exceptions over traditional C error handling.

To get the most out of this book

The reader should have a general knowledge of C and C++ and be capable of writing, compiling, and executing C and C++ applications on Linux. In order to execute the examples in this book, the reader should also have access to an Intel-based computer running Ubuntu Linux 17.10 or higher. The reader should also ensure that GCC 7.0 or higher is installed using the following:

```
sudo apt-get install build-essential
```

Download the example code files

You can download the example code files for this book from your account at www.packtpub.com. If you purchased this book elsewhere, you can visit www.packtpub.com/support and register to have the files emailed directly to you.

You can download the code files by following these steps:

1. Log in or register at www.packtpub.com.
2. Select the **SUPPORT** tab.
3. Click on **Code Downloads & Errata**.
4. Enter the name of the book in the **Search** box and follow the onscreen instructions.

Once the file is downloaded, please make sure that you unzip or extract the folder using the latest version of:

- WinRAR/7-Zip for Windows
- Zipeg/iZip/UnRarX for Mac
- 7-Zip/PeaZip for Linux

The code bundle for the book is also hosted on GitHub at `https://github.com/PacktPublishing/Hands-On-System-Programming-with-CPP/`. In case there's an update to the code, it will be updated on the existing GitHub repository.

We also have other code bundles from our rich catalog of books and videos available at `https://github.com/PacktPublishing/`. Check them out!

Conventions used

There are a number of text conventions used throughout this book.

`CodeInText`: Indicates code words in text, database table names, folder names, filenames, file extensions, pathnames, dummy URLs, user input, and Twitter handles. Here is an example: "For example, look at the difference between using an `std::array{}` or a `std::vector{}` command."

A block of code is set as follows:

```
int array[10];

auto r1 = array + 1;
auto r2 = *(array + 1);
auto r3 = array[1];
```

When we wish to draw your attention to a particular part of a code block, the relevant lines or items are set in bold:

```
int main()
{
    auto ptr1 = mmap_unique_server<int>(42);
    auto ptr2 = mmap_unique_client<int>();
    std::cout << *ptr1 << '\n';
    std::cout << *ptr2 << '\n';
}
```

Any command-line input or output is written as follows:

```
> cmake -DCMAKE_BUILD_TYPE=Release ..
> make
```

Bold: Indicates a new term, an important word, or words that you see on screen. For example, words in menus or dialog boxes appear in the text like this. Here is an example: "Select **System info** from the **Administration** panel."

Warnings or important notes appear like this.

Tips and tricks appear like this.

Get in touch

Feedback from our readers is always welcome.

General feedback: Email feedback@packtpub.com and mention the book title in the subject of your message. If you have questions about any aspect of this book, please email us at questions@packtpub.com.

Errata: Although we have taken every care to ensure the accuracy of our content, mistakes do happen. If you have found a mistake in this book, we would be grateful if you would report this to us. Please visit www.packtpub.com/submit-errata, selecting your book, clicking on the Errata Submission Form link, and entering the details.

Piracy: If you come across any illegal copies of our works in any form on the internet, we would be grateful if you would provide us with the location address or website name. Please contact us at `copyright@packtpub.com` with a link to the material.

If you are interested in becoming an author: If there is a topic that you have expertise ini and you are interested in either writing or contributing to a book, please visit `authors.packtpub.com`.

Reviews

Please leave a review. Once you have read and used this book, why not leave a review on the site that you purchased it from? Potential readers can then see and use your unbiased opinion to make purchase decisions, we at Packt can understand what you think about our products, and our authors can see your feedback on their book. Thank you!

For more information about Packt, please visit `packtpub.com`.

1
Getting Started with System Programming

In this chapter, we will discuss what system programming is (that is, the act of making system calls to the operating system to perform an action on your behalf), and go into the pros and cons of both system programming, and system programming with C++.

In this chapter, we will review the following:

- System calls, including what they are, how to execute them, and the potential security risks associated with them
- The benefits of using C++ when system programming

Technical requirements

In order to follow the examples in this chapter, the reader must have:

- A Linux-based system capable of compiling and executing C++17 (for example, Ubuntu 17.10+)
- GCC 7+
- CMake 3.6+
- An internet connection

Understanding system calls

An operating system is a piece of software designed to execute one or more applications simultaneously, while also providing the resources needed for those applications to execute. To accomplish this, the operating system must be capable of dividing hardware resources between all the applications executing on the system at the same time.

For example, most **personal computers** (**PCs**) have a single hard disk that stores all the files being used by the owner of the PC. On modern PCs, it's likely the user will want to execute several applications at once—for example, a web browser and an office suite.

Both of these applications will need exclusive access to the hard disk at various times while executing. In the case of the web browser, this might be to cache websites to disk, while in the case of the office suite, this might be to store documents.

It's the operating system's responsibility to manage the applications and their access to the hard disk, to ensure that both the web browser and the office suite are able to execute properly.

To accomplish this, operating systems provide an **application programming interface** (**API**) that applications can leverage to accomplish their tasks. Accessing the hard disk is an example of one of these tasks. The read() and write() functions are examples of APIs provided by POSIX-compliant operating systems for reading from and writing data to file descriptors.

Under the hood, these APIs make calls to the operating system using an **application binary interface** (**ABI**) called a **system call**. The act of making system calls to accomplish tasks provided by the operating system is called **system programming**, which is the main focus of this book.

The anatomy of a system call

For the purposes of this section, we will focus our examples on the Intel x86 architecture, although these examples apply to most other CPU architectures.

The original x86 architecture leveraged interrupts to provide system call ABIs. The APIs provided by the operating system would program specific registers on the CPU, and make a call to the operating system using an interrupt.

For example, using BIOS, an application could read data from a hard disk using int 0x13 with the following register layout:

- AH = 2
- AL: Sectors to read
- CH: Cylinder
- CL: Sector
- DH: Head
- DL: Drive
- ES:BX: Buffer address

The application author would use the read() API command to read this data, while under the hood, read() would perform the system call using the preceding ABI. When int 0x13 executed, the application would be paused by the hardware, and the operating system (in this case, BIOS) would execute on behalf of the application to read data from the disk and return the result in the buffer provided by the application.

Once complete, BIOS would execute iret (interrupt return) to return to the application, which would then have the data read from disk waiting in its buffer to be used.

With this approach, the application doesn't need to know how to physically interface with the hard disk on that specific computer in order to read data; a task that is meant to be handled by the operating system and its device drivers.

The application doesn't have to worry about other applications that may be executing either. It can simply leverage the provided API (or ABI, depending on the operating system), and the rest of the gory details are handled by the operating system.

In other words, system calls provide a clean delineation between applications, to help the user accomplish specific tasks, and to help the operating system whose job it is to manage these applications and the hardware resources they require.

Interrupts are, however, slow. The hardware makes no assumptions about how the operating system is written, or how the applications the operating system is executing are written or organized. For this reason, interrupts must save the CPU state before the interrupt handler is executed, and restore this state when the iret command is executed, leading to poor performance.

As will be shown, applications make a lot of system calls when attempting to perform their job, and this poor performance became a bottleneck on x86 architectures (as well as other CPU architectures).

To solve this issue, modern versions of Intel x86 CPU provided *fast system call* instructions. These instructions were designed specifically to address the performance bottleneck of interrupt-driven system calls. However, they require coordination between the CPU, the operating system, and the applications executing on that operating system to reduce overhead.

Specifically, the operating system must structure the memory layout of itself and the applications it's running in a specific way, dictated by the CPU. By predefining the memory layout of the operating system and its associated applications, the CPU no longer needs to save and restore as much CPU state when performing a system call, reducing overhead. How this is accomplished is different depending on whether you're executing on an Intel or AMD x86 CPU.

The most important thing to understand with respect to how a system call is performed is that a system call is not cheap. Even with fast system call support, a system call has to perform a lot of work. In the case of reading data from a hard disk via the `read()` API, the CPU register state must be set up and a system call instruction must be executed. CPU control is handed off to the operating system to read data from the disk.

Since more than one application might be executing, and attempting to read data from the disk at the same time, the operating system might have to pause the application so that it can service another.

Once the operating system is ready to service the application, it must first figure out what data the application is attempting to read, which ultimately determines which physical device it needs to work with. In our example, this is a hard disk, but on a POSIX-compliant system it could be any type of block device.

Next, the operating system must leverage one of its device drivers to read data from this disk. This takes time, as the operating system has to physically program the hard disk to ask for data from a specific location, over a hardware bus that almost certainly is not executing at the same speed as the CPU itself.

Once the hard disk finally provides the operating system with the requested data, the operating system can provide this information back to the application and return control, restoring the CPU state to the application. All of this insanity is obscured by a single call to `read()`.

For this reason, system calls should be executed sparingly, and only when absolutely needed, to prevent the poor performance of the resulting application.

It should be noted that this type of optimization requires a deep understanding of the APIs the application leverages, as higher-level APIs make their own system calls on the API's behalf. For example, allocating memory, as will be discussed later, is another type of system call.

For example, look at the difference between using an `std::array{}` or a `std::vector{}` command. `std::vector{}` supports resizing of the array being managed under the hood, which requires memory allocation. This can not only lead to memory fragmentation (a topic that will be discussed later on in this book), but also poor performance, as the memory allocation might have to ask the operating system for more system RAM.

Learning about different types of system calls

Almost every application that executes on a POSIX-compliant operating system must make a couple of system calls. Here, we outline some of the system call types that will be explored in this book.

Console input/output

If you have ever executed a command-line application, you willbe familiar with the concept of console-based input/output. This is especially true with respect to POSIX-compliant operating systems. When outputting to the console, you can either output to `stdout` (typically used for normal output) or `stderr` (typically used for outputting error messages).

Outputting to `stdout` and `stderr` is accomplished by an application performing a system that asks the operating system to deliver a character buffer to these output devices. (It should be noted that, in this book, we typically state that we are *outputting to* `stdout`, not *printing to the console*.)

The reason for this is that, on POSIX-compliant systems, your application doesn't actually know where it is sending the text to. The application leverages an API to output to `stdout`. This can be accomplished by:

- Writing to a dedicated file handle (that is, `stdout`)
- Using C APIs such as `printf`
- Using C++ APIs such as `std::cout`
- Forking an application that outputs to `stdout` for you (for example, by using `echo`)

Most of these examples, when all is said and done, make a system call to the operating system to transfer a character buffer to a device that manages stdout or stderr. In some cases, this causes the operating system to relay the resulting character buffer to the parent process (likely your shell), which will ultimately make another system call to display the character buffer on the screen.

However your operating system decides to handle this, a device driver exists in the operating system that manages the physical monitor used to display text, and the simple APIs the application calls to output text (for example, printf and std::cout) eventually provide this device driver with the requested character buffer.

Although, on most systems, the text being output to stdout is usually provided to your shell and eventually displayed on the screen, this doesn't have to be the case. Since the application is making a system call to output the character buffer, the operating system is free to forward this data to a serial device, log file, as input to another application, and so on.

This flexibility is one of the reasons POSIX-compliant operating systems are so powerful, and why learning how to properly make system calls is so important.

Memory allocation

Memory is another resource that an application must request using a system call. Most applications are given global and stack memory resources when the application is first executed, along with a small heap of memory that the application can use when calls to functions such as malloc() and free() are made.

If the application only uses the memory that it is initially given in this heap, no extra memory needs to be requested by the application. If, however, heap memory runs out, the application's malloc() or free() engine will have to ask the operating system (via a system call) for more memory.

To do this, the operating system will extend the end of the application by adding more physical memory to the application. The malloc() or free() engine is then able to make use of this additional memory, until more is needed.

On systems with limited RAM, when a request for additional memory is made, the operating system has to take memory from other applications that aren't currently executing. It does this by swapping these applications to disk, an operation that is expensive to perform.

For this reason, on resource-constrained systems, calls to `malloc()` or `free()` should not be made in time-critical code, as the time it takes to execute these functions can vary greatly.

We will go into further detail on memory management in Chapter 7, *A Comprehensive Look at Memory Management*.

File input/output

Reading and writing to a file is another common use case for most applications that requires making system calls.

It should be noted that on POSIX-compliant systems, reading and writing to a file descriptor doesn't always mean reading and writing to a file on a storage device. Instead, the system calls you make write to *character* or *block* devices. This could be a storage device, but could also be a console device, or even a virtual device such as /dev/random, which provides random data when read.

In Chapter 8, *Learning to Program File Input/Output*, we will provide more information about file input/output system programming.

Networking

Networking is another common use case that requires making system calls. On POSIX-compliant systems, we perform network-based system programming by working with POSIX sockets. Sockets provide an API for programming the **Network Interface Controller (NIC)**, and support logic (for example, the TCP/IP stack) within the operating system.

Networking itself is an extremely complicated topic, deserving of its own book, but thankfully, the system calls needed to perform this type of programming are simple, with the majority of the gory details being handled by the operating system.

In Chapter 10, *Programming POSIX Sockets Using C++*, we will go into further detail on how to make these types of system calls using the socket API.

Time

Some readers might find it surprising to know that even performing simple tasks such as getting the current date and time require system calls to ask the operating system for this information. Even to this day, a dedicated chip (with a battery, in case of loss of power) is provided on the system to maintain the current date and time.

If this information is needed, a system call must be made to request it. When this happens, the operating system will ask the device driver responsible for managing the chip what date and time it is currently storing, and then this information will be returned to the application.

It should be noted that not all time interfaces require system calls. For example, most high-resolution timers, which are designed to compare a high-resolution number before and after an operation has taken place, do not need the operating system to perform this action. This is because these high-resolution timers usually exist directly in the CPU, and their values can be extracted using a simple instruction.

The downside to these types of timers is that their values in and of themselves are usually meaningless (that is, the difference between the values returned is what provides meaning, not the values themselves). Essentially, these timers are usually nothing more than a counter that increments each time the CPU ticks (that is, executes an instruction).

Since modern CPUs can dynamically change their frequency, the values these counters store depends on how long the CPU has executed since the previous power cycle, and at what frequency the CPU was set while it was executing.

There isn't even a guarantee that the value in one counter will be the same as the value read in another counter on another physical core, as each physical core is capable of changing its own frequency independently of other cores on multi-core CPUs.

The benefit of high-resolution timers is that they can be executed extremely quickly (as you are just executing an instruction that reads a counter in the CPU). The difference between two measured values can be used to carry out tasks such as measuring how long it takes to execute small functions—a task that usually doesn't work with standard timers, as they don't have enough granularity.

In Chapter 11, *Time Interfaces in Unix*, we will go over these details and even provide an example of how to do this yourself.

Threading and process creation

Executing multiple tasks simultaneously can be accomplished by asking the operating system to create additional threads (or even new processes). This is a common task in system programming, and there are numerous system calls to get the job done.

A process is a unit of execution that has a set of resources assigned to it (for example, memory, file descriptors, and so on.) Each application is made up of at least one process, but they can contain more than one (for example, a shell is an application that is specifically designed to run several child processes).

Each process is scheduled by the operating system to execute for a limited amount of time before the next process is given access to the CPU, and this cycle continues as needed.

Threads are like processes, but they share the same resources as other threads of the same process. Threads provide an application with an opportunity to create tasks that are capable of executing in parallel, without the need for inter-process communication methods. In Chapter 12, *Learning to Program POSIX and C++ Threads*, we will learn how to program threads using both POSIX and C++ APIs.

System call security risks

System calls are not without their security risks. Even on modern hardware, and using CPU architectures other than Intel, executing more than one process within an operating system with full isolation between processes is nearly impossible.

Although modern hardware and modern operating systems work hard to provide the best possible isolation and security, it should always be assumed that other, malicious processes executing alongside yours may be able to spy on what you're doing, including sensitive tasks such as decrypting user data.

This is another topic that deserves its own book, but here, we will briefly discuss two different, recent security vulnerabilities that affect system programming.

SYSRET

The *fast system call* interface provided by Intel and AMD was not without its issues. As stated previously, for fast system calls to work, the hardware, operating system, and applications must coordinate. This is to ensure that ABI information is handled properly, to allow the operating system to execute a system call without the need for the hardware to save the entire CPU state before execution begins.

The same applies when the system call is complete, and control must be handed back to the application. To accomplish this, the operating system must load the application's stack, and then execute the SYSRET instruction, which returns control to the application.

The problem with this approach is that a **non-maskable interrupt** (**NMI**) could fire between the operating system loading the application's stack and the execution of SYSRET. The result of this race condition is that an NMI (which is code that executes with root privileges) would be executed using the application's stack and not the kernel's stack, resulting in a possible security vulnerability or corruption.

Thankfully, there are ways for modern operating systems to prevent this type of attack, which most operating systems, such as Linux, can and do leverage.

Meltdown and Spectre

The Meltdown and Spectre attacks are a modern examples of just how complicated system calls are to implement. To support the fast execution of system calls, the kernel's memory is mapped into each application using a memory layout technical called the 3:1 split, which refers to the three-to-one ratio of application memory to kernel memory.

To prevent an application from reading/writing kernel memory, which may or may not contain highly-sensitive information such as encryption keys and passwords, modern CPU architectures provide a mechanism to lock down the kernel portion of this memory, such that only the kernel is capable of seeing it all. The application is only able to see its deprivileged portion of that memory.

To improve the performance of these modern CPUs, most architectures, including Intel, AMD, and ARM, incorporate a technology called **speculative execution**. For example, look at the following code:

```
if (x) {
    do_y();
}

do_z();
```

The CPU doesn't know whether x is true or false until it executes this instruction. If the CPU assumes that x is true, it can enhance performance by saving some CPU cycles. If x does, in fact, end up being true, the CPU saves cycles, whereas if x is actually false, the penalty is usually worth the risk, especially if the CPU can make an educated guess as to the likelihood of x being true instead of false (for example, if the CPU executed this statement in the past and x was true).

This type of optimization is called *speculative execution*. The CPU is executing code, even though it's possible the code may later turn out to be invalid and need to be undone.

Speculative execution attacks such as Meltdown and Spectre exploit this process to bypass the memory protections that protect the system call interface between an application and its kernel. This is done by convincing the CPU to speculatively execute an instruction that would typically cause a security violation (for example, attempting to read a password from kernel memory).

If the CPU speculatively executes this type of instruction, there will be a gap between the CPU loading the password into the CPU's cache, and the CPU figuring out that a security violation has occurred. If the CPU is interrupted during this gap (using what is called a transient instruction), the password will be left in the CPU's cache, even though the instruction never actually completed its execution.

To recover the password from the cache, attackers leverage additional attacks on the CPU called **side-channel attacks**, which are specifically designed to read the contents of a CPU's cache without performing a direct memory operation.

The end result is that an attacker is capable of setting up an elaborate set of conditions that will eventually allow them to recover sensitive information stored in the kernel, using nothing more than an unprivileged application (which could be a website you happened to click on while looking for cat videos).

If this seems complicated, that's because it is. These types of attacks are extremely sophisticated. The goal of these examples is to provide a brief overview of why system calls are not without their issues. Depending on the CPU and operating system you're executing on, you might have to take special care when handling sensitive information while system programming.

Benefits of using C++ when system programming

Although the focus of this book is on system programming and not C++, and we do provide a lot of examples in C, there are several benefits to system programming in C++ compared to standard C.

Note that this section assumes some general knowledge of C++. A more complete explanation of the C++ standard will be provided in Chapter 2, *Learning the C, C++17, and POSIX Standards*.

Type safety in C++

Standard C is not a type-safe language. Type safety refers to protections put in place to prevent one type from being confused with another type. Some languages, such as ADA, are extremely type-safe, providing so many protections that the language, at times, can be frustrating to work with.

Conversely, languages such as C are so type-unsafe that hard-to-find type errors occur frequently, and often lead to instability.

C++ provides a compromise between the two approaches, encouraging reasonable type safety by default, while providing mechanisms to circumvent this when needed.

For example, consider the following code:

```
/* Example: C */
int *p = malloc(sizeof(int));

// Example: C++
auto p = new int;
```

Allocating an integer on the heap in C requires the use of `malloc()`, which returns `void *`. There are several issues with this code that are addressed in C++:

- C automatically converts the `void *` type to `int *`, meaning that an implicit type conversion has occurred even though there is no connection between the type the user stated and the type returned. The user could easily allocate `short` (which is not the same thing as `int`, a topic we will discuss in Chapter 3, *System Types for C and C++*). The type conversion would still be applied, meaning that the compiler would not have the proper context to detect that the allocation was not large enough for the type the user was attempting to allocate.
- The size of the allocation must be stated by the programmer. Unlike C++, C has no understanding of the type that is being allocated. Thus, it is unaware of the size of the type, and so the programmer must explicitly state this. The problem with this approach is that hard-to-find allocation bugs can be introduced. Often, the type that is provided to `sizeof()` is incorrect (for example, the programmer might provide a pointer instead of the type itself, or the programmer might change the code later on, but forget to change the value being provided to `sizeof()`). As stated previously, there is no connection between what `malloc()` allocates and returns, and the type the user attempts to allocate, providing an opportunity to introduce a hard-to-find logic error.

- The type must be explicitly stated twice. `malloc()` returns `void *`, but C implicitly converts to whatever pointer type the user states—which means a type has been declared twice (in this case, `void *` and `int *`). In C++, the use of `auto` means that the type is only declared once (in this case, `int` states the type is an `int *`), and `auto` will take on whatever type is returned. The use of `auto` and the removal of implicit type conversions means whatever type is declared in the allocation is what the `p` variable will take on. If the code after this allocation expects a different type to the one `p` takes on, the compiler will know about it at compile time in C++, while a bug like this would likely not be caught in C until runtime, when the program crashes (we hope this code is not controlling an airplane!).

In addition to the preceding example of the dangers of implicit type casting, C++ also provides **run-time type information** (**RTTI**). This information has many uses, but the most important use case involves the `dynamic_cast<>` operator, which performs runtime type checking.

Specifically, converting from one type to another can be checked during runtime, to ensure a type error doesn't occur. This is often seen when performing the following:

- **Polymorphic type conversions**: In C, polymorphism is possible, but it must be done manually, a pattern that is seen often in kernel programming. C, however, doesn't have the ability to determine whether a pointer was allocated for a base type or not, resulting in the potential for a type error. Conversely, C++ is capable of determining at runtime whether a provided pointer is being cast to the proper type, including when using polymorphism.
- **Exception support**: When catching an exception, C++ uses RTTI (essentially `dynamic_cast<>`), to ensure that the exception being thrown is caught by the proper handler.

Objects of C++

Although C++ supports object-oriented programming with built-in constructs, object-oriented programming is a design pattern that is often used in C as well, and in POSIX in general. Take the following example:

```
/* Example: C */

struct point
{
    int x;
```

```
        int y;
};

void translate(point *p; int val)
{
    if (p == NULL) {
        return;
    }

    p->x += val;
    p->y += val;
}
```

In the preceding example, we have a struct that stores a point{}, which contains x and y positions. We then offer a function that is capable of translating this point{} in both the x and y positions, using a given value (that is, a diagonal translation).

There are a couple of notes with respect to this example:

- Often, people will claim to dislike object-oriented programming, but then you see this sort of thing in their code, which is, in fact, an object-oriented design. The use of class isn't the only way to create an object-oriented design. The difference with C++ is that the language provides additional constructs for cleanly and safely working with objects, while with C this same functionality must be done by hand—a process that is prone to error.
- The translate() function is only related to the point{} object because it takes a point{} as a parameter. As a result, the compiler has no contextual information to understand how to manipulate a point{} struct, without translate() being given a pointer to it as a parameter. This means that every single public-facing function that wishes to manipulate a point{} struct must take a pointer to it as its first parameter, and verify that the pointer is valid. Not only is this a clunky interface, it's slow.

In C++, the preceding example can be written as the following:

```
// Example: C++

struct point
{
    int x;
    int y;

    void translate(int val)
    {
        p->x += val;
```

```
        p->y += val;
    }
};
```

In this example, a struct is still used. The only difference between a class and a struct in C++ is that all variables and functions are public by default with a struct, while they are private by default with a class.

The difference is that the `translate()` function is a member of `point{}`, which means it has access to the contents of its structure, and so no pointers are needed to perform the translation. As a result, this code is safer, more deterministic, and easier to reason about, as there is never the fear of a null dereference.

Finally, objects in C++ provide construction and destruction routines that help prevent objects from not being properly initialized or properly deconstructed. Take the following example:

```
// Example: C++

struct myfile
{
    int fd{0};

    ~myfile() {
        close(fd);
    }
};
```

In the preceding example, we create a custom file object that holds a file descriptor, often seen and used when system programming with POSIX APIs.

In C, the programmer would have to remember to manually set the file descriptor to 0 on initialization, and close the file descriptor when it is no longer in scope. In C++, using the preceding example, both of these operations would be done for you any time you use `myfile`.

This is an example of the use of **Resource Acquisition Is Initialization (RAII)**, a topic that will be discussed in more detail in Chapter 4, *C++, RAII, and the GSL Refresher*, as this pattern is used a lot by C++. We will leverage this technique when system programming to avoid a lot of common POSIX-style pitfalls.

Templates used in C++

Template programming is often an undervalued, misunderstood addition to C++ that is not given enough credit. Most programmers need to look no further than attempting to create a generic linked list to understand why.

C++ templates provides you with the ability to define your code without having to define type information ahead of time.

One way to create a linked list in C is to use pointers and dynamic memory allocation, as seen in this simple example:

```
struct node
{
    void *data;
    node next;
};

void add_data(node *n, void *val);
```

In the preceding example, we store data in the linked list using void *. An example of how to use this is as follows:

```
node head;
add_data(&head, malloc(sizeof(int)));
*(int*)head.data = 42;
```

There are a few issues with this approach:

- This type of linked list is clearly not type-safe. The use of the data and the data's allocation are completely unrelated, requiring the programmer using this linked list to manage all of this without error.
- A dynamic memory allocation is needed for both the nodes and the data. As was discussed earlier, memory allocations are slow as they require system calls.
- In general, this code is hard to read and clunky.

Another way to create a generic linked list is to use macros. There are several implementations of these types of linked lists (and other data structures) floating around on the internet, which provide a generic implementation of a linked list without the need for dynamically allocating data. These macros provide the user with a way to define the data type the linked list will manage at compile time.

The problem with these approaches, other than reliability, is these implementations use macros to implement template programming in a way that is far less elegant. In other words, the solution to adding generic data structures to C is to use C's macro language to manually implement template programming. The programmer would be better off just using C++ templates.

In C++, a data structure like a linked list can be created without having to declare the type the linked list is managing until it is declared, as follows:

```
template<typename T>
class mylinked_list
{
    struct node
    {
        T data;
        node *next;
    };

public:

    . . .

private:

    node m_head;
};
```

In the preceding example, not only are we able to create a linked list without macros or dynamic allocations (and all the problems that come with the use of void * pointers), but we are also able to encapsulate the functionality, providing a cleaner implementation and user API.

One complaint that is often made about template programming is the amount of code it generates. Most code bloat from templates typically originates as a programming error. For example, a programmer might not realize that integers and unsigned integers are not the same types, resulting in code bloat when templates are used (as a definition for each type is created).

Even aside from that issue, the use of macros would produce the same code bloat. There is no free lunch. If you want to avoid the use of dynamic allocation and type casting while still providing generic algorithms, you have to create an instance of your algorithm for each type you plan to use. If reliability is your goal, allowing the compiler to generate the code needed to ensure your program executes properly outweighs the disadvantages.

Functional programming associated with C++

Functional programming is another addition to C++ that provides the user with compiler assistance, in the form of lambda functions. Currently, this must be carried out by hand in C.

In C, a functional programming construct can be achieved using a callback. For example, consider the following code:

```
void
guard(void (*ptr)(int *val), int *val)
{
    lock();
    ptr(val);
    unlock();
}

void
inc(int *val)
{
    *val++;
}

void
dec(int *val)
{
    *val--;
}

void
foo()
{
    int count = 0;
    guard(inc, &count);
    guard(dec, &count);
}
```

In the preceding code example, we create a `guard` function that locks a mutex, calls a function that operates on a value, and then unlocks the mutex on exit. We then create two functions, one that increments a value given to it, and one that decrements a value given to it. Finally, we create a function that instantiates a count, and then increments the count and decrements the count using the guard function.

There are a couple of issues with this code:

- The first issue is the need for pointer logic to ensure we can manipulate the variable we wish to operate on. We are also required to manually pass this pointer around to keep track of it. This makes the APIs clunky, as we have a lot of extra code that we have to write manually for such a simple example.
- The function signature of the helper functions is static. The guard function is a simple one. It locks a mutex, calls a function, and then unlocks it. The problem is that, since the parameters of the function must be known while writing the code instead of at compile time, we cannot reuse this function for other tasks. We will need to hand-write the same function for each function signature type we plan to support.

The same example can be written using C++ as follows:

```
template<typename FUNC>
guard(FUNC f)
{
    lock();
    f();
    unlock();
}

void
foo()
{
    int count = 0;
    guard(inc, [&]{ count++ });
    guard(inc, [&]{ count-- });
}
```

In the preceding example, the same functionality is provided, but without the need for pointers. In addition, the guard function is generic and can be used for more than one case. This is accomplished by leveraging both template programming and functional programming.

The lambda provides the callback, but the parameters of the callback are encoded into the lambda's function signature, which is absorbed by the use of a template function. The compiler is capable of generating a version of the guard function for use that takes the parameters (in this case, a reference to the count variable) and storing it in the code itself, removing the need for users to do this by hand.

The preceding example will be used a lot in this book, especially when creating benchmarking examples, as this pattern gives you the ability to wrap functionality in code designed to time the execution of your callback.

Error handling mechanism in C++

Error handling is another issue with C. The problem, at least until set jump exceptions were added, was that the only ways to get an error code from a function were as follows:

- Constrain the output of a function, so that certain output values from the function could be considered an error
- Get the function to return a structure, and then manually parse that structure

For example, consider the following code:

```
struct myoutput
{
    int val;
    int error_code;
}

struct myoutput myfunc(int val)
{
    struct myoutput = {0};

    if (val == 42) {
        myoutput.error_code = -1;
    }

    myoutput.val = val;
    return myoutput;
}

void
foo(void)
{
    struct myoutput = myfunc(42);

    if (myoutput.error_code == -1) {
        printf("yikes\n");
        return;
    }
}
```

The preceding example provides a simple mechanism for outputting an error from a function without having to constrain the output of the function (for example, by assuming that -1 is always an error).

In C++, this can be implemented using the following C++17 logic:

```
std::pair<int, int>
myfunc(int val)
{
    if (val == 42) {
        return {0, -1};
    }

    return {val, 0};
}

void
foo(void)
{
    if (auto [val, error_code] = myfunc(42); error_code == -1) {
        printf("yikes\n");
        return;
    }
}
```

In the preceding example, we were able to remove the need for a dedicated structure by leveraging `std::pair{}`, and we were able to remove the need to work with `std::pair{}` by leveraging an `initializer_list{}` and C++17-structured bindings.

There is, however, an even easier method for handling errors without the need for checking the output of every function you execute, and that is to use exceptions. C provides exceptions through the set jump API, while C++ provides C++ exception support. Both of these will be discussed at length in Chapter 13, *Error - Handling with Exceptions*.

APIs and C++ containers in C++

As well as the language primitives that C++ provides, it also comes with a **Standard Template Library** (**STL**) and associated APIs that greatly aid system programming. A good portion of this book will focus on these APIs, and how they support system programming.

It should be noted that the focus of this book is system programming and not C++, and for this reason, we do not cover C++ containers in any detail, but instead assume the reader has some general knowledge of what they are and how they work. With that said, C++ containers support system programming by preventing the user from having to re-write them manually.

We teach students how to write their own data structures, not so that when they need a data structure they know how to write one, but instead so that, when they need one, they know which data structure to use and why. C++ already provides most, if not all, of the data structures you might need when system programming.

Summary

In this chapter, we learned what system programming is. We covered the general anatomy of a system call, different types of system calls, and some recent security issues with system calls.

In addition, we covered the advantages of system programming with C++ instead of strictly using standard C. In the next chapter, we will cover the C, C++, and POSIX standards in detail and how they relate to system programming.

Questions

1. What is system programming?
2. Prior to *fast system calls*, how were system calls executed?
3. What key change was made to support *fast system calls*?
4. Does allocating memory always result in a system call?
5. What type of execution do the Meltdown and Spectre attacks exploit?
6. What is type safety?
7. Provide at least one benefit to template programming in C++?

Further reading

- https://www.packtpub.com/application-development/c17-example
- https://www.packtpub.com/application-development/getting-started-c17-programming-video

2
Learning the C, C++17, and POSIX Standards

As stated in Chapter 1, *Getting Started with System Programming*, system programming is the act of making system calls to perform various actions in coordination with the underlying operating system. Each operating system has its own set of system calls, and how these system calls are made is different.

To prevent the system programmer from having to rewrite their program for each different operating system, several standards have been put into place that wrap the operating system's ABI with a well-defined API.

In this chapter, we will discuss three standards—the C standard, the C++ standard, and the POSIX standard. The C and POSIX standards provide the fundamental language syntax and APIs that wrap an operating system's ABI. Specifically, the C standard defines program linking and execution, the standard C syntax (which a number of higher-level languages, such as C++, are based on), and the C libraries that provide the ABI-to-API wrappers.

The C libraries can be thought of as a subset of the greater POSIX standard, which defines a much larger subset of APIs, including, but not limited to, filesystem, network, and threading libraries.

Finally, the C++ standard defines the C++ syntax, program linking and execution, and the C++ libraries that provide higher-level abstractions of the C and POSIX standards. The majority of this book will revolve around these standard APIs and how to use them with C++17.

This chapter has the following objectives:

- Learning about the C, C++, and POSIX standards
- Understanding program linking and execution, and the differences between C and C++
- Providing a brief overview of the facilities these standards provide, each of which will be discussed in greater detail later in the book

Technical requirements

In order to follow the examples in this chapter, the reader must have:

- A Linux-based system capable of compiling and executing C++17 (for example, Ubuntu 17.10+)
- GCC 7+
- CMake 3.6+
- An internet connection

To download all the code in this chapter, including the examples and code snippets, go to the following link: https://github.com/PacktPublishing/Hands-On-System-Programming-with-CPP/tree/master/Chapter02.

Beginning with the C standard language

The C programming language is one of the oldest languages available. Unlike other higher-level languages, C is similar enough to assembly language programming, while still providing some high-level programming abstractions, that it has become a firm favorite among system, embedded, and kernel-level programmers alike.

Almost every major operating system is rooted in C. In addition, most higher-level languages, including C++, build upon C to provide their higher-level constructs, and therefore still require some of the components of the C standard.

The C standard is a huge standard that is managed by the **International Organization for Standardization** (**ISO**). We assume the reader has some basic knowledge of the C standard and how to write C code: http://www.open-std.org/jtc1/sc22/wg14/www/docs/n1256.pdf.

For these reasons, the goal of this section is to discuss some topics that are discussed in lesser detail in other books, as well as portions of the C standard that are relevant to this book and system programming, but are missing from the other chapters.

For additional information on the C programming language and how to write C programs, please see the *Further reading* section of this chapter.

How the standard is organized

The specification is broken up into three sections:

- Environment
- Language
- Libraries

Let's briefly discuss the purpose of each section. After that, we will discuss specific portions of the C standard that are relevant to system programming but are not discussed elsewhere in this book.

Environment

The Environment section of the standard provides information that is mainly needed by compiler writers to better understand how to create a compiler for C.

It describes the minimum limitations the compiler must adhere to (such as the minimum number of nested `if()` statements that must be supported), as well as how programs are linked and started.

In this chapter, we will discuss program linking and execution to provide a better understanding of what is required to create a C program.

Language

The Language section of the standard provides all the details associated with the C syntax, including what a variable is, how to write a function, the difference between a `for()` loop and a `while()` loop, and all of the operators that are supported and how they work.

This book assumes the reader has general knowledge of this section of the standard, and only touches on system programming-specific nuances of the standard C syntax that the reader is likely to run into (such as issues associated with pointers).

Libraries

The Libraries section of the standard describes all of the library facilities that are provided by the standard C language. This includes facilities such as outputting strings to `stdout`, allocating memory, and working with time.

System programming largely revolves around these library facilities, and the bulk of this book will focus on these libraries, what they provide, and how to use them.

How a C program starts

One part of the standard that is relevant to system programming, but is not as widely discussed in literature, is how a C program starts. A common misconception is that a C program starts with the following two entry points:

```
int main(void) {}
int main(int argc, char *argv[]) {}
```

Although this is, in fact, the first function call that a C programmer provides, it is not the first function called when your C program starts. It is not the first code that executes either, nor is it the first code provided by the user that executes.

A lot of work is carried out, both by the operating system and the standard C environment, as well as the user, prior to the `main()` function ever executing.

Let's look at how your compiler creates a simple `Hello World\n` example:

```
#include <stdio.h>

int main(void)
{
    printf("Hello World\n");
}
```

To better understand the start up process of a C program, let's look at how this simple program is compiled:

```
> gcc -v scratchpad.c; ./a.out

Using built-in specs.
COLLECT_GCC=gcc
COLLECT_LTO_WRAPPER=/usr/lib/gcc/x86_64-linux-gnu/7/lto-wrapper
OFFLOAD_TARGET_NAMES=nvptx-none
OFFLOAD_TARGET_DEFAULT=1
Target: x86_64-linux-gnu
```

```
Configured with: ...
...
```

By adding the –v option to GCC, we are able to see each step the compiler takes to compile our simple `Hello World\n` program.

To start, the compiler converts the program to a format that can be processed by `gnu-as`:

```
/usr/lib/gcc/x86_64-linux-gnu/7/cc1 -quiet -v -imultiarch x86_64-linux-gnu
scratchpad.c -quiet -dumpbase scratchpad.c -mtune=generic -march=x86-64 -
auxbase scratchpad -version -fstack-protector-strong -Wformat -Wformat-
security -o /tmp/ccMSWHgC.s
```

Not only can you see how the initial compilation is performed, but you can see the default flags that your operating system provides.

Next, the compiler converts the output to an object file, as follows:

```
/usr/bin/x86_64-linux-gnu-as -v --64 -o /tmp/cc9oaJWV.o /tmp/ccMSWHgC.s
```

Finally, the last step links the resulting object files into a single executable using the `collect2` utility, which is a wrapper around the linker:

```
/usr/lib/gcc/x86_64-linux-gnu/7/collect2 -plugin /usr/lib/gcc/x86_64-linux-
gnu/7/liblto_plugin.so -plugin-opt=/usr/lib/gcc/x86_64-linux-gnu/7/lto-
wrapper -plugin-opt=-fresolution=/tmp/ccWQB2Gf.res -plugin-opt=-pass-
through=-lgcc -plugin-opt=-pass-through=-lgcc_s -plugin-opt=-pass-through=-
lc -plugin-opt=-pass-through=-lgcc -plugin-opt=-pass-through=-lgcc_s --
sysroot=/ --build-id --eh-frame-hdr -m elf_x86_64 --hash-style=gnu --as-
needed -dynamic-linker /lib64/ld-linux-x86-64.so.2 -pie -z now -z relro
/usr/lib/gcc/x86_64-linux-gnu/7/../../../x86_64-linux-gnu/Scrt1.o
/usr/lib/gcc/x86_64-linux-gnu/7/../../../x86_64-linux-gnu/crti.o
/usr/lib/gcc/x86_64-linux-gnu/7/crtbeginS.o -L/usr/lib/gcc/x86_64-linux-
gnu/7 -L/usr/lib/gcc/x86_64-linux-gnu/7/../../../x86_64-linux-gnu -
L/usr/lib/gcc/x86_64-linux-gnu/7/../../../../lib -L/lib/x86_64-linux-gnu -
L/lib/../lib -L/usr/lib/x86_64-linux-gnu -L/usr/lib/../lib -
L/usr/lib/gcc/x86_64-linux-gnu/7/../../.. /tmp/cc9oaJWV.o -lgcc --push-
state --as-needed -lgcc_s --pop-state -lc -lgcc --push-state --as-needed -
lgcc_s --pop-state /usr/lib/gcc/x86_64-linux-gnu/7/crtendS.o
/usr/lib/gcc/x86_64-linux-gnu/7/../../../x86_64-linux-gnu/crtn.o
```

There are a couple of important things to take note of here with respect to how the program is linked:

- `-lc`: The use of this flag tells the linker to link in `libc`. Like the rest of the libraries being discussed here, we didn't tell the compiler to link against `libc`. By default, GCC links `libc` for us.
- `-lgcc_s`: This is a static library that is linked automatically by GCC to provide support for compiler-specific operations including 64-bit operations on a 32-bit CPU, and facilities such as exception unwinding (a topic that will be discussed in `Chapter 13`, *Error - Handling with Exceptions*).
- `Scrt1.o`, `crti.o`, `crtbeginS.o`, `crtendS.o`, and `crtn.o`: These libraries provide the code needed to start and stop your application.

Specifically, the **C run-time libraries** (**CRT**) libraries are the libraries of interest here. These libraries provide the code that is needed to bootstrap the application, including:

- Executing global constructors and destructors (as GCC supports constructors and destructors in C, even though this is not a standard C facility).
- Setting up unwinding to support exception supporting. Although this is mainly needed for C++ exceptions, which are not needed in a standard C-only application, they are still needed for linking in the set jump exception logic, a topic that will be explained in `Chapter 13`, *Error - Handling with Exceptions*.
- Providing the `_start` function, which is the actual entry point to any C-based application using a default GCC compiler.

Finally, all these libraries are responsible for providing the `main()` function with the arguments that are passed to it, as well as intercepting the return value of the `main()` function, and executing the `exit()` function on your behalf, as needed.

The most important takeaway here is that the first piece of code to execute in your program is not the `main()` function, and if you register a global constructor, it is not the first piece of code that you provide that executes either. While system programming, if you experience issues with the initialization of your program, this is where to look first.

All about linking

Linking is an extremely complex topic that varies from operating system to operating system. For example, Windows links programs quite differently to Linux. For this reason, we will limit our discussion to Linux.

When a C source file is compiled, it is compiled into what is called an **object file**, which contains the compiled source code with each function that is defined in the program in a binary format, as follows:

```
> gcc -c scratchpad.c; objdump -d scratchpad.o

...

0000000000000000 <main>:
   0: 55 push %rbp
   1: 48 89 e5 mov %rsp,%rbp
   4: 48 8d 3d 00 00 00 00 lea 0x0(%rip),%rdi # b <main+0xb>
   b: e8 00 00 00 00 callq 10 <main+0x10>
  10: b8 00 00 00 00 mov $0x0,%eax
  15: 5d pop %rbp
  16: c3 retq
```

As shown here, the compiler creates an object file, which contains the compiler (that is, binary) version of the source code. An important note here is that that the main() function is labeled *main*, in plain text.

Let's expand this example to include another function:

```
int test(void)
{
    return 0;
}

int main(void)
{
    return test();
}
```

Compiling this source, we get the following:

```
> gcc -c scratchpad.c; objdump -d scratchpad.o

...

0000000000000000 <test>:
   0: 55 push %rbp
   1: 48 89 e5 mov %rsp,%rbp
   4: b8 00 00 00 00 mov $0x0,%eax
   9: 5d pop %rbp
   a: c3 retq

000000000000000b <main>:
   b: 55 push %rbp
```

```
   c: 48 89 e5 mov %rsp,%rbp
   f: e8 00 00 00 00 callq 14 <main+0x9>
  14: 5d pop %rbp
  15: c3 retq
```

As shown here, each function that is compiled is labeled using the same name as the function. That is, the name of each function is not *mangled* (unlike in C++). Name mangling will be explained in further detail in the next section, as well as why this is important with respect to linking.

Going beyond a simple source file, a C program is split into groups of source files that are compiled and linked together. Specifically, an executable is the combination of object files and libraries. Libraries are a combination of additional object files, divided into two different types:

- **Static libraries**: libraries that are linked at compile time
- **Dynamic libraries**: libraries that are linked at load time

Static libraries

Static libraries are a collection of object files that are linked at compile time. In Linux (and most UNIX-based systems), static libraries are nothing more than an archive of object files. You can easily take an existing static library and use the AR tool to extract the original object files.

Unlike object files that are linked as part of your program, object files that are linked as part of a static library only include the source code needed by that static library, providing optimization that removes unused code from your program, ultimately reducing the total size of your program.

The downside to this approach is that the order in which a program is linked using static libraries matters. If a library is linked before the code that needs the library is provided (on the command line, that is), a link error will occur, as the code from the static library will be optimized out.

Libraries provided by the operating system usually do not support static linking either, and, typically, static linking of operating system libraries is not needed as those libraries are likely to have been loaded into memory by your operating system.

Dynamic libraries

Dynamic libraries are libraries that are linked at load time. Dynamic libraries are more like executables without an entry point. They contain code needed by your program, and the load-time linker is responsible for providing the location of each required function to your program while your program is being loaded.

It is also possible for your program to link itself while it executes during runtime as an optimization, only linking functions that are needed (a process known as **lazy loading**).

Most of the libraries provided by the operating system are dynamic libraries. To see which dynamic libraries are needed by your program, you can use the LDD tool, as follows:

```
> ldd a.out
  linux-vdso.so.1 (0x00007ffdc5bfd000)
  libc.so.6 => /lib/x86_64-linux-gnu/libc.so.6 (0x00007f92878a0000)
  /lib64/ld-linux-x86-64.so.2 (0x00007f9287e93000)
```

In this example, we used the LDD tool to list the dynamic libraries needed by our simple `Hello World\n` example. As shown, the following libraries are needed:

- `vdso`: a library provided by the operating system to speed up the process of making system calls
- `libc`: the standard C library
- `ld-linux-x86-64`: the dynamic linker itself, responsible for lazy-loading

Scope

One addition to the C language that distinguishes it dramatically from assembly language programming is the use of *scope*. In assembly, a function prefix and postfix must be hand-coded, and the process for doing this depends entirely on the **instruction set architecture (ISA)** your CPU provides, and the ABI the programmer decides to use.

In C, the scope of a function is defined automatically for you using the `{}` syntax. For example:

```c
#include <stdio.h>

int main(void)
{
    printf("Hello World\n");
}
```

In our simple `Hello World\n` example, scope is used to define the start and end of our `main()` function. The scope of other primitives can also be defined using the `{}` syntax. For example:

```
#include <stdio.h>

int main(void)
{
    int i;

    for (i = 0; i < 10; i++) {
        printf("Hello World: %d\n", i);
    }
}
```

In the previous example, we define the scope of both our `main()` function and our `for()` loop.

The `{}` syntax can also be used to create *scope* for anything. For example:

```
#include <stdio.h>

int main(void)
{
    {
        int i;
        ...
    }

    {
        int i;
        ...
    }
}
```

In the previous example, we are able to use the `i` variable twice without accidentally redefining it, because we wrapped the definition of `i` in a `{}`. Not only does this tell the compiler the scope of `i`, it also tells the compiler to automatically create a prefix and postfix for us if they are needed (as optimizations can remove the need for a prefix and postfix).

Scope is also used to define what the compiler exposes with respect to linking. In standard C, the `static` keyword tells the compiler that a variable is only visible (that is, scoped) to the object file it is being compiled to, providing not only an optimization to the linker, but also preventing two global variables or functions from colliding with each other.

For this reason, if a function is not intended to be called by another source file (or library), it should be labeled static.

In the context of system programming, scope is important because system programming typically requires the acquisition of system-level resources. As will be seen in Chapter 4, *C++, RAII, and the GSL Refresher*, C++ provides the ability to create objects whose life can be scoped using standard C { } syntax, providing a safe mechanism for resource acquisition and release.

Pointers and arrays

In school, I had a teacher who once told me:

"No matter how experienced you are, nobody truly understands pointers completely."

No statement could be truer. In standard C, a pointer is a variable whose value points to a location in memory. The problem with standard C is that this location in memory is not associated with a particular type. Instead, the pointer type itself defines the type of memory the pointer is pointing to, as in the following example:

```
int main(void)
{
    int i;
    int *p = &i;
}

// > gcc scratchpad.c; ./a.out
```

In the previous example, we created an integer, and then created a pointer and pointed it at the previously-defined integer. We could, however, do the following:

```
int main(void)
{
    int i;
    void *p = &i;

    int *int_p = p;
    float *float_p = p;
}

// > gcc scratchpad.c; ./a.out
```

In this program, we create a pointer to an integer, but we define the pointer type as `void *`, which tells the compiler we are creating a pointer with no type. We then create two additional pointers—a pointer to an integer, and a pointer to a floating point number. Both of these additional pointers are initialized using the `void *` pointer we created earlier.

The problem with this example is that the standard C compiler is performing automatic type casting, changing a `void *` into both an integer pointer and a floating point number pointer. If both of these pointers were used, corruption would occur in a couple of ways:

- Depending on the architecture, a buffer overflow could occur, as an integer could be larger than a float and vice versa. It depends on the CPU being used; a topic that will be discussed in more detail in `Chapter 3`, *System Types for C and C++*.
- Under the hood, an integer and a floating point number are stored differently in the same memory, meaning any attempt to set one value would corrupt the other.

Thankfully, modern C compilers have flags that are capable of detecting this type of type casting error, but these warnings must be enabled as they are not on by default, as shown previously.

The obvious issue with pointers is not just that they can point to anything in memory and redefine that memory's meaning, but that they can also take on a null value. In other words, pointers are considered optional. They either optionally contain a valid value and point to memory, or they are null.

For this reason, pointers should not be used until their value is determined to be valid, as follows:

```c
#include <stdio.h>

int main(void)
{
    int i = 42;
    int *p = &i;

    if (p) {
        printf("The answer is: %d\n", *p);
    }
}

// > gcc scratchpad.c; ./a.out
// The answer is: 42
```

In the previous example, we create a pointer to an integer that is initialized with the location of a previously-defined integer with an initial value of 42. We check to make sure p is not a null pointer, and then output its value to stdout.

The addition of the if() statement is not only cumbersome—it isn't performant. For this reason, most programmers would leave out the if() statement, knowing that, in this example, p is never a null pointer.

The problem with this is, at some point, the programmer could add code to this simple example that contradicts this assumption, while simultaneously forgetting to add the if() statement, resulting in code that has the potential to generate a hard-to-find segmentation fault.

As will be shown in the next section, the C++ standard addresses this issue by introducing the notion of a *reference*, which is a non-optional pointer, meaning it is a pointer that must always point to a valid, typed, memory location. To address this issue in standard C, null pointer checks are usually (although not always) checked by public-facing APIs. Private APIs typically do not check for null pointers to improve performance, making the assumption, that so long as the public-facing API cannot accept a null pointer, it's likely the private API will never see an invalid pointer.

Standard C arrays are similar to pointers. The only difference is that a C array leverages a syntax capable of indexing into the memory pointed to by a pointer, as in the following example:

```
#include <stdio.h>

int main(void)
{
    int i[2] = {42, 43};
    int *p = i;

    if (p) {
        // method #1
        printf("The answer is: %d and %d\n", i[0], p[0]);
        printf("The answer is: %d and %d\n", i[1], p[1]);

        // method #2
        printf("The answer is: %d and %d\n", *(i + 0), *(p + 0));
        printf("The answer is: %d and %d\n", *(i + 1), *(p + 1));
    }
}

// > gcc scratchpad.c; ./a.out
// The answer is: 42 and 42
```

```
// The answer is: 43 and 43
// The answer is: 42 and 42
// The answer is: 43 and 43
```

In the previous example, we create an array of integers with 2 elements initialized to the values 42 and 43. We then create a pointer that points to the array. Note that the & is no longer needed. This is because the array is a pointer, thus, we are simply setting one pointer to the value of another (instead of having to extract a pointer from an existing memory location).

Finally, we print the value of each element in the array using both the array itself and the pointer to the array using pointer arithmetic.

As will be discussed in Chapter 4, *C++, RAII, and the GSL Refresher*, there is little difference between an array and a pointer. Both perform what is known as **pointer arithmetic** when an attempt is being made to access an element in an array.

With respect to system programming, pointers are used extensively. Examples include the following:

- Since standard C doesn't contain the notion of a *reference* as C++ does, system APIs that must be passed by a reference because they are too large to be passed by a value, or must be modified by the API, must be passed by a pointer, resulting in the heavy use of pointers when making system calls.
- System programming often involves interacting with pointers to a location in memory, designed to define the layout of that memory. Pointers provide a convenient way to accomplish this.

Libraries

Standard C not only defines a syntax, the environment, and how programs are linked, it also provides a set of libraries that may be leveraged by a programmer to perform system programming. Some of these libraries are as follows:

- errno.h: Provides the code needed for working with errors. This library will be discussed in further detail in Chapter 13, *Error - Handling with Exceptions*.
- inttypes.h: Provides type information, which will be discussed in Chapter 3, *System Types for C and C++*.
- limits.h: Provides information about the limits of each type, which will be discussed in Chapter 3, *System Types for C and C++*.

- `setjump.h`: Provides the APIs for C-style exception handling, which will be discussed in Chapter 13, *Error - Handling with Exceptions*.
- `signal.h`: Provides APIs for handling signals sent from the system to your program, which will be discussed in Chapter 5, *Programming Linux/Unix Systems*.
- `stdbool.h`: Provides type information, which will be discussed in Chapter 3, *System Types for C and C++*.
- `stddef.h`: Provides type information, which will be discussed in Chapter 3, *System Types for C and C++*.
- `stdint.h`: Provides type information, which will be discussed in Chapter 3, *System Types for C and C++*.
- `stdio.h`: Provides functions for working with input and output while system programming, which will be discussed in Chapter 6, *Learning to Program Console Input/Output*, and Chapter 8, *Learning to Program File Input/Output*.
- `stdlib.h`: Provides various utilities, including dynamic memory allocation APIs, which will be discussed in Chapter 7, *A Comprehensive Look at Memory Management*.
- `time.h`: Provides facilities for working with clocks, which will be discussed in Chapter 11, *Time Interfaces in Unix*.

As stated previously, the bulk of this book will focus on these facilities and how they support system programming.

Learning about the C++ standard

The C++ programming language (originally called C with Classes) was designed specifically to provide higher-level facilities than C, including better type safety and object-oriented programming, with system programming in mind. Specifically, C++ aims to provide the performance and efficiency of C programs, while still providing the features of higher-level languages.

Today, C++ is one of the most popular programming languages in the world, used in everything from avionics to banking.

Like the C standard, the C++ standard is huge and is managed by the ISO. We assume the reader has some basic knowledge of the C++ standard and how to write C code: http://www.open-std.org/jtc1/sc22/wg21/docs/papers/2017/n4713.pdf.

For these reasons, the goal of this section is to discuss some topics that are discussed in lesser detail in other books, as well as portions of the C++ standard that are relevant to this book and system programming but are missing from the other chapters. Please see the *Further reading* section of this chapter for additional information on the C++ programming language, and how to write C++ programs.

How the standard is organized

Like the C standard specification, the C++ specification is broken up into three major groups of sections:

- General conventions and concepts
- Language syntax
- Libraries

It should be noted that the C++ standard is considerably larger than the C standard.

General conventions and concepts

The first four sections in the standard are dedicated to conventions and concepts. They define types, program start-up and shutdown, memory, and linking. They also outline all of the definitions and keywords that are needed to understand the rest of the specification.

As in the standard C specification, there are a lot of things defined in these sections that are important to system programmers, as they define what the compiler will output when a program is compiled, and how that program will be executed.

Language syntax

The next 12 sections in the specification define the C++ language syntax itself. This includes C++ features such as classes, overloading, templates, and exception handling. There are entire books written on just these sections of the specification.

We assume the reader has a general understanding of C++ and we do not go over this part of the specification in the book, except the C++17-specific modifications in `Chapter 4`, *C++, RAII, and the GSL Refresher*.

Libraries

The remaining 14 sections in the specification define the libraries that C++ provides as part of the specification. It should be noted that the bulk of this book revolves around this part of the specification.

Specifically, we discuss in great detail the facilities that C++ provides for system programmers, and how to use those facilities in practice.

Linking C++ applications

As in C, C++ applications typically start from a `main()` function with the same signatures that C already provides. Also, as in C programs, the actual entry point of the code is actually the `_start` function.

Unlike in C, however, C++ is far more complicated, including a lot more code for a simple example. To demonstrate this, let's look at a simple `Hello World\n` example:

```
#include <iostream>

int main(void)
{
    std::cout << "Hello World\n";
}

// > g++ scratchpad.cpp; ./a.out
// Hello World
```

First and foremost, the C++ application example is slightly longer than the equivalent C example from the previous section:

```
> gcc scratchpad.c -o c_example
> g++ scratchpad.cpp -o cpp_example
> stat -c "%s %n" *
8352 c_example
8768 cpp_example
```

If we look at the symbols in our example, we get the following:

```
> nm -gC cpp_example
                 U __cxa_atexit@@GLIBC_2.2.5
                 w __cxa_finalize@@GLIBC_2.2.5
00000000000008f4 T _fini
0000000000000688 T _init
00000000000007fa T main
```

```
00000000000006f0 T _start
                 U std::ios_base::Init::Init()@@GLIBCXX_3.4
                 U std::ios_base::Init::~Init()@@GLIBCXX_3.4
0000000000201020 B std::cout@@GLIBCXX_3.4
                 U std::basic_ostream<char, std::char_traits<char> >&
std::operator<< <std::char_traits<char> >(std::basic_ostream<char,
std::char_traits<char> >&, char const*)@@GLIBCXX_3.4

...
```

As previously stated, our program contains a `main()` function and a `_start()` function. The `_start()` function is the actual entry point of the application, while the `main()` function is called by the `_start()` function after initialization has completed.

The `_init()` and `_fini()` functions are responsible for global construction and destruction. In the case of our example, the `_init()` function creates the code needed by the C++ library to support `std::cout`, while the `_fini()` function is responsible for destroying these global objects. To do this, the global objects register with the `__cxa_atexit()` function, and are eventually destroyed using the `__cxa_finalize()` function.

The rest of the symbols make up the code for `std::cout`, including references to `ios_base{}` and `basic_ostream{}`.

The important thing to note here is that, as in C, there is a lot of code that executes both before and after the `main()` function, and using global objects in C++ only adds to the complexity of starting and stopping your application.

In the preceding example, we use the `_C` option to demangle our function names. Let's look at the same output with this option:

```
> nm -gC cpp_example
                 U __cxa_atexit@@GLIBC_2.2.5
                 w __cxa_finalize@@GLIBC_2.2.5
00000000000008f4 T _fini
0000000000000688 T _init
00000000000007fa T main
00000000000006f0 T _start
                 U _ZNSt8ios_base4InitC1Ev@@GLIBCXX_3.4
                 U _ZNSt8ios_base4InitD1Ev@@GLIBCXX_3.4
0000000000201020 B _ZSt4cout@@GLIBCXX_3.4
                 U
_ZStlsISt11char_traitsIcEERSt13basic_ostreamIcT_ES5_PKc@@GLIBCXX_3.4

...
```

As shown, some of these functions are still readable, while others are not. Specifically, the C++ specification dictates that certain support functions are linked using C linkage, preventing mangling. In our example, this includes the __cxa_xxx() functions, _init(), _fini(), main(), and _start().

The C++ library functions that support std::cout, however, are managed with an almost unreadable syntax. On most POSIX-compliant systems, these mangled names can be demangled using the c++filt command, as follows:

```
> c++filt _ZSt4cout
std::cout
```

These names are mangled because they contain the entire function signature in their name, including the arguments and specializations (for example, the noexcept keyword). To demonstrate this, let's create two function overloads:

```
void test(void) {}
void test(bool b) {}

int main(void)
{
    test();
    test(false);
}

// > g++ scratchpad.cpp; ./a.out
```

In the previous example, we created two functions with the same name, but with different function signatures, a process known as **function overloading**, which is specific to C++.

Now let's look at the symbols in our test application:

```
> nm -g a.out
...

0000000000000601 T _Z4testb
00000000000005fa T _Z4testv
```

There are a couple of reasons why function names are mangled in C++:

- Encoding function arguments in the function's name means functions can be overloaded, and the compiler and the linker will know which function does what. Without name mangling, two functions with the same name but different arguments would look identical to the linker, and errors would occur.
- By encoding this type of information in the function name, the linker is able to identify whether a function for a library was compiled using a different signature. Without this information, it would be possible for the linker to link, for example, a library compiled with a different signature (and therefore a different implementation) to the same function name, which would lead to a hard-to-find error, and likely corruption.

The biggest issue with C++ name mangling is that small changes to a public-facing API result in a library no longer being able to link with already-existing code.

There are many ways to overcome this problem, but, in general, it's simply important to understand that C++ encodes a lot of information about how you write your code in a function's name, making it imperative that public-facing APIs do not change unless a version change is expected.

Scope

One major difference between C and C++ is how the construction and destruction of an object is handled. Let's take the following example:

```cpp
#include <iostream>

struct mystruct {
    int data1{42};
    int data2{42};
};

int main(void)
{
    mystruct s;
    std::cout << s.data1 << '\n';
}

// > g++ scratchpad.cpp; ./a.out
// 42
```

Unlike in C, in C++ we are able to use the { } operator to define how we would like the data values of the structure to be initialized. This is possible because, in C++, objects (both structures and classes) contain constructors and destructors that define how the object is initialized on construction and destroyed on destruction.

When system programming, this scheme will be used extensively, and the idea of the construction and destruction of objects will be leveraged throughout this book when handling system resources. Specifically, a scope will be leveraged to define the lifetime of an object, and thus the system resource that the object owns, using a concept called **Resource Acquisition is Initialization (RAII)**.

Pointers versus references

In the previous section, we discussed pointers in length, including how pointers can take on two values—valid or null (assuming corruption is not part of the equation).

The problem with this is that the user must check whether the pointer is valid or not. This is normally not an issue when using pointers to define the contents of memory (for example, laying out memory using a data structure), but often, pointers in C must be used simply to reduce the overhead of passing a large object to a function, as in the following example:

```cpp
struct mystruct {
    int data1{};
    int data2{};
    int data3{};
    int data4{};
    int data5{};
    int data6{};
    int data7{};
    int data8{};
};

void test(mystruct *s)
{
}

int main(void)
{
    mystruct s;
    test(&s);
}

// > g++ scratchpad.cpp; ./a.out
```

In the previous example, we create a structure that has eight variables in it. Passing this type of structure with a value would result in the use of the stack (that is, several memory accesses). It is far more efficient to pass this structure with a pointer in C to reduce the cost of passing the structure to a single register, likely removing all memory accesses entirely.

The problem is that, now, the test function must check to make sure the pointer is valid before it can use it. Therefore, the function trades a set of memory accesses for a branch statement and possible pipeline flush in the CPU, when all we are trying to do is reduce the cost of passing a large object to a function.

As stated in the previous section, the solution is to simply not verify the validity of the pointer. In C++, however, we have another option, and that is to pass the structure with a reference, as follows:

```cpp
struct mystruct {
    int data1{};
    int data2{};
    int data3{};
    int data4{};
    int data5{};
    int data6{};
    int data7{};
    int data8{};
};

void test(mystruct &s)
{
}

int main(void)
{
    mystruct s;
    test(s);
}

// > g++ scratchpad.cpp; ./a.out
```

In the previous example, our `test()` function takes a reference to `mystruct{}` instead of a pointer. When we call the `test()` function, there is no need to get the address of the structure, as we are not using a pointer.

C++ references will be leveraged heavily throughout this book, as they greatly increase both the performance and stability of a program, especially while system programming, where resources, performance, and stability are critical.

Libraries

C++ not only defines the basic environment and language syntax—it also provides a set of libraries that may be leveraged by a programmer to perform system programming. These include the following:

- **Console input/output libraries**: These include the iostream, iomanip, and string libraries, which provide the ability to work with strings, format them, and output them (or grab input from the user). We will discuss most of these libraries in Chapter 6, *Learning to Program Console Input/Output.*
- **Memory management libraries**: These include the memory library, which contains memory management utilities that help to prevent dangling pointers. They will be discussed in Chapter 7, *A Comprehensive Look at Memory Management.*
- **File input/output libraries**: These include the fstream and filesystem (new to C++17) libraries, which will be discussed in Chapter 8, *Learning to Program File Input/Output.*
- **Time libraries**: These include the chrono library, which will be discussed in Chapter 11, *Time Interfaces in Unix.*
- **Threading libraries**: These include the thread, mutex, and conditional_variable libraries, which will be discussed in Chapter 12, *Learn to Program POSIX and C++ Threads.*
- **Error-handling libraries**: These include the exception support libraries, which will be discussed in Chapter 13, *Error - Handling with Exceptions*

Beginning with the POSIX standard

The POSIX standard defines all of the functionality a POSIX-compliant operating system must implement. With respect to system programming, the POSIX standard defines the system call interface (that is, the APIs, not the ABIs) that the operating system must support.

Under the hood, most of the system-level APIs that C and C++ provide actually execute POSIX functions, or are POSIX functions themselves (as is this case with a lot of C library APIs). In fact, libc is generally considered to be a subset of the greater POSIX standard, while C++ leverages libc and POSIX to implement its higher-level APIs such as threading, memory management, error handling, file operations, and input/output. For more information, refer to https://ieeexplore.ieee.org/document/8277153/.

In this section, we will discuss some components of the POSIX standard that are relevant to system programming. All of these topics will be discussed in further detail in later chapters.

Memory management

All of the memory management functions that `libc` provides are considered POSIX APIs as well. In addition, there are some POSIX-specific memory management functions that `libc` doesn't provide, such as aligned memory.

For example, the following demonstrates how to allocate aligned dynamic (heap) memory using POSIX:

```
#include <iostream>

int main()
{
    void *ptr;

    if (posix_memalign(&ptr, 0x1000, 42 * sizeof(int))) {
        std::clog << "ERROR: unable to allocate aligned memory\n";
        ::exit(EXIT_FAILURE);
    }

    std::cout << ptr << '\n';
    free(ptr);
}

// > g++ -std=c++17 scratchpad.cpp; ./a.out
// 0x55c5d31d1000
```

In this example, we use the `posix_memalign()` function to allocate an array of 42 integers, which is aligned to a page. This is a POSIX-specific function.

In addition, we leverage the `std::clog()` function to output an error to `stderr`, which, under the hood, leverages POSIX-specific functions for outputting character strings to `stderr`. We also use `::exit()`, which is a `libc` and POSIX function for exiting an application.

Finally, we leverage both the `std::cout()` and `free()` functions. `std::cout()` uses POSIX functions to output character strings to `stdout`, while `free()` is both a `libc` and POSIX-specific function for freeing up memory.

In this simple example, we are leveraging several C, C++, and POSIX-specific functionalities to perform system programming. Throughout this book, we will discuss how to leverage POSIX heavily to program the system to accomplish specific tasks.

Filesystems

POSIX not only defines how to read and write a file from a POSIX-compliant operating system, it also defines where files should be located on the filesystem. In Chapter 8, *Learning to Program File Input/Output*, we will go into great detail about how to read and write to a filesystem using C, C++, and POSIX.

With respect to the layout of the filesystem, POSIX defines where files should be located, including common folders such as the following:

- /bin: for binaries used by all users
- /boot: for files needed to boot the operating system
- /dev: for physical and virtual devices
- /etc: for configuration files needed by the operating system
- /home: for user-specific files
- /lib: for libraries needed by executables
- /mnt and /media: used as temporary mount points
- /sbin: for system-specific binaries
- /tmp: for files that are deleted on reboot
- /usr: for user-specific versions of the preceding folders

Sockets

To perform networking on a POSIX-compliant operating system, you need to leverage the POSIX sockets API. The socket programming interface provided by POSIX is a good example of a set of APIs that is provided by neither C nor C++, but is needed for networking on POSIX-compliant operating systems.

In Chapter 10, *Programming POSIX Sockets Using C++*, we will discuss how to perform networking using the POSIX sockets API, while leveraging C++. Specifically, we will show how C++ can be leveraged to simplify the implementation of socket-based networking, and provide several examples of how to perform networking.

Threading

Threads provide a system programmer with a means to perform parallel execution. Specifically, a thread is a unit of execution that the operating system schedules when it deems appropriate. Both C++ and POSIX provide APIs for working with threads, with the C++ APIs arguably being easier to work with.

It should be noted that, under the hood, C++ leverages the POSIX threads library (pthreads)—so, even though C++ provides a set of APIs for working with threads, in the end, POSIX threads are responsible for threading in all cases.

The reason for this is simple. POSIX defines the interface a program leverages to talk to the operating system. In this case, if you wish to tell the operating system to create a thread, you must do so by leveraging the APIs defined by the operating system. If the operating system is POSIX-compliant, those interfaces are POSIX, regardless of any abstractions that might be put in place to make working with the APIs easier.

Summary

In this chapter, we learned about three different standards: C, C++, and POSIX. The C standard defines the popular C syntax, C-style program linking and execution, and the standard C libraries that provide cross-platform APIs to wrap an operating system's ABIs.

We also learned about the C++ standard, and how it defines the C++ syntax, program linking and execution, and the high-level C++ APIs that wrap underlying C and POSIX APIs to C++.

Finally, we saw how the POSIX standard provides additional APIs that go beyond C. These APIs include (but are not limited to) memory management, networking, and threading. In general, the POSIX standard defines all the standards needed for an application to perform its functions in a cross-platform way on any POSIX-compliant operating system.

The remainder of this book will focus on the APIs defined in these standards, and how they can be used to perform system programming in C++17. In the next chapter specifically, we will cover the system types provided by C, C++, and POSIX, and how they affect system programming.

Questions

1. Is the C standard part of the POSIX standard? If so, name an API that is common to both standards.
2. What is the difference between the _start() and main() functions?
3. List one of the responsibilities of the C runtime?
4. Are global constructors executed before or after the main() function?
5. What is C++ name mangling, and why is it needed?
6. Name one difference between C and C++ program linking.
7. What is the difference between a pointer and a reference?

Further reading

- https://www.packtpub.com/application-development/c17-example
- https://www.packtpub.com/application-development/getting-started-c17-programming-video

System Types for C and C++ 3

With a system program, simple things, such as integer types, become complicated. This entire chapter is devoted toward common problems that arise when performing system programming, especially when performing system programming for multiple CPU architectures, operating systems, and user space/kernel communications, such as system calls.

This chapter consists of the following topics:

- An explanation of the default types that C and C++ provide, including types that most programmers are familiar with, such as `char` and `int`
- A review of some of the standard integer types provided by `stdint.h` to address limitations with the default types
- Structure packing and the complications associated with optimizations and type conversions

Technical requirements

To compile and execute the examples in this chapter, the reader must have the following:

- A Linux-based system capable of compiling and executing C++17 (for example, Ubuntu 17.10+)
- GCC 7+
- CMake 3.6+
- An internet connection

To download all of the code in this chapter, including the examples and code snippets, please go to the following link: `https://github.com/PacktPublishing/Hands-On-System-Programming-with-CPP/tree/master/Chapter03`.

Exploring C and C++ default types

The C and C++ languages come with several built-in types that come with the language, without the need for additional header files or language features. In this section, we will be discussing the following:

- `char`, `wchar_t`
- `short int`, `int`, `long int`
- `float`, `double`, `long double`
- `bool` (C++ only)

Character types

The most basic type in C and C++ is the following character type:

```cpp
#include <iostream>

int main(void)
{
    char c = 0x42;
    std::cout << c << '\n';
}

// > g++ scratchpad.cpp; ./a.out
// B
```

A `char` is an integer type that, on most platforms, is 8 bits in size, and must be capable of taking on the value range of [0, 255] for unsigned, and [-127, 127] for signed. The difference between a `char` and the other integer types is that a `char` has a special meaning, corresponding with the **American Standard Code for Information Interchange** (**ASCII**). In the preceding example, the uppercase letter B is represented by the 8-bit value `0x42`. It should be noted that although a `char` can be used to simply represent an 8-bit integer type, its default meaning is a character type; that's why it has a special meaning. For example, consider the following code:

```cpp
#include <iostream>

int main(void)
{
    int i = 0x42;
    char c = 0x42;

    std::cout << i << '\n';
```

```
        std::cout << c << '\n';
}

// > g++ scratchpad.cpp; ./a.out
// 66
// B
```

In the previous example, we represented the same integer type, 0x42, using both an int (to be explained later) and a char. These two values are, however, output to stdout in two different ways. The integer is output as an integer while, using the same APIs, the char is output as its ASCII representation. In addition, arrays of char types are considered to be an ASCII string type in both C and C++, which also has a special meaning. The following code shows this:

```
#include <iostream>

int main(void)
{
    const char *str = "Hello World\n";
    std::cout << str;
}

// > g++ scratchpad.cpp; ./a.out
// Hello World
```

From the preceding example, we understand the following. We define an ASCII string using a char pointer (an unbounded array type would also work in this case); std::cout understands how to handle this type by default, and a char array has a special meaning. Changing the array type to an int would not compile, as the compiler would not know how to convert the string to an array on integers, and std::cout would not know, by default, how to handle the array of integers, even though, on some platforms, an int and a char might actually be the same type.

Like a bool and short int, the character type is not always the most efficient type to use when representing an 8-bit integer, and as alluded to in the previous code, on some platforms, it is possible for a char to actually be larger than 8 bits, a topic that will be discussed in further detail when we discuss integers.

To further investigate the char type, as well as the other types being discussed in this section, let's leverage the std::numeric_limits{} class. This class provides a simple wrapper around limits.h, which provides us with a means to query how a type is implemented on a given platform in real time using a collection of static member functions.

For example, consider the following code:

```cpp
#include <iostream>

int main(void)
{
    auto num_bytes_signed = sizeof(signed char);
    auto min_signed = std::numeric_limits<signed char>().min();
    auto max_signed = std::numeric_limits<signed char>().max();

    auto num_bytes_unsigned = sizeof(unsigned char);
    auto min_unsigned = std::numeric_limits<unsigned char>().min();
    auto max_unsigned = std::numeric_limits<unsigned char>().max();

    std::cout << "num bytes (signed): " << num_bytes_signed << '\n';
    std::cout << "min value (signed): " << +min_signed << '\n';
    std::cout << "max value (signed): " << +max_signed << '\n';

    std::cout << '\n';

    std::cout << "num bytes (unsigned): " << num_bytes_unsigned << '\n';
    std::cout << "min value (unsigned): " << +min_unsigned << '\n';
    std::cout << "max value (unsigned): " << +max_unsigned << '\n';
}

// > g++ scratchpad.cpp; ./a.out
// num bytes (signed): 1
// min value (signed): -128
// max value (signed): 127

// num bytes (unsigned): 1
// min value (unsigned): 0
// max value (unsigned): 255
```

In the preceding example, we leverage `std::numeric_limits{}` to tell us the min and max value for both a signed and unsigned `char` (it should be noted that all examples in this book were performed on a standard Intel 64-bit CPU, and it is assumed that these same examples can, in fact, be executed on different platforms for which the values being returned might be different). The `std::numeric_limits{}` class can provide real-time information about a type, including the following:

- Signed or unsigned
- Conversion limits, such as rounding and the total number of digits needed to represent the type
- Min and max information

As shown in the preceding example, a `char` on a 64-bit Intel CPU is 1 byte in size (that is, 8 bits), and takes on the values [0, 255] for an unsigned `char` and [-127, 127] for a signed `char`, as stated by the specification. Let's look at a wide `char` or `wchar_t`:

```
#include <iostream>

int main(void)
{
    auto num_bytes_signed = sizeof(signed wchar_t);
    auto min_signed = std::numeric_limits<signed wchar_t>().min();
    auto max_signed = std::numeric_limits<signed wchar_t>().max();

    auto num_bytes_unsigned = sizeof(unsigned wchar_t);
    auto min_unsigned = std::numeric_limits<unsigned wchar_t>().min();
    auto max_unsigned = std::numeric_limits<unsigned wchar_t>().max();

    std::cout << "num bytes (signed): " << num_bytes_signed << '\n';
    std::cout << "min value (signed): " << +min_signed << '\n';
    std::cout << "max value (signed): " << +max_signed << '\n';

    std::cout << '\n';

    std::cout << "num bytes (unsigned): " << num_bytes_unsigned << '\n';
    std::cout << "min value (unsigned): " << +min_unsigned << '\n';
    std::cout << "max value (unsigned): " << +max_unsigned << '\n';
}

// > g++ scratchpad.cpp; ./a.out
// num bytes (signed): 4
// min value (signed): -2147483648
// max value (signed): 2147483647

// num bytes (unsigned): 4
// min value (unsigned): 0
// max value (unsigned): 4294967295
```

A `wchar_t` represents Unicode characters and its size depends on the operating system. On most Unix-based systems, a `wchar_t` is 4 bytes, and can represent a UTF-32 character type, as shown in the previous example, while on Windows, a `wchar_t` is 2 bytes in size, and can represent a UTF-16 character type. Executing the previous example on either of these operating systems will result in a different output.

This is extremely important, and this issue defines the fundamental theme of this entire chapter; the default types that C and C++ provide are different depending on the CPU architecture, the operating system, and in some cases, if the application is running in user space or in the kernel (for example, when a 32-bit application is executing on a 64-bit kernel). Never assume, while system programming, that when interfacing with a system call, that your application's definition of a specific type is the same as the type the API assumes. Quite often, this assumption will prove to be invalid.

Integer types

To further explain how the default C and C++ types are defined by their environment, and not by their size, let's look at the integer types. There are three main integer types—short int, int, and long int (excluding long long int, which on Windows is actually a long int).

A short int is typically smaller than an int, and on most platforms, represents 2 bytes. For example, go through the following code:

```cpp
#include <iostream>

int main(void)
{
    auto num_bytes_signed = sizeof(signed short int);
    auto min_signed = std::numeric_limits<signed short int>().min();
    auto max_signed = std::numeric_limits<signed short int>().max();

    auto num_bytes_unsigned = sizeof(unsigned short int);
    auto min_unsigned = std::numeric_limits<unsigned short int>().min();
    auto max_unsigned = std::numeric_limits<unsigned short int>().max();

    std::cout << "num bytes (signed): " << num_bytes_signed << '\n';
    std::cout << "min value (signed): " << min_signed << '\n';
    std::cout << "max value (signed): " << max_signed << '\n';

    std::cout << '\n';

    std::cout << "num bytes (unsigned): " << num_bytes_unsigned << '\n';
    std::cout << "min value (unsigned): " << min_unsigned << '\n';
    std::cout << "max value (unsigned): " << max_unsigned << '\n';
}

// > g++ scratchpad.cpp; ./a.out
// num bytes (signed): 2
// min value (signed): -32768
```

```
// max value (signed): 32767

// num bytes (unsigned): 2
// min value (unsigned): 0
// max value (unsigned): 65535
```

As shown in the previous example, the code gets the min, max, and size of both a signed `short int` and an unsigned `short int`. The results of this code demonstrates that on an Intel 64-bit CPU running Ubuntu, a `short int`, whether it is signed or unsigned, returns a 2 byte representation.

Intel CPUs provide an interesting advantage over other CPU architectures, as an Intel CPU is known as a **complex instruction set computer** (**CISC**), meaning that the Intel **instruction set architecture** (**ISA**) provides a long list of complicated instructions, designed to provide both compilers and by-hand authors of Intel assembly with advanced features. Among these features is the ability for an Intel processor to perform **arithmetic logic unit** (**ALU**) operations (including memory-based operations) at the byte level, even though most Intel CPUs are either 32-bit or 64-bit. Not all CPU architectures provide this same level of granularity.

To explain this better, let's look at the following example involving a `short int`:

```cpp
#include <iostream>

int main(void)
{
    short int s = 42;

    std::cout << s << '\n';
    s++;
    std::cout << s << '\n';
}

// > g++ scratchpad.cpp; ./a.out
// 42
// 43
```

In the previous example, we take a `short int`, set it to the value `42`, output this value to `stdout` using `std::cout`, increment the `short int` by `1`, and then output the result to `stdout` using `std::cout` again. This is a simple example, but under the hood, a lot is occurring. In this case, a 2 byte value, executing on a system that contains 8 byte (that is, 64 bit) registers must be initialized to `42`, stored in memory, incremented, and then stored in memory again to be output to `stdout`. All of these operations must involve CPU registers to perform these actions.

On an Intel-based CPU (either 32-bit or 64-bit), these operations likely involve the use of the 2 byte versions of the CPU's registers. Specifically, Intel's CPUs might be 32-bit or 64-bit, but they provide registers that are 1, 2, 4, and 8 bytes in size (specifically on 64-bit CPUs). In the previous example, this means that the CPU loads a 2 byte register with 42, stores this value to memory (using a 2 byte memory operation), increments the 2 byte register by 1, and then stores the 2 byte register back into memory again.

On a **reduced instruction set computer** (**RISC**), this same operation might be far more complicated, as 2 byte registers do not exist. To load, store, increment, and store again only 2 bytes of data would require the use of additional instructions. Specifically, on a 32 bit CPU, a 32 bit value would have to be loaded into a register, and when this value is stored in memory, the upper 32 bit (or lower, depending on alignment) would have to be saved and restored to ensure that only 2 bytes of memory were actually being affected. The additional alignment checks, that is, memory reading, masking, and storing, would result in a substantial performance impact if a lot of operations were taking place.

For this reason, C and C++ provide the default `int` type, which typically represents a CPU register. That is, if the architecture is 32 bit, an `int` is 32 bit and vice versa (with the exception of 64 bit, which will be explained shortly). It should be noted that CISC architectures, such as Intel, are free to implement ALU operations with granularity smaller than the CPU's register size however they wish, which means that under the hood, the same alignment checks and masking operations could still be taking place. The take home point is that unless you have a very specific reason to use a `short int` (for which there are a few reasons to do so; a topic we will discuss at the end of this chapter), instead of an `int`, an `int` type is, in most cases, more efficient than using a smaller type; even if you don't need a full 4 or 8 bytes, it's still faster.

Let's look at the `int` type:

```
#include <iostream>

int main(void)
{
    auto num_bytes_signed = sizeof(signed int);
    auto min_signed = std::numeric_limits<signed int>().min();
    auto max_signed = std::numeric_limits<signed int>().max();

    auto num_bytes_unsigned = sizeof(unsigned int);
    auto min_unsigned = std::numeric_limits<unsigned int>().min();
    auto max_unsigned = std::numeric_limits<unsigned int>().max();

    std::cout << "num bytes (signed): " << num_bytes_signed << '\n';
    std::cout << "min value (signed): " << min_signed << '\n';
    std::cout << "max value (signed): " << max_signed << '\n';
```

```
    std::cout << '\n';

    std::cout << "num bytes (unsigned): " << num_bytes_unsigned << '\n';
    std::cout << "min value (unsigned): " << min_unsigned << '\n';
    std::cout << "max value (unsigned): " << max_unsigned << '\n';
}

// > g++ scratchpad.cpp; ./a.out
// num bytes (signed): 4
// min value (signed): -2147483648
// max value (signed): 2147483647

// num bytes (unsigned): 4
// min value (unsigned): 0
// max value (unsigned): 4294967295
```

In the previous example, an `int` is showing as 4 bytes on a 64 bit Intel CPU. The reason for this is backward compatibility, meaning that on some RISC architectures, the default register size, resulting in the most efficient processing, might not be an `int` but rather a `long int`. The problem is that to determine this in real time is painful (as the instructions being used are done so at compile-time). Let's look at the `long int` to explain this further:

```
#include <iostream>

int main(void)
{
    auto num_bytes_signed = sizeof(signed long int);
    auto min_signed = std::numeric_limits<signed long int>().min();
    auto max_signed = std::numeric_limits<signed long int>().max();

    auto num_bytes_unsigned = sizeof(unsigned long int);
    auto min_unsigned = std::numeric_limits<unsigned long int>().min();
    auto max_unsigned = std::numeric_limits<unsigned long int>().max();

    std::cout << "num bytes (signed): " << num_bytes_signed << '\n';
    std::cout << "min value (signed): " << min_signed << '\n';
    std::cout << "max value (signed): " << max_signed << '\n';

    std::cout << '\n';

    std::cout << "num bytes (unsigned): " << num_bytes_unsigned << '\n';
    std::cout << "min value (unsigned): " << min_unsigned << '\n';
    std::cout << "max value (unsigned): " << max_unsigned << '\n';
}

// > g++ scratchpad.cpp; ./a.out
// num bytes (signed): 8
```

```
// min value (signed): -9223372036854775808
// max value (signed): 9223372036854775807

// num bytes (unsigned): 8
// min value (unsigned): 0
// max value (unsigned): 18446744073709551615
```

As shown in the preceding code, on a 64 bit Intel CPU running on Ubuntu, the `long int` is an 8 byte value. This is not true on Windows, which represents a `long int` as 32 bit, with the `long long int` being 64 bits (once again for backward compatibility).

When system programming, the size of the data you are working with is usually extremely important, and as shown in this section, unless you know exactly what CPU, operating system, and mode your application will be running on, it's nearly impossible to know the size of your integer types when using the default types provided by C and C++. Most of these types should not be used when system programming with the exception of `int`, which almost always represents a data type with the same bit width as the registers on your CPU, or at a minimum, a data type that doesn't require additional alignment checks and masking to perform simple arithmetic operations. In the next section, we will discuss additional types that overcome these size issues, and we will discuss their pros and cons.

Floating – point numbers

When system programming, floating point numbers are rarely used, but we will briefly discuss them here for reference. Floating point numbers increase the size of the possible value that can be stored by reducing the accuracy. For example, with a floating point number, it is possible to store a number that represents $1.79769e+308$, which is simply not possible with an integer value, even with a `long long int`. To accomplish this, however, it is not possible to subtract this value by `1` and see a difference in the number's value, and the floating point number cannot represent such a large value while still maintaining the same granularity as an integer value. Another benefit of floating point numbers is their ability to represent sub-integer numbers, which is useful when dealing with more complicated, mathematical calculations (a task that is rarely needed for system programming, as most kernels don't work with floating point numbers to prevent floating point errors from occurring within the kernel, ultimately resulting in a lack of system calls that take floating point values).

There are mainly three different types of floating point numbers—`float`, `double`, and `long double`. For example, consider the following code:

```cpp
#include <iostream>

int main(void)
{
    auto num_bytes = sizeof(float);
    auto min = std::numeric_limits<float>().min();
    auto max = std::numeric_limits<float>().max();

    std::cout << "num bytes: " << num_bytes << '\n';
    std::cout << "min value: " << min << '\n';
    std::cout << "max value: " << max << '\n';
}

// > g++ scratchpad.cpp; ./a.out
// num bytes: 4
// min value: 1.17549e-38
// max value: 3.40282e+38
```

In the previous example, we leverage `std::numeric_limits` to examine the `float` type, which on an Intel 64 bit CPU is a 4 byte value. The `double` is as follows:

```cpp
#include <iostream>

int main(void)
{
    auto num_bytes = sizeof(double);
    auto min = std::numeric_limits<double>().min();
    auto max = std::numeric_limits<double>().max();

    std::cout << "num bytes: " << num_bytes << '\n';
    std::cout << "min value: " << min << '\n';
    std::cout << "max value: " << max << '\n';
}

// > g++ scratchpad.cpp; ./a.out
// num bytes: 8
// min value: 2.22507e-308
// max value: 1.79769e+308
```

With the `long double`, the code is as follows:

```cpp
#include <iostream>

int main(void)
{
```

```
    auto num_bytes = sizeof(long double);
    auto min = std::numeric_limits<long double>().min();
    auto max = std::numeric_limits<long double>().max();

    std::cout << "num bytes: " << num_bytes << '\n';
    std::cout << "min value: " << min << '\n';
    std::cout << "max value: " << max << '\n';
}

// > g++ scratchpad.cpp; ./a.out
// num bytes: 16
// min value: 3.3621e-4932
// max value: 1.18973e+4932
```

As shown in the previous code, on an Intel 64 bit CPU, the `long double` is a 16 byte value (or 128 bits), which can store an absolutely massive number.

Boolean

The standard C language doesn't define a Boolean type natively. C++, however, does, and is defined using the `bool` keyword. When writing in C, a Boolean can be represented using any integer type, with `false` typically representing 0, and `true` typically representing 1. As an interesting side note, some CPUs are capable of comparing a register or memory location to 0 faster than 1, meaning that on some CPUs, it's actually faster for Boolean arithmetic and branching to result in `false` in the *typical* case.

Let's look at a `bool` using the following code:

```
#include <iostream>

int main(void)
{
    auto num_bytes = sizeof(bool);
    auto min = std::numeric_limits<bool>().min();
    auto max = std::numeric_limits<bool>().max();

    std::cout << "num bytes: " << num_bytes << '\n';
    std::cout << "min value: " << min << '\n';
    std::cout << "max value: " << max << '\n';
}

// > g++ scratchpad.cpp; ./a.out
// num bytes: 1
// min value: 0
// max value: 1
```

As shown in the preceding code, a Boolean using C++ on a 64 bit Intel CPU is 1 byte in size, and can take on a value of 0 or 1. It should be noted, for the same reasons as already identified, a Boolean could be 32-bits or even 64-bits, depending on the CPU architecture. On an Intel CPU, which is capable of supporting register sizes of 8 bits (that is, 1 byte), a Boolean only needs to be 1 byte in size.

The total size of a Boolean is important to note, with respect to storing Booleans in a file on disk. A Boolean technically only needs a single bit to store its value, but rarely (if any) CPU architectures support bit-style register and memory access, meaning a Boolean typically consumes more than a single bit, and in some cases could consume as many as 64 bits. If the size of your resulting file is important, storing a Boolean using the built-in Boolean type may not be preferred (ultimately resulting in the need for bit masking).

Learning standard integer types

To address the uncertainty of the default types provided by C and C++, both provide the standard integer types, which are accessible from the `stdint.h` header file. This header defines the following types:

- `int8_t`, `uint8_t`
- `int16_t`, `uint16_t`
- `int32_t`, `uint32_t`
- `int64_t`, `uint64_t`

In addition, `stdint.h` provides both *least* and *fast* versions of the aforementioned types, and a max type and integer pointer type, which is all out-of-scope for this book. The previous types do exactly what you would expect; they define the width of integer types with a specific number of bits. For example, an `int8_t` is a signed 8 bit integer. No matter what the CPU architecture, operating system, or mode is, these types are always the same (with the only thing not being defined is their endianness, which is usually only needed when working with networking and external devices).

In general, if the size of the data type you are working with is important, use the standard integer types instead of the default types provided by the language. Although the standard types do solve a lot of the problems already identified, they do have their own issues. Specifically, `stdint.h` is a compiler provided header file, with a different header being defined for each CPU architecture and operating system combination possible. The types defined in this file are typically represented using the default types under the hood. This can be done because the compiler knows if an `int32_t` is an `int`, or a `long int`. To demonstrate this, let's create an application that's capable of comparing integer types.

We will start with the following headers:

```
#include <typeinfo>
#include <iostream>

#include <string>
#include <cstdint>
#include <cstdlib>
#include <cxxabi.h>
```

The `typeinfo` header will provide us with C++ supported type information, which will ultimately provide us with the root type for a specific integer type. The problem is that `typeinfo` provides us with the mangled versions of this type information. To demangle this information, we will need the `cxxabi.h` header, which provides access to the demangler built into C++ itself:

```
template<typename T>
std::string type_name()
{
    int status;
    std::string name = typeid(T).name();

    auto demangled_name =
        abi::__cxa_demangle(name.c_str(), nullptr, nullptr, &status);

    if (status == 0) {
        name = demangled_name;
        std::free(demangled_name);
    }

    return name;
}
```

The previous function returns the root name for a provided type `T`. This is done by first getting the type's name from C++, and then using the demangler to convert the mangled type information into its human-readable form. Finally, the resulting name is returned:

```
template<typename T1, typename T2>
void
are_equal()
{
    #define red "\033[1;31m"
    #define reset "\033[0m"

    std::cout << type_name<T1>() << " vs "
              << type_name<T2>() << '\n';
```

```
    if (sizeof(T1) == sizeof(T2)) {
        std::cout << " - size: both == " << sizeof(T1) << '\n';
    }
    else {
        std::cout << red " - size: "
                      << sizeof(T1)
                      << " != "
                      << sizeof(T2)
                      << reset "\n";
    }

    if (type_name<T1>() == type_name<T2>()) {
        std::cout << " - name: both == " << type_name<T1>() << '\n';
    }
    else {
        std::cout << red " - name: "
                      << type_name<T1>()
                      << " != "
                      << type_name<T2>()
                      << reset "\n";
    }
}
```

The previous function checks to see if both the name and size of the type are the same, as they do not need to be the same (for example, the size could be the same, but the type's root might not be). It should be noted that we add some strange characters to the output of this function (which outputs to stdout). These strange characters tell the console to output in the color red in the event that a match was not found, providing a simple means to see which types are the same, and which types are not the same:

```
int main()
{
    are_equal<uint8_t, int8_t>();
    are_equal<uint8_t, uint32_t>();

    are_equal<signed char, int8_t>();
    are_equal<unsigned char, uint8_t>();

    are_equal<signed short int, int16_t>();
    are_equal<unsigned short int, uint16_t>();
    are_equal<signed int, int32_t>();
    are_equal<unsigned int, uint32_t>();
    are_equal<signed long int, int64_t>();
    are_equal<unsigned long int, uint64_t>();
    are_equal<signed long long int, int64_t>();
    are_equal<unsigned long long int, uint64_t>();
}
```

Finally, we will compare each standard integer type with the expected (or more appropriately stated, *typical*) default type to see if the types are in fact the same on any given architecture. This example can be run on any architecture to see what the differences are between the default types and the standard integer types so that we can look for discrepancies if this information is needed when system programming.

The results are as follow (for an Intel-based 64 bit CPU on Ubuntu) for a `uint8_t`:

```
are_equal<uint8_t, int8_t>();
are_equal<uint8_t, uint32_t>();

// unsigned char vs signed char
// - size: both == 1
// - name: unsigned char != signed char

// unsigned char vs unsigned int
// - size: 1 != 4
// - name: unsigned char != unsigned int
```

The following shows the results of a `char`:

```
are_equal<signed char, int8_t>();
are_equal<unsigned char, uint8_t>();

// signed char vs signed char
// - size: both == 1
// - name: both == signed char

// unsigned char vs unsigned char
// - size: both == 1
// - name: both == unsigned char
```

Finally, the following code shows the results for the remaining `int` types:

```
are_equal<signed short int, int16_t>();
are_equal<unsigned short int, uint16_t>();
are_equal<signed int, int32_t>();
are_equal<unsigned int, uint32_t>();
are_equal<signed long int, int64_t>();
are_equal<unsigned long int, uint64_t>();
are_equal<signed long long int, int64_t>();
are_equal<unsigned long long int, uint64_t>();

// short vs short
// - size: both == 2
// - name: both == short

// unsigned short vs unsigned short
```

```
// - size: both == 2
// - name: both == unsigned short

// int vs int
// - size: both == 4
// - name: both == int

// unsigned int vs unsigned int
// - size: both == 4
// - name: both == unsigned int

// long vs long
// - size: both == 8
// - name: both == long

// unsigned long vs unsigned long
// - size: both == 8
// - name: both == unsigned long

// long long vs long
// - size: both == 8
// - name: long long != long

// unsigned long long vs unsigned long
// - size: both == 8
// - name: unsigned long long != unsigned long
```

All of the types are the same, with some notable exceptions:

- The first two tests were provided specifically to ensure that an error would, in fact, be detected.
- On Ubuntu, an int64_t is implemented using long and not a long long, which means that on Ubuntu, a long and a long long mean the same thing. This is not the case with Windows.

The most important thing to recognize with this demonstration is that the output doesn't include the standard integer type names, but instead only contains the default type names. This is because, as previously demonstrated, the compiler implements an int32_t on an Intel 64 bit CPU on Ubuntu using an int, and to the compiler, these types are one and the same. The difference is, on another CPU architecture and operating system, an int32_t might be implemented using a long int.

If you care about the size of an integer type, use a standard integer type, and let the header file pick which default type to use for you. If you don't care about the size of the integer type, or an API dictates the type, leverage the default type instead. In the next section, we will show you how even standard integer types do not guarantee a specific size, and the rules just described can break down using a common system programming pattern.

Structure packing

The standard integers provide a compiler-supported method for dictating the size of an integer type at compile time. Specifically, they map bit widths to default types so that the coder doesn't have to do this manually. The standard types, however, do not always guarantee the width of a type, and structures are a good example of this. To better understand this issue, let's look at a simple example of a structure with some data in it:

```cpp
#include <iostream>

struct mystruct {
    uint64_t data1;
    uint64_t data2;
};

int main()
{
    std::cout << "size: " << sizeof(mystruct) << '\n';
}

// > g++ scratchpad.cpp; ./a.out
// size: 16
```

In the previous example, we created a structure with two 64 bit integers in it. We then, using the `sizeof()` function, output the size of the structure to `stdout` using `std::cout`. As expected, the total size, in bytes, of the structure is `16`. It should be noted that, like the rest of this book, the examples in this section are all being executed on a 64 bit Intel CPU.

Now, let's look at the same example, but with one of the data types being changed to a 16 bit integer instead of a 64 bit integer, as follows:

```cpp
#include <iostream>

struct mystruct {
    uint64_t data1;
    uint16_t data2;
};
```

```
int main()
{
    std::cout << "size: " << sizeof(mystruct) << '\n';
}

// > g++ scratchpad.cpp; ./a.out
// size: 16
```

As shown in the preceding example, we have a structure that has two data types, but they do not match. We then output the size of the data structure to stdout using std::cout, and the reported size is 16 bytes. The problem is that we expect 10 bytes, as we defined the structure as being the combination of a 64-bit (8 bytes) and a 16-bit (2 bytes) integer.

Under the hood, the compiler is replacing the 16 bit integer with a 64 bit integer. The reason for this is the base type for C and C++ is an int, and the compiler is allowed to change a type smaller than an int with an int, even though we explicitly declared the second integer as a 16 bit integer. To explain this in other words, the use of unit16_t does not demand the use of a 16 bit integer, but rather it is a typedef for short int on a 64 bit Intel-based CPU running Ubuntu, and based on the C and C++ specifications, the compiler is allowed to change a short int to an int at will.

The order in which we specify our integers also does not matter:

```
#include <iostream>

struct mystruct {
    uint16_t data1;
    uint64_t data2;
};

int main()
{
    std::cout << "size: " << sizeof(mystruct) << '\n';
}

// > g++ scratchpad.cpp; ./a.out
// size: 16
```

As seen in the previous example, the compiler once again states that the total size of the structure is 16 bytes when, in fact, we expect 10. In this example, the compiler is even more likely to make this type of substitution because it is capable of identifying that there is an alignment issue. Specifically, the CPU this code was compiled on was a 64 bit CPU, which means that replacing the `uint16_t` with a `unit64_t` could possibly improve memory caching, and align `data2` on a 64 bit boundary instead of a 16 bit boundary, which would span two 64 bit memory locations if the structure is properly aligned in memory.

Structures are not the only way to reproduce this type of substitution. Let's examine the following example:

```
#include <iostream>

int main()
{
    int16_t s = 42;
    auto result = s + 42;
    std::cout << "size: " << sizeof(result) << '\n';
}

// > g++ scratchpad.cpp; ./a.out
// size: 4
```

In the previous example, we created a 16-bit integer and set it to `42`. We then created another integer and set it to our 16-bit integer plus `42`. The value `42` can be represented as an 8-bit integer, but it's not. Instead, the compiler represents `42` as an `int`, which in this case means that the system this code was compiled on is 4 bytes in size.

The compiler represents `42` as an `int`, and `int` plus an `int16_t`, which results in an `int`, as that is the higher width type. In the previous example, we define our `result` variable using `auto`, which ensures that the resulting type reflects the type the compiler created as a consequence of this arithmetic. We could have defined `result` as another `int16_t`, which would have worked unless we turned on integer type conversion warnings. Doing so would have resulted in a conversion warning as the compiler constructs an `int` as a consequence of adding `s` plus `42`, and then would have to automatically convert the resulting `int` back to an `int16_t`, which would be performing a narrowing conversion, which could result in an overflow (hence the warning).

All of these issues are a consequence of the compiler's ability to perform type conversions from a smaller width type to a higher width type in order to optimize performance to reduce the possibility of overflows. In this case, a numeric value is always an `int` unless the value requires more storage (for example, replace `42` with `0xFFFFFFFF00000000`).

This type of conversion is not always guaranteed. Consider the following example:

```cpp
#include <iostream>

struct mystruct {
    uint16_t data1;
    uint16_t data2;
};

int main()
{
    std::cout << "size: " << sizeof(mystruct) << '\n';
}

// > g++ scratchpad.cpp; ./a.out
// size: 4
```

In the previous example, we have a structure with two 16 bit integers. The total size of the structure is reported as 4 bytes, which is exactly what we would expect. In this case, the compiler doesn't see a benefit to changing the size of either of the integers and thus leaves them alone.

Bit fields also do not change the compiler's ability to perform this type of conversion, as shown in the following example:

```cpp
#include <iostream>

struct mystruct {
    uint16_t data1 : 2, data2 : 14;
    uint64_t data3;
};

int main()
{
    std::cout << "size: " << sizeof(mystruct) << '\n';
}

// > g++ scratchpad.cpp; ./a.out
// size: 16
```

In the previous example, we created a structure with two integers (a 16-bit integer and a 64-bit integer), but instead of just defining the 16-bit integer, we also defined bit fields, giving us direct access to specific bits within the integer (a practice that should be avoided when system programming for reasons that are about to be explained). Defining these bit fields does not prevent the compiler from changing the total size of the first integer from 16 bits to 64 bits.

The problem with the previous example is that bit fields are often a pattern used by system programmers when interfacing directly with hardware. In the previous example, the second 64-bit integer is expected to be at 2 bytes from the top of the structure. In this case, however, the second 64-bit integer is actually 8 bytes from the top of the structure. If we used this structure to interface directly with hardware, a hard to find logic bug would be the result.

The way to overcome this problem is to pack the structure. The following example demonstrates how to do this:

```
#include <iostream>

#pragma pack(push, 1)
struct mystruct {
    uint64_t data1;
    uint16_t data2;
};
#pragma pack(pop)

int main()
{
    std::cout << "size: " << sizeof(mystruct) << '\n';
}

// > g++ scratchpad.cpp; ./a.out
// size: 10
```

The previous example is similar to the first example in this section. A structure was created with a 64 bit integer and a 16 bit integer. In the previous example, the resulting size of the structure was 16 bytes, as the compiler replaced the 16 bit integer with a 64 bit integer instead. In the previous example, to fix this issue, we wrap the structure with the `#pragma pack` and `#pragma pop` macros. These macros tell the compiler (since we passed a 1 to the macro, which indicates a byte) to pack the structure using a byte granularity, telling the compiler it is not allowed to make a substitution optimization.

Using this method, changing the order of the variables to the more likely scenario for which the compiler would attempt this type of optimization still results in a structure that is not converted, as shown in the following example:

```
#include <iostream>

#pragma pack(push, 1)
struct mystruct {
    uint16_t data1;
    uint64_t data2;
};
```

```
#pragma pack(pop)

int main()
{
    std::cout << "size: " << sizeof(mystruct) << '\n';
}

// > g++ scratchpad.cpp; ./a.out
// size: 10
```

As seen in the previous example, the size of the structure is still 10 bytes, regardless of the order of the integers.

Combining structure packing with the standard integer types is sufficient (assuming endianness is not an issue) to directly interface with the hardware, but this type of pattern is still discouraged in favor of building accessors and leveraging bit masks that provide the user with a means to ensure that direct access to hardware registers is occurring in a controlled manner without the compiler getting in the way, or optimizations producing undesired results.

To explain why packed structures and bit fields should be avoided, let's look at an alignment issue with the following example:

```
#include <iostream>

#pragma pack(push, 1)
struct mystruct {
    uint16_t data1;
    uint64_t data2;
};
#pragma pack(pop)

int main()
{
    mystruct s;
    std::cout << "addr: " << &s << '\n';
}

// > g++ scratchpad.cpp; ./a.out
// addr: 0x7fffd11069cf
```

In the previous example, we created a structure with a 16 bit integer and a 64-bit integer, and then packed the structure to ensure the total size of the structure is 10 bytes, and each data field is properly aligned. The total alignment of the structure is, however, not cache aligned, which is demonstrated in the previous example by creating an instance of the structure on the stack and then outputting the structure's address to `stdout` using `std::cout`. As shown, the address is byte aligned, not cache aligned.

To cache align the structure, we will leverage the `alignas()` function, which will be explained in Chapter 7, *A Comprehensive Look at Memory Management*:

```
#include <iostream>

#pragma pack(push, 1)
struct alignas(16) mystruct {
    uint16_t data1;
    uint64_t data2;
};
#pragma pack(pop)

int main()
{
    mystruct s;
    std::cout << "addr: " << &s << '\n';
    std::cout << "size: " << sizeof(mystruct) << '\n';
}

// > g++ scratchpad.cpp; ./a.out
// addr: 0x7fff44ee3f40
// size: 16
```

In the previous example, we added the `alignas()` function to the definition of the structure, which cache aligns the structure on the stack. We also output the total size of the structure as with previous examples, and as shown, the structure is no longer packed. In other words, the use of `#pragma pack#` does not guarantee the structure will, in fact, be packed. As in all cases, the compiler is free to make changes as needed, and even the `#pragma pack` macro is a hint, not a requirement.

In the previous case, it should be noted that the compiler actually adds additional memory to the end of the structure, meaning that the data members in the structure are still in their correct locations, as follows:

```
#include <iostream>

#pragma pack(push, 1)
struct alignas(16) mystruct {
    uint16_t data1;
```

```
        uint64_t data2;
};
#pragma pack(pop)

int main()
{
    mystruct s;
    std::cout << "addr data1: " << &s.data1 << '\n';
    std::cout << "addr data2: " << &s.data2 << '\n';
}

// > g++ scratchpad.cpp; ./a.out
// addr data1: 0x7ffc45dd8c90
// addr data2: 0x7ffc45dd8c92
```

In the previous example, the address of each data member is output to stdout, and as expected, the first data member is aligned to 0, and the second data member is 2 bytes from the top of the structure, even though the total size of the structure is 16 bytes, meaning that the compiler is getting the extra 6 bytes by adding addition integers to the bottom of the structure. Although this might seem benign if an array of these structures were created, and it was assumed the structures were 10 bytes in size due to the use of #pragma pack, a hard to find logic bug would be introduced.

To conclude this chapter, a note about pointers should be provided with respect to their size. Specifically, the size of a pointer depends entirely on the CPU architecture, operating system, and mode the application is running in. Let's examine the following example:

```
#include <iostream>

#pragma pack(push, 1)
struct mystruct {
    uint16_t *data1;
    uint64_t data2;
};
#pragma pack(pop)

int main()
{
    std::cout << "size: " << sizeof(mystruct) << '\n';
}

// > g++ scratchpad.cpp; ./a.out
// size: 16
```

In the previous example, we stored a pointer and an integer and output the total size of the structure to `stdout` using `std::cout`. The resulting size of this structure is 16 bytes on a 64-bit Intel CPU running Ubuntu. The total size of this structure on a 32-bit Intel CPU running Ubuntu would be 12 bytes, as the pointer would only be 4 bytes in size. Worse, if the application were compiled as a 32-bit application, but executed on a 64-bit kernel, the application would see this structure as 12 bytes, and the kernel would see this structure as 16 bytes. Attempting to pass this structure to the kernel would result in a bug, as the application and kernel would see the structure differently.

Summary

In this chapter, we reviewed the different integer types (and briefly reviewed the floating point types) that are provided by C and C++ for system programming. We started with a discussion on the default types provided by C and C++ and the pros and cons associated with these types, including the common `int` type, explaining what it is, and how it is used. Next, we discussed the standard integer types provided by `stdint.h` and how they address some of the issues with the default types. Finally, we concluded this chapter with a discussion on structure packing and the issues associated with type conversions and optimizations that the compiler can make in different scenarios.

In the next chapter, we will cover changes made by C++17, a C++ specific technique called **Resource Acquisition Is Initialization** (**RAII**) and provide an overview of the **Guideline Support Library** (**GSL**).

Questions

1. What is the difference between a `short int` and an `int`?
2. What is the size of an `int`?
3. Is the size of a `signed int` and an `unsigned int` different?
4. What is the difference between an `int32_t` and an `int`?
5. Is an `int16_t` guaranteed to be 16 bits?
6. What does `#pragma pack` do?
7. Is it possible to guarantee structure packing in all cases?

Further reading

- https://www.packtpub.com/application-development/c17-example
- https://www.packtpub.com/application-development/getting-started-c17-programming-video

C++, RAII, and the GSL Refresher

4

In this chapter, we will provide an overview of some of the recent advancements of C++ that are leveraged in this book. We will start by providing an overview of the changes made to C++ in the C++17 specification. We will then briefly cover a C++ design pattern called **Resource Acquisition Is Initialization** (**RAII**), how it is used by C++, and why it is so important to not only C++ but many other languages that leverage the same design pattern. This chapter will conclude with an introduction to the **Guideline Support Library** (**GSL**) and how it can help to increase the reliability and stability of system programming by helping to adhere to the C++ Core Guidelines.

In this chapter, we will cover the following topics:

- Discussing the advancements made in C++17
- Outlining RAII
- Introducing the GSL

Technical requirements

In order to compile and execute the examples in this chapter, the reader must have the following:

- A Linux-based system capable of compiling and executing C++17 (for example, Ubuntu 17.10+)
- GCC 7+
- CMake 3.6+
- An internet connection

To download all of the code in this chapter, including the examples and code snippets, go to the following link: `https://github.com/PacktPublishing/Hands-On-System-Programming-with-CPP/tree/master/Chapter04`.

A brief overview of C++17

The goal of this section is to provide a brief overview of C++17 and the features added to C++. For a more comprehensive and in-depth look at C++17, please see the *Further reading* section of this chapter, which list additional books from Packt Publishing on the topic.

Language changes

There were several changes made to the C++17 language and syntax. The following are some examples.

Initializers in if/switch statements

In C++17, it is now possible to define a variable and initialize it in the definition of an `if` and `switch` statement, as follows:

```
#include <iostream>

int main(void)
{
    if (auto i = 42; i > 0) {
        std::cout << "Hello World\n";
    }
}

// > g++ scratchpad.cpp; ./a.out
// Hello World
```

In the preceding example, the `i` variable is defined and initialized inside the `if` statement using a semicolon (`;`) inside the branch itself. This is especially useful for C- and POSIX-style functions that return error codes, as the variable that stores the error code can be defined in the proper context.

What makes this feature so important and useful is that the variable is only defined when the condition is met. That is, in the preceding example, `i` only exists if `i` is greater than 0.

This is extremely helpful in ensuring that variables are available when they are valid, helping to reduce the likelihood of working with an invalid variable.

The same type of initialization can occur with `switch` statements as follows:

```cpp
#include <iostream>

int main(void)
{
    switch(auto i = 42) {
        case 42:
            std::cout << "Hello World\n";
            break;

        default:
            break;
    }
}

// > g++ scratchpad.cpp; ./a.out
// Hello World
```

In the preceding example, the `i` variable is created only in the context of the `switch` statement. Unlike the `if` statement, the `i` variable exists for all cases, meaning the `i` variable is available in the `default` state, which could represent the invalid state.

Additions to compile-time facilities

With C++11, `constexpr` was added as a statement to the compiler that a variable, function, and so on, can be evaluated at compile time and optimized, reducing the complexity of the code at runtime and improving performance overall. In some cases, the compiler was smart enough to extend `constexpr` statements to other components, including branch statements, for example:

```cpp
#include <iostream>

constexpr const auto val = true;

int main(void)
{
    if (val) {
        std::cout << "Hello World\n";
    }
}
```

In this example, we have created a `constexpr` variable, and we only output `Hello World` to `stdout` if `constexpr` is `true`. Since, in this example, it's always true, the compiler will remove the branch from the code entirely, as shown here:

```
push %rbp
mov %rsp,%rbp
lea 0x100(%rip),%rsi
lea 0x200814(%rip),%rdi
callq 6c0 <...cout...>
mov $0x0,%eax
pop %rbp
retq
```

As you can see, the code loads a couple of registers and calls `std::cout` without checking whether `val` is true, since the compiler completely removed the code from the resulting binary. The issue with C++11 was that the author could assume that this type of optimization was taking place, when in fact it might not be.

To prevent this type of error, C++17 adds a `constexpr if` statement, which tells the compiler to specifically optimize the branch at compile time. If the compiler cannot optimize the `if` statement, an explicit compile-time error will occur, telling the user that optimization could not be done, providing the user with an opportunity to fix the issue (instead of assuming the optimization was taking place when in fact it might not be), for example:

```cpp
#include <iostream>

int main(void)
{
    if constexpr (constexpr const auto i = 42; i > 0) {
        std::cout << "Hello World\n";
    }
}

// > g++ scratchpad.cpp; ./a.out
// Hello World
```

In the preceding example, we have a more complicated `if` statement that leverages both a compile-time `constexpr` optimization as well as an `if` statement initializer. The resulting binary is as follows:

```
push %rbp
mov %rsp,%rbp
sub $0x10,%rsp
movl $0x2a,-0x4(%rbp)
lea 0x104(%rip),%rsi
lea 0x200809(%rip),%rdi
callq 6c0 <...cout...>
mov $0x0,%eax
leaveq
retq
```

As you can see, the branch has been removed from the resulting binary, and more specifically, if the expression was not a constant, the compiler would have thrown an error stating that this code could not be compiled as stated.

It should be noted that this result is not the same binary as previously as one might expect. It would appear that GCC 7.3 has some additional improvements to make in its optimization engine, as the `constexpr i` variable that was defined and initialized inside the binary was not removed (as stack space was allocated for `i` in this code when it didn't need to be).

Another compile-time change was a different version of the `static_assert` compile-time function. In C++11, the following was added:

```cpp
#include <iostream>

int main(void)
{
    static_assert(42 == 42, "the answer");
}

// > g++ scratchpad.cpp; ./a.out
//
```

The goal of the `static_assert` function is to ensure that certain compile-time assumptions are true. This is especially helpful when programming a system to do things such as making sure a structure is a specific size in bytes, or that a certain code path is taken, depending on the system you're compiling for. The problem with this assert was that it required the addition of a description that would be output during compile time, which likely just describes the assertion in English without providing any additional information. In C++17, another version of this assert was added, which removed the need for the description, as follows:

```cpp
#include <iostream>

int main(void)
{
    static_assert(42 == 42);
}

// > g++ scratchpad.cpp; ./a.out
//
```

Namespaces

A welcome change to C++17 is the addition of nested namespaces. Prior to C++17, nested namespaces had to be defined on different lines, as follows:

```cpp
#include <iostream>

namespace X
{
namespace Y
{
namespace Z
{
    auto msg = "Hello World\n";
}
}
}

int main(void)
{
    std::cout << X::Y::Z::msg;
}

// > g++ scratchpad.cpp; ./a.out
// Hello World
```

In the preceding example, we define a message that is output to stdout in a nested namespace. The problem with this syntax is obvious—it takes up a lot of space. In C++17, this limitation was removed by giving us the ability to declare nested namespaces on the same line, as follows:

```
#include <iostream>

namespace X::Y::Z
{
    auto msg = "Hello World\n";
}

int main(void)
{
    std::cout << X::Y::Z::msg;
}

// > g++ scratchpad.cpp; ./a.out
// Hello World
```

In the preceding example, we are able to define a nested namespace without the need for separate lines.

Structured bindings

My favorite addition to C++17 is something called **structured bindings**. Prior to C++17, complex structures, such as a struct or std::pair, could be used to return more than one value as the output of a function, but the syntax was cumbersome, for example:

```
#include <utility>
#include <iostream>

std::pair<const char *, int>
give_me_a_pair()
{
    return {"The answer is: ", 42};
}

int main(void)
{
    auto p = give_me_a_pair();
    std::cout << std::get<0>(p) << std::get<1>(p) << '\n';
}

// > g++ scratchpad.cpp; ./a.out
// The answer is: 42
```

In the preceding example, the `give_me_a_pair()` function returns `std::pair` with a `The answer is:` string and an integer of `42`. The result of this function is stored in a variable named `p` in the `main` function, and `std::get()` is needed to get the first and second portion of `std::pair`. This code is both cumbersome and inefficient without aggressive optimizations, as additional function calls are needed to retrieve the results of `give_me_a_pair()`.

In C++17, structured bindings provide us with a means to retrieve individual fields of a struct or `std::pair`, as follows:

```
#include <iostream>

std::pair<const char *, int>
give_me_a_pair()
{
    return {"The answer is: ", 42};
}

int main(void)
{
    auto [msg, answer] = give_me_a_pair();
    std::cout << msg << answer << '\n';
}

// > g++ scratchpad.cpp; ./a.out
// The answer is: 42
```

In the preceding example, the `give_me_a_pair()` function returns the same `std::pair` as before, but this time, we retrieve the results of `give_me_a_pair()` using structured bindings. The `msg` and `answer` variables are initialized to the results of `std::pair`, providing us with direct access to the results without the need for `std::get()`.

The same is also possible with structures, as follows:

```
#include <iostream>

struct mystruct
{
    const char *msg;
    int answer;
};

mystruct
give_me_a_struct()
{
    return {"The answer is: ", 42};
```

```
}

int main(void)
{
    auto [msg, answer] = give_me_a_struct();
    std::cout << msg << answer << '\n';
}

// > g++ scratchpad.cpp; ./a.out
// The answer is: 42
```

In the preceding example, we create a structure that is returned by `give_me_a_struct()`. The results of this function are acquired using structured bindings instead of `std::get()`.

Inline variables

A more controversial addition to C++17 is the inclusion of inline variables. As time progresses, more and more header-only libraries are being developed by various members of the C++ community. These libraries offer the ability to provide complex functionality to C++ without the need to install and link against the library (simply include the library and you're done). The issue with these types of libraries is that they have to play fancy tricks to include global variables in the library itself.

Inline variables remove this issue, as follows:

```
#include <iostream>

inline auto msg = "Hello World\n";

int main(void)
{
    std::cout << msg;
}

// > g++ scratchpad.cpp; ./a.out
// Hello World
```

In the preceding example, the `msg` variable is declared as `inline`. This type of variable can be defined in a header (that is, a `.h` file) and included several times without multiple definitions being defined during linking. It should be noted that inline variables also remove the need for the following:

```
extern const char *msg;
```

Often, a global variable is needed by multiple source files and the preceding pattern is used to expose the variable to all of these source files. The preceding code is added to a header file that is included by all of the source files and then one source file actually defines the variable, for example:

```
const char *msg = "Hello World\n";
```

Although this works, this approach is cumbersome and it's not always clear which source file should actually define the variable. Using inline variables removes this issue, as the header both defines the variable and exposes the symbol to all of the source files that need it, removing the ambiguity.

Changes in the library

In addition to changes to the language's syntax, some library changes were also made. The following are some of the notable changes.

String View

As will be discussed in the *GSL* section of this chapter, there is a push within the C++ community to remove direct access to both pointers and arrays. Most segfaults and vulnerabilities discovered in applications can be attributed to the mishandling of pointers and arrays. As programs become more and more complex, and modified by multiple people without a complete picture of the application and how it uses each and every pointer and/or array, the likelihood of an error being introduced increases.

To address this, the C++ community has adopted the C++ Core Guidelines: `https://github.com/isocpp/CppCoreGuidelines`.

The goal of the C++ Core Guidelines is to define a set of best practices that help to prevent common mistakes that are made when programming with C++, to limit the total number of errors that are introduced into a program. C++ has been around for years and, although it has a lot of facilities to prevent mistakes, it still maintains backward-compatibility, allowing old programs to coexist with new ones. The C++ Core Guidelines helps new and expert users navigate the many features that are available to help create safer and more robust applications.

One of the features that was added to C++17 in support of this effort is the `std::string_view{}` class. `std::string_view` is a wrapper around a character array, similar to `std::array`, that helps to make working with basic C strings safer and easier, for example:

```
#include <iostream>
#include <string_view>

int main(void)
{
    std::string_view str("Hello World\n");
    std::cout << str;
}

// > g++ scratchpad.cpp; ./a.out
// Hello World
```

In the preceding example, we create `std::string_view{}` and initialize it to an ASCII C string. We then output the string to `stdout` using `std::cout`. Like `std::array`, `std::string_view{}` provides accessors to the underlying array, as follows:

```
#include <iostream>
#include <string_view>

int main(void)
{
    std::string_view str("Hello World");

    std::cout << str.front() << '\n';
    std::cout << str.back() << '\n';
    std::cout << str.at(1) << '\n';
    std::cout << str.data() << '\n';
}

// > g++ scratchpad.cpp; ./a.out
// H
// d
// e
// Hello World
```

In the preceding example, the `front()` and `back()` functions can be used to get the first and last character in the string, while the `at()` function can be used to get any character in the string; if the index is out of range (that is, the index provided to `at()` is longer than the string itself), an `std::out_of_range{}` exception is thrown. Finally, the `data()` function can be used to get direct access to the underlying array. Although, this function should be used with care, as its use negates the safety benefits of `std::string_view{}`.

In addition to the accessors, the `std::string_view{}` class provides information about the size of the string:

```
#include <iostream>
#include <string_view>

int main(void)
{
    std::string_view str("Hello World");

    std::cout << str.size() << '\n';
    std::cout << str.max_size() << '\n';
    std::cout << str.empty() << '\n';
}

// > g++ scratchpad.cpp; ./a.out
// 11
// 4611686018427387899
// 0
```

In the preceding example, the `size()` function returns the total number of characters in the string, while the `empty()` function returns `true` if `size() == 0` and `false` otherwise. The `max_size()` function defines the maximum size `std::string_view{}` can hold, which in most cases is unattainable or realistic. In the preceding example, the maximum string size is more than a million terabytes in size.

Unlike a `std::array`, the `std::string_view{}` provides the ability to reduce the size of the view of the string by removing characters from the front or back of the string, as follows:

```
#include <iostream>
#include <string_view>

int main(void)
{
    std::string_view str("Hello World");

    str.remove_prefix(1);
    str.remove_suffix(1);
    std::cout << str << '\n';
}

// > g++ scratchpad.cpp; ./a.out
// ello Worl
```

In the preceding example, the `remove_prefix()` and `remove_suffix()` functions are used to remove one character from both the front and back of the string, resulting in `ello Worl` being outputted to `stdout`. It should be noted that this simply changes the starting character and repositions the ending null character pointer without having to reallocate memory. For more advanced functionality, `std::string{}` should be used, but it comes with the resulting performance hits of additional memory allocations.

It is also possible to access substrings, as follows:

```
#include <iostream>
#include <string_view>

int main(void)
{
    std::string_view str("Hello World");
    std::cout << str.substr(0, 5) << '\n';
}

// > g++ scratchpad.cpp; ./a.out
// Hello
```

In the preceding example, we access the `Hello` substring using the `substr()` function.

It is also possible to compare strings:

```
#if SNIPPET13

#include <iostream>
#include <string_view>

int main(void)
{
    std::string_view str("Hello World");

    if (str.compare("Hello World") == 0) {
        std::cout << "Hello World\n";
    }

    std::cout << str.compare("Hello") << '\n';
    std::cout << str.compare("World") << '\n';
}

// > g++ scratchpad.cpp; ./a.out
// Hello World
// 6
// -1
```

Like the `strcmp()` function, the compare function returns 0 when the two strings are compared, and a difference when they do not.

Finally, search functions are provided as follows:

```
#include <iostream>

int main(void)
{
    std::string_view str("Hello this is a test of Hello World");

    std::cout << str.find("Hello") << '\n';
    std::cout << str.rfind("Hello") << '\n';
    std::cout << str.find_first_of("Hello") << '\n';
    std::cout << str.find_last_of("Hello") << '\n';
    std::cout << str.find_first_not_of("Hello") << '\n';
    std::cout << str.find_last_not_of("Hello") << '\n';
}

// > g++ scratchpad.cpp; ./a.out
// 0
// 24
// 0
// 33
// 5
// 34
```

The results of this example are as follows:

- The `find()` function returns the location in the string of the first occurrence of Hello which in this case is 0.
- `rfind()` returns the location of the last occurrence of the provided string, which, in this case, is 24.
- `find_first_of()` and `find_last_of()` find the first and last occurrence of any of the characters provided (not the string as a whole). In this case, H is in the provided string, and H is the first character in msg, which means `find_first_of()` returns 0 since the 0 is the first index in the string.
- In the case of `find_last_of()`, l is the last-occurring letter, at position 33.
- `find_first_not_of()` and `find_last_not_of()` are the opposite of `find_first_of()` and `find_last_of()`, returning the first and last occurrence of any character not in the provided string.

std::any, std::variant, and std::optional

Other welcome additions to C++17 are the `std::any{}`, `std::variant{}`, and `std::optional{}` classes. `std::any{}` is capable of storing any value at any time. Special accessors are needed to retrieve the data in `std::any{}`, but they are capable of holding any value in a type-safe manner. To accomplish this, `std::any{}` leverages an internal pointer, and memory must be allocated each time the type is changed, for example:

```cpp
#include <iostream>
#include <any>

struct mystruct {
    int data;
};

int main(void)
{
    auto myany = std::make_any<int>(42);
    std::cout << std::any_cast<int>(myany) << '\n';

    myany = 4.2;
    std::cout << std::any_cast<double>(myany) << '\n';

    myany = mystruct{42};
    std::cout << std::any_cast<mystruct>(myany).data << '\n';
}

// > g++ scratchpad.cpp; ./a.out
// 42
// 4.2
// 42
```

In the preceding example, we create `std::any{}` and set it to an `int` with the value of 42, a double with the value of 4.2, and a struct with the value of 42.

`std::variant` is more like a type-safe union. A union reserves storage space for all of the types that are stored within the union at compile time (so no allocations is needed, but all of the possible types must be known at compile time). The problem with a standard C union is that there is no way to know what type is stored at any given time. Storing both an int and a `double` at the same time is problematic, since using both simultaneously will lead to corruption. With `std::variant`, this type of issue can be avoided, as `std::variant` is aware of what type it is currently storing, and attempting to access the data as a different type is not allowed (hence, `std::variant` is type-safe), for example:

```cpp
#include <iostream>
#include <variant>
```

```
int main(void)
{
    std::variant<int, double> v = 42;
    std::cout << std::get<int>(v) << '\n';

    v = 4.2;
    std::cout << std::get<double>(v) << '\n';
}

// > g++ scratchpad.cpp; ./a.out
// 42
// 4.2
```

In the preceding example, `std::variant` is used to store both an `integer` and a `double`, and we can safely retrieve the data in `std::variant` without corruption.

`std::optional` is a nullable value type. A pointer is a nullable reference type in which the pointer is either invalid or is valid and stores a value. To make a pointer value, memory must be allocated (or at least pointed to). `std::optional` is a value type, meaning the memory for `std::optional` doesn't have to be allocated, and under the hood, construction is only performed when the optional is valid, removing the overhead of constructing a default value type when it is not actually set. For complex objects, this not only provides the ability to determine whether an object is valid, it allows us to skip construction in the invalid case, which increases performance, for example:

```
#include <iostream>
#include <optional>

class myclass
{
public:
    int val;

    myclass(int v) :
        val{v}
    {
        std::cout << "constructed\n";
    }
};

int main(void)
{
    std::optional<myclass> o;
    std::cout << "created, but not constructed\n";

    if (o) {
        std::cout << "Attempt #1: " << o->val << '\n';
```

```
    }

    o = myclass{42};

    if (o) {
        std::cout << "Attempt #2: " << o->val << '\n';
    }
}

// > g++ scratchpad.cpp; ./a.out
// created, but not constructed
// constructed
// Attempt #2: 42
```

In the preceding example, we create a simple class that stores an `integer`. In this class, we output a string to stdout when the class is constructed. We then create an instance of this class using `std::optional`. We attempt to access this `std::optional` before and after we actually set the class to a valid value. As shown, the class is not constructed until we actually set the class to a valid value. Since `sts::unique_ptr` used to be the common method for creating optionals, it should be no surprise that `std::optional` shares a common interface.

Resource Acquisition Is Initialization (RAII)

RAII is arguably one of the more notable differences between C and C++. RAII sets the foundation and design patterns for the entire C++ library, and has been the inspiration for countless other languages. This simple concept provides C++ with an unmatched level of safety when compared to C, and this concept will be leveraged throughout this book when C and POSIX must be used in place of C++ (for example, when a C++ alternative either doesn't exist or is incomplete).

The idea behind RAII is simple. If a resource is allocated, it is allocated during the construction of an object, and when the object is destroyed, the resource is released. To accomplish this, RAII leverages the construction and destruction features of C++, for example:

```
#include <iostream>

class myclass
{
public:
    myclass()
    {
```

```
            std::cout << "Hello from constructor\n";
    }

    ~myclass()
    {
            std::cout << "Hello from destructor\n";
    }
};

int main(void)
{
    myclass c;
}

// > g++ scratchpad.cpp; ./a.out
// Hello from constructor
// Hello from destructor
```

In the preceding example, we create a class that, on construction and destruction, outputs to stdout. As shown, when the class is instantiated, the class is constructed, and when the class loses focus, the class is destroyed.

This simple concept can be leveraged to guard a resource, as follows:

```
#include <iostream>

class myclass
{
    int *ptr;

public:
    myclass() :
        ptr{new int(42)}
    { }

    ~myclass()
    {
        delete ptr;
    }

    int get()
    {
        return *ptr;
    }
};

int main(void)
{
```

```
    myclass c;
    std::cout << "The answer is: " << c.get() << '\n';
}

// > g++ scratchpad.cpp; ./a.out
// The answer is: 42
```

In the preceding example, a pointer is allocated when `myclass{}` is constructed, and freed when `myclass{}` is destroyed. This pattern provides many advantages:

- So long as the instance of `myclass{}` is visible (that is, can be accessed), the pointer is valid. So, any attempt to access the memory in the class is guaranteed to be safe as the deallocation of the memory only occurs when the scope of the class is lost, which would result in an inability to access the class (assuming pointers and references to the class are not used).
- No leaking of memory can occur. If the class is visible, the memory that the class allocated will be valid. Once the class is no longer visible (that is, loses scope), the memory is freed and no leak occurs.

Specifically, RAII ensures that the acquisition of a resource occurs at the initialization of the object, and the release of the resources occurs when the object is no longer needed. As will be shown later on in `Chapter 7`, *A Comprehensive Look at Memory Management*, `std::unique_ptr[]` and `std::shared_ptr{}` leverage this exact design pattern (although, these classes go above and beyond the preceding example to enforce ownership in addition to acquisition).

RAII does not just apply to pointers; it can be used for any resource that must be acquired and then released, for example:

```cpp
#include <iostream>

class myclass
{
    FILE *m_file;

public:
    myclass(const char *filename) :
        m_file{fopen(filename, "rb")}
    {
        if (m_file == 0) {
            throw std::runtime_error("unable to open file");
        }
    }

    ~myclass()
```

```
        {
            fclose(m_file);
            std::clog << "Hello from destructor\n";
        }
    };

    int main(void)
    {
        myclass c1("test.txt");

        try {
            myclass c2("does_not_exist.txt");
        }
        catch(const std::exception &e) {
            std::cout << "exception: " << e.what() << '\n';
        }
    }

    // > g++ scratchpad.cpp; touch test.txt; ./a.out
    // exception: unable to open file
    // Hello from destructor
```

In the preceding example, we create a class that opens a file and stores its handle on construction, and then closes the file on destruction and releases the handle. In the main function, we create an instance of the class that is both constructed and destructed as normal, leveraging RAII to prevent the file from leaking.

In addition to the normal case, we create a second class, which attempts to open a file that doesn't exist. In this case, an exception is thrown. The important thing to note here is the destructor is not called for this second instance. The is because the construction failed and threw an exception. As a result, no resource was acquired, thus, no destruction is required. That is, the acquisition of the resource is directly tied to the initialization of the class itself, and a failure to construct the class safely prevents the destruction of a resource that was never allocated in the first place.

RAII is a simple yet powerful feature of C++ that is leveraged extensively in C++, and this design pattern will be expanded upon in this book.

The Guideline Support Library (GSL)

As stated before, the goal of the C++ Core Guidelines is to provide a set of best practices associated with programming C++. The GSL is a library designed to assist in maintaining compliance with these guidelines. In general, there are some overall themes associated with the GSL:

- **Pointer ownership**: Defining who owns a pointer is a simple way to prevent memory leaks and pointer corruption. In general, the best way to define ownership is through the use of `std::unique_ptr{}` and `std::shared_ptr{}`, which will be explained in depth in Chapter 7, *A Comprehensive Look at Memory Management*, but in some cases, these cannot be used and the GSL helps to deal with these edge cases.
- **Expectation management**: The GSL also helps to define what a function should expect for input and what it ensures for output, with the goal being to transition these concepts to C++ contracts.
- **No pointer arithmetic**: Pointer arithmetic is one of the leading causes of program instability and vulnerabilities. Removing pointer arithmetic (or at least confining pointer arithmetic to well-tested support libraries) is a simple way to remove these types of issues.

Pointer ownership

Classical C++ doesn't distinguish between who owns a pointer (that is, the code or object responsible for releasing the memory associated with a pointer) and who is simply accessing memory using a pointer, for example:

```
void init(int *p)
{
    *p = 0;
}

int main(void)
{
    auto p = new int;
    init(p);
    delete p;
}

// > g++ scratchpad.cpp; ./a.out
//
```

In the preceding example, we allocate a pointer to an integer, and then pass that pointer to a function called `init()`, which initializes the pointer. Finally, we delete the pointer after it has been used by the `init()` function. If the `init()` function were located in another file, it would not be clear whether the `init()` function should delete the pointer. Although in this simple example it might be obvious that this is not the case, in complicated projects with lots of code, this intent can be lost. Future modifications to such code can result in improper use of pointers whose ownership is not well-defined.

To overcome this, the GSL provides a `gsl::owner<>{}` decoration that is used to document whether a given variable is an owner of the pointer, for example:

```
#include <gsl/gsl>

void init(int *p)
{
    *p = 0;
}

int main(void)
{
    gsl::owner<int *> p = new int;
    init(p);
    delete p;
}

// > g++ scratchpad.cpp; ./a.out
//
```

In the preceding example, we document that p in the `main` function is the owner of the pointer, meaning once p is no longer needed, the pointer should be released. Another issue with the preceding example is that the `init()` function expects the pointer to not be null. If the pointer were null, a null dereference would occur.

There are two common methods for overcoming the possibility of a null dereference. The first choice would be to check for a `nullptr` and throw an exception. The problem with this approach is you would have to perform this null pointer check on every function. These types of checks are costly and clutter code. The other option is to use a `gsl::not_null<>{}` class. Like `gsl::owner<>{}`, `gsl::not_null<>{}` is a decoration that can be compiled out of the code when debugging is not used. However, if debugging is enabled, `gsl::not_null<>{}` will throw an exception, `abort()`, or in some cases, refuse to compile if the variable is set to null. Using `gsl::not_null<>{}`, it is possible for a function to state explicitly whether or not null pointers are allowed and safely handled, for example:

```
#include <gsl/gsl>

gsl::not_null<int *>
test(gsl::not_null<int *> p)
{
    return p;
}

int main(void)
{
    auto p1 = std::make_unique<int>();
    auto p2 = test(gsl::not_null(p1.get()));
}

// > g++ scratchpad.cpp; ./a.out
//
```

In the preceding example, we create a pointer using `std::unique_ptr{}`, and then pass the resulting pointer to a function called `test()`. The `test()` function does not support a null pointer, and therefore states this using `gsl::not_null<>{}`. In turn, the `test()` function returns `gsl::not_null<>{}`, telling the user that the `test()` function ensures that the result of the function is not null (which is why the `test` function doesn't support a null pointer in the first place).

Pointer arithmetic

Pointer arithmetic is a common source of bugs that lead to instability and vulnerabilities. For this reason, the C++ Core Guidelines discourages the use of this type of arithmetic. Here are some examples of pointer arithmetic:

```
int array[10];

auto r1 = array + 1;
auto r2 = *(array + 1);
auto r3 = array[1];
```

The last example is likely the most surprising. The subscript operator is, in fact, pointer arithmetic, and its use can lead to out-of-range bugs. To overcome this, the GSL provides the `gsl::span{}` class, which gives us a safe interface for working with pointers, including arrays, for example:

```
#define GSL_THROW_ON_CONTRACT_VIOLATION
#include <gsl/gsl>
#include <iostream>

int main(void)
{
    int array[5] = {1, 2, 3, 4, 5};
    auto span = gsl::span(array);

    for (const auto &elem : span) {
        std::clog << elem << '\n';
    }

    for (auto i = 0; i < 5; i++) {
        std::clog << span[i] << '\n';
    }

    try {
        std::clog << span[5] << '\n';
    }
    catch(const gsl::fail_fast &e) {
        std::cout << "exception: " << e.what() << '\n';
    }
}

// > g++ scratchpad.cpp; ./a.out
// 1
// 2
// 3
// 4
```

```
// 5
// 1
// 2
// 3
// 4
// 5
// exception: GSL: Precondition failure at ...
```

Let's see how the preceding example works:

1. We create an array and initialize it with a set of integers.
2. We create a span into that array so that we can interact with the array safely. We output the array to `stdout` using a range-based `for` loop (as a span includes an iterator interface).
3. We output the array a second time to `stdout`, using a traditional index and subscript operator (that is, the `[]` operator). The difference with this subscript operator is each array access is checked for out-of-range errors. To demonstrate this, we attempt to access the array out of bounds and `gsl::span{}` throws a `gsl::fail_fast{}` exception. It should be noted that `GSL_THROW_ON_CONTRACT_VIOLATION` is used to tell the GSL to throw exceptions, instead of executing `std::terminate` or ignoring the bounds checks completely.

In addition to `gsl::span{}`, the GSL also contains specializations of `gsl::span{}`, which help us when working with common types of arrays. For example, the GSL provides `gsl::cstring_span{}`, as follows:

```cpp
#include <gsl/gsl>
#include <iostream>

int main(void)
{
    gsl::cstring_span<> str = gsl::ensure_z("Hello World\n");
    std::cout << str.data();

    for (const auto &elem : str) {
        std::clog << elem;
    }
}

// > g++ scratchpad.cpp; ./a.out
// Hello World
// Hello World
```

`gsl::cstring_span{}` is a `gsl::span{}` that contains a standard C-style string. In the preceding example, we load `gsl::cstring_span{}` with a standard C-style string, using the `gsl::ensure_z()` function to ensure the string ends in a null character before continuing. We then output the standard C-style string using a regular `std::cout call`, and also by using a range-based loop.

Contracts

C++ contracts provide the user with a means to state what a function expects as input, and what that function ensures as output. Specifically, a C++ contract documents a contract between the author of an API and the user of the API, it also provides compile-time and runtime validation of that contract.

Future versions of C++ will have built-in support for contracts, but until then, the GSL provides a library-based implementation of C++ contracts by providing the `expects()` and `ensures()` macros, for example:

```
#define GSL_THROW_ON_CONTRACT_VIOLATION
#include <gsl/gsl>
#include <iostream>

int main(void)
{
    try {
        Expects(false);
    }
    catch(const gsl::fail_fast &e) {
        std::cout << "exception: " << e.what() << '\n';
    }
}

// > g++ scratchpad.cpp; ./a.out
// exception: GSL: Precondition failure at ...
```

In the preceding example, we use the `Expects()` macro and pass it as `false`. Like the `assert()` function that is provided by the standard C library, the `Expects()` macro fails on `false`. Unlike `assert()`, `Expects()` will execute `std::terminate()` even when debugging is disabled, if the expression passed to `Expects()` evaluates to `false`. In the preceding example, we state that `Expects()` should throw a `gsl::fail_fast{}` exception instead of executing `std::terminate()`.

The `Ensures()` macro is the same as `Expects()`, with the only difference being the name, which is meant to document the contract's output instead of its input, for example:

```cpp
#define GSL_THROW_ON_CONTRACT_VIOLATION
#include <gsl/gsl>
#include <iostream>

int
test(int i)
{
    Expects(i >= 0 && i < 41);
    i++;

    Ensures(i < 42);
    return i;
}

int main(void)
{
    test(0);

    try {
        test(42);
    }
    catch(const gsl::fail_fast &e) {
        std::cout << "exception: " << e.what() << '\n';
    }
}

// > g++ scratchpad.cpp; ./a.out
// exception: GSL: Precondition failure at ...
```

In the preceding example, we create a function that expects the input to be greater than or equal to 0 and less than 41. The function then operates on the input and ensures the resulting output is always less than 42. A properly-written function will define its expectations such that the `Ensures()` macros will never trigger. Instead, the `Expects()` checks will likely trigger instead, if the input would lead to an output that violates the contract.

Utilities

The GSL also provides some helper utilities that are useful in creating a more reliable and readable code. One example of these utilities is the `gsl::finally{}` API, as follows:

```
#define concat1(a,b) a ## b
#define concat2(a,b) concat1(a,b)
#define ____ concat2(dont_care, __COUNTER__)

#include <gsl/gsl>
#include <iostream>

int main(void)
{
    auto ____ = gsl::finally([]{
        std::cout << "Hello World\n";
    });
}

// > g++ scratchpad.cpp; ./a.out
// Hello World
```

`gsl::finally{}` provides a simple means to execute code just prior to a function exiting, by leveraging a C++ destructor. This is helpful when a function has to perform cleanup before exiting. It should be noted that `gsl::finally{}` is most useful in the presence of exceptions. Often, cleanup code is forgotten when an exception is fired, preventing the cleanup logic from ever executing. The `gsl::finally{}` API will always execute, even if an exception is fired, so long as it is defined just prior to performing an action that might generate an exception.

In the preceding code, we also include a useful macro that allows the use of ____ to define the name of the `gsl::finally{}` to use. Specifically, the user of `gsl::finally{}` must store an instance of the `gsl::finally{}` object so that the object can be destroyed on exiting the function, but having to name the `gsl::finally{}` object is cumbersome and pointless, as there are no APIs to interact with the `gsl::finally{}` object (its only purpose is to execute on `exit`). This macro provides a simple way of saying, *I don't care what the variable's name is.*

Other utility that the GSL provides are `gsl::narrow<>()` and `gsl::narrow_cast<>()`, for example:

```
#include <gsl/gsl>
#include <iostream>

int main(void)
```

```
{
    uint64_t val = 42;

    auto val1 = gsl::narrow<uint32_t>(val);
    auto val2 = gsl::narrow_cast<uint32_t>(val);
}

// > g++ scratchpad.cpp; ./a.out
//
```

Both of these APIs are the same as a regular static_cast<>(), with the only difference being that gsl::narrow<>() performs an overflow check while gsl::narrow_cast<>() is just a synonym for static_cast<>(), which documents that a narrowing of an integer is taking place (that is, converting an integer with a larger number of bits into an integer with fewer bits), for example:

```
#endif

#if SNIPPET30

#define GSL_THROW_ON_CONTRACT_VIOLATION
#include <gsl/gsl>
#include <iostream>

int main(void)
{
    uint64_t val = 0xFFFFFFFFFFFFFFFF;

    try {
        gsl::narrow<uint32_t>(val);
    }
    catch(...) {
        std::cout << "narrow failed\n";
    }
}

// > g++ scratchpad.cpp; ./a.out
// narrow failed
```

In the preceding example, we attempt to convert a 64-bit integer into a 32-bit integer using the gsl::narrow<>() function, which performs an overflow check. Since an overflow does occur, an exception is thrown.

Summary

In this chapter, we provided an overview of some of the recent advancements in C++ that are leveraged in this book. We started with an overview of the changes made to C++ in the C++17 specification. We then briefly covered a C++ design pattern called RAII, and how it is used by C++. Finally, we introduced the GSL and how it can help to increase the reliability and stability of system programming by helping to adhere to the C++ Core Guidelines.

In the next chapter, we will go over UNIX-specific topics such as UNIX processes and signals, and a comprehensive overview of the System V specification, which is used to define how programs are written for UNIX on Intel CPUs.

Questions

1. What are structured bindings?
2. What changes did C++17 make to nested namespaces?
3. What changes did C++17 make to the `static_assert()` function?
4. What is an `if` statement initializer?
5. What does RAII stand for?
6. What is RAII used for?
7. What does `gsl::owner<>{}` do?
8. What is the purpose of `Expects()` and `Ensures()`?

Further Reading

- https://www.packtpub.com/application-development/c17-example
- https://www.packtpub.com/application-development/getting-started-c17-programming-video

5
Programming Linux/Unix Systems

The goal of this chapter is to explain the foundations of programming on Linux/Unix-based systems. This will provide a more complete picture of how a program executes on a Unix/Linux system, how to write more efficient code, and where to look when hard-to-find bugs arise.

To that end, this chapter starts by taking a comprehensive look at the Linux ABI, or more specifically, the System V ABI. In this section, we will review everything from the register and stack layout, to the System V calling conventions and ELF binary object specification.

The next section will briefly cover the Linux filesystem, including the standard layout and permissions. We will then provide a comprehensive review of Unix processes and how to program them, including considerations such as forking new processes and interprocess communication.

Finally, this chapter will conclude with a brief overview of Unix-based signals and how to work with them (both sending them and receiving them).

In this chapter, we will address the following:

- The Linux ABI
- The Unix filesystem
- Unix process APIs
- Unix signal APIs

Technical requirements

In order to follow the examples in this chapter, you must have the following:

- A Linux-based system capable of compiling and executing C++17 (for example, Ubuntu 17.10+)
- GCC 7+
- CMake 3.6+
- An internet connection

To download all the code in this chapter, including the examples and code snippets, go to the following link: `https://github.com/PacktPublishing/Hands-On-System-Programming-with-CPP/tree/master/Chapter05`.

The Linux ABI

In this section, we will discuss the Linux ABI (which is actually called the **System V ABI**), as well as the ELF standard and its use in Linux/Unix.

We will also dive into some of the details associated with ELF files, how to read and interpret them, and some of the implications of specific components within an ELF file.

The System V ABI

Unix System V was one of the first versions of Unix available, and largely defined Unix for years. Under the hood, System V leveraged the System V ABI. As Linux and BSD (Unix-like operating systems) became more widely used, the popularity of System V declined. However, the System V ABI remained popular, as operating systems such as Linux adopted this specification for Intel-based PCs.

In this chapter, we will focus on the System V ABI for Intel platforms on the Linux operating system. It should be noted, however, that other architectures and operating systems might use different ABIs. For example, ARM has its own ABI, which is largely based on System V (and, oddly, the Itanium 64 specification), but has several key differences.

The goal of this section is to expose the inner workings of a single Unix ABI, which in turn should make learning other ABIs easier, if needed.

Most of the specifications discussed in this chapter can be found at the following link: `https://refspecs.linuxfoundation.org/`.

The System V ABI defines most of the low-level details of a program (which in turn define the interfaces for system programming), including:

- The register layout
- The stack frame
- Function prologs and epilogs
- The calling convention (that is, parameter passing)
- Exception handling
- Virtual memory layout
- Debugging
- The binary object format (in this case, ELF)
- Program loading and linking

In `Chapter 2`, *Learning the C, C++17, and POSIX Standards*, we discussed the details of program linking and dynamic loading, and we devoted an entire section to the binary object format (ELF).

The following is a brief description of the remaining details of the System V specification, with respect to the Intel 64-bit architecture.

The register layout

For the purpose of keeping this topic simple, we will focus on Intel 64-bit. A whole book could be written on the different register layouts for each ABI, operating system, and architecture combination.

The Intel 64-bit architecture (which is usually referred to as AMD64, as AMD actually wrote it) defines several registers, of which a few have defined meanings within the instruction set.

The instruction pointer `rip` defines a program's current location in executable memory. Specifically, as a program executes, it executes from the location stored in `rip`, and each time an instruction is retired, `rip` advances to the next instruction.

The stack pointer and the base pointer (`rsp` and `rbp` respectively) are used to define the current location in the stack, as well as the location of the beginning of a stack frame (we will provide more information on this later).

The following are the remaining general-purpose registers. These have different meanings, which will be discussed in the rest of this section: `rax`, `rbx`, `rcx`, `rdx`, `rdi`, `rsi`, `r8`, `r9`, `r10`, `r11`, `r12`, `r13`, `r14`, and `r15`.

It should be noted before we continue that there are several other registers defined on the system that have very specific purposes, including floating-point registers and wide registers (which are used by special instructions designed to speed up certain types of calculations; for example, SSE and AVX). These are out of scope for the purpose of this discussion.

Finally, some of the registers end with letters, while others end with numbers, because versions of Intel's x86 processors only had letter-based registers, and the only true, general-purpose registers were AX, BX, CX, and DX.

When 64-bit was introduced by AMD, the number of general-purpose registers doubled, and to keep things simple, the register names were given numbers.

The stack frame

The stack frame is used to store the return address of each function, and to store function parameters and stack-based variables. It is a resource used heavily by all program, and it takes the following form:

```
high |----------| <- top of stack
     |          |
     |   Used   |
     |          |
     |----------| <- Current frame (rbp)
     |          | <- Stack pointer (rsp)
     |----------|
     |          |
     |  Unused  |
     |          |
 low |----------|
```

The stack frame is nothing more than an array of memory that grows from top to bottom. That is to say, on an Intel PC, pushing to the stack *subtracts* from the stack pointer, while popping from the stack *adds* to the stack pointer—which means that memory actually grows down (assuming your view is that memory grows upward as an address increases, as in the previous diagram).

The System V ABI states that the stack is made up of stack *frames*. Each frame looks like the following:

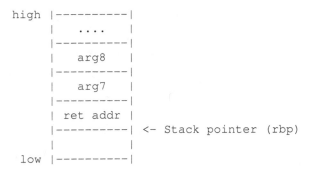

```
high |----------|
     |   ....   |
     |----------|
     |   arg8   |
     |----------|
     |   arg7   |
     |----------|
     | ret addr |
     |----------| <- Stack pointer (rbp)
     |          |
 low |----------|
```

Each frame represents a function call, and starts with any arguments to a function beyond the first six being called (the first six arguments are passed as registers—this will be discussed in more detail later). Finally, the return address is pushed to the stack, and the function is called.

Memory after the return address belongs to variables that are scoped to the function itself. This is why we call variables defined in a function *stack-based variables*. The remaining stack is used by functions that will be called in the future. Each time one function calls another, the stack grows, while each time a function returns, the stack shrinks.

It is the job of the operating system to manage the size of the stack, ensuring that it always has enough memory. For example, if an application is trying to use too much memory, the operating system will kill the program.

Finally, it should be noted that on most CPU architectures, special instructions are provided that return from a function call and automatically pop the return address of the stack. In the case of Intel, the `call` instruction will jump to a function and push the current `rip` to the stack as the return address, and then `ret` will pop the return address from the stack and jump the address that was popped.

Function prologs and epilogs

Each function comes with a stack frame that, as stated previously, stores function parameters, function variables, and return addresses. The code that manages these resources is called the function's *prolog* (beginning) and *epilog* (ending).

To better explain this, let's create a simple example and examine the resulting binary:

```
int test()
{
    int i = 1;
    int j = 2;

    return i + j;
}

int main(void)
{
    test();
}

// > g++ scratchpad.cpp; ./a.out
//
```

If we disassemble the resulting binary, we get the following:

```
...
00000000000005fa <_Z4testv>:
 push %rbp
 mov %rsp,%rbp
 movl $0x1,-0x8(%rbp)
 movl $0x2,-0x4(%rbp)
 mov -0x8(%rbp),%edx
 mov -0x4(%rbp),%eax
 add %edx,%eax
 pop %rbp
 retq
...
```

In our test function, the first two instructions are the function's prolog. The prolog is pushing the current stack frame (which is the previous function's stack frame), and then setting the current stack pointer to rbp, which is in turn creating a new stack frame.

From there, the next two instructions are using the unused portion of the stack to create the variables i and j. Finally, the resulting stack-based variables are loaded into registers, and the result is added and returned in rax (which is the return register for most ABIs defined for Intel).

The function's epilog is the final two instructions in this example. Specifically, the location of the previous stack frame (which was pushed to the stack in the prolog) is popped from the stack and stored in rbp, effectively changing to the previous stack frame, and then the ret instruction is used to return to the previous function (just after the function call).

A keen eye might have noticed that space was not reserved on the stack by moving rsp for the variables i and j. This is because the 64-bit version of the System V ABI defines what is called the **red zone**. The red zone only applies to leaf functions (in our case, the test function is a leaf function, meaning it doesn't call any other functions).

Leaf functions will never grow the stack any further, which means that the remaining stack can be used by the function without having to advance the stack pointer, as all remaining memory is fair game.

When system programming, this can sometimes be a problem if you are programming in the kernel. Specifically, if an interrupt fires (using the current stack pointer as its stack), corruption can occur if the stack was not properly reserved, therefore the interrupt would corrupt a leaf function's stack-based variables.

To overcome this, the red zone must be turned off using the −mno−red−zone flag with GCC. For example, if we compile the previous example with this flag, we get the following binary output:

```
. . .
00000000000005fa <_Z4testv>:
 push %rbp
 mov %rsp,%rbp
 sub $0x10,%rsp
 movl $0x1,-0x8(%rbp)
 movl $0x2,-0x4(%rbp)
 mov -0x8(%rbp),%edx
 mov -0x4(%rbp),%eax
 add %edx,%eax
 leaveq
 retq
. . .
```

As shown, the resulting binary is very similar to the original. There are two major differences, however. The first is the sub instruction, which is used to move the stack pointer, which in turn reserves stack space instead of using the red zone.

The second difference is the use of the leave instruction. This instruction pops rbp just as in the previous example, but also restores the stack pointer, which has been moved to make space for stack-based variables. In this example, the leave and ret instructions are the new epilog.

The calling convention

A calling convention dictates which registers are *volatile*, which registers are *non-volatile*, which registers are used for parameter passing and in which order, and which register is used to return the result of a function.

A non-volatile register is a register that is restored to its original value just prior to a function leave (that is, in its epilog). The System V ABI defines rbx, rbp, r12, r13, r14, and r15 as non-volatile. By contrast, a volatile register is one that a called function can change at will, without having to restore its value on return.

To demonstrate this, let's look at the following example:

```
0000000000000630 <__libc_csu_init>:
push %r15
push %r14
mov %rdx,%r15
push %r13
push %r12
```

As shown in the previous example, the __libc_csu_init() function (which is used by libc to initialize) touches r12, r13,r14, and r15. As such, it must push the original values of these registers to the stack before performing its initialization procedure.

In addition, in the middle of this code, the compiler stores rdx in r15. As will be shown later, the compiler is preserving the third argument to the function. Just based on this code, we know that this function takes at least three arguments.

A quick Google search will reveal that this function has the following signature:

```
__libc_csu_init (int argc, char **argv, char **envp)
```

Since this function touches *non-volatile* registers, it must restore these registers to their original values before leaving. Let's look at the function's epilog:

```
pop %rbx
pop %rbp
pop %r12
pop %r13
pop %r14
pop %r15
retq
```

As shown previously, the __libc_csu_init() function restores all the non-volatile registers before leaving. This means that, somewhere in the middle of the function, rbx was also clobbered (with its original value being pushed to the stack beforehand).

In addition to volatile and non-volatile registers being defined, System V's calling convention also defines which registers are used to pass function parameters. Specifically, the registers rdi, rsi, rdx, rcx, r8, and r9 are used to pass parameters (in the order provided).

To demonstrate this, let's look at the following example:

```
int test(int val1, int val2)
{
    return val1 + val2;
}

int main(void)
{
    auto ret = test(42, 42);
}

// > g++ scratchpad.cpp; ./a.out
//
```

In the previous example, we created a test function that takes two arguments, adds them together, and returns the result. Let's now look at the resulting binary for the main() function:

```
000000000000060e <main>:
push %rbp
mov %rsp,%rbp
sub $0x10,%rsp
mov $0x2a,%esi
mov $0x2a,%edi
callq 5fa <_Z4testii>
mov %eax,-0x4(%rbp)
mov $0x0,%eax
leaveq
retq
```

The first thing the main() function does is provide its prolog (as described in previous chapters, the main() function is not the first function to execute, and thus, a prolog and epilog are needed just like any other function).

The main() function then reserves space on the stack for the return value of the test() function, and fills in esi and edi with the parameters being passed to test() just before calling test().

The call instruction, as previously stated, pushes the return address onto the stack and then jumps to the test() function. The result of the test() function is stored on the stack (an operation that would be removed if optimization were enabled), and then 0 is placed in eax just before returning.

As we can see, we did not provide our main function with a return value. This is because, if no return value is provided, the compiler will automatically insert a return 0 for us, which is what we see in this code, as rax is the return register for System V.

Now let's look at the test function binary:

```
00000000000005fa <_Z4testii>:
push %rbp
mov %rsp,%rbp
mov %edi,-0x4(%rbp)
mov %esi,-0x8(%rbp)
mov -0x4(%rbp),%edx
mov -0x8(%rbp),%eax
add %edx,%eax
pop %rbp
retq
```

The test function sets up a prolog, and then stores the function's parameters on the stack (an operation that would be removed with optimizations turned on). The stack variables are then placed into volatile registers (to prevent them from having to be saved and restored), the registers are added together, and the result is stored in eax. Finally, the function returns with an epilog.

As stated previously, the return register for System V is rax, which means that every function that returns a value will do so using rax. To return more than one value, rdx can also be used. For example, see the following:

```
#include <cstdint>

struct mystruct
{
    uint64_t data1;
    uint64_t data2;
};

mystruct test()
```

```
{
    return {1, 2};
}

int main(void)
{
    auto ret = test();
}

// > g++ scratchpad.cpp; ./a.out
//
```

In the previous example, we create a `test` function that returns a structure that has two 64-bit integers. We choose two 64-bit integers because if we used regular ints, the compiler would attempt to store the contents of the struct in a single 64-bit register.

The resulting binary for the `test()` function is as follows:

```
00000000000005fa <_Z4testv>:
push %rbp
mov %rsp,%rbp
mov $0x1,%eax
mov $0x2,%edx
pop %rbp
retq
```

As previously shown, the `test` function stores the results in `rax` and `rdx` before returning. If more than 128 bits of data are returned, both the `main()` function and the `test()` function get way more complicated. This is because stack space must be reserved by the `main()` function, and then the `test()` function must leverage this stack space to return the results of the function.

The specific details of how this works are beyond the scope of this book, but, in short, the address of the stack space reserved for the return value actually becomes the first argument to the function, all of which is defined by the System V ABI.

It should be noted that the examples make heavy use of registers that are prefixed with e rather than r. This is because e denotes a 32-bit register, while r denotes a 64-bit register. The reason e versions are used so much is that we leverage integer-based literals such as 1, 2, and 42. These are all of type `int`, as defined by the C and C++ specifications (as stated in previous chapters), which, by default on an Intel 64 bit CPU, is a 32-bit value.

Exception handling and debugging

C++ exceptions provide a way to return an error to a `catch` handler somewhere in the call stack. We will cover C++ exceptions in great detail in `Chapter 13`, *Error - Handling with Exceptions*.

For now, we will work with the following simple example:

```
#include <iostream>
#include <exception>

void test(int i)
{
    if (i == 42) {
        throw 42;
    }
}

int main(void)
{
    try {
        test(1);
        std::cout << "attempt #1: passed\n";

        test(21);
        std::cout << "attempt #2: passed\n";
    }
    catch(...) {
        std::cout << "exception catch\n";
    }
}

// > g++ scratchpad.cpp; ./a.out
// attempt #1: passed
// exception catch
```

In the previous example, we create a simple `test()` function that takes an input. If the input is equal to `42`, we throw an exception. This will cause the function to return (and every calling function to continue to return) until a `try` or `catch` block is encountered. Any code executed in the `try` portion of the block will execute the `catch` portion of the block if an exception is thrown.

It should be noted that the return value of the called function is not considered or used. This provides a means to throw an error at any point in the execution of a call stack of functions, and catch possible errors at any point (most likely when the error can be safely handled or the program can be safely aborted).

As shown in the preceding example, the first attempt to execute the test() function succeeds, and the attempt #1: passed string is output to stdout. The second attempt to execute the test() function fails when the function throws an exception, and as a result, the attempt #2: passed string is not output to stdout as this code is never executed. Instead, the catch block is executed, which handles the error (by ignoring it).

The details of exception handling (and debugging) are exceptionally difficult (pun intended), and therefore the goal of this section is to explain how the System V specification dictates the ABI associated with exception (and debugging) support.

I provide more detail about the inner workings of C++ exceptions in the following video, recorded at CppCon: https://www.youtube.com/watch?v=uQSQy-7lveQ.

At the end of this section, the following should be clear:

- C++ exceptions are expensive to execute, and therefore should never be used for control flow (only error handling).
- C++ exceptions consume a lot of space in the executable and if they are not used, the -fno-exceptions flag should be passed to GCC to reduce the overall size of the resulting code. This also means that no library facilities that could possibly throw an exception should be used.

To support the previous example, the stack has to be *unwound*. That is, for the program to jump to the catch block, the non-volatile registers need to be set to appear as though the test() function was never executed in the first place. To do this, we, in a way, execute the test() function in reverse, using a set of instructions provided by the compiler.

Before we get into the details of this information, let's first look at the assembly code associated with our previous example:

```
0000000000000c11 <main>:
push %rbp
mov %rsp,%rbp
push %rbx
sub $0x8,%rsp
mov $0x1,%edi
callq b9a <test>
...
callq a30 <std::cout>
...
mov $0x0,%eax
jmp c90
...
callq 9f0 <__cxa_begin_catch@plt>
...
```

```
callq a70 <_Unwind_Resume@plt>
add $0x8,%rsp
pop %rbx
pop %rbp
retq
```

To keep this easy to understand, the previous code has been simplified. Let's start at the top. The first thing this function does is set up the function prolog (that is, the stack frame), and then reserve some space on the stack. Once this is done, the code moves `0x1` into `edi`, which passes a `1` to the `test()` function.

Next, the `test()` function is called. Next, some stuff happens (the details are not important), and then `std::cout` is called (which attempts to output the `attempt #1: passed` string to `stdout`). This process is repeated for `test(42)` as well.

The next bit of code is where the `main()` function gets interesting. `mov $0x0,%eax` sets `eax` to `0`, which, as we know, is the return register. This code sets up the return value for the `main()` function, but what is interesting is that the next instruction does a relative jumps to `c90` in the `main()` function, which is the `add $0x8,%rsp` code. This is the beginning of the epilog of the function, which cleans up the stack and restores the non-volatile registers.

The code in between is our `catch` block. This is the code that is executed if an exception is thrown. If an exception is not thrown, the `jmp c90` code is executed, which skips the `catch` block.

The `test` function is far more simple:

```
0000000000000a6a <_Z4testi>:
push %rbp
mov %rsp,%rbp
sub $0x10,%rsp
mov %edi,-0x4(%rbp)
cmpl $0x2a,-0x4(%rbp)
jne a9f
mov $0x4,%edi
callq 8e0 <__cxa_allocate_exception@plt>
...
callq 930 <__cxa_throw@plt>
nop
leaveq
retq
```

In the `test` function, the function prolog is set up, and stack space is reserved (which would likely be removed if optimizations were enabled). The input is then compared to `42`, and if they are not equal (as shown by the use of `jne`), the function jumps to the epilog and returns. If they are equal, a C++ exception is allocated and thrown.

The important thing to note here is that the `__cxa_throw()` function does not return, which means that the function's epilog is never executed. The reason for this is that, when an exception is thrown, the programmer is stating that the remaining portion of the function cannot execute, and instead, `__cxa_throw()` needs to jump to a `catch` block in the call stack (in this case, in the `main()` function), or terminate the program if a `catch` block cannot be found.

Since the function's epilog is never executed, the non-volatile registers need to be restored to their original state somehow. This brings us to the DWARF specification, and the `.eh_frame` table that is embedded in the application itself.

As will be shown later on in this chapter, most Unix-based applications are compiled to a binary format called **ELF**. Any ELF application that was compiled with C++ exception support contains a special table called the `.eh_frame` table (this stands for exception handling framework).

For example, if you run `readelf` on the previous application, you will see the `.eh_frame` table, as follows:

```
> readelf -SW a.out
There are 31 section headers, starting at offset 0x2d18:

Section Headers:
...
  [18] .eh_frame PROGBITS 0000000000000ca8 000ca8 000190 00 A 0 0 8
...
```

The DWARF specification (which doesn't officially stand for anything) provides all the information needed to debug an application. When debugging is enabled by GCC, several debugging tables are added to the application to assist GDB.

The DWARF specification is also used to define the instructions needed to reverse the stack; in other words, to execute a function in reverse with respect to the contents of the non-volatile registers.

Let's look at the contents of the `.eh_frame` table using `readelf`, as follows:

```
> readelf --debug-dump=frames a.out
...
00000088 000000000000001c 0000005c FDE ...
  DW_CFA_advance_loc: 1 to 0000000000000a6b
  DW_CFA_def_cfa_offset: 16
  DW_CFA_offset: r6 (rbp) at cfa-16
  DW_CFA_advance_loc: 3 to 0000000000000a6e
  DW_CFA_def_cfa_register: r6 (rbp)
  DW_CFA_advance_loc: 51 to 0000000000000aa1
  DW_CFA_def_cfa: r7 (rsp) ofs 8
  DW_CFA_nop
  DW_CFA_nop
  DW_CFA_nop
...
```

An entire book could be written on what this code does, but the goal here is to keep this simple. For every single function in the program (which could be hundreds of thousands of functions for programs with a lot of code), a block like the previous one is provided in `.eh_frame`.

The preceding block (which was located by matching addresses found using `objdump`) is the **Frame Description Entry** (**FDE**) for our `test()` function. This FDE describes how to reverse the stack using DWARF instructions, which are compressed instructions designed to be as small as possible (to reduce the size of the `.eh_frame` table).

The FDE provides the stack reversal instructions based on the location of the throw. That is to say, as a function executes, it continues to touch the stack. If more than one throw is present in a function, it is possible that more of the stack has been touched in between each throw, which means that more stack reversal instructions are needed to properly return the stack back to normal.

Once a function's stack has been reversed, the next function in the call stack needs to be reversed. This process continues until a `catch` block is located. The problem is that the `.eh_frame` table is a list of these FDEs, which means that reversing the stack is an $O(N^2)$ operation.

Optimizations have been carried out, including the use of a hash table, but two things remain true:

- Reversing the stack is a slow process.
- Using C++ exceptions takes up a lot of space. This is because each function defined in the code not only has to contain the code for that function, it must also contain an FDE that tells the code how to unwind the stack in the event that an exception is fired.

Virtual memory layout

Virtual memory layout is also provided by the System V specification. In the next section, we will discuss the details of the ELF format, which will provide more information about the virtual memory layout and how it can be changed.

Executable and Linkable Format (ELF)

The **Executable and Linkable Format** (**ELF**) is the main format used in most Unix-based operating systems, including Linux. Every ELF file begins with the hex number 0x7F, and continues with the ELF string.

For example, let's look at the following program:

```
int main(void)
{
}

// > g++ scratchpad.cpp; ./a.out
//
```

If we look at a hexdump of the resulting a.out ELF file, we see the following:

```
> hexdump -C a.out
00000000 7f 45 4c 46 02 01 01 00 00 00 00 00 00 00 00 00  |.ELF............|
00000010 03 00 3e 00 01 00 00 00 f0 04 00 00 00 00 00 00  |..>.............|
00000020 40 00 00 00 00 00 00 00 e8 18 00 00 00 00 00 00  |@...............|
00000030 00 00 00 00 40 00 38 00 09 00 40 00 1c 00 1b 00  |....@.8...@.....|
```

As shown, the `ELF` string is at the very beginning.

Every ELF file contains an ELF header, which describes some of the critical components of the ELF file itself. The following can be used to view an ELF file's header:

```
> readelf -hW a.out
ELF Header:
  Magic: 7f 45 4c 46 02 01 01 00 00 00 00 00 00 00 00 00
  Class: ELF64
  Data: 2's complement, little endian
  Version: 1 (current)
  OS/ABI: UNIX - System V
  ABI Version: 0
  Type: DYN (Shared object file)
  Machine: Advanced Micro Devices X86-64
  Version: 0x1
  Entry point address: 0x4f0
  Start of program headers: 64 (bytes into file)
  Start of section headers: 6376 (bytes into file)
  Flags: 0x0
  Size of this header: 64 (bytes)
  Size of program headers: 56 (bytes)
  Number of program headers: 9
  Size of section headers: 64 (bytes)
  Number of section headers: 28
  Section header string table index: 27
```

As shown, the ELF file that we compiled was linked to an ELF-64 file that adheres to the Unix System V ABI for Intel 64-bit. Near the bottom of the header, you might notice the mention of program headers and section headers.

Every ELF file can be viewed in terms of either its segments or its sections. To visualize this, let's look at an ELF file from both points of view, as follows:

```
       Segments          Sections
    |------------|    |------------|
    |   Header   |    |   Header   |
    |------------|    |------------|
    |            |    |            |
    |            |    |------------|
    |            |    |            |
    |            |    |            |
    |------------|    |------------|
    |            |    |            |
    |            |    |------------|
    |            |    |            |
    |------------|    |------------|
```

As previously shown, each ELF file is composed of sections. The sections are then grouped into segments, which are used to define which sections need to be loaded, and how (for example, some sections need to be loaded as read-write, others as read-execute, or, in some sub-optimal cases, read-write-execute).

ELF sections

To see a list of all of the sections, use the following command:

```
> readelf -SW a.out
```

This will result in the following output:

```
●  ●  ●                    user: ~/Hands-On-System-Programming-with-CPP/Chapter05
user:~/Hands-On-System-Programming-with-CPP/Chapter05$ readelf -SW a.out
There are 28 section headers, starting at offset 0x18e8:

Section Headers:
  [Nr] Name              Type            Address          Off    Size   ES Flg Lk Inf Al
  [ 0]                   NULL            0000000000000000 000000 000000 00      0   0  0
  [ 1] .interp           PROGBITS        0000000000000238 000238 00001c 00   A  0   0  1
  [ 2] .note.ABI-tag     NOTE            0000000000000254 000254 000020 00   A  0   0  4
  [ 3] .note.gnu.build-id NOTE           0000000000000274 000274 000024 00   A  0   0  4
  [ 4] .gnu.hash         GNU_HASH        0000000000000298 000298 00001c 00   A  5   0  8
  [ 5] .dynsym           DYNSYM          00000000000002b8 0002b8 000090 18   A  6   1  8
  [ 6] .dynstr           STRTAB          0000000000000348 000348 00007d 00   A  0   0  1
  [ 7] .gnu.version      VERSYM          00000000000003c6 0003c6 00000c 02   A  5   0  2
  [ 8] .gnu.version_r    VERNEED         00000000000003d8 0003d8 000020 00   A  6   1  8
  [ 9] .rela.dyn         RELA            00000000000003f8 0003f8 0000c0 18   A  5   0  8
  [10] .init             PROGBITS        00000000000004b8 0004b8 000017 00  AX  0   0  4
  [11] .plt              PROGBITS        00000000000004d0 0004d0 000010 10  AX  0   0 16
  [12] .plt.got          PROGBITS        00000000000004e0 0004e0 000008 08  AX  0   0  8
  [13] .text             PROGBITS        00000000000004f0 0004f0 000192 00  AX  0   0 16
  [14] .fini             PROGBITS        0000000000000684 000684 000009 00  AX  0   0  4
  [15] .rodata           PROGBITS        0000000000000690 000690 000004 04  AM  0   0  4
  [16] .eh_frame_hdr     PROGBITS        0000000000000694 000694 00003c 00   A  0   0  4
  [17] .eh_frame         PROGBITS        00000000000006d0 0006d0 000108 00   A  0   0  8
  [18] .init_array       INIT_ARRAY      0000000000200df0 000df0 000008 08  WA  0   0  8
  [19] .fini_array       FINI_ARRAY      0000000000200df8 000df8 000008 08  WA  0   0  8
  [20] .dynamic          DYNAMIC         0000000000200e00 000e00 0001c0 10  WA  6   0  8
  [21] .got              PROGBITS        0000000000200fc0 000fc0 000040 08  WA  0   0  8
  [22] .data             PROGBITS        0000000000201000 001000 000010 00  WA  0   0  8
  [23] .bss              NOBITS          0000000000201010 001010 000008 00  WA  0   0  1
  [24] .comment          PROGBITS        0000000000000000 001010 000024 01  MS  0   0  1
  [25] .symtab           SYMTAB          0000000000000000 001038 0005b8 18     26  42  8
  [26] .strtab           STRTAB          0000000000000000 0015f0 0001f8 00      0   0  1
  [27] .shstrtab         STRTAB          0000000000000000 0017e8 0000f9 00      0   0  1
Key to Flags:
  W (write), A (alloc), X (execute), M (merge), S (strings), I (info),
  L (link order), O (extra OS processing required), G (group), T (TLS),
  C (compressed), x (unknown), o (OS specific), E (exclude),
  l (large), p (processor specific)
user:~/Hands-On-System-Programming-with-CPP/Chapter05$
```

As shown, even in a simple example, there are several sections. Some of these sections contain information that has already been talked about in previous chapters:

- `eh_frame/.eh_frame_hdr`: These contain the FDE information for reversing the stack when dealing with exceptions, as just discussed. The `eh_frame_hdr` section contains additional information for improving the performance of C++ exceptions, including a hash table that can be used to locate an FDE instead of looping through the list of FDEs (which would be an $O(n^2)$ operation otherwise).

- `.init_array/.fini_array/.init/.fini`: These contain the constructors and destructors that are executed by the code, including any libraries that are linked to your code (as discussed, there could be many libraries linked to your application under the hood). It should also be noted that these sections contain code capable of performing runtime relocations, which must be executed at the very beginning of any application to ensure that code is properly linked and relocated.

- `.dynsym`: This contains all the symbols used for dynamic linking. As discussed earlier, if GCC is used, these symbols will all contain C runtime linking names, whereas if G++ is used, they will also contain mangled names. We will explore this section in more detail shortly.

A lot can be learned from the output of the sections in `readelf`. For example, the addresses all start with `0`, and not some address in higher memory. This means the application was compiled using the `-pie` flag during linking, which means that the application is relocatable. Specifically, **Position Independent Executable** (**PIE**) (and as such, the ELF file) contains the `.plt` and `.got` sections that are used to relocate the executable in memory.

This can also be seen from the inclusion of the `.rela.xxx` sections, which contain the actual relocation commands used by the ELF loader to relocate the executable in memory. To prove that this application was compiled using the `-pie` flag, let's look at the application's compilation flags:

```
> g++ scratchpad.cpp -v
...
/usr/lib/gcc/x86_64-linux-gnu/7/collect2 -plugin /usr/lib/gcc/x86_64-linux-
gnu/7/liblto_plugin.so -plugin-opt=/usr/lib/gcc/x86_64-linux-gnu/7/lto-
wrapper -plugin-opt=-fresolution=/tmp/ccmBVeIh.res -plugin-opt=-pass-
through=-lgcc_s -plugin-opt=-pass-through=-lgcc -plugin-opt=-pass-through=-
lc -plugin-opt=-pass-through=-lgcc_s -plugin-opt=-pass-through=-lgcc --
sysroot=/ --build-id --eh-frame-hdr -m elf_x86_64 --hash-style=gnu --as-
needed -dynamic-linker /lib64/ld-linux-x86-64.so.2 -pie -z now -z relro
/usr/lib/gcc/x86_64-linux-gnu/7/../../../x86_64-linux-gnu/Scrt1.o
/usr/lib/gcc/x86_64-linux-gnu/7/../../../x86_64-linux-gnu/crti.o
```

```
/usr/lib/gcc/x86_64-linux-gnu/7/crtbeginS.o -L/usr/lib/gcc/x86_64-linux-
gnu/7 -L/usr/lib/gcc/x86_64-linux-gnu/7/../../../x86_64-linux-gnu -
L/usr/lib/gcc/x86_64-linux-gnu/7/../../../../lib -L/lib/x86_64-linux-gnu -
L/lib/../lib -L/usr/lib/x86_64-linux-gnu -L/usr/lib/../lib -
L/usr/lib/gcc/x86_64-linux-gnu/7/../../.. /tmp/ccZU6K8e.o -lstdc++ -lm -
lgcc_s -lgcc -lc -lgcc_s -lgcc /usr/lib/gcc/x86_64-linux-gnu/7/crtendS.o
/usr/lib/gcc/x86_64-linux-gnu/7/../../../x86_64-linux-gnu/crtn.o
...
```

As previously shown, the -pie flag was provided.

Another thing to note is that the sections start at address 0 and progress, but, at some point, the address jumps to 0x200000 and continues from there. This means that the application is 2 MB aligned, which is typical for 64-bit applications as they have a much larger address space to work with.

As will be shown, the point at which the jump to 0x200000 starts is the beginning of a new program segment in the ELF file, and denotes a change in the permissions of the sections being loaded.

There are some notable sections that should also be pointed out:

- .text: This contains most, if not all, of the code associated with the program. This section is usually located in a segment marked as read-execute, and, ideally, is not given write permissions.
- .data: This contains global variables that are initialized to a value other than 0. As shown, this section exists in the ELF file itself, and, for this reason, these types of variables should be used sparingly as they increase the size of the resulting ELF file (which reduces the load time of the application and consumes additional space on the disk). It should also be noted that some compilers will place uninitialized variables in this section—so, if a variable should be 0, initialize it as such.
- .bss: This section contains all the global variables that should be initialized to 0 (assuming C and C++ is used). This section is always the last section to be loaded (that is to say, it is the last section marked by a segment), and does not actually exist in the ELF file itself. Instead, when an ELF file is loaded into memory, the size of the ELF file is extended to include the total size of this section, and the extra memory is initialized to 0 by the ELF loader (or the C runtime).

- .dynstr/.strtab: These tables contain the strings that are used for symbol names (that is, variable and function names). The .dynstr table contains all the strings that are needed during dynamic linking, while the .strtab section contains all the symbols in the program. The key point here is that the strings show up twice. The use of static in front of a variable or function prevents the variable's symbol from showing up in the .dynsym section, which in turn means it will not show up in the .dynstr section. The downside of this is that the variable cannot be seen during dynamic linking, which means that, if another library attempts to use extern on that variable, it will fail. By default, all variables and functions should be labeled static unless you intend them to be externally assessable, reducing the total size of the file on disk and in memory. This also speeds up linking time, as it reduces the size of the .dynsym section, which is used for dynamic linking.

To further examine how strings are stored in an ELF file, let's create a simple example with a string that is easy to look up, as follows:

```
#include <iostream>

int main(void)
{
    std::cout << "The answer is: 42\n";
}

// > g++ scratchpad.cpp; ./a.out
// The answer is: 42
```

As previously shown, this example outputs The answer is: 42 to stdout.

Let's now look for this string in the ELF file itself, using the following:

```
> hexdump -C a.out | grep "The" -B1 -A1
000008f0 f3 c3 00 00 48 83 ec 08 48 83 c4 08 c3 00 00 00 |....H...H.......|
00000900 01 00 02 00 00 54 68 65 20 61 6e 73 77 65 72 20 |.....The answer |
00000910 69 73 3a 20 34 32 0a 00 01 1b 03 3b 4c 00 00 00 |is: 42.....;L...|
```

As previously shown, the string exists in our program and is located at `0x905`. Now let's look at the ELF sections for this application:

```
                        user: ~/Hands-On-System-Programming-with-CPP/Chapter05
user:~/Hands-On-System-Programming-with-CPP/Chapter05$ readelf -SW a.out
There are 29 section headers, starting at offset 0x1b00:

Section Headers:
  [Nr] Name              Type            Address          Off    Size   ES Flg Lk Inf Al
  [ 0]                   NULL            0000000000000000 000000 000000 00      0   0  0
  [ 1] .interp           PROGBITS        0000000000000238 000238 00001c 00   A  0   0  1
  [ 2] .note.ABI-tag     NOTE            0000000000000254 000254 000020 00   A  0   0  4
  [ 3] .note.gnu.build-id NOTE           0000000000000274 000274 000024 00   A  0   0  4
  [ 4] .gnu.hash         GNU_HASH        0000000000000298 000298 000024 00   A  5   0  8
  [ 5] .dynsym           DYNSYM          00000000000002c0 0002c0 000108 18   A  6   1  8
  [ 6] .dynstr           STRTAB          00000000000003c8 0003c8 000117 00   A  0   0  1
  [ 7] .gnu.version      VERSYM          00000000000004e0 0004e0 000016 02   A  5   0  2
  [ 8] .gnu.version_r    VERNEED         00000000000004f8 0004f8 000040 00   A  6   2  8
  [ 9] .rela.dyn         RELA            0000000000000538 000538 000108 18   A  5   0  8
  [10] .rela.plt         RELA            0000000000000640 000640 000048 18   AI 5  22  8
  [11] .init             PROGBITS        0000000000000688 000688 000017 00   AX 0   0  4
  [12] .plt              PROGBITS        00000000000006a0 0006a0 000040 10   AX 0   0 16
  [13] .plt.got          PROGBITS        00000000000006e0 0006e0 000008 08   AX 0   0  8
  [14] .text             PROGBITS        00000000000006f0 0006f0 000202 00   AX 0   0 16
  [15] .fini             PROGBITS        00000000000008f4 0008f4 000009 00   AX 0   0  4
  [16] .rodata           PROGBITS        0000000000000900 000900 000018 00   A  0   0  4
  [17] .eh_frame_hdr     PROGBITS        0000000000000918 000918 00004c 00   A  0   0  4
  [18] .eh_frame         PROGBITS        0000000000000968 000968 000148 00   A  0   0  8
  [19] .init_array       INIT_ARRAY      0000000000200d88 000d88 000010 08   WA 0   0  8
  [20] .fini_array       FINI_ARRAY      0000000000200d98 000d98 000008 08   WA 0   0  8
  [21] .dynamic          DYNAMIC         0000000000200da0 000da0 000200 10   WA 6   0  8
  [22] .got              PROGBITS        0000000000200fa0 000fa0 000060 08   WA 0   0  8
  [23] .data             PROGBITS        0000000000201000 001000 000010 00   WA 0   0  8
  [24] .bss              NOBITS          0000000000201020 001010 000118 00   WA 0   0 32
  [25] .comment          PROGBITS        0000000000000000 001010 000024 01   MS 0   0  1
  [26] .symtab           SYMTAB          0000000000000000 001038 0006a8 18      27  47  8
  [27] .strtab           STRTAB          0000000000000000 0016e0 000321 00      0   0  1
  [28] .shstrtab         STRTAB          0000000000000000 001a01 0000fe 00      0   0  1
Key to Flags:
  W (write), A (alloc), X (execute), M (merge), S (strings), I (info),
  L (link order), O (extra OS processing required), G (group), T (TLS),
  C (compressed), x (unknown), o (OS specific), E (exclude),
  l (large), p (processor specific)
user:~/Hands-On-System-Programming-with-CPP/Chapter05$
```

If we look at the addresses within the sections, we can see that the string exists in a section called `.rodata`, which contains *constant* data.

Now let's look at the assembly for this application using `objdump`, which disassembles the code in the `.text` section, as follows:

```
 user: ~/Hands-On-System-Programming-with-CPP/Chapter05
7f4:    5d                          pop     %rbp
7f5:    e9 66 ff ff ff              jmpq    760 <register_tm_clones>

00000000000007fa <main>:
7fa:    55                          push    %rbp
7fb:    48 89 e5                    mov     %rsp,%rbp
7fe:    48 8d 35 00 01 00 00        lea     0x100(%rip),%rsi      # 905 <_ZStL19piecewise_construct+0x1>
805:    48 8d 3d 14 08 20 00        lea     0x200814(%rip),%rdi       # 201020 <_ZSt4cout@@GLIBCXX_3.4>
80c:    e8 af fe ff ff              callq   6c0 <_ZStlsISt11char_traitsIcEERSt13basic_ostreamIcT_ES5_PKc@plt>
811:    b8 00 00 00 00              mov     $0x0,%eax
816:    5d                          pop     %rbp
817:    c3                          retq

0000000000000818 <_Z41__static_initialization_and_destruction_0ii>:
818:    55                          push    %rbp
819:    48 89 e5                    mov     %rsp,%rbp
```

As previously shown, the code loads `rsi` with the address of the string (at `0x905`), which is the second parameter, just prior to calling `std::cout`. It should be noted that, as before, this application was compiled using the `-pie` command, which means that the application itself will be relocated. This ultimately means that the address of the string will not be at `0x905`, but instead will be at `# + 0x905`.

To prevent the need for a relocation entry (that is, an entry in the **Global Offset Table (GOT)**), the program uses an instruction pointer relative offset. In this case, the instruction to load `rsi` is at `0x805`, and the offset `0x100` is used, which in turn returns `0x905 + rip`. This means that, no matter where in memory the application is loaded, the code can locate the string without a relocation entry being needed.

ELF segments

As previously stated, ELF segments group the sections into loadable components, and describe how and where to load the ELF file in memory. The ideal ELF loader would only have to read ELF segments to load an ELF file, and (in the case of a relocatable ELF file) also have to load the dynamic sections and relocation sections.

To see an ELF's segments, use the following code:

```
user: ~/Hands-On-System-Programming-with-CPP/Chapter05
user:~/Hands-On-System-Programming-with-CPP/Chapter05$ readelf -lW a.out

Elf file type is DYN (Shared object file)
Entry point 0x6f0
There are 9 program headers, starting at offset 64

Program Headers:
  Type           Offset   VirtAddr           PhysAddr           FileSiz MemSiz  Flg Align
  PHDR           0x000040 0x0000000000000040 0x0000000000000040 0x0001f8 0x0001f8 R   0x8
  INTERP         0x000238 0x0000000000000238 0x0000000000000238 0x00001c 0x00001c R   0x1
      [Requesting program interpreter: /lib64/ld-linux-x86-64.so.2]
  LOAD           0x000000 0x0000000000000000 0x0000000000000000 0x000ab0 0x000ab0 R E 0x200000
  LOAD           0x000d88 0x0000000000200d88 0x0000000000200d88 0x000288 0x0003b0 RW  0x200000
  DYNAMIC        0x000da0 0x0000000000200da0 0x0000000000200da0 0x000200 0x000200 RW  0x8
  NOTE           0x000254 0x0000000000000254 0x0000000000000254 0x000044 0x000044 R   0x4
  GNU_EH_FRAME   0x000918 0x0000000000000918 0x0000000000000918 0x00004c 0x00004c R   0x4
  GNU_STACK      0x000000 0x0000000000000000 0x0000000000000000 0x000000 0x000000 RW  0x10
  GNU_RELRO      0x000d88 0x0000000000200d88 0x0000000000200d88 0x000278 0x000278 R   0x1

 Section to Segment mapping:
  Segment Sections...
   00
   01     .interp
   02     .interp .note.ABI-tag .note.gnu.build-id .gnu.hash .dynsym .dynstr .gnu.version .gnu.
version_r .rela.dyn .rela.plt .init .plt .plt.got .text .fini .rodata .eh_frame_hdr .eh_frame
   03     .init_array .fini_array .dynamic .got .data .bss
   04     .dynamic
   05     .note.ABI-tag .note.gnu.build-id
   06     .eh_frame_hdr
   07
   08     .init_array .fini_array .dynamic .got
user:~/Hands-On-System-Programming-with-CPP/Chapter05$
```

As shown previously, the simple example has several program segments. The first segment describes the program header (which defines the segments) and, for the most part, can be ignored.

The second segment tells the ELF loader which relocator it is expecting to use. Specifically, the program that is described in this segment is used for lazy relocations. When a program is dynamically linked, the symbols in the GOT and **Procedure Linkage Table** (**PLT**) contain the actual address in memory for each symbol, and the code references the entries in this table instead of directly referencing a symbol.

This is necessary, as the compiler has no way of knowing the location of a symbol in another library, so the ELF loader fills in the location of each symbol by loading the GOT and PLT for symbols that exist in other libraries (or symbols that are not marked as static).

The problem is that a large program can have hundreds or thousands of these GOT or PLT entries and, as a result, loading a program could take a long time. What makes this problem even worse is that a lot of symbols from external libraries may never be called, which means the ELF loader would need to fill in an entry in the GOT or PLT with a symbol location that is not even needed.

To overcome these issues, the ELF loader loads the GOT and PLT with the location of a lazy loader, instead of the symbol itself. The lazy loader (which is the program you see in the second segment) loads the location of a symbol once it is used for the first time, reducing program load times.

The third segment, marked as LOAD, tells the ELF loader to load the following portion of the ELF file into memory. As shown in the previous output, this segment contains several sections, all of which are marked as read-execute. For example, the .text section exists in this section.

All the ELF loader has to do is follow the instructions by loading the portion of the ELF file marked by the segment into the virtual address provided (with the memory size provided).

The fourth segment is the same as the third, but instead of the read-execute sections being marked, the read-write sections are marked, including sections such as .data.

It should be noted that the offset in memory to load the fourth segment increases by 0x200000. As previously stated, this is because the program is 2 MB aligned. More specifically, Intel 64-bit CPUs support 4 KB, 2 MB, and 1 GB pages.

Since the first loadable segment is marked read-execute, the second loadable segment cannot be on the same page as the first (otherwise, it too would have to be marked read-execute). As a result, the second loadable segment is designed to start on the next available page, which in this case, is 2 MB in memory. This allows the operating system to mark the first loadable segment as read-execute and the second loadable segment as read-write, and the CPU can enforce these permissions.

The next segment defines the location of the dynamic section, which is used by the ELF loader to perform dynamic relocations. This is necessary because the executable was compiled using -pie. It should be noted that the ELF loader could scan the ELF sections to find this data, but the goal of the program segments is to define all of the information needed to load an ELF file without the need for scanning the sections. Sadly, in practice, this is not always true, but, ideally, this should be the case.

The *notes* segment can safely be ignored. The following segments provide the ELF loader with the location of the exception information (as described); the permissions for the stack that the executable expects; which, ideally, would always be read-write and not read-write-execute, and the location of the read-only section, which can have its permissions changed to read-only once loaded.

The Unix filesystem

The Unix filesystem, which is used by most Unix-based operating systems, including Linux, consists of a virtual filesystem tree, which is the frontend to the user and applications. The tree starts with the root (that is, /), and all files, devices, and other resources are located within this single root directory.

From there, a physical filesystem is usually mapped onto the virtual filesystem, providing a mechanism by which files are stored and retrieved. It should be noted that this physical filesystem does not have to be a disk; it could also be RAM or some other type of storage device.

To perform this mapping, the operating system has a mechanism for instructing the OS to perform this mapping. On Linux, this is done using /etc/fstab, as follows:

```
> cat /etc/fstab
UUID=... / ext4 ...
UUID=... /boot/efi vfat ...
```

As shown in this example, the root filesystem maps to a specific physical device (denoted with a UUID), which contains an ext4 filesystem. In addition, within this root filesystem, another physical partition is mapped to /boot/efi and contains a VFAT filesystem.

What this means is that all access to the virtual filesystem defaults to the ext4 partition, while access to anything below /boot/efi is redirected to a separate VFAT partition that contains files specific to UEFI (which is the specific BIOS being used in the textbox used to write this book).

Any node within the virtual filesystem can be remapped to any device or resource. The brilliance behind this design is that applications do not need to be concerned with what type of device the virtual filesystem is currently mapping, as long as the application has permissions for the portion of the filesystem it is trying to access, and has the ability to open a file and read and write to it.

For example, let's look at the following:

```
> ls /dev/null
/dev/null
```

On most Linux-based systems, a file called /dev/null exists. This file doesn't actually map to a real file. Instead, the virtual filesystem maps this file to a device driver that ignores all writes and returns nothing when read. For example, see the following:

```
> echo "Hello World" > /dev/null
> hexdump -n16 /dev/null
<nothing>
```

Most Linux-based systems also provide a /dev/zero, which returns all zeros when read, as follows:

```
> hexdump -n16 /dev/zero
0000000 0000 0000 0000 0000 0000 0000 0000 0000
0000010
```

There is also /dev/random, which returns a random number when read, as follows:

```
> hexdump -n16 /dev/random
0000000 3ed9 25c2 ad88 bf62 d3b3 0f72 b32a 32b3
0000010
```

As discussed previously, in Chapter 2, *Learning the C, C++17, and POSIX Standards*, the layout of the filesystem that POSIX defines is as follows:

- /bin: for binaries used by all users
- /boot: for files needed to boot the operating system
- /dev: for physical and virtual devices
- /etc: for configuration files needed by the operating system
- /home: for user-specific files
- /lib: for libraries needed by executables
- /mnt and /media: used as temporary mount points
- /sbin: for system-specific binaries
- /tmp: for files that are deleted on reboot
- /usr: for user-specific versions of the preceding folders

Typically, the files under /boot point to a physical partition that is different to the root partition, the /dev folder contains files that are mapped to devices (rather than files that are stored and retrieved on a disk), and /mnt or /media is used to mount temporary devices such as USB storage devices and CD-ROMs.

On some systems, /home could be mapped to a completely separate hard drive, allowing the user to completely format and reinstall the root filesystem (that is, to reinstall the OS), without losing any personal files or configurations.

The Unix filesystem also maintains an entire set of permissions that define who is allowed to read, write, and execute files. See the following example:

```
> ls -al
total 40
drwxrwxr-x 3  user user ... .
drwxrwxr-x 16 user user ... ..
-rwxrwxr-x 1  user user ... a.out
drwxrwxr-x 3  user user ... build
-rw-rw-r-- 1  user user ... CMakeLists.txt
-rw-rw-r-- 1  user user ... scratchpad.cpp
```

The filesystem defines the permissions for the file's owner, the file's group, and others (users who are neither the owner nor part of the file's group).

The first column in the preceding example defines a file's permissions. The d defines whether or not a node is a directory or a file. The first of the three characters define the read/write/execute permissions for a file's owner, while the second defines the permissions for a file's group, and finally, the third defines the permissions for others.

The third column in the preceding example defines the name of the owner, while the second column defines the name of the group (which, in most cases, is also the owner).

Using this permission model, the Unix filesystem can control access to any file or directory for any given user, a group of users, and everyone else.

Unix processes

A process on a Unix-based system is a userspace application executed and scheduled by the operating system. In this book, we will refer to processes and userspace applications interchangeably.

As will be shown, most Unix-based processes that are running at any given time are children of some other parent process, and each kernel implements processes under the hood differently, but the same basic commands for creating and managing processes are provided by all Unix operating systems.

In this section, we will discuss how to create and manage Unix-based processes using commonly-seen POSIX interfaces.

The fork() function

On a Unix-based system, the fork() function is used to create processes. The fork() function is a relatively simple system call provided by the operating system that takes the current process, and creates a duplicate child version of the process. Everything about the parent and child processes is the same, including opened file handles, memory, and so on, with the key difference being that the child process has a new process ID.

In Chapter 12, *Learning to Program POSIX and C++ Threads*, we will discuss threads (which are more commonly used for system programming than processes). Both threads and processes are scheduled by the operating system; the main difference between a thread and a process is that a child and parent process do not have access to one another's memory, while threads do.

Even though fork() creates a new process with the same resources and memory layout, the memory that is shared between the parent and child processes are marked as copy-on-write. This means that, as the parent and child process executes, any attempt to write to memory that might have been shared causes the child process to create its own copies of memory that only it can write to. As a result, the parent process is unable to see modifications to the memory made by the child.

This is not true for threads, as threads maintain the same memory layout and are not marked as copy-on-write. As a result, a thread is capable of seeing the changes made to the memory by another thread (or parent process).

Let's look at the following example:

```cpp
#include <unistd.h>
#include <iostream>

int main(void)
{
    fork();
    std::cout << "Hello World\n";
}
```

```
// > g++ scratchpad.cpp; ./a.out
// Hello World
// Hello World
```

In this example, we use the `fork()` system call to create a duplicate process. The duplicate, child, process outputs `Hello World` to `stdout` using `std::cout`. As shown, the result of this example is that `Hello World` is output twice.

The `fork()` system call returns the process ID in the parent process for the child, and in the child 0, is returned. If an error occurs, `-1` is returned and `errno` is set to the appropriate error code. See the following example:

```
#include <unistd.h>
#include <iostream>

int main(void)
{
    if (fork() != 0) {
        std::cout << "Hello\n";
    }
    else {
        std::cout << "World\n";
    }
}

// > g++ scratchpad.cpp; ./a.out
// Hello
// World
```

In this example, the parent process outputs `Hello` while the child process outputs `World`.

To examine how shared memory is handled between the parent and child process, as described, let's look at the following example:

```
#include <unistd.h>
#include <iostream>

int data = 0;

int main(void)
{
    if (fork() != 0)
    {
        data = 42;
    }

    std::cout << "The answer is: " << data << '\n';
```

```
}

// > g++ scratchpad.cpp; ./a.out
// The answer is: 42
// The answer is: 0
```

In this example, we output the `The answer is:` string for both the parent and child processes. Both processes have access to a global variable called `data`, which is initialized to `0`. The difference is that the parent process sets the `data` variable to `42` and the child does not.

The parent process completes its job before the operating system schedules the child process, and, as a result, `The answer is: 42` is output to `stdout` first.

Once the child process has a chance to execute, it too outputs this string, but the answer is `0` and not `42`. This is because, as far as the child is concerned, the data variable was never set. Both the child process and the parent process have access to their own memory (at least, the memory that is written), and as such, `42` was set in the memory for the parent, not the child.

On most Unix-based operating systems, the first process to execute is `init`, which starts the rest of the processes on the system using `fork()`. This means the `init` process is the root-level parent for userspace applications (sometimes referred to as the grandparent). As such, the `fork()` system call can be used to create complex trees of processes.

See the following example:

```cpp
#include <unistd.h>
#include <iostream>

int main(void)
{
    fork();
    fork();
    std::cout << "Hello World\n";
}

// > g++ scratchpad.cpp; ./a.out
// Hello World
// Hello World
// Hello World
// Hello World
```

In the preceding example, we execute the `fork()` system call twice, which generates three additional processes. To understand why three processes are created instead of two, let's make a simple modification to the example, to highlight the tree structure that is created, as follows:

```
#include <unistd.h>
#include <iostream>

int main(void)
{
    auto id1 = fork();
    std::cout << "id1: " << id1 << '\n';

    auto id2 = fork();
    std::cout << "id2: " << id2 << '\n';
    std::cout << "-----------\n";
}

// > g++ scratchpad.cpp; ./a.out
// id1: 14181
// id2: 14182
// -----------
// id1: 0
// id2: 14183
// -----------
// id2: 0
// -----------
// id2: 0
// -----------
```

In this example, we execute `fork()` twice, as previously, with the main difference being that we output the ID for each process that is created. The parent process executes `fork()`, outputs the ID, executes `fork()` again, and then outputs the ID again before executing.

Since the IDs are not 0 (in fact, they are 14181 and 14182), we know that this is the parent process, and, as expected, it creates two child processes. The next IDs that are shown are 0 and 14183. This is the first child process (14181), which occurs at the first call to `fork()` by the parent.

This child process then continues to create its own child process (which has the ID 14183, as stated). The parent process and the child process each created an additional process (14182 and 14183) when the second `fork()` was executed, which both output 0 for id2. This accounts for the last two outputs.

It should be noted that this example might need to be executed several times to get a clean result, as each additional child process increases the chance that one child process will execute at the same time as the other child processes, corrupting the output. As processes do not share memory, implementing methods to synchronize the output in an example like this is non-trivial.

The use of `fork()` creates n^2 processes, with n being the total number of times `fork()` is called. For example, if `fork()` were called three times instead of two, as in the simplified preceding example, we would expect `Hello World` to output eight times instead of four, as shown here:

```
#include <unistd.h>
#include <iostream>

int main(void)
{
    fork();
    fork();
    fork();
    std::cout << "Hello World\n";
}

// > g++ scratchpad.cpp; ./a.out
// Hello World
// Hello World
// Hello World
// Hello World
// Hello World
// Hello World
// Hello World
// Hello World
```

In addition to the exponential growth of processes shown, some processes might choose to create a child while others might not, resulting in a complex process tree structure.

See the following example:

```
#include <unistd.h>
#include <iostream>

int main(void)
{
    if (fork() != 0) {
        std::cout << "The\n";
    }
    else {
        if (fork() != 0) {
```

```
            std::cout << "answer\n";
        }
        else {
            if (fork() != 0) {
                std::cout << "is\n";
            }
            else {
                std::cout << 42 << '\n';
            }
        }
    }
}

// > g++ scratchpad.cpp; ./a.out
// The
// answer
// is
// 42
```

In this example, the parent process creates child processes, while each child process does nothing. This results in the The answer is 42 string being output to stdout solely by the parent process.

The wait() function

As stated, each process is executed by the operating system in whatever order the operating system chooses. As a result, it is possible that the parent process could finish its execution prior to the child process completing. On some operating systems, this could result in corruption, as some operating systems require the parent process to be alive for the child process to successfully complete.

To handle this, POSIX provides the wait() function:

```
#include <unistd.h>
#include <iostream>
#include <sys/wait.h>

int main(void)
{
    if (fork() != 0) {
        std::cout << "parent\n";
        wait(nullptr);
    }
    else {
        std::cout << "child\n";
```

```
      }
}

// > g++ scratchpad.cpp; ./a.out
// parent
// child
```

In this example, we create a child process that outputs `child` to `stdout`. Meanwhile, the parent outputs `parent` to `stdout` and then executes the `wait()` function, which tells the parent to wait for a child to complete its execution.

We pass `nullptr` to the `wait()` function, as that tells the `wait()` function that we are not interested in an error code.

The `wait()` function waits for *any* child process to complete. It doesn't wait for a *specific* child process to complete. As a result, if more than one child process has been created, `wait()` must be executed more than once.

See the following example:

```
#include <unistd.h>
#include <iostream>
#include <sys/wait.h>

int main(void)
{
    int id;

    auto id1 = fork();
    auto id2 = fork();
    auto id3 = fork();

    while(1)
    {
        id = wait(nullptr);

        if (id == -1)
            break;

        if (id == id1)
            std::cout << "child #1 finished\n";

        if (id == id2)
            std::cout << "child #2 finished\n";

        if (id == id3)
            std::cout << "child #3 finished\n";
```

```
        }

    if (id1 != 0 && id2 != 0 && id3 != 0)
        std::cout << "parent done\n";
}

// > g++ scratchpad.cpp; ./a.out
// child #3 finished
// child #3 finished
// child #3 finished
// child #3 finished
// child #2 finished
// child #2 finished
// child #1 finished
// parent done
```

In the preceding example, we create eight child processes. As previously stated, the total number of processes created is 2^(the number of times `fork` is called). In this example, however, we are interested in making sure that the grandparent, which is the root parent process, is the last process to finish executing.

Remember that, when we call `fork()` like this, the first call creates the first child. The second call to `fork()` makes another child, but the first child now becomes a parent as it calls `fork()`. The same happens (but even more so) when we call `fork()` a third time. The grandparent is the root parent process.

Regardless of which process is the grandparent process, we want to ensure that all child processes finish before their parents do. To accomplish this, we record the process ID each time `fork()` is executed. For child processes, this ID is set to 0.

The next thing we do is enter a `while(1)` loop, and then call `wait()`. The `wait()` function will exit as soon as a child process is complete. Once the process is complete, we output which child process exited to `stdout`. If the process ID that we get from `wait()` is -1, we know that no more child processes exist, and we can exit the `while(1)` loop.

Finally, if none of the process IDs are equal to 0, we know that the process is the grandparent, and we output when it exits just to show that it is the last process to exit.

Since the `wait()` function will not return 0, we know that when a child process exits, we will only ever output the child process that exited within our `while(1)` loop. As shown, we see that one child with `id1` exits, two children with `id2` exit, and four children with `id3` exit. This is as expected, based on the math that we performed previously.

It should also be noted that this example ensures that all child processes are completed before the parent completes. This means that the grandparent must wait for its children to complete. Since the child processes of the grandparent also create their own processes, the grandparent must first wait for the parent process to complete, which must wait in turn for its children to complete.

This results in a cascading effect of child processes completing before their parents, all the way until the grandparent process finally completes.

Finally, it should also be noted that, although parents have to wait for their children to complete, it doesn't mean that all children with id3 will exit before children with id2 exit. This is because one half of the child tree could complete without issue before the other half completes, or in any order. As a result, it's possible to get outputs like this:

```
child #3 finished
child #3 finished
child #3 finished
child #2 finished
child #2 finished
child #3 finished
child #1 finished
parent done
```

In this example, the last `child #3` to complete was the process that was created by the last call to `fork()` by the grandparent process.

Interprocess communication (IPC)

In one of our preceding examples, we demonstrated how `fork()` can be used to create a child process from a parent process, as shown here:

```cpp
#include <unistd.h>
#include <iostream>
#include <sys/wait.h>

int main(void)
{
    if (fork() != 0) {
        std::cout << "parent\n";
        wait(nullptr);
    }
    else {
        std::cout << "child\n";
    }
}
```

```
// > g++ scratchpad.cpp; ./a.out
// parent
// child
```

The reason we see `parent` output before `child` in this example is merely the result of the operating system taking longer to start the child process than it takes to output from the child process. If the parent process were to take longer, `child` would output first.

See the following example:

```cpp
#include <unistd.h>
#include <iostream>
#include <sys/wait.h>

int main(void)
{
    if (fork() != 0) {
        sleep(1);
        std::cout << "parent\n";
        wait(nullptr);
    }
    else {
        std::cout << "child\n";
    }
}

// > g++ scratchpad.cpp; ./a.out
// child
// parent
```

This is identical to the previous example, with the exception that a `sleep()` command was added to the parent process, which tells the operating system to yield the execution of the parent for one second. As a result, the child process has plenty of time to execute, resulting in `child` being output first.

To prevent the child from executing first, we need to set up a communication channel between the parent and child process so that the child process knows to wait for the parent to finish outputting to `stdout` before the child does. This is called **synchronization**.

For more information about synchronization, how to handle it, and the issues that arise from synchronization, such as deadlock and race conditions, please see the *Further reading* section in this chapter.

In this section, the mechanism we will use to synchronize the parent and child process is called **Interprocess communication** (**IPC**). It should be noted before we continue that creating multiple processes and using IPC to synchronize them is a heavy-handed way of creating and coordinating more than one task on the operating system. Unless separate processes are absolutely needed, a better approach is to use threading, a topic that we cover in great detail in `Chapter 12`, *Learning to Program POSIX and C++ Threads*.

There are several different types of IPC that can be leveraged in a Unix system. Here, we will cover two of the most popular methods:

- Unix pipes
- Unix shared memory

Unix pipes

A pipe is a mechanism for sending information from one process to another. In its simplest form, a pipe is a file (in RAM) that one process can write to, and the other can read from. The file starts out empty, and no bytes can be read from the pipe until bytes are written to it.

Let's look at the following example:

```cpp
#include <string.h>
#include <unistd.h>
#include <sys/wait.h>

#include <array>
#include <iostream>
#include <string_view>

class mypipe
{
    std::array<int, 2> m_handles;

public:
    mypipe()
    {
        if (pipe(m_handles.data()) < 0) {
            exit(1);
        }
    }

    ~mypipe()
    {
        close(m_handles.at(0));
```

```cpp
            close(m_handles.at(1));
    }

    std::string
    read()
    {
        std::array<char, 256> buf;
        std::size_t bytes = ::read(m_handles.at(0), buf.data(),
buf.size());

        if (bytes > 0) {
            return {buf.data(), bytes};
        }

        return {};
    }

    void
    write(const std::string &msg)
    {
        ::write(m_handles.at(1), msg.data(), msg.size());
    }
};

int main(void)
{
    mypipe p;

    if (fork() != 0) {
        sleep(1);
        std::cout << "parent\n";

        p.write("done");
        wait(nullptr);
    }
    else {
        auto msg = p.read();

        std::cout << "child\n";
        std::cout << "msg: " << msg << '\n';
    }
}

// > g++ scratchpad.cpp -std=c++17; ./a.out
// parent
// child
// msg: done
```

This example is similar to the previous example, with the addition of a Unix pipe. This is used to ensure that even if the parent takes a while to execute, the parent outputs to stdout before the child executes. To accomplish this, we create a class that leverages **Resource Acquisition Is Initialization** (**RAII**) to encapsulate the Unix pipe, ensuring that the details of the C APIs are properly abstracted and the handles that are opened to support Unix pipes are closed when the mypipe class loses scope.

The first thing we do in the class is to open the pipe, as follows:

```
mypipe()
{
    if (pipe(m_handles.data()) < 0) {
        exit(1);
    }
}
```

The pipe itself is an array of two file handles. The first handle is used to read from the pipe, while the second handle is used to write to the pipe. The pipe() function will return −1 if an error occurs.

It should be noted that if the pipe() function succeeds, the result is two file handles that should be closed when they are no longer used. To support this, we close the file handles that were opened in the destructor of the class, so that when the pipe loses scope, the pipe is closed, as follows:

```
~mypipe()
{
    close(m_handles.at(0));
    close(m_handles.at(1));
}
```

We then provide a read() function as follows:

```
std::string
read()
{
    std::array<char, 256> buf;
    std::size_t bytes = ::read(m_handles.at(0), buf.data(), buf.size());

    if (bytes > 0) {
        return {buf.data(), bytes};
    }

    return {};
}
```

The `read()` function creates a buffer that can be read to, and we read from the pipe and place the results in the buffer. Notice how we read from the first file handle, as stated.

It should be noted that the `read()` and `write()` functions that we leverage here will be covered in detail in Chapter 8, *Learning to Program File Input/Output*. For now, it is important to note that the `read()` function, in this case, is a blocking function, and will not return until data is read from the pipe. If an error occurs (for example, the pipe is closed), −1 will be returned.

To account for this, we only return the data that is read from the pipe if actual bytes are read; otherwise, we return a null string, which can be used by the user of this class to detect an error (or we could use a C++ exception, as covered in Chapter 13, *Error - Handling with Exceptions*).

Finally, we also add a `write()` function to the pipe, as follows:

```
void
write(const std::string &msg)
{
    ::write(m_handles.at(1), msg.data(), msg.size());
}
```

The `write()` function is far simpler, writing to the write side of the pipe using the `write()` Unix function.

In the parent process we do the following:

```
sleep(1);
std::cout << "parent\n";

p.write("done");
wait(nullptr);
```

The first thing we do is sleep for one second, which ensures that the parent takes a long time to execute. If synchronization were not used, the child process would output to `stdout` before the parent process as a result of the use of this `sleep()` function.

The next thing we do is to output to `stdout` and then write the `done` message to the pipe. Finally, we wait for the child process to finish before exiting.

The child process does the following:

```
auto msg = p.read();

std::cout << "child\n";
std::cout << "msg: " << msg << '\n';
```

As stated, the read() function is a blocking function, which means that it will not return until data is read from the file handle (or an error occurs). We assume that no errors will occur, and store the resulting string in a variable called msg.

Since the read() function is blocking, the child process will wait until the parent process outputs to stdout, and then writes to the pipe. No matter what the parent process does before the write to the pipe, the child process will wait.

Once the call to read() returns, we output to stdout *child* and the message that was sent by the parent, and exit.

Using this simple example, we are able to send information from one process to another. In this case, we use this communication to synchronize the parent and child processes.

Unix shared memory

Unix shared memory is another popular form of IPC. Unlike Unix pipes, Unix shared memory provides a buffer that can be read and written to by both processes.

Let's examine the following example:

```
#include <string.h>
#include <unistd.h>
#include <sys/shm.h>
#include <sys/wait.h>

#include <iostream>

char *
get_shared_memory()
{
    auto key = ftok("myfile", 42);
    auto shm = shmget(key, 0x1000, 0666 | IPC_CREAT);

    return static_cast<char *>(shmat(shm, nullptr, 0));
}

int main(void)
{
    if (fork() != 0) {
        sleep(1);
        std::cout << "parent\n";

        auto msg = get_shared_memory();
        msg[0] = 42;
```

```
            wait(nullptr);
    }
    else {
  auto msg = get_shared_memory();
  while(msg[0] != 42);

  std::cout << "child\n";
    }
}


// > g++ scratchpad.cpp; ./a.out
// parent
// child
```

In the preceding example, we create the following function which is responsible for opening the shared memory between the parent and child processes:

```
char *
get_shared_memory()
{
    auto key = ftok("myfile", 42);
    auto shm = shmget(key, 0x1000, 0666 | IPC_CREAT);

    return static_cast<char *>(shmat(shm, nullptr, 0));
}
```

This function starts by creating a unique key, which is used by the operating system to associate the shared memory between the parent and child processes. Once this key is generated, shmget() is used to open the shared memory.

0x1000 tells shmget() that we would like to open 4 KB of memory, and 0666 | IPC_CREATE is used to tell shmget() that we would like to open the memory with read and write permissions, and create the shared memory file if it doesn't exist.

The result of shmget() is a handle that can be used by shmat() to return a pointer to the shared memory.

It should be noted that a more complete example would wrap this shared memory in a class so that RAII can be used as well as leveraging the GSL to properly protect the buffer that is shared between both processes.

In the parent process, we do the following:

```
sleep(1);
std::cout << "parent\n";

auto msg = get_shared_memory();
```

```
msg[0] = 42;

wait(nullptr);
```

As in the previous example, the parent sleeps for one second before outputting to `stdout`. Next, the parent gets the shared memory region, and writes `42` to the buffer. Finally, the parent waits for the child to complete before exiting.

The child process does the following:

```
auto msg = get_shared_memory();
while(msg[0] != 42);

std::cout << "child\n";
```

As shown, the child process gets the shared memory buffer and waits for the buffer to have the value `42`. Once it does, which means the parent process has finished outputting to `stdout`, the child outputs to `stdout` and exits.

The exec() function

Up until this point, all the child processes that we have created were copies of the parent process, with the same code and memory structure. Although this can be done, it is far less likely, as POSIX threads provide the same functionality without the issues with shared memory and IPC. POSIX threads will be discussed in more detail in `Chapter 12`, *Learning to Program POSIX and C++ Threads*.

Instead, it is more likely that calls to `fork()` will be followed by calls to `exec()`. The `exec()` system call is used to override the existing process with a completely new process. See the following example:

```
#include <unistd.h>
#include <iostream>

int main(void)
{
    execl("/bin/ls", "ls", nullptr);
    std::cout << "Hello World\n";
}

// > g++ scratchpad.cpp; ./a.out
// <output of ls>
```

In the preceding example, we make a call to `execl()`, which is a specific version of the `exec()` family of system calls. The `execl()` system call executes the first argument to the function, and passes the remaining arguments to the process as `argv[]`. The last argument always has to be `nullptr`, just as the last argument in `argv[]` is always `nullptr`.

The call to `exec()` (and friends) replaces the current process with the new process being executed. As a result, the call to output `Hello World` to `stdout` is not called. This is because this call is part of the `a.out` program, not the `ls` program, and since `exec()` replaces the current process with the new executable, the output never occurs.

This is why `fork()` and `exec()` are usually called together. The call to `fork()` creates a new process, while the call to `exec()` takes that new process and executes the desired program as that new process.

This is how the `system()` system call works:

```
#include <unistd.h>
#include <iostream>

int main(void)
{
    system("ls");
    std::cout << "Hello World\n";
}

// > g++ scratchpad.cpp; ./a.out
// <output of ls -al>
// Hello World
```

When calling `system()`, the `ls` executable is run, and the `system()` function waits until the executable is complete. Once it is complete, the execution continues and the call to output `Hello World` to `stdout` is made.

This is because the `system()` call forks a new process and runs `exec()` from that new process. The parent process runs `wait()` and returns when the child process is complete.

To demonstrate this, we can make our own version of the system call, as follows:

```
#include <unistd.h>
#include <iostream>
#include <sys/wait.h>

void
mysystem(const char *command)
{
```

```
        if (fork() == 0) {
            execlp(command, command, nullptr);
        }
        else {
            wait(nullptr);
        }
    }

int main(void)
{
    mysystem("ls");
    std::cout << "Hello World\n";
}

// > g++ scratchpad.cpp; ./a.out
// <output of ls>
// Hello World
```

In the `mysystem()` function, we execute `fork()` to create a new child process and then execute `execlp()` to execute `ls`. (The call to `execlp()` will be explained later.)

The parent process calls `wait()`, and waits for the newly-created child process to complete. Once it is complete, the call to `mysystem()` finishes, allowing the output of `Hello World` to execute.

It should be noted that there are a couple of improvements that would make this function more complete. The actual `system()` function passes arguments to the `exec()` call, which our version does not.

The `wait()` call doesn't check to make sure that the child process that completed was the process that was forked either. Instead, the call to `wait()` should loop until the child process that was forked actually completes.

To pass arguments to the child process, we can do the following using `execl()`:

```
#include <unistd.h>
#include <iostream>

int main(void)
{
    execl("/bin/ls", "ls", "-al", nullptr);
}

// > g++ scratchpad.cpp; ./a.out
// <output of ls -al>
```

In this example, we execute `/bin/ls` and pass `-al` to the process.

The second argument, which is `ls`, is the same as `argv[0]`, which is always the name of the process. And just as with `argv[argc] == nullptr`, our last argument is `nullptr`.

As mentioned earlier, there are different versions of `exec()`. See the following example:

```
#include <unistd.h>
#include <iostream>

int main(void)
{
    const char *envp[] = {"ENV1=1", "ENV2=2", nullptr};
    execle("/bin/ls", "ls", nullptr, envp);
}

// > g++ scratchpad.cpp; ./a.out
// <output of ls>
```

The `execle()` version does the same thing as `execl()`, but also provides the ability to pass in environment variables. In this case, we provide `ls` with the process-specific environment variables `ENV1` and `ENV2`.

The `execl()` function so far have taken an absolute path to `ls`. Instead of using the absolute path, the `PATH` environment variable can be used to locate the executable, as follows:

```
#include <unistd.h>
#include <iostream>

int main(void)
{
    execlp("ls", "ls", nullptr);
}

// > g++ scratchpad.cpp; ./a.out
// <output of ls>
```

The call to `execlp()` locates `ls` using `PATH`, instead of using an absolute path.

Alternatively, the `exec()` family also provides the ability to detail the `argv[]` arguments using a variable, instead of directly as a function argument to `exec()`, as follows:

```
#include <unistd.h>
#include <iostream>

int main(void)
```

```
{
    const char *argv[] = {"ls", nullptr};
    execv("/bin/ls", const_cast<char **>(argv));
}

// > g++ scratchpad.cpp; ./a.out
// <output of ls>
```

As shown here, the `execv()` calls allow you to define `argv[]` as a separate variable.

One issue with the `execv()` family of calls is that `argv[]` is technically an array of pointers to C-style strings, which take the form `const char *` in C++. However, calls to `execv()` and friends take `char**`, not `const char**`, which means that `const_cast` is needed to convert the arguments.

The `execv()` family also provides the ability to pass in environment variables, just like `execl()`, as follows:

```
#include <unistd.h>
#include <iostream>

int main(void)
{
    const char *argv[] = {"ls", nullptr};
    const char *envp[] = {"ENV1=1", "ENV2=2", nullptr};

    execve(
        "/bin/ls",
        const_cast<char **>(argv),
        const_cast<char **>(envp)
    );
}

// > g++ scratchpad.cpp; ./a.out
// <output of ls>
```

In the preceding example, we pass in the `argv[]` arguments and the environment variables using `execve()`.

Finally, it is also possible to use the path to locate the executable, instead of using an absolute value, as follows:

```
\#include <unistd.h>
#include <iostream>

int main(void)
{
```

```
        const char *argv[] = {"ls", nullptr};
        execvp("ls", const_cast<char **>(argv));
    }

// > g++ scratchpad.cpp; ./a.out
// <output of ls>
```

In this example, the PATH environment variable is used to locate ls.

Output redirection

In this chapter, we have outlined all the system calls that are needed to write your own shell. You can now create your own processes, load an arbitrary executable, and wait for the process to complete.

There are still a couple of things needed to create a complete shell. One of these is Unix signals, which will be discussed shortly; the other is capturing the output of a child process.

To do this, we will leverage a Unix pipe for IPC and tell the child process to redirect its output to this pipe so that the parent process can receive it.

See the following example:

```
#include <string.h>
#include <unistd.h>
#include <sys/wait.h>

#include <array>
#include <iostream>
#include <string_view>

class mypipe
{
    std::array<int, 2> m_handles;

public:
    mypipe()
    {
        if (pipe(m_handles.data()) < 0) {
            exit(1);
        }
    }

    ~mypipe()
    {
        close(m_handles.at(0));
```

```
                close(m_handles.at(1));
        }

        std::string
        read()
        {
                std::array<char, 256> buf;
                std::size_t bytes = ::read(m_handles.at(0), buf.data(),
buf.size());

                if (bytes > 0) {
                        return {buf.data(), bytes};
                }

                return {};
        }

        void
        redirect()
        {
                dup2(m_handles.at(1), STDOUT_FILENO);
                close(m_handles.at(0));
                close(m_handles.at(1));
        }
};

int main(void)
{
        mypipe p;

        if(fork() == 0) {
                p.redirect();
                execlp("ls", "ls", nullptr);
        }
        else {
                wait(nullptr);
                std::cout << p.read() << '\n';
        }
}

// > g++ scratchpad.cpp; ./a.out
// <output of ls>
```

In the preceding example, we use the same Unix pipe class that we created in the previous example. The difference, however, is that the child process will not write to the Unix pipe, but will output to stdout. So, we need to redirect the output of stdout to our Unix pipe.

To do this, we replace the `write()` function with `redirect()`, as follows:

```
void
redirect()
{
    dup2(m_handles.at(1), STDOUT_FILENO);
    close(m_handles.at(0));
    close(m_handles.at(1));
}
```

In this `redirect()` function, we tell the operating system to redirect all writes to `stdout` that are made to our pipe (the write side of the pipe). As a result, when the child process writes to `stdout`, the writes are redirected to the read side of the pipe for the parent process.

As a result, the pipe handles for the child process are no longer needed (and are closed before executing the child process).

The rest of the example is similar to our call to our custom `mysystem()` call, as follows:

```
if(fork() == 0) {
    p.redirect();
    execlp("ls", "ls", nullptr);
}
else {
    wait(nullptr);
    std::cout << p.read() << '\n';
}
```

A child process is created. Before we execute the `ls` command, we redirect the output of the child process. The parent process, just like `mysystem()`, waits for the child process to complete, and then reads the contents of the pipe.

To create your own complete shell, a lot more functionality would be needed, including providing asynchronous access to a child process's output for both `stdout` and `stderr`, the ability to execute processes in the foreground and background, parsing arguments, and so on. However, the bulk of the concepts that are needed have been provided here.

In the next section, we will discuss how Unix signals work.

Unix signals

Unix signals provide the ability to interrupt a given process, and allow a child to receive this interruption and handle it any way they wish.

Specifically, Unix signals provide the user with the ability to handle specific types of control flow and errors that might occur, such as a Terminal attempting to close your program, or a segmentation fault that might be recoverable.

See the following example:

```
#include <unistd.h>
#include <iostream>

int main(void)
{
    while(true) {
        std::cout << "Hello World\n";
        sleep(1);
    }
}

// > g++ scratchpad.cpp; ./a.out
// Hello World
// Hello World
// Hello World
// ...
// ^C
```

In the preceding example, we create a process that executes forever, outputting `Hello World` every second. To stop this application, we must use the `CTRL+C` command, which tells the shell to terminate the process. This is done using a Unix signal.

We can trap this signal as follows:

```
#include <signal.h>
#include <unistd.h>
#include <iostream>

void handler(int sig)
{
    if (sig == SIGINT)
    {
        std::cout << "handler called\n";
    }
}
```

```
int main(void)
{
    signal(SIGINT, handler);

    for (auto i = 0; i < 10; i++)
    {
        std::cout << "Hello World\n";
        sleep(1);
    }
}

// > g++ scratchpad.cpp; ./a.out
// Hello World
// Hello World
// ^Chandler called
// Hello World
// ^Chandler called
// Hello World
// ^Chandler called
// Hello World
// ^Chandler called
// Hello World
// Hello World
// Hello World
// Hello World
// Hello World
```

In this example, we create a loop that outputs Hello World to stdout every second, and does so 10 times. We then install a signal handler using the signal() function. This signal handler tells the operating system that we would like to call the handler() function any time SIGINT is called.

As a result, now, if we use CTRL+C, the signal handler is called instead, and we see handler called output to stdout.

It should be noted that, since we successfully handled SIGINT, using CTRL+C no longer kills the process, which is why we used a for() loop instead of a while(1) loop. You could also use CTRL+/ to send SIGSTOP instead of SIGINT, which would also kill the application in the preceding example.

Another way to overcome this would be to use a global variable capable of stopping the loop, as follows:

```
#include <signal.h>
#include <unistd.h>
#include <iostream>
```

```
auto loop = true;

void handler(int sig)
{
    if (sig == SIGINT)
    {
        std::cout << "handler called\n";
        loop = false;
    }
}

int main(void)
{
    signal(SIGINT, handler);

    while(loop) {
        std::cout << "Hello World\n";
        sleep(1);
    }
}

// > g++ scratchpad.cpp; ./a.out
// Hello World
// Hello World
// ^Chandler called
```

This example is identical to our previous example, except that we use a `while()` loop, which loops until the `loop` variable is `false`. In our signal handler, we set the `loop` variable to `true`, which stops the loop. This works because the signal handler is not executed in the same thread as the `while()` loop.

This is important to understand, as deadlock, corruption, and race conditions can occur when using signal handlers if these types of issues are not addressed. For more information on threading, see Chapter 12, *Learning to Program POSIX and C++ Threads*.

Finally, before we conclude, the `kill()` function can be used to send a signal to a child process, as follows:

```
#include <signal.h>
#include <unistd.h>
#include <sys/wait.h>

#include <iostream>

void
mysystem(const char *command)
{
```

```
        if(auto id = fork(); id > 0) {
            sleep(2);
            kill(id, SIGINT);
        }
        else {
            execlp(command, command, nullptr);
        }
    }

    int main(void)
    {
        mysystem("b.out");
    }

    // > g++ scratchpad.cpp -std=c++17; ./a.out
    //
```

In this example, we created our `mysystem()` function call again, but this time, in the parent, we killed the child process after two seconds instead of waiting for it to complete. We then compiled our `while(1)` example and renamed it `b.out`.

We then executed the child process, which will execute forever, or until the parent sends the `kill` command.

Summary

In this chapter, we provided a comprehensive overview of the Linux (System V) ABI. We discussed the register and stack layout, the System V calling convention, and the ELF specification.

We then reviewed the Unix filesystem, including the standard filesystem layout and permissions.

Next, we reviewed how to work with Unix processes, including common functions such as `fork()`, `exec()`, and `wait()`, as well as IPC.

Finally, this chapter concluded with a brief overview of Unix-based signals and how to work with them.

In the next chapter, we will provide a comprehensive look at console input and output using C++.

Questions

1. What is the first return register for the System V architecture (64-bit) on Intel?
2. What is the first argument register for the System V architecture (64-bit) on Intel?
3. When pushing to the stack on Intel, do you add or subtract the stack pointer?
4. What is the difference between segments and sections in ELF?
5. What is stored in the `.eh_frame` section in an ELF file?
6. What is the difference between `fork()` and `exec()`?
7. When creating a Unix pipe, which file handle is the write file handle? The first, or the second?
8. What is the return value of the `wait()` system call?

Further reading

- https://www.packtpub.com/application-development/c-multithreading-cookbook

6
Learning to Program Console Input/Output

Console IO is essential for any program. It can be used to get user input, provide an output, and support debugging and diagnostics. A common cause of program instability also generally originates from poorly written IO, which is only exacerbated by the overuse of standard C `printf()`/`scanf()` IO functions. In this chapter, we will discuss the pros and cons of using C++ IO, commonly referred to as stream-based IO, compared to the standard C-style alternatives. In addition, we will provide a high-level introduction to C++ manipulators and how they can be used in place of standard C-style format strings. We will conclude this chapter with a set of examples designed to guide the reader through the use of both `std::cout` and `std::cin`.

The chapter has the following objectives:

- Learning about stream-based IO
- User-defined type-manipulators
- An example of echoes
- The Serial Echo server example

Technical requirements

In order to compile and execute the examples in this chapter, the reader must have:

- A Linux-based system capable of compiling and executing C++17 (for example, Ubuntu 17.10+)
- GCC 7+
- CMake 3.6+
- An internet connection

To download all of the code in this chapter, including the examples and code snippets, please see the following GitHub link: `https://github.com/PacktPublishing/Hands-On-System-Programming-with-CPP/tree/master/Chapter06`.

Learning about stream-based IO

In this section, we are going to learn about the basics and some advantages and disadvantages of stream-based IO.

The basics of stream

Unlike the C-style `printf()` and `scanf()` functions, C++ IO uses streams (`std::ostream` for output and `std::istream` for input) that leverage the << and >> operators. For example, the following code outputs `Hello World` to `stdout` using a non-member << overload of `basic_ostream` for `const char *` strings:

```
#include <iostream>

int main()
{
    std::cout << "Hello World\n";
}

> g++ -std=c++17 scratchpad.cpp; ./a.out
Hello World
```

By default, the `std::cout` and `std::wcout` objects, which are instantiations of `std::ostream`, output data to the standard C `stdout`, with the only difference being that `std::wcout` provides support for Unicode, while `std::cout` provides support for ASCII. In addition to several non-member overloads, C++ provides the following arithmetic-style member overloads:

```
basic_ostream &operator<<(short value);
basic_ostream &operator<<(unsigned short value);
basic_ostream &operator<<(int value);
basic_ostream &operator<<(unsigned int value);
basic_ostream &operator<<(long value);
basic_ostream &operator<<(unsigned long value);
basic_ostream &operator<<(long long value);
basic_ostream &operator<<(unsigned long long value);
basic_ostream &operator<<(float value);
basic_ostream &operator<<(double value);
```

```
basic_ostream &operator<<(long double value);
basic_ostream &operator<<(bool value);
basic_ostream &operator<<(const void* value);
```

These overloads can be used to stream numbers of various types to `stdout` or `stderr`. Consider the following example:

```cpp
#include <iostream>

int main()
{
    std::cout << "The answer is: " << 42 << '\n';
}

> g++ -std=c++17 scratchpad.cpp; ./a.out
The answer is: 42
```

Using `stdin` by default, input is performed via `std::cin` and `std::wcin`. Unlike `std::cout`, `std::cin` uses the `>>` stream operator, instead of the `<<` stream operator. The following accepts input from `stdin` and outputs the result to `stdout`:

```cpp
#include <iostream>

int main()
{
    auto n = 0;

    std::cin >> n;
    std::cout << "input: " << n << '\n';
}

> g++ -std=c++17 scratchpad.cpp; ./a.out
42 ↵
input: 42
```

Advantages and disadvantages of C++ stream-based IO

There are many pros and cons to using C++ for IO instead of standard C functions.

Advantages of C++ stream-based IO

C++ streams are generally preferred over the standard C functions that leverage format specifiers, because C++ streams are:

- Capable of handling user-defined types providing cleaner, type-safe IO
- Safer, preventing a larger number of accidental-buffer overflow vulnerabilities as not all format-specifier bugs can be detected by the compiler or prevented using the _s C function variants added to C11
- Capable of providing implicit memory management, and do not require variadic functions

For these reasons, format specifiers are discouraged by the C++ Core Guidelines including functions such as printf(), scanf(), and others. Although there are many advantages to using C++ streams, there are some disadvantages.

Disadvantages of C++ stream-based IO

The two most common complaints about C++ streams are as follows:

- Standard C functions (specifically printf()) often outperform C++ streams (an issue that largely depends on your operating system and C++ implementation)
- Format specifiers are often more flexible than #include <iomanip>

Although these are typically valid complaints, there are ways to address these issues without having to sacrifice the advantages of C++ streams, which we will explain in the following sections.

Beginning with user-defined types

C++ streams provide the ability to overload the << and >> operators for user-defined types. This provides the ability to create custom, type-safe IO for any data type, including system-level data types, structures, and even more complicated types such as classes. For example, the following provides an overload for the << stream operator to print an error code provided by a POSIX-style function:

```
#include <fcntl.h>
#include <string.h>
#include <iostream>

class custom_errno
```

```
{ };

std::ostream &operator<<(std::ostream &os, const custom_errno &e)
{ return os << strerror(errno); }

int main()
{
    if (open("filename.txt", O_RDWR) == -1) {
        std::cout << custom_errno{} << '\n';
    }
}

> g++ -std=c++17 scratchpad.cpp; ./a.out
No such file or directory
```

In this example, we create an empty class that provides us with a custom type and overload the << operator for this custom type. We then use `strerror()` to output the error string for `errno` to the provided output stream. Although this could be achieved by directly outputting the result of `strerror()` to the stream, it demonstrates how user-defined types can be created and used with streams.

In addition to more complicated types, user-defined types can also be leveraged by input streams. Consider the following example:

```
#include <iostream>

struct object_t
{
    int data1;
    int data2;
};

std::ostream &operator<<(std::ostream &os, const object_t &obj)
{
    os << "data1: " << obj.data1 << '\n';
    os << "data2: " << obj.data2 << '\n';
    return os;
}

std::istream &operator>>(std::istream &is, object_t &obj)
{
    is >> obj.data1;
    is >> obj.data2;
    return is;
}

int main()
```

```
{
    object_t obj;

    std::cin >> obj;
    std::cout << obj;
}

> g++ -std=c++17 scratchpad.cpp; ./a.out
42 ↵
43 ↵
data1: 42
data2: 43
```

In this example, we create a structure that stores two integers. We then overload both the << and >> operators for this user-defined type, exercise these overloads by reading data into an instance of our type, and then output the results. With our overloads, we have instructed both std::cin and std::cout on how to handle the input and output of our user-defined type.

Safety and implicit memory management

Although vulnerabilities are still possible with C++ streams, they are less likely compared to their standard C counterparts. The classic example of a buffer overflow using the standard C scanf() function is as follows:

```
#include <stdio.h>

int main()
{
    char buf[2];
    scanf("%s", buf);
}

> g++ -std=c++17 scratchpad.cpp; ./a.out
The answer is 42 ↵
*** stack smashing detected ***: <unknown> terminated
Aborted (core dumped)
```

The buffer being input by the user is larger than the space allocated for this buffer, resulting in a buffer overflow situation. Increasing the size of `buf` will not solve the problem in this example as the user can always input a string larger than the provided buffer. This issue can be addressed by specifying a length limit on `scanf()`:

```
#include <stdio.h>

int main()
{
    char buf[2];
    scanf("%2s", buf);
}


> g++ -std=c++17 scratchpad.cpp; ./a.out
The answer is 42 ↵
```

Here, we provide the size of `buf` to the `scanf()` function, preventing the buffer overflow. The problem with this approach is the size of `buf` is declared twice. If only one of these is changed, a buffer overflow could be reintroduced. C-style macros could be used to address this issue, but the decoupling of the buffer and its size is still present.

Although there are other ways to solve this using C, one way to address the preceding issues with C++ is as follows:

```
#include <iomanip>
#include <iostream>

template<std::size_t N>
class buf_t
{
    char m_buf[N];

public:

    constexpr auto size()
    { return N; }

    constexpr auto data()
    { return m_buf; }
};

template<std::size_t N>
std::istream &operator>>(std::istream &is, buf_t<N> &b)
{
    is >> std::setw(b.size()) >> b.data();
    return is;
}
```

```
int main()
{
    buf_t<2> buf;
    std::cin >> buf;
}

> g++ -std=c++17 scratchpad.cpp; ./a.out
The answer is 42 ↵
```

Instead of using a * char, we create a user-defined type that encapsulates a * char and its length. The total size of the buffer is coupled with the buffer itself, preventing accidental buffer overflows. Still, if memory-allocation is allowed (which is not always the case when programming systems, we can do better:

```
#include <string>
#include <iostream>

int main()
{
    std::string buf;
    std::cin >> buf;
}

> g++ -std=c++17 scratchpad.cpp; ./a.out
The answer is 42 ↵
```

In this example, we use `std::string` to store the input from `std::cin`. The difference here is that `std::string` dynamically allocates memory as needed to store the input, preventing a possible buffer overflow. If more memory is needed, more memory is allocated or `std::bad_alloc` is thrown and the program aborts. User-defined types with C++ streams provide safer mechanisms for handling IO.

Common debugging patterns

In programming systems, one of the main uses of console output is debugging. C++ streams provide two different global objects—`std::cout` and `std::cerr`. The first option, `std::cout`, is typically buffered, sent to `stdout`, and only flushed when either `std::flush` or `std::endl` is sent to the stream. The second option, `std::cerr`, provides the same functionality as `std::cout`, but is sent to `stderr` instead of `stdout`, and is flushed on every call to the global object. Take a look at the following example:

```
#include <iostream>

int main()
```

```
{
    std::cout << "buffered" << '\n';
    std::cout << "buffer flushed" << std::endl;
    std::cerr << "buffer flushed" << '\n';
}

> g++ -std=c++17 scratchpad.cpp; ./a.out
buffer
buffer flushed
buffer flushed
```

For this reason, error logic is usually sent to stderr using std::cerr to ensure all error console output is received in the event of a catastrophic issue. Likewise, general output, including debug logic is sent to stdout using std::cout to take advantage of buffering to speed up console output, and '\n' is used to send a newline instead of std::endl unless an explicit flush is required.

The following shows a typical pattern in C for debugging:

```
#include <iostream>

#ifndef NDEBUG
#define DEBUG(...) fprintf(stdout, __VA_ARGS__);
#else
#define DEBUG(...)
#endif

int main()
{
    DEBUG("The answer is: %d\n", 42);
}

> g++ -std=c++17 scratchpad.cpp; ./a.out
The answer is: 42
```

If debugging is enabled, which usually means that NDEBUG is defined, the DEBUG macro can be used to send debug statements to the console. NDEBUG is used because this is the macro that is defined when most compilers are set to Release mode, disabling assert() in standard C. Another common debugging pattern is to provide the debug macro with a debug level that allows the developer to dial in how verbose the program is while debugging:

```
#include <iostream>

#ifndef DEBUG_LEVEL
#define DEBUG_LEVEL 0
```

```
#endif

#ifndef NDEBUG
#define DEBUG(level,...) \
    if(level <= DEBUG_LEVEL) fprintf(stdout, __VA_ARGS__);
#else
#define DEBUG(...)
#endif

int main()
{
    DEBUG(0, "The answer is: %d\n", 42);
    DEBUG(1, "The answer no is: %d\n", 43);
}

> g++ -std=c++17 scratchpad.cpp; ./a.out
The answer is: 42
```

The problem with this logic is the overuse of macros to achieve debugging, a pattern that is discouraged by the C++ Core Guidelines (https://github.com/isocpp/CppCoreGuidelines/blob/master/CppCoreGuidelines.md#Res-macros2). A simple approach to debugging with C++17 is as follows:

```
#include <iostream>

#ifdef NDEBUG
constexpr auto g_ndebug = true;
#else
constexpr auto g_ndebug = false;
#endif

int main()
{
    if constexpr (!g_ndebug) {
        std::cout << "The answer is: " << 42 << '\n';
    }
}

> g++ -std=c++17 scratchpad.cpp; ./a.out
The answer is: 42
```

Even with C++17, some macro logic is needed to handle the NDEBUG macro that is provided by the compiler when debugging is enabled. In this example, the NDEBUG macro is converted into constexpr, which is then used in the source code to handle debugging. A debug level can also be implemented using the following:

```
#include <iostream>

#ifdef DEBUG_LEVEL
constexpr auto g_debug_level = DEBUG_LEVEL;
#else
constexpr auto g_debug_level = 0;
#endif

#ifdef NDEBUG
constexpr auto g_ndebug = true;
#else
constexpr auto g_ndebug = false;
#endif

int main()
{
    if constexpr (!g_ndebug && (0 <= g_debug_level)) {
        std::cout << "The answer is: " << 42 << '\n';
    }

    if constexpr (!g_ndebug && (1 <= g_debug_level)) {
        std::cout << "The answer is not: " << 43 << '\n';
    }
}

> g++ -std=c++17 scratchpad.cpp; ./a.out
The answer is: 42
```

Since changing the debug level is a compile-time feature in this example, it would be passed to the compiler using -DDEBUG_LEVEL=xxx, and as such, still requires macro logic to convert the C macro into a C++ constexpr. As can be seen in this example, the C++ implementation is far more complicated than a simple DEBUG macro that leverages fprintf() and friends. To overcome this complexity, we will leverage encapsulation, without sacrificing compile-time optimizations:

```
#include <iostream>

#ifdef DEBUG_LEVEL
constexpr auto g_debug_level = DEBUG_LEVEL;
#else
constexpr auto g_debug_level = 0;
```

```
#endif

#ifdef NDEBUG
constexpr auto g_ndebug = true;
#else
constexpr auto g_ndebug = false;
#endif

template <std::size_t LEVEL>
constexpr void debug(void(*func)()) {
    if constexpr (!g_ndebug && (LEVEL <= g_debug_level)) {
        func();
    };
}

int main()
{
    debug<0>([] {
        std::cout << "The answer is: " << 42 << '\n';
    });

    debug<1>([] {
        std::cout << "The answer is not: " << 43 << '\n';
    });
}

> g++ -std=c++17 scratchpad.cpp; ./a.out
The answer is: 42
```

In this example, the debug logic is encapsulated into a constexpr function that takes a Lambda. The debug level is defined using a template parameter to maintain constancy. Unlike the typical standard C debugging pattern, this implementation will accept any debug logic that can fit into a void(*func)() function or lambda and, like the standard C version, will be compiled out and removed when the compiler is set to Release mode (that is, when NDEBUG is defined, and typically optimizations are enabled). To show this, GCC 7.3 outputs the following when Release mode is enabled:

```
> g++ -std=c++17 -O3 -DNDEBUG scratchpad.cpp; ./a.out
> ls -al a.out
-rwxr-xr-x 1 user users 8600 Apr 13 18:23 a.out

> readelf -s a.out | grep cout
```

GCC 7.3 outputs the following when `#undef NDEBUG` is added to the source code (ensuring the only difference is the debug logic is disabled, but the compile flags remain the same):

```
> g++ -std=c++17 scratchpad.cpp; ./a.out
> ls -al a.out
-rwxr-xr-x 1 user users 8888 Apr 13 18:24 a.out

> readelf -s a.out | grep cout
    23: 0000000000201060 272 OBJECT GLOBAL DEFAULT 24 _ZSt4cout@GLIBCXX_3.4
(5)
    59: 0000000000201060 272 OBJECT GLOBAL DEFAULT 24
_ZSt4cout@@GLIBCXX_3.4
```

The extra 288 bytes come from the debug logic that is completely removed by the compiler thanks to the constancy observed by the additions of `constexpr` to C++17, providing a cleaner approach to debugging, without the need for the extensive use of macros.

Another common debugging pattern is to include both the current line number and the filename into debugging statements for additional context. The `__LINE__` and `__FILE__` macros are used to provide this information. Sadly, without the Source Location TS (`http://en.cppreference.com/w/cpp/experimental/source_location`), which was not included in C++17, there is no way to provide this information without these macros and the inclusion of something like the following pattern:

```
#include <iostream>

#ifndef NDEBUG
#define DEBUG(fmt, args...) \
    fprintf(stdout, "%s [%d]: " fmt, __FILE__, __LINE__, args);
#else
#define DEBUG(...)
#endif

int main()
{
    DEBUG("The answer is: %d\n", 42);
}

> g++ -std=c++17 scratchpad.cpp; ./a.out
scratchpad.cpp [11]: The answer is: 42
```

In this example, the DEBUG macro automatically inserts the file name and line number into the standard C-style fprintf() function. This works because wherever the compiler sees the DEBUG macro, it inserts fprintf(stdout, "%s [%d]: " fmt, __FILE__, __LINE__, args);, and then must evaluate the line and file macros, resulting in the expected output. One example of how to convert this same pattern to our existing C++ example is as follows:

```cpp
#include <iostream>

#ifdef DEBUG_LEVEL
constexpr auto g_debug_level = DEBUG_LEVEL;
#else
constexpr auto g_debug_level = 0;
#endif

#ifdef NDEBUG
constexpr auto g_ndebug = true;
#else
constexpr auto g_ndebug = false;
#endif

#define console std::cout << __FILE__ << " [" << __LINE__ << "]: "

template <std::size_t LEVEL>
constexpr void debug(void(*func)()) {
    if constexpr (!g_ndebug && (LEVEL <= g_debug_level)) {
        func();
    };
}

int main()
{
    debug<0>([] {
        console << "The answer is: " << 42 << '\n';
    });
}

> g++ -std=c++17 scratchpad.cpp; ./a.out
scratchpad.cpp [27]: The answer is: 42
```

Instead of using std::cout in our debug lambdas, we add a console macro that uses std::cout, but also adds the file name and line number to the debug statement to provide the same functionality as the standard C version. Unlike the standard C version, an additional C macro function is not needed as the console macro will properly provide the file name and line number where used.

Finally, to complete our C++17 debugging patterns, we add a debug, warning, and fatal version of the preceding example with color, and an overload for the `fatal` function that defaults to exiting with −1 on error.

To start, we leverage the same standard C macros as used in the preceding code snippets:

```
#ifdef DEBUG_LEVEL
constexpr auto g_debug_level = DEBUG_LEVEL;
#else
constexpr auto g_debug_level = 0;
#endif

#ifdef NDEBUG
constexpr auto g_ndebug = true;
#else
constexpr auto g_ndebug = false;
#endif
```

These macros convert standard C-style macros, which are needed for command-line compatibility, to C++-style constant expressions. Next, we create a template function called debug, capable of accepting a lambda function. This debug function first outputs a green colored debug to stdout, and then executes the lambda function, if (and only if) debugging is enabled and the debugging level matches that which was provided to the debug function itself. If debugging is not enabled, the debug function is compiled without impacting the size of the program, or its performance:

```
template <std::size_t LEVEL>
constexpr void debug(void(*func)()) {
    if constexpr (!g_ndebug && (LEVEL <= g_debug_level)) {
        std::cout << "\033[1;32mDEBUG\033[0m ";
        func();
    };
}
```

This same debug function is repeated to provide a warning, and a fatal version of this function, with the only difference being color (which is platform-specific, and in this case is intended for UNIX operating systems), and the fatal function exits the program after the lambda function is executed with either a user-defined error code or −1:

```
template <std::size_t LEVEL>
constexpr void warning(void(*func)()) {
    if constexpr (!g_ndebug && (LEVEL <= g_debug_level)) {
        std::cout << "\033[1;33mWARNING\033[0m ";
        func();
    };
}
```

```
template <std::size_t LEVEL>
constexpr void fatal(void(*func)()) {
    if constexpr (!g_ndebug && (LEVEL <= g_debug_level)) {
        std::cout << "\033[1;31mFATAL ERROR\033[0m ";
        func();
        ::exit(-1);
    };
}

template <std::size_t LEVEL>
constexpr void fatal(int error_code, void(*func)()) {
    if constexpr (!g_ndebug && (LEVEL <= g_debug_level)) {
        std::cout << "\033[1;31mFATAL ERROR\033[0m ";
        func();
        ::exit(error_code);
    };
}
```

Finally, these debugging patterns are exercised in a `main()` function to demonstrate how they can be used:

```
int main()
{
    debug<0>([] {
        console << "The answer is: " << 42 << '\n';
    });

    warning<0>([] {
        console << "The answer might be: " << 42 << '\n';
    });

    fatal<0>([] {
        console << "The answer was not: " << 42 << '\n';
    });
}

> g++ -std=c++17 scratchpad.cpp; ./a.out
DEBUG scratchpad.cpp [54]: The answer is: 42
WARNING scratchpad.cpp [58]: The answer might be: 42
FATAL ERROR scratchpad.cpp [62]: The answer was not: 42
```

Performance of C++ streams

A common complaint about C++ streams is performance, a problem that has largely been mitigated over the years. To ensure C++ streams perform at their best, there are some optimizations that can be applied:

- **Disable std::ios::sync_with_stdio:** C++ streams by default synchronize themselves with standard C functions, such as `printf()` and others. If these functions are not being used, this synchronization feature should be disabled as it will result in a noticeable improvement in performance.

- **Avoid flushing**: Where possible, avoid flushing C++ streams and let `libc++` and the OS handle flushing for you. This includes not using `std::flush`, and using `'\n'` instead of `std::endl`, which flushes after it outputs a newline. When flushing is avoided, all output is buffered for you, reducing the number of calls to the OS to deliver the output.

- **Use std::cout and std::clog instead of std::cerr**: For the same reason, `std::cerr` will flush on destruction, increasing the number of times the OS is delivered output. When possible, `std::cout` should be used, with `std::cerr` only being used for fatal errors followed by control-flow changes, such as exits, exceptions, assertions, and possible crashes.

It's impossible to provide a general answer to the question, *Which is faster*, `printf()` *or* `std::cout`? But in practice, if the preceding optimizations are used, `std::cout` can often outperform standard C `printf()`, but this is highly dependent on your environment and use case.

In addition to the preceding example, one way to avoid unwanted flushing to increase performance is to use `std::stringstream` instead of `std::cout`:

```
#include <sstream>
#include <iostream>

int main()
{
    std::stringstream stream;
    stream << "The answer is: " << 42 << '\n';

    std::cout << stream.str() << std::flush;
}

> g++ -std=c++17 scratchpad.cpp; ./a.out
The answer is: 42
```

By using `std::stringstream`, all output is directed to your controlled buffer until you are ready to send the output to the OS via `std::cout` and manual flushing. This can also be used to buffer output to `std::cerr`, reducing the total number of flushes. Another way to avoid flushing is to use `std::clog`:

```
#include <iostream>

int main()
{
    std::clog << "The answer is: " << 42 << '\n';
}

> g++ -std=c++17 scratchpad.cpp; ./a.out
The answer is: 42
```

`std::clog` operates like `std::cout`, but instead of sending output to `stdout`, `std::clog` sends output to `stderr`.

Learning about manipulators

C++ streams have several different manipulators that may be used to control both input and output, some of which have already been discussed. The most common manipulator is `std::endl`, which outputs a newline and then flushes the output stream:

```
#include <iostream>

int main()
{
    std::cout << "Hello World" << std::endl;
}

> g++ -std=c++17 scratchpad.cpp; ./a.out
Hello World
```

Another way to write this same logic is to use the `std::flush` manipulator:

```cpp
#include <iostream>

int main()
{
    std::cout << "Hello World\n" << std::flush;
}

> g++ -std=c++17 scratchpad.cpp; ./a.out
Hello World
```

Both are the same, although '\n' should always be used unless a flush is explicitly needed. For example, if multiple lines are needed, the following is preferred:

```cpp
#include <iostream>

int main()
{
    std::cout << "Hello World\n";
    std::cout << "Hello World\n";
    std::cout << "Hello World\n";
    std::cout << "Hello World" << std::endl;
}

> g++ -std=c++17 scratchpad.cpp; ./a.out
Hello World
Hello World
Hello World
Hello World
```

Compared to the preceding code, the following is not preferred:

```cpp
#include <iostream>

int main()
{
    std::cout << "Hello World" << std::endl;
    std::cout << "Hello World" << std::endl;
    std::cout << "Hello World" << std::endl;
    std::cout << "Hello World" << std::endl;
}

> g++ -std=c++17 scratchpad.cpp; ./a.out
Hello World
Hello World
Hello World
Hello World
```

It should be noted that the trailing flush is not needed, as `::exit()` flushes `stdout` on exit for you, which is called when main completes.

A common manipulator that is set at the beginning of any program is `std::boolalpha`, which causes Booleans to be outputted as `true` or `false` instead of 1 or 0 (with `std::noboolalpha` providing the inverse, which is also the default):

```
#include <iostream>

int main()
{
    std::cout << std::boolalpha;
    std::cout << "The answer is: " << true << '\n';
    std::cout << "The answer is: " << false << '\n';

    std::cout << std::noboolalpha;
    std::cout << "The answer is: " << true << '\n';
    std::cout << "The answer is: " << false << '\n';
}

> g++ -std=c++17 scratchpad.cpp; ./a.out
The answer is: true
The answer is: false
The answer is: 1
The answer is: 0
```

Another common set of manipulators is numeric base manipulators—`std::hex`, `std::dec`, and `std::oct`. These manipulators are similar to `%d`, `%x`, and `%o` used by standard C-format specifiers (for example, those used by `printf()`). Unlike the standard C versions, these manipulators are global, and thus should be used with caution, especially in libraries. To use these manipulators, simply add them to the stream prior to adding a number for the desired base:

```
#include <iostream>

int main()
{
    std::cout << "The answer is: " << 42 << '\n' << std::hex
              << "The answer is: " << 42 << '\n';
    std::cout << "The answer is: " << 42 << '\n' << std::dec
              << "The answer is: " << 42 << '\n';
    std::cout << "The answer is: " << 42 << '\n' << std::oct
              << "The answer is: " << 42 << '\n';
}

> g++ -std=c++17 scratchpad.cpp; ./a.out
```

```
The answer is: 42
The answer is: 2a
The answer is: 2a
The answer is: 42
The answer is: 42
The answer is: 52
```

The first number, 42, is printed as 42 as no numeric base-manipulators have been used yet. The second number is printed as 2a as the std::hex manipulator was used resulting in 2a as that is the hex value for 42. The third number that is printed is also 2a as numeric base manipulators are global and thus, even though std::cout is called a second time, the stream is still told to use hex values instead of decimal. This pattern continues for both std::dec (for example, decimal numbers) and std::oct (for example, octal numbers), resulting in 42, 2a, 2a, 42, 42, and finally 52.

It is also possible to use the uppercase version of std::hex instead of the default, lowercase version seen in the previous example. To accomplish this, use std::uppercase and std::nouppercase (std::uppercase shows alphanumeric characters in uppercase while std::nouppercase does not, which is the default):

```cpp
#include <iostream>

int main()
{
    std::cout << std::hex << std::uppercase << "The answer is: "
            << 42 << '\n';
}
```

```
> g++ -std=c++17 scratchpad.cpp; ./a.out
The answer is: 2A
```

In this example, instead of 42 being outputted as 2a, it was outputted as 2A, with the alphanumeric characters being uppercase.

Typically, especially with respect to programming systems, hexadecimal and octal numbers are printed with their base identifiers (for example, 0x and 0). To accomplish this, use the std::showbase and std::noshowbase manipulators (std::showbase shows the base while std::noshowbase does not, which is the default):

```cpp
#include <iostream>

int main()
{
    std::cout << std::showbase;
    std::cout << std::hex << "The answer is: " << 42 << '\n';
```

```
        std::cout << std::dec << "The answer is: " << 42 << '\n';
        std::cout << std::oct << "The answer is: " << 42 << '\n';
}

> g++ -std=c++17 scratchpad.cpp; ./a.out
The answer is: 0x2a
The answer is: 42
The answer is: 052
```

As seen from this example, `std::hex` now outputs `0x2a` instead of `2a`, and `std::oct` outputs `052` instead of `52`, while `std::dec` continues to output `42` as expected (since decimal numbers do not have base identifiers). Unlike numbers, pointers always output in hexadecimal, lowercase, and with their base being shown, and `std::uppercase, std::noshowbase, std::dec,` and `std::oct` do not affect the output. One solution to this problem is to cast the pointer to a number, and then the preceding manipulators may be used as shown in the following example, but this type of logic is discouraged by the C++ Core Guidelines since `reinterpret_cast` is required, which is frowned upon:

```
#include <iostream>

int main()
{
    int i = 0;
    std::cout << &i << '\n';
    std::cout << std::hex << std::showbase << std::uppercase
              << reinterpret_cast<uintptr_t>(&i) << '\n';
}

> g++ -std=c++17 scratchpad.cpp; ./a.out
0x7fff51d370b4
0X7FFF51D370B4
```

One issue with outputting pointers is that their total length (that is, the total number of characters) changes from pointer to pointer. This can often be distracting when outputting several pointers at the same time, as their base modifiers are likely not to match up. To overcome this, `std::setw` and `std::setfill` may be used. `std::setw` sets the total width (that is, the total number of characters) in the next output. If the next output is not at least the size of the value passed to `std::setw`, the stream will automatically add spaces to the stream:

```
#include <iomanip>
#include <iostream>

int main()
{
```

```
    std::cout << "The answer is: " << std::setw(18) << 42 << '\n';
}

> g++ -std=c++17 scratchpad.cpp; ./a.out
The answer is:                 42
```

In this example, the width is set to `18`. Since the next addition to the stream is two characters (from the number `42`), `16` total spaces are added prior to adding `42` to the stream. To change the characters that are added to the stream by `std::setw`, use `std::setfill`:

```
#include <iomanip>
#include <iostream>

int main()
{
    std::cout << "The answer is: " << std::setw(18) << std::setfill('0')
              << 42 << '\n';
}

> g++ -std=c++17 scratchpad.cpp; ./a.out
The answer is: 00000000000000042
```

As can be seen, instead of spaces being added to the stream (which is the default), `'0'` characters are added to the stream. The direction of the characters being added to the stream can be controlled using `std::left`, `std::right`, and `std::internal`:

```
#include <iomanip>
#include <iostream>

int main()
{
    std::cout << "The answer is: "
              << std::setw(18) << std::left << std::setfill('0')
              << 42 << '\n';

    std::cout << "The answer is: "
              << std::setw(18) << std::right << std::setfill('0')
              << 42 << '\n';
}

> g++ -std=c++17 scratchpad.cpp; ./a.out
The answer is: 420000000000000000
The answer is: 000000000000000042
```

std::left first outputs to the stream, and then fills in the stream with the remaining characters, while std::right fills in the stream with unused characters, and then outputs to the stream. std::internal is specific to text that uses base identifiers such as std::hex and std::oct with std::showbase or pointers that automatically show the base identifier, as follows:

```
#include <iomanip>
#include <iostream>

int main()
{
    int i = 0;

    std::cout << std::hex
              << std::showbase;

    std::cout << "The answer is: "
              << std::setw(18) << std::internal << std::setfill('0')
              << 42 << '\n';

    std::cout << "The answer is: "
              << std::setw(18) << std::internal << std::setfill('0')
              << &i << '\n';
}

> g++ -std=c++17 scratchpad.cpp; ./a.out
The answer is: 0x000000000000002a
The answer is: 0x00007ffc074c9be4
```

Often, especially in libraries, it can be useful to set some manipulators, and then restore the stream to its original state. For example, if you're writing a library and you want to output a number in `hex`, you would need to use the `std::hex` manipulator, but doing so would cause all of the numbers your user outputs from that point on to also be outputted in `hex`. The problem is, you cannot simply use `std::dec` to set the stream back to decimal because the user might actually be using `std::hex` in the first place. One way to deal with this issue is to use the `std::cout.flags()` function, which allows you to both get and set the stream's internal flags:

```
#include <iostream>

int main()
{
    auto flags = std::cout.flags();
    std::cout.flags(flags);
}
```

```
> g++ -std=c++17 scratchpad.cpp; ./a.out
```

In general, all of the manipulators that have been discussed, as well as some others, can be enabled/disabled using the `std::cout.flags()` function, and the manipulators discussed are simply wrappers around this function to reduce verbosity. Although this function can be used to configure the manipulators (which should be avoided), the `std::cout.flags()` function is a convenient way to restore the manipulators after the stream has been changed. It should also be noted that the preceding methods work for all of the streams, not just `std::cout`. One way to simplify restoring the manipulators is to use a little functional programming, and wrap a user function with the save/restore logic, as follows:

```
#include <iomanip>
#include <iostream>

template<typename FUNC>
void cout_transaction(FUNC f)
{
    auto flags = std::cout.flags();
    f();
    std::cout.flags(flags);
}

int main()
{
    cout_transaction([]{
        std::cout << std::hex << std::showbase;
        std::cout << "The answer is: " << 42 << '\n';
```

```
    });

    std::cout << "The answer is: " << 42 << '\n';
}

> g++ -std=c++17 scratchpad.cpp; ./a.out
The answer is: 0x2a
The answer is: 42
```

In this example, we wrap the use of std::cout in cout_transation. This wrapper stores the current state of the manipulators, calls the user-provided function (which changes the manipulators), and then restores the manipulators prior to completing. As a result, the manipulators are unaffected after the completion of the transaction, which means the second std::cout in this example outputs 42 instead of 0x2a.

Finally, to simplify the use of manipulators, it can sometimes be useful to create your own user-defined manipulators that can encapsulate your custom logic:

```
#include <iomanip>
#include <iostream>

namespace usr
{
    class hex_t { } hex;
}

std::ostream &
operator<<(std::ostream &os, const usr::hex_t &obj)
{
    os << std::hex << std::showbase << std::internal
        << std::setfill('0') << std::setw(18);

    return os;
}

int main()
{
    std::cout << "The answer is: " << usr::hex << 42 << '\n';
}

> g++ -std=c++17 scratchpad.cpp; ./a.out
The answer is: 0x000000000000002a
```

As can be seen from this example, by simply using usr::hex instead of std::hex, 42 is outputted using std::hex, std::showbase, std::internal, std::setfill('0'), and std::setw(18), reducing verbosity and simplifying multiple uses of this same logic.

Recreating the echo program

In this hands-on example, we will be recreating the popular echo program found on almost all POSIX systems. The echo program takes all of the input provided to the program and echoes it back to stdout. This program is very simple, with the following program options:

- -n: Prevents echo from outputting a newline on exit
- --help: Prints the Help menu
- --version: Prints some version information

There are two other options, -e and -E; we have omitted them here to keep things simple, but, if desired, would serve as a unique exercise for the reader.

To see the full sources for this example, please see the following: https://github.com/PacktPublishing/Hands-On-System-Programming-with-CPP/blob/master/Chapter06/example1.cpp.

The main function presented here is a useful pattern to add to all programs and deviates slightly from the original echo program as exceptions (which are highly unlikely in this example) could generate error messages not seen in the original echo program; however, it is still useful:

```
int
main(int argc, char **argv)
{
    try {
        return protected_main(argc, argv);
    }
    catch (const std::exception &e) {
        std::cerr << "Caught unhandled exception:\n";
        std::cerr << " - what(): " << e.what() << '\n';
    }
    catch (...) {
        std::cerr << "Caught unknown exception\n";
    }

    return EXIT_FAILURE;
}
```

The goal of this logic is to catch any exceptions prior to the program exiting and outputting the exception description to stderr before exiting with a failure status.

Consider the following example:

```
catch (const std::exception &e) {
    std::cerr << "Caught unhandled exception:\n";
    std::cerr << " - what(): " << e.what() << '\n';
}
```

The preceding code catches all `std::exceptions` and outputs a catch exception's description (that is, `e.what()`) to `stderr`. Note that `std::cerr` is used here (instead of `std::clog`) just in case the use of exceptions generates instability, ensuring a flush occurs. When using error-handling logic, it's always better to be on the safe side and ensure all debugging output is delivered with performance being a secondary concern.

Consider the following example:

```
catch (...) {
    std::cerr << "Caught unknown exception\n";
}
```

The preceding code catches all unknown exceptions, which in this program should almost certainly never happen, and was added purely for completeness:

```
try {
    return protected_main(argc, argv);
}
```

The `try` block attempts to execute the `protected_main()` function, and if it fails with an exception, executes the `catch` blocks as described previously; otherwise, it returns from the `main` function, ultimately exiting the program.

The goal of the `protected_main()` function is to parse the arguments provided to the program, and handle each argument as expected:

```
int
protected_main(int argc, char **argv)
{
    using namespace gsl;

    auto endl = true;
    auto args = make_span(argv, argc);

    for (int i = 1, num = 0; i < argc; i++) {
        cstring_span<> span_arg = ensure_z(args.at(i));

        if (span_arg == "-n") {
            endl = false;
            continue;
```

```
        }

        if (span_arg == "--help") {
            handle_help();
        }

        if (span_arg == "--version") {
            handle_version();
        }

        if (num++ > 0) {
            std::cout << " ";
        }

        std::cout << span_arg.data();
    }

    if (endl) {
        std::cout << '\n';
    }

    return EXIT_SUCCESS;
}
```

Here is the first line:

```
auto endl = true;
```

It is used to control whether a newline is added to stdout on exit, just like the original echo program, and is controlled by the -n program argument. Here is the next line:

```
auto args = make_span(argv, argc);
```

The preceding code converts the standard C argv and argc arguments into a C++ GSL span, allowing us to safely process the program arguments in a C++-Core-Guideline-compliant fashion. The span is nothing more than a list (specifically, it is very similar to std::array), with the bounds of this list being checked each time we access the list (unlike std::array). If our code attempts to access an argument that doesn't exist, an exception will be thrown, and the program will safely exit with an error code, telling us via stderr that we attempted to access an element in the list that does not exist (via the try/catch logic in the main function.

Here is the next part:

```
for (int i = 1, num = 0; i < argc; i++) {
    cstring_span<> span_arg = ensure_z(args.at(i));
```

It loops through each argument in the list. Normally, we would loop through each element in a list using the ranged `for` syntax:

```
for (const auto &arg : args) {
    ...
}
```

But this syntax cannot be used because the first argument in the argument list is always the program name, and in our case should be ignored. For this reason, we start from 1 (instead of 0) as can be seen previously, and then we loop through the remaining elements in the list. The second line in this snippet creates `cstring_span{}` from each program argument in the list. `cstring_span{}` is nothing more than a standard C-style string wrapped in a GSL span to protect any accesses to the string to make C-style string access C++-Core-Guideline-compliant. This wrapper will later be used to compare the string to look for our program options, such as `-n`, `--help`, and `--version`, in a safe and compliant way. The `ensure_z()` function ensures that the string is complete, preventing possible unwanted corruption.

The next step is to compare each argument to the list of arguments we plan to support:

```
if (span_arg == "-n") {
    endl = false;
    continue;
}
```

Since we are using `cstring_span{}` instead of a standard C-style string, we can directly compare the argument to the `"-n"` literal string safely without having to use an unsafe function such as `strcmp()`, or direct character comparisons, which is what the original echo implementation does (and since we only support one single character option, performance is the same). If the argument is `-n`, we instruct our implementation that no newline should be added to `stdout` when the program exits by setting `endl` to `false`, and then we continue looping through the arguments until they are all processed.

Here are the next two blocks of code:

```
if (span_arg == "--help") {
    handle_help();
}

if (span_arg == "--version") {
    handle_version();
}
```

They check whether the arguments are `--help` or `--version`. If either of these is provided by the user, a special `handle_help()` or `handle_version()` function is executed. It should be noted that `handle_xxx()` functions exit the program when they are done, so no further logic is needed and it should be assumed that these functions never return (as the program exits).

At this point, all of the optional arguments have been processed. All other arguments should be outputted to `stdout`, just like the original echo program. The problem is that the user could provide more than one argument that they wish to be outputted to `stdout`. Consider the following example:

```
> echo Hello World
Hello World
```

In this example, the user has provided two arguments—`Hello` and `World`. The expected output is `Hello World` (with a space), not `HelloWorld` (without a space), and some additional logic is needed to ensure that a space is outputted to `stdout` as needed.

Here is the next block:

```
if (num++ > 0) {
    std::cout << " ";
}
```

This outputs a space to `stdout` after the first argument has already been outputted, but right before the next argument is about to be outputted (and all remaining arguments). It does this because `num` starts as 0 (and 0 is equal to 0, not greater than 0, and thus the space is not outputted on the first argument), and then `num` is incremented. When the next argument is processed, `num` is 1 (or larger) which is greater than 0, and thus the space is added to `stdout`.

Finally, the argument is added to `stdout` by providing `std::cout` with the argument's data, which is nothing more than the unsafe, standard C version of the argument that `std::cout` can safely handle for us:

```
std::cout << span_arg.data();
```

The last block in the `protected_main()` function is:

```
if (endl) {
    std::cout << '\n';
}

return EXIT_SUCCESS;
```

By default, endl is true, and thus a newline is added to stdout before the program exits. If, however, the user had provided –n, then endl would have been set to false by the following:

```
if (span_arg == "-n") {
    endl = false;
    continue;
}
```

In the preceding code, the program would exit without adding the newline to stdout. If --help was provided by the user, the handle_help() function would be executed as follows:

```
void
handle_help()
{
    std::cout
            << "Usage: echo [SHORT-OPTION]... [STRING]...\n"
            << " or: echo LONG-OPTION\n"
            << "Echo the STRING(s) to standard output.\n"
            << "\n"
            << " -n do not output the trailing newline\n"
            << " --help display this help and exit\n"
            << " --version output version information and exit\n";

    ::exit(EXIT_SUCCESS);
}
```

This function outputs the Help menu to stdout using std::cout, and then exits the program successfully. The handle_version() function does the same thing if --version is provided by the user:

```
void
handle_version()
{
    std::cout
            << "echo (example) 1.0\n"
            << "Copyright (C) ???\n"
            << "\n"
            << "Written by Rian Quinn.\n";

    ::exit(EXIT_SUCCESS);
}
```

To compile this example, we use CMake:

```
# -----------------------------------------------------------------------
-----
# Header
# -----------------------------------------------------------------------
-----

cmake_minimum_required(VERSION 3.6)
project(chapter6)

include(ExternalProject)
find_package(Git REQUIRED)

set(CMAKE_CXX_STANDARD 17)

# -----------------------------------------------------------------------
-----
# Guideline Support Library
# -----------------------------------------------------------------------
-----

list(APPEND GSL_CMAKE_ARGS
    -DGSL_TEST=OFF
    -DCMAKE_INSTALL_PREFIX=${CMAKE_BINARY_DIR}
)

ExternalProject_Add(
    gsl
    GIT_REPOSITORY https://github.com/Microsoft/GSL.git
    GIT_SHALLOW 1
    CMAKE_ARGS ${GSL_CMAKE_ARGS}
    PREFIX ${CMAKE_BINARY_DIR}/external/gsl/prefix
    TMP_DIR ${CMAKE_BINARY_DIR}/external/gsl/tmp
    STAMP_DIR ${CMAKE_BINARY_DIR}/external/gsl/stamp
    DOWNLOAD_DIR ${CMAKE_BINARY_DIR}/external/gsl/download
    SOURCE_DIR ${CMAKE_BINARY_DIR}/external/gsl/src
    BINARY_DIR ${CMAKE_BINARY_DIR}/external/gsl/build
)

# -----------------------------------------------------------------------
-----
# Executable
# -----------------------------------------------------------------------
-----
```

```
include_directories(${CMAKE_BINARY_DIR}/include)
add_executable(example1 example1.cpp)
add_dependencies(example1 gsl)
```

Here is the header portion of this CMakeLists.txt file:

```
cmake_minimum_required(VERSION 3.6)
project(chapter6)

include(ExternalProject)
find_package(Git REQUIRED)

set(CMAKE_CXX_STANDARD 17)
```

This sets up CMake to require version 3.6 (since we use GIT_SHALLOW), gives the project a name, includes the ExternalProject module (which provided ExternalProject_Add), and sets the C++ standard to C++17.

Here is the next section:

```
# ----------------------------------------------------------------------
-----
# Guideline Support Library
# ----------------------------------------------------------------------
-----

list(APPEND GSL_CMAKE_ARGS
    -DGSL_TEST=OFF
    -DCMAKE_INSTALL_PREFIX=${CMAKE_BINARY_DIR}
)

ExternalProject_Add(
    gsl
    GIT_REPOSITORY https://github.com/Microsoft/GSL.git
    GIT_SHALLOW 1
    CMAKE_ARGS ${GSL_CMAKE_ARGS}
    PREFIX ${CMAKE_BINARY_DIR}/external/gsl/prefix
    TMP_DIR ${CMAKE_BINARY_DIR}/external/gsl/tmp
    STAMP_DIR ${CMAKE_BINARY_DIR}/external/gsl/stamp
    DOWNLOAD_DIR ${CMAKE_BINARY_DIR}/external/gsl/download
    SOURCE_DIR ${CMAKE_BINARY_DIR}/external/gsl/src
    BINARY_DIR ${CMAKE_BINARY_DIR}/external/gsl/build
)
```

It uses CMake's `ExternalProject_Add` to download and install the GSL from its Git repository at GitHub using a depth of 1 (that is, `GIT_SHALLOW 1`) to speed up the download process. The arguments provided to `ExternalProject_Add` (that is, `GSL_CMAKE_ARGS`) tell the GSL's build system to turn off unit testing (which our project does not need) and to install the resulting headers into our build directory (which places them in an `include` folder in our `build` directory). The remaining arguments provided to `ExternalProject_Add` are optional, simply serve to clean up the output of `ExternalProject_Add`, and can be ignored, or even removed if desired.

Finally, here is the last block:

```
include_directories(${CMAKE_BINARY_DIR}/include)
add_executable(example1 example1.cpp)
```

It tells the build system where to find our newly-installed GSL headers, and then creates an executable called `example1` from the `example1.cpp` source code. To compile and run this example, simply execute:

```
> mkdir build; cd build
> cmake ..; make
...
> ./example1 Hello World
Hello World
```

Understanding the Serial Echo server example

In this hands-on example, we will be creating a serial-based echo server. An echo server (regardless of the type) takes an input and echoes the input to the program's output (similar to the first example, but in this case using a server-style application over a serial port).

To see the full sources for this example, please see the following: https://github.com/PacktPublishing/Hands-On-System-Programming-with-CPP/blob/master/Chapter06/example2.cpp.

```cpp
#include <fstream>
#include <iostream>

#include <gsl/gsl>
using namespace gsl;

void
```

```cpp
redirect_output(
    const std::ifstream &is,
    const std::ofstream &os,
    std::function<void()> f)
{
    auto cinrdbuf = std::cin.rdbuf();
    auto coutrdbuf = std::cout.rdbuf();

    std::cin.rdbuf(is.rdbuf());
    std::cout.rdbuf(os.rdbuf());

    f();

    std::cin.rdbuf(cinrdbuf);
    std::cout.rdbuf(coutrdbuf);
}

auto
open_streams(cstring_span<> port)
{
    std::ifstream is(port.data());
    std::ofstream os(port.data());

    if (!is || !os) {
        std::clog << "ERROR: unable to open serial port:" << port.data() <<
'\n';
        ::exit(EXIT_FAILURE);
    }

    return std::make_pair(std::move(is), std::move(os));
}

int
protected_main(int argc, char** argv)
{
    auto args = make_span(argv, argc);

    if (argc != 2) {
        std::clog << "ERROR: unsupported number of arguments\n";
        ::exit(EXIT_FAILURE);
    }

    auto [is, os] = open_streams(
        ensure_z(args.at(1))
    );

    redirect_output(is, os, []{
        std::string buf;
```

```
        std::cin >> buf;
        std::cout << buf << std::flush;
    });

    return EXIT_SUCCESS;
}
```

The `main` function is the same as the first example. Its sole purpose is to catch any exceptions that might fire, output the exception's description to `stderr`, and safely exit the program with a failure status. For more information on how this works, please see the first example. The `protected_main()` function's purpose is to open the serial port, read in an input, and echo the input to the output:

```
int
protected_main(int argc, char** argv)
{
    auto args = make_span(argv, argc);

    if (argc != 2) {
        std::clog << "ERROR: unsupported number of arguments\n";
        ::exit(EXIT_FAILURE);
    }

    auto [is, os] = open_streams(
        ensure_z(args.at(1))
    );

    redirect_output(is, os, []{
        std::string buf;

        std::cin >> buf;
        std::cout << buf << std::flush;
    });

    return EXIT_SUCCESS;
}
```

Here is the first line:

```
auto args = make_span(argv, argc);
```

It does the same thing the first example does, which wraps the `argc` and `argv` argument parameters in a GSL span, providing a safe mechanism for parsing the arguments provided by the user.

Here is the second block:

```
if (argc != 2) {
    std::clog << "ERROR: unsupported number of arguments\n";
    ::exit(EXIT_FAILURE);
}
```

It checks to make sure that one, and only one, argument was provided by the user. The reason the total number of arguments (`argc`) is 2 and not 1 is because the first argument is always the name of the program and in this case should be ignored, and thus 1 argument provided by the user is actually equal to an `argc` of 2. Furthermore, we use `std::clog` instead of `std::cerr` as instability is unlikely in this case, and a flush will be performed for us by `libc` when `::exit()` is called.

Here is the second block:

```
auto [is, os] = open_streams(
    ensure_z(args.at(1))
);
```

It opens the serial port and returns input and output streams that can be used by `std::cout` and `std::cin` to use the serial port instead of `stdout` and `stdin`. To do this, the `open_streams()` function is used:

```
auto
open_streams(cstring_span<> port)
{
    std::ifstream is(port.data());
    std::ofstream os(port.data());

    if (!is || !os) {
        std::clog << "ERROR: unable to open serial port:" << port.data() << '\n';
        ::exit(EXIT_FAILURE);
    }

    return std::make_pair(std::move(is), std::move(os));
}
```

This function takes in a `cstring_span{}` that stores the serial port to open (for example, /dev/ttyS0).

Next we move on the following streams:

```
std::ifstream is(port.data());
std::ofstream os(port.data());
```

The preceding code opens an input and output stream tied to this serial port. Both `ifstream{}` and `ofstream{}` are file streams, which are outside the scope of this chapter (they will be explained in later chapters), but in short, these open the serial device and provide a stream object that `std::cout` and `std::cin` can use as if they were using `stdout` and `stdin` (which are also technically file streams on a POSIX system).

Here is the next block:

```
if (!is || !os) {
    std::clog << "ERROR: unable to open serial port:" << port.data() <<
'\n';
    ::exit(EXIT_FAILURE);
}
```

It verifies that both the input stream and the output steam were successfully opened, which is important because this type of error could happen (for example, an invalid serial port is provided, or the user doesn't have access to the serial port). If an error occurs, the user is informed via a message outputted to `std::clog`, and the program exits with a failure status.

Finally, if the input stream and output stream are successfully opened, they are returned in a pair, which is read by the `protected_main()` function using a structured binding syntax (a feature added in C++17).

Here is the next block in the `protected_main()` function:

```
redirect_output(is, os, []{
    std::string buf;

    std::cin >> buf;
    std::cout << buf << std::flush;
});
```

It redirects `std::cout` and `std::cin` to the serial port, and then echos input into the program to the program's output, in effect echoing the serial port provided by the user. To perform the redirection, the `redirect_output()` function is used:

```
void
redirect_output(
    const std::ifstream &is,
    const std::ofstream &os,
    std::function<void()> f)
{
    auto cinrdbuf = std::cin.rdbuf();
    auto coutrdbuf = std::cout.rdbuf();
```

```
    std::cin.rdbuf(is.rdbuf());
    std::cout.rdbuf(os.rdbuf());

    f();

    std::cin.rdbuf(cinrdbuf);
    std::cout.rdbuf(coutrdbuf);
}
```

The `redirect_output()` function takes an input and output stream as a parameter, as well as a function to execute and the final parameter. The first thing `redirect_function()` does is save the current buffers for `std::cin` and `std::cout`:

```
auto cinrdbuf = std::cin.rdbuf();
auto coutrdbuf = std::cout.rdbuf();
```

Next we see:

```
std::cin.rdbuf(is.rdbuf());
std::cout.rdbuf(os.rdbuf());
```

Both `std::cin` and `std::cout` are redirected to the provided input and output streams. Once this is done, the function that was provided is executed. Any use of `std::cin` and `std::cout` will be redirected to the provided serial port instead of the standard `stdout` and `stdin`. When the `f()` function is finished, `std::cin` and `std::cout` are restored to their original buffers, redirecting them back to `stdout` and `stdin`:

```
std::cin.rdbuf(cinrdbuf);
std::cout.rdbuf(coutrdbuf);
```

Finally, the program exits with success. To compile this example, we use CMake:

```
# ---------------------------------------------------------------------
-----
# Header
# ---------------------------------------------------------------------
-----

cmake_minimum_required(VERSION 3.6)
project(chapter6)

include(ExternalProject)
find_package(Git REQUIRED)

set(CMAKE_CXX_STANDARD 17)
```

```
# -----------------------------------------------------------------------
-----
# Guideline Support Library
# -----------------------------------------------------------------------
-----

list(APPEND GSL_CMAKE_ARGS
    -DGSL_TEST=OFF
    -DCMAKE_INSTALL_PREFIX=${CMAKE_BINARY_DIR}
)

ExternalProject_Add(
    gsl
    GIT_REPOSITORY https://github.com/Microsoft/GSL.git
    GIT_SHALLOW 1
    CMAKE_ARGS ${GSL_CMAKE_ARGS}
    PREFIX ${CMAKE_BINARY_DIR}/external/gsl/prefix
    TMP_DIR ${CMAKE_BINARY_DIR}/external/gsl/tmp
    STAMP_DIR ${CMAKE_BINARY_DIR}/external/gsl/stamp
    DOWNLOAD_DIR ${CMAKE_BINARY_DIR}/external/gsl/download
    SOURCE_DIR ${CMAKE_BINARY_DIR}/external/gsl/src
    BINARY_DIR ${CMAKE_BINARY_DIR}/external/gsl/build
)

# -----------------------------------------------------------------------
-----
# Executable
# -----------------------------------------------------------------------
-----

include_directories(${CMAKE_BINARY_DIR}/include)
add_executable(example2 example2.cpp)
add_dependencies(example2 gsl)
```

This CMakeLists.txt is identical to the CMakeLists.txt in the first example (minus the user of example2 instead of example1). For a complete explanation of how this works, please see the first example in this chapter.

To compile and use this example, two computers are needed, one that acts as the echo server and a second one that acts as the client, with both computers' serial ports connected to each other. On the echo server computer, use the following:

```
> mkdir build; cd build
> cmake ..; make
...
> ./example2 /dev/ttyS0
```

Note that your serial port device might be different. On the client computer, open two terminals. In the first terminal, run the following:

```
> cat < /dev/ttyS0
```

This code waits for the serial device to output data. In the second terminal, run:

```
> echo "Hello World" > /dev/ttyS0
```

This sends data through the serial port to the echo server. When you press *Enter*, you will see the `example2` program that we wrote on the echo server close successfully, and the first terminal on the client will show `Hello World`:

```
> cat < /dev/ttyS0
Hello World
```

Summary

In this chapter, we learned how to perform console-based IO, a common system-programming requirement, using C++17. Unlike standard C-style IO functions, such as `printf()` and `scanf()`, C++ uses stream-based IO functions, such as `std::cout` and `std::cin`. There are many advantages and some disadvantages to using stream-based IO. For example, stream-based IO provides a type-safe mechanism for performing IO, while raw, POSIX-style `write()` functions can often outperform stream-based IO due to a lack of calls to `malloc()` and `free()`.

In addition, we looked at stream-based manipulators, which provide stream-based IO with a similar feature set to standard C-style format strings, but without the common instability issues found with the C equivalents. In addition to manipulating the format of numbers and Boolean values, we explored field properties, including width and justification.

Finally, we finished this chapter with two different examples. The first example showed how to implement the popular POSIX *echo* program in C++ rather than in C. The second created an *echo* server for the serial port that takes input from the serial port using `std::cin` and sends that input back over the serial port as an output using `std::cout`.

In the next chapter we will provide a comprehensive overview of the memory management facilities provided by C, C++, and POSIX including aligned memory and C++ smart pointers.

Questions

1. How does `std::cin` help to prevent buffer overflows compared to the standard C `scanf`?
2. Name at least one advantage from using C++ streams compared to the standard C-style `printf`/`scanf`.
3. Name at least on disadvantage to using C++ streams compared to the standard C-style `printf`/`scanf`.
4. When should `std::endl` be used instead of `\n`?
5. What is the difference between `std::cerr` and `std::clog`, and when should `std::cerr` be used?
6. How does one output extra characters between a base identifier and a hex value?
7. How does one output a number in octal and upper case?
8. How can standard C-style program arguments be safely parsed using C++ and the GSL?
9. How does one save/restore the read buffer for `std::cin`?

Further reading

- https://www.packtpub.com/application-development/c17-example
- https://www.packtpub.com/application-development/getting-started-c17-programming-video

7
A Comprehensive Look at Memory Management

In this chapter, we will step the reader through how to properly and safely perform C++-style memory management, while also adhering to the C++ Core Guidelines whenever possible, leveraging additions to the C++ standard template library in C++11, C++14, and C++17 to increase the safety, reliability, and stability of the reader's system program. We will start by first introducing the `new()` and `delete()` functions, and how they may be used to allocate type-safe memory, including aligned memory. Next, this chapter will discuss the safety issues with using `new()` and `delete()` directly and how these safety concern may be handled using smart pointers, including their impact on C++ Core Guideline compliance. How to perform memory mapping and permissions will also be discussed, with the chapter concluding with a brief discussion on fragmentation.

Technical requirements

In order to compile and execute the examples in this chapter, the reader must have the following:

- A Linux-based system capable of compiling and executing C++17 (for example, Ubuntu 17.10+)
- GCC 7+
- CMake 3.6+
- An internet connection

To download all of the code in this chapter, including the examples, and code snippets, please visit: `https://github.com/PacktPublishing/Hands-On-System-Programming-with-CPP/tree/master/Chapter07`.

Learning about the new and delete functions

In this section, the reader will learn how to allocate and deallocate memory using C++17. You will learn how to use `new()` and `delete()` instead of `malloc()`/`free()` to increase the type-safety of allocations and deallocations. Various versions of these functions will be explained, including array, aligned, and placement-style allocations.

The basics for writing a program

When writing a program, including system programming, there are a few different types of memory that can be leveraged by the author:

- Global memory
- Stack memory
- Heap memory

Global memory exists in the program itself, is allocated by the OS's loader, and generally exists in two different locations (assuming ELF binaries):

- `.bss`: zero-initialized (or uninitialized) memory
- `.data`: value-initialized memory

Consider the following example:

```
#include <iostream>

int bss_mem = 0;
int data_mem = 42;

int main()
{
    std::cout << bss_mem << '\n';
    std::cout << data_mem << '\n';
}

// > g++ -std=c++17 scratchpad.cpp; ./a.out
// 0
// 42
```

Although used a lot in system programming, global memory is usually discouraged in favor of stack memory and dynamic memory. Special care should be taken when using value-initialized global memory, as this form of memory usage increases the size of the program on disk, resulting in a larger storage impact, as well as long load times, while the zero-initialized memory is provided by the OS-loader during linking.

Stack memory is the memory that is allocated on the stack:

```
#include <iostream>

int main()
{
    int stack_mem = 42;
    std::cout << stack_mem << '\n';
}

// > g++ -std=c++17 scratchpad.cpp; ./a.out
// 42
```

As shown in this example, `stack_mem` is allocated on the stack instead of globally because it exists in the `main()` function. Stack memory is bound to the scope in which it was created—in this case, the `main()` function. Besides being scoped, another advantage of stack memory is that when the memory's scope is complete, the memory will be released automatically for you. Care should be taken when using stack memory as this memory is limited in size.

It should be noted that the total size of the stack is entirely system-dependent and can vary widely. Unless you know the size of the stack, it should be assumed to be small, and used with caution as there is no simple way to determine when the stack runs out. Unlike dynamic memory allocation, which usually returns an error of some kind when memory is not available, on most systems when the stack runs out, your program will simply crash.

For example, on our test system, when attempting to allocate an integer array of `268435456` on the stack as shown in the following code:

```
#include <iostream>

int main()
{
    int stack_mem[268435456];
    std::cout << stack_mem[0] << '\n';
}
```

```
// > g++ -std=c++17 scratchpad.cpp; ./a.out
// Segmentation fault (core dumped)
```

This results in a segmentation fault as the stack_mem variable exceeds the total size of the stack.

The third form of memory and the main topic of this chapter is dynamic memory (also called **heap memory**). Like the stack, each program is given a pool of heap memory by the OS, which often can grow based on demand. Unlike the stack, and even global memory, heap memory allocations can be quite large if the physical system and OS can support it. In addition, unlike stack and global memory, heap memory is slow to allocate and any memory that is allocated on-demand by the user must also be released back to the heap by the user when complete. In C++, the fundamental method for allocating heap memory is through the use of the new() and delete() operator functions, as shown here:

```
#include <iostream>

int main()
{
    auto ptr = new int;
    std::cout << ptr << '\n';
    delete ptr;
}

// > g++ -std=c++17 scratchpad.cpp; ./a.out
// 0x5639c77e4e70
```

In this simple example, an integer (whose size is architecture-dependent, but assumed to be 4 bytes here) is allocated on the heap using the new operator. The address of the newly-allocated memory is outputted to stdout, and then the memory is released back to the heap using the delete() operator. In addition to single objects, arrays can also be allocated/deallocated using the new()/delete() operators, as shown here:

```
#include <iostream>

int main()
{
    auto ptr = new int[42];
    std::cout << ptr << '\n';
    delete [] ptr;
}

// > g++ -std=c++17 scratchpad.cpp; ./a.out
// 0x5594a7d47e70
```

In this example, an array of integers is allocated a size of 42. Note that, unlike `malloc()` in standard C, the new operator automatically calculates the total number of bytes needed for an object or array of objects. Assuming that an integer is 4 bytes, in this example, the new operator allocates $42 * sizeof(int) == 42 * 4 == 11088$ bytes. In addition to the use of `new[]()` to allocate an array, the `delete []()` operator is used instead of the `delete` operator. The delete operator calls the destructor for a single object while the `delete []()` operator calls the destructor for each object in the array:

```cpp
#include <iostream>

class myclass
{
public:
    ~myclass()
    {
        std::cout << "my delete\n";
    }
};

int main()
{
    auto ptr = new myclass[2];
    std::cout << ptr << '\n';
    delete [] ptr;
}

// > g++ -std=c++17 scratchpad.cpp; ./a.out
// 0x56171064ae78
// my delete
// my delete
```

It's important to note that some systems may use different pools to allocate single objects versus arrays of objects versus aligned objects, and more. Care should be taken to ensure that the deallocation routine matches the allocation routine. For example, if `new []()` is used, `delete []()` should always be used instead of `delete()`. If a mismatch occurs, systems that share the same pools will function without issue, but a crash could occur on systems that do not share these pools as you would be attempting to release memory to a pool to which the memory did not originally belong. The easiest way to prevent these types of errors is to use `std::unique_ptr{}` and `std::shared_ptr{}`, which will be discussed in the *Understanding smart pointers and ownership* section.

Aligning memory

When programming systems, often allocating aligned memory (that is, memory that is divisible by a specific alignment) is required. Specifically, when memory is allocated, the resulting address that points to said allocated memory can be any value. When programming systems, however, this can often be problematic as some APIs and physical devices require memory to be allocated with a certain minimum granularity. Consider the following example:

```
0x0ABCDEF123456789 // Unaligned
0x0ABCDEF12345F000 // 4 Kb aligned
```

Aligned memory may be allocated using all three memory types:

- Globally
- On the stack
- Dynamically

To allocate aligned memory globally using C++, use the `alignas()` specifier:

```cpp
#include <iostream>

alignas(0x1000) int ptr[42];

int main()
{
    std::cout << ptr << '\n';
}

// > g++ -std=c++17 scratchpad.cpp; ./a.out
// 0x560809897000
```

In this example, an integer array of size `42` is allocated globally, and the `alignas()` specifier is used to align the array to a 4k page boundary. The array's address is then outputted, and as shown, the address is divisible by a 4k page (that is, the first 12 bits are zero). To allocate aligned memory on the stack, you can also use the `alignas()` specifier:

```cpp
#include <iostream>

int main()
{
    alignas(0x1000) int ptr[42];
    std::cout << ptr << '\n';
}

// > g++ -std=c++17 scratchpad.cpp; ./a.out
// 0x560809897000
```

Instead of the array being allocated globally, the array is moved into the `main` function's scope and is therefore allocated using the stack when the `main` function executes, and automatically released when the `main` function completes. This type of allocation should be used with care as the compiler has to add code to the program's executable to move the stack pointer in order to align this memory. As a result, aligned allocations on the stack indirectly allocate additional, unusable memory to ensure the pointer is aligned (shown on Intel's x86_64 using GCC 7.3):

```
> objdump -d | grep main
...
00000000000008da <main>:
 8da: 4c 8d 54 24 08    lea 0x8(%rsp),%r10
 8df: 48 81 e4 00 f0 ff ff    and $0xfffffffffffff000,%rsp
 8e6: 41 ff 72 f8    pushq -0x8(%r10)
```

As can be seen, the stack pointer (that is, the RSP register in this case), is moved to align the integer array. If this type of allocation is done a lot, or the alignment is high (say a 2 MB alignment), stack space could run out quickly. Another way to allocate aligned memory (regardless of the type) is to manually calculate an aligned position within an existing character buffer:

```cpp
#include <iostream>

int main()
{
    char buffer[0x2000];
    auto ptr1 = reinterpret_cast<uintptr_t>(buffer);
    auto ptr2 = ptr1 - (ptr1 % 0x1000) + 0x1000;

    std::cout << std::hex << std::showbase;
```

```
        std::cout << ptr1 << '\n';
        std::cout << ptr2 << '\n';
}

// > g++ -std=c++17 scratchpad.cpp; ./a.out
// 0x7ffd160dec20
// 0x7ffd160df000
```

In this example, a character buffer of ample size is allocated on the stack. The character buffer's address is then converted into an unsigned integer pointer type, an operation that is discouraged by the C++ Core Guidelines as `reinterpret_cast()` should be avoided, and then arithmetic on the character buffer's pointer is performed to locate a page-aligned address inside the buffer, another operation that is discouraged by the C++ Core Guidelines as pointer arithmetic should be avoided as well. Both the original and resulting pointers are outputted to `stdout`, and as shown, the calculated pointer is aligned to a 4k page boundary within the character buffer. To see how this algorithm works, see the following:

```
// ptr1 = 0x7ffd160dec20
// ptr1 % 0x1000 = 0xc20
// ptr1 - (ptr1 % 0x1000) = 0x7ffd160de000
// ptr1 - (ptr1 % 0x1000) + 0x1000 = 0x7ffd160df000
```

This type of process works, and has been used for years, but should be avoided as there are better ways to accomplish this same task using `alignas()` without the need for type-casting and pointer arithmetic that is prone to error and discouraged by the C++ Core Guidelines.

Finally, the third way to allocate aligned memory is to use dynamic allocations. Prior to C++17, this was done using `posix_memalign()` or the newer C11 `aligned_alloc()`, as shown here:

```cpp
#include <iostream>

int main()
{
    int *ptr;

    if (posix_memalign(reinterpret_cast<void **>(&ptr), 0x1000, 42 *
sizeof(int))) {
        std::clog << "ERROR: unable to allocate aligned memory\n";
        ::exit(EXIT_FAILURE);
    }

    std::cout << ptr << '\n';
    free(ptr);
}
```

```
// > g++ -std=c++17 scratchpad.cpp; ./a.out
// 0x55c5d31d1000
```

The `posix_memalign()` API is a bit clunky. First, a pointer must be declared, the alignment and size (which must be manually calculated) are provided, and then the function returns 0 upon success. Finally, `reinterpret_cast()` is needed to tell the `posix_memalign()` function that the provided pointer is `void **` and not `int**`. Since the `posix_memalign()` function is a C-style function, `free()` is used to release the memory.

Another way to allocate aligned memory is to use the relatively new `aligned_alloc()` function, which provides a less clunky, more portable implementation:

```cpp
#include <iostream>

int main()
{
    if (auto ptr = aligned_alloc(0x1000, 42 * sizeof(int))) {
        std::cout << ptr << '\n';
        free(ptr);
    }
}

// > g++ -std=c++17 scratchpad.cpp; ./a.out
// 0x55c5d31d1000
```

As shown, `aligned_alloc()` functions like a regular `malloc()` but with an additional alignment parameter. This API still suffers from the same size issue as `malloc()` and `posix_memalign()`, where the total size of the array must be manually calculated.

To solve these issues, C++17 added aligned allocation versions of the `new()` and `delete()` operators that leverage `alignas()` as follows:

```cpp
#include <iostream>

using aligned_int alignas(0x1000) = int;

int main()
{
    auto ptr = new aligned_int;
    std::cout << ptr << '\n';
    delete ptr;
}

// > g++ -std=c++17 scratchpad.cpp; ./a.out
// 0x55e32ece1000
```

In this example, we allocate a single integer using `alignas()` and the `new()` and `delete()` operators. To accomplish this, we create a new type, called `aligned_int`, that leverages `alignas()` in the type definition. The following can also be used to allocate an aligned array:

```
#include <iostream>

using aligned_int alignas(0x1000) = int;

int main()
{
    auto ptr = new aligned_int[42];
    std::cout << ptr << '\n';
    delete [] ptr;
}

// > g++ -std=c++17 scratchpad.cpp; ./a.out
// 0x5649c0597000
```

The same aligned integer type is used, with the only difference being the use of `new [] ()` and `delete [] ()` instead of `new()` and `delete()`. Unlike the C APIs shown in the preceding code, `new()` and `delete()`, including the aligned versions added to C++17, automatically calculate the total number of bytes that need to be allocated for you, removing potential errors.

nothrow

The `new()` and `delete()` operators are allowed to throw exceptions. In fact, if an allocation fails, the default new operator throws `std::bad_alloc` instead of returning `nullptr`. In some situations, often seen when programming systems, an exception on an invalid allocation is unwanted, and for this reason, a `nothrow` version has been provided:

```
#include <iostream>

int main()
{
    auto ptr = new (std::nothrow) int;
    std::cout << ptr << '\n';
    delete ptr;
}

// > g++ -std=c++17 scratchpad.cpp; ./a.out
// 0x55893e230e70
```

Specifically, `new (std::nothrow)` is used instead of `new()`, which tells C++ that you would like `nullptr` to be returned on an invalid allocation instead of `new()` throwing `std::bad_alloc`. The array version was also provided as follows:

```
#include <iostream>

int main()
{
    auto ptr = new (std::nothrow) int[42];
    std::cout << ptr << '\n';
    delete [] ptr;
}

// > g++ -std=c++17 scratchpad.cpp; ./a.out
// 0x5623076e9e70
```

And as one might expect, the aligned allocation versions of these functions were also provided for single-object allocations:

```
#include <iostream>

using aligned_int alignas(0x1000) = int;

int main()
{
    auto ptr = new (std::nothrow) aligned_int;
    std::cout << ptr << '\n';
    delete ptr;
}

// > g++ -std=c++17 scratchpad.cpp; ./a.out
// 0x55e36201a000
```

There's also array-style allocations:

```
#include <iostream>

using aligned_int alignas(0x1000) = int;

int main()
{
    auto ptr = new (std::nothrow) aligned_int[42];
    std::cout << ptr << '\n';
    delete [] ptr;
}

// > g++ -std=c++17 scratchpad.cpp; ./a.out
// 0x557222103000
```

It should be noted that `nullptr` is only returned for types provided by C++. For user-defined types, if an exception is thrown during construction, the `nothrow` version of `new()`, which is marked `nothrow`, will call `std::terminate` and abort:

```
#include <iostream>

class myclass
{
public:
    myclass()
    {
        throw std::runtime_error("the answer was not 42");
    }
};

int main()
{
    auto ptr = new (std::nothrow) myclass;
    std::cout << ptr << '\n';
    delete ptr;
}

// > g++ -std=c++17 scratchpad.cpp; ./a.out
// terminate called after throwing an instance of 'std::runtime_error'
// what(): the answer was not 42
// Aborted (core dumped)
```

To overcome this issue, class-specific `new` and `delete` operators may be used (a topic to be explained in the *Overloading* section).

Placement of new

In addition to aligned allocations and `nothrow` specifiers, C++ also provides the ability to allocate memory from an existing, user-controlled buffer, a situation that can often be seen while programming systems. For example, suppose you have mapped a buffer from a physical device. Now suppose you wish to allocate from this buffer an integer, the `new()` placement operator may be used to accomplish this:

```
#include <iostream>

char buf[0x1000];

int main()
{
    auto ptr = new (buf) int;
```

```
        std::cout << ptr << '\n';
}

// > g++ -std=c++17 scratchpad.cpp; ./a.out
// 0x5567b8884000
```

In this example, we leverage the new() placement operator to allocate memory from an existing user-controlled buffer. The new() placement operator provides the object to be allocated with the address that is provided, and then, as usual, calls the object's constructor. It should be noted that the delete() operator is not needed in this case because the memory to the object being allocated is user-defined, in which case there is no heap memory to return to the heap when complete. Furthermore, the new() placement operator doesn't manage the memory provided to a set of objects, a task that must be performed by the user. To demonstrate this, see the following:

```
#include <iostream>

char buf[0x1000];

int main()
{
    auto ptr1 = new (buf) int;
    auto ptr2 = new (buf) int;
    std::cout << ptr1 << '\n';
    std::cout << ptr2 << '\n';
}

// > g++ -std=c++17 scratchpad.cpp; ./a.out
// 0x558044c66180
// 0x558044c66180
```

In this example, the new() placement is used twice. As shown, the address that is provided is the same since we have not manually advanced the address provided to the new() placement, demonstrating that C++ doesn't automatically manage user-defined memory when the new() placement is used. Typically, this type of example would lead to undefined behavior if executed (in this case it doesn't since we are not actually using the newly allocated memory). For these reasons, the new() placement should be used with special care. In addition to single allocations, array allocations are also provided:

```
#include <iostream>

char buf[0x1000];

int main()
{
    auto ptr = new (buf) int[42];
```

```
        std::cout << ptr << '\n';
}

// > g++ -std=c++17 scratchpad.cpp; ./a.out
// 0x55594aff0000
```

Since C++ doesn't manage `new()` placement allocations, aligned allocations must be provided by the user as well. The alignment algorithm provided in the preceding code could be used to provide aligned allocations from a user-defined buffer, the memory that is already aligned (for example, when interfacing with a physical device via `mmap()`) could be used, or `alignas()` could also be used, as follows:

```
#include <iostream>

alignas(0x1000) char buf[0x1000];

int main()
{
    auto ptr = new (buf) int;
    std::cout << ptr << '\n';
}

// > g++ -std=c++17 scratchpad.cpp; ./a.out
// 0x5567b8884000
```

In this example, since the buffer is aligned using `alignas()`, the resulting new placement allocation is also aligned when this buffer is provided. This same type of allocation also works for array allocation:

```
#include <iostream>

alignas(0x1000) char buf[0x1000];

int main()
{
    auto ptr = new (buf) int[42];
    std::cout << ptr << '\n';
}

// > g++ -std=c++17 scratchpad.cpp; ./a.out
// 0x55594aff0000
```

Overloading

Often when programming systems, the default allocation scheme provided by C++ is undesirable. Examples include (but are not limited to):

- Custom memory layouts
- Fragmentation
- Performance optimizations
- Debugging and statistics

One way to overcome these issues is to leverage C++ allocators, a complex topic that will be discussed in Chapter 9, *A Hands-On Approach to Allocators*. Another, more heavy-handed, way to achieve this is to leverage the new() and delete() operators' user-defined overloads:

```cpp
#include <iostream>

void *operator new (std::size_t count)
{
    // WARNING: Do not use std::cout here
    return malloc(count);
}

void operator delete (void *ptr)
{
    // WARNING: Do not use std::cout here
    return free(ptr);
}

int main()
{
    auto ptr = new int;
    std::cout << ptr << '\n';
    delete ptr;
}

// > g++ -std=c++17 scratchpad.cpp; ./a.out
// 0x55f204617e70
```

In this example, a custom new() and delete() operator overload is provided. Instead of your program using the default allocation scheme provided by the new() and delete() functions, your user-defined versions will be used instead.

These overloads affect all allocations, including those used by the C++ library, so care should be taken when leveraging these overloads as infinite cyclic recursions could occur if an allocation is performed inside these functions. For example, data structures such as `std::vector` and `std::list`, or debugging functions such as `std::cout` and `std::cerr` cannot be used as these facilities use the `new()` and `delete()` operators to allocate memory.

In addition to the single-object `new()` and `delete()` operators, all of the other operators may also be overloaded, including the array allocation versions:

```
#include <iostream>

void *operator new[](std::size_t count)
{
    // WARNING: Do not use std::cout here
    return malloc(count);
}

void operator delete[](void *ptr)
{
    // WARNING: Do not use std::cout here
    return free(ptr);
}

int main()
{
    auto ptr = new int[42];
    std::cout << ptr << '\n';
    delete [] ptr;
}

// > g++ -std=c++17 scratchpad.cpp; ./a.out
// 0x55e5e2c62e70
```

Debugging and statistics are a common reason to overload the new() and delete() operators, providing useful information about the types of allocations that are occurring. For example, suppose you wish to record the total number of allocations larger than, or equal to, a page:

```cpp
#include <iostream>

std::size_t allocations = 0;

void *operator new (std::size_t count)
{
    if (count >= 0x1000) {
        allocations++;
    }

    return malloc(count);
}

void operator delete (void *ptr)
{
    return free(ptr);
}

int main()
{
    auto ptr = new int;
    std::cout << allocations << '\n';
    delete ptr;
}

// > g++ -std=c++17 scratchpad.cpp; ./a.out
// 0
```

As shown, no allocations larger than a page were performed by our program, including allocations made by the C++ library. Let's see what happens if we allocate a page as shown here:

```cpp
#include <iostream>

std::size_t allocations = 0;

void *operator new (std::size_t count)
{
    if (count >= 0x1000) {
        allocations++;
    }
```

```
        return malloc(count);
}

void operator delete (void *ptr)
{
        return free(ptr);
}

struct mystruct
{
        char buf[0x1000];
};

int main()
{
        auto ptr = new mystruct;
        std::cout << allocations << '\n';
        delete ptr;
}

// > g++ -std=c++17 scratchpad.cpp; ./a.out
// 1
```

We get a single allocation larger than, or equal to, a page, as expected. This type of use of
new() and delete() overloaded can be extremely useful for debugging memory leaks,
locating allocation optimizations, and more. It should be noted however that care should be
taken when writing these types of overloads. If you accidentally allocate memory (for
example, when using a C++ data structure such as std::vector{}, or when using
std::cout), you could end up in an infinite loop, or adding to statistics you might be
trying to record.

In addition to global operator new and delete operator overloads, class-specific versions
are also provided:

```
#include <iostream>

class myclass
{
public:
    void *operator new (std::size_t count)
    {
        std::cout << "my new\n";
        return ::operator new (count);
    }

    void operator delete (void *ptr)
    {
```

```
        std::cout << "my delete\n";
        return ::operator delete (ptr);
    }
};

int main()
{
    auto ptr = new myclass;
    std::cout << ptr << '\n';
    delete ptr;
}

// > g++ -std=c++17 scratchpad.cpp; ./a.out
// my new
// 0x5561cac52280
// my delete
```

When class-specific operators are used, the only allocations that are directed to your overloads are allocations for the specific class or classes that you provide overloads for. As shown in the preceding example, the allocations made by std::cout are not directed to our class-specific overloads, preventing infinite recursion. The only allocation and deallocation that uses overload are the ones for myclass.

As expected, all of the global operators also exist for the class-specific operators, including versions such as aligned allocations:

```
#include <iostream>

class myclass
{
public:
    void *operator new[](std::size_t count, std::align_val_t al)
    {
        std::cout << "my new\n";
        return ::operator new (count, al);
    }

    void operator delete[](void *ptr, std::align_val_t al)
    {
        std::cout << "my delete\n";
        return ::operator delete (ptr, al);
    }
};

using aligned_myclass alignas(0x1000) = myclass;

int main()
```

```
{
    auto ptr1 = new aligned_myclass;
    auto ptr2 = new aligned_myclass[42];
    std::cout << ptr1 << '\n';
    std::cout << ptr2 << '\n';
    delete ptr1;
    delete [] ptr2;
}

// > g++ -std=c++17 scratchpad.cpp; ./a.out
// my new
// 0x563b49b74000
// 0x563b49b76000
// my delete
```

Understanding smart pointers and ownership

In this section, the reader will learn how to use smart pointers to increase the safety, reliability, and stability of their program, while also adhering to the C++ Core Guidelines.

The std::unique_ptr{} pointer

It should be clear by now that C++ provides an extensive set of APIs for allocating and deallocating dynamic memory. It should also be clear that whether you are using malloc()/free() or new()/delete(), errors are not only possible but likely in large applications. For example, you might forget to release memory back to the heap:

```
#include <iostream>

int main()
{
    auto ptr = new int;
    std::cout << ptr << '\n';
}

// > g++ -std=c++17 scratchpad.cpp; valgrind ./a.out
// ==8627== LEAK SUMMARY:
// ==8627== definitely lost: 4 bytes in 1 blocks
// ==8627== indirectly lost: 0 bytes in 0 blocks
// ==8627== possibly lost: 0 bytes in 0 blocks
// ==8627== still reachable: 0 bytes in 0 blocks
```

```
// ==8627== suppressed: 0 bytes in 0 blocks
// ==8627== Rerun with --leak-check=full to see details of leaked memory
```

Or you could use `delete` instead of `delete []` when allocating an array:

```
#include <iostream>

int main()
{
    auto ptr = new int[42];
    std::cout << ptr << '\n';
    delete ptr;
}

// > g++ -std=c++17 scratchpad.cpp; valgrind ./a.out
// ==8656== Mismatched free() / delete / delete []
// ==8656== at 0x4C2E60B: operator delete(void*) (vg_replace_malloc.c:576)
// ==8656== by 0x108960: main (in /home/user/examples/chapter_7/a.out)
// ==8656== Address 0x5aebc80 is 0 bytes inside a block of size 168 alloc'd
// ==8656== at 0x4C2DC6F: operator new[](unsigned long)
(vg_replace_malloc.c:423)
// ==8656== by 0x10892B: main (in /home/user/examples/chapter_7/a.out)
```

To overcome this, C++11 introduced the concept of pointer ownership with two classes:

- `std::unique_ptr{}`: Defines a pointer uniquely owned by a single entity. Copying this pointer is not allowed and is explicitly prevented by the compiler, and deallocations are automatically handled by C++.
- `std::shared_ptr{}`: Defines a pointer that may be owned by one or more entities. Copying this pointer is allowed, and deallocation only occurs when all of the owners have released their ownership.

The C++ Core Guidelines, in general, discourage any dynamic allocations that are not performed by these two classes. For most cases where `new` and `delete` would normally be used, `std::unique_ptr{}` should be used instead. Consider the following example:

```
#include <memory>
#include <iostream>

int main()
{
    auto ptr = std::make_unique<int>(42);
    std::cout << *ptr << '\n';
}

// > g++ -std=c++17 scratchpad.cpp; ./a.out
// 42
```

To create both `std::unique_ptr{}` and `std::shared_ptr`, C++ provides the following:

- `std::make_unique()`: Creates `std::unique_ptr{}`
- `std::make_shared()`: Creates `std::shared_ptr{}`

If you plan to provide C++ Core Guideline compliance, get used to these functions. As shown, to create `std::unique_ptr{}`, you must provide the object type you plan to allocate, and the object's initial value, as a template argument. Also, as shown, there is no need to manually call the `delete()` operator, as this is done for you. To demonstrate this, see the following:

```cpp
#include <memory>
#include <iostream>

class myclass
{
public:
    ~myclass()
    {
        std::cout << "my delete\n";
    }
};

int main()
{
    auto ptr = std::make_unique<myclass>();
    std::cout << ptr.get() << '\n';
}

// > g++ -std=c++17 scratchpad.cpp; ./a.out
// 0x5621eb029e70
// my delete
```

Using `std::unique_ptr{}` in this example, both memory leaks and memory API mismatching have been prevented. In addition, this smart allocation and deallocation is scoped. Consider the following example:

```cpp
#include <memory>
#include <iostream>

class myclass1
{
public:
    ~myclass1()
    {
        std::cout << "my delete\n";
```

```
    }
};

class myclass2
{
    std::unique_ptr<myclass1> m_data;

public:
    myclass2() :
        m_data{std::make_unique<myclass1>()}
    { }
};

int main()
{
    myclass2();
    std::cout << "complete\n";
}

// > g++ -std=c++17 scratchpad.cpp; ./a.out
// my delete
// complete
```

myclass1 is stored as a member variable of myclass2. In the main function, myclass2 is created and destroyed immediately, and as a result, when myclass2 is destroyed, myclass1 is also released back to the heap.

std::unique_ptr{} accepts a pointer to previously-allocated memory (for example, via the new() operator), and then, on destruction, releases the memory it was given via the delete() operator by default. If the memory provided to std::unique_ptr{} is allocated using new[]() instead of new(), the [] version of std::unique_ptr{} should be used to ensure it releases the allocated memory using delete[]() instead of delete():

```
#include <memory>
#include <iostream>

class myclass1
{
public:
    ~myclass1()
    {
        std::cout << "my delete\n";
    }
};

int main()
{
```

```
        std::unique_ptr<myclass1[]>(new myclass1[2]);
}

// > g++ -std=c++17 scratchpad.cpp; ./a.out
// my delete
// my delete
```

The more C++-Core-Guideline-compliant method for allocating and deallocating an array using `std::unique_ptr{}` is to use the array version of `std::make_unique()`:

```cpp
#include <memory>
#include <iostream>

int main()
{
    auto ptr = std::make_unique<int[]>(42);
    std::cout << ptr.get() << '\n';
}

// > g++ -std=c++17 scratchpad.cpp; ./a.out
// 0x55b25f224e70
// my delete
```

Instead of manually allocating the array, `std::make_unique()` allocates the array for you. The difference between a single-object allocation and an array allocation with `std::make_unique()` is as follows:

- `std::make_unique<type>(args)`: To perform a single-object allocation, the type is provided as the template argument, and the object's constructor arguments are provided as the arguments to `std::make_unique()`
- `std::make_unique<type[]>(size)`: To perform an array allocation, the array type is provided as the template argument, and the size of the array is provided as the argument to `std::make_unique()`

In some cases, the memory provided to `std::unique_ptr{}` cannot be released using `delete()` or `delete[]()` (for example, a `mmap()` buffer, placement `new()`, and more). To support these types of scenarios, `std::unique_ptr{}` accepts custom deleters:

```cpp
#include <memory>
#include <iostream>

class int_deleter
{
public:
    void operator()(int *ptr) const
    {
```

```
            std::cout << "my delete\n";
            delete ptr;
        };
};

int main()
{
    auto ptr = std::unique_ptr<int, int_deleter>(new int, int_deleter());
    std::cout << ptr.get() << '\n';
}

// > g++ -std=c++17 scratchpad.cpp; ./a.out
// 0x5615be977e70
// my delete
```

In the preceding example, a `deleter` class is created, and a functor (that is, `operator ()`) is provided, which performs the custom deletion. When it's time to release the allocated memory, the functor is called by `std::unique_ptr{}`.

One disadvantage of `std::unqiue_ptr{}` in C++17 is that the alignment versions of the `new` and `delete` operators were not extended to `std::unique_ptr{}` (or `std::shared_pointer{}`). Since there is no alignment version for `std::unique_ptr{}`, if aligned memory is required, it must be allocated manually (hopefully an issue that will be resolved in future versions of C++ as this allocation style is typically discouraged by the C++ Core Guidelines):

```
#include <memory>
#include <iostream>

using aligned_int alignas(0x1000) = int;

int main()
{
    auto ptr = std::unique_ptr<int>(new aligned_int);
    std::cout << ptr.get() << '\n';
}

// > g++ -std=c++17 scratchpad.cpp; ./a.out
// 0x560eb6a0a000
```

Like a normal C++-style pointer, * and -> may be used to dereference at `std::unique_ptr{}`:

```
#include <memory>
#include <iostream>

struct mystruct {
    int data{42};
};

int main()
{
    auto ptr1 = std::make_unique<int>(42);
    auto ptr2 = std::make_unique<mystruct>();
    std::cout << *ptr1 << '\n';
    std::cout << ptr2->data << '\n';
}

// > g++ -std=c++17 scratchpad.cpp; ./a.out
// 42
// 42
```

To get `std::unique_ptr{}` to release its allocation, the pointer needs to lose scope, causing the destructor of `std::unique_ptr{}` to be called, which in turn releases the allocation back to the heap. `std::unique_ptr{}` also provides the `reset()` function, which explicitly tells the pointer to release its memory on demand, without having to lose scope:

```
#include <memory>
#include <iostream>

int main()
{
    auto ptr = std::make_unique<int>();
    std::cout << ptr.get() << '\n';
    ptr.reset();
    std::cout << ptr.get() << '\n';
}

// > g++ -std=c++17 scratchpad.cpp; ./a.out
// 0x55bcfa2b1e70
// 0
```

In this example, `std::unique_ptr{}` is reset, and as a result, the pointer it is storing is equivalent to `nullptr`. `std::unique_ptr{}` does not check to ensure that the pointer is valid when it is dereferenced using operators such as `->` and `*`. For this reason, the `reset()` function should be used with care, and used only when needed (for example, when the order in which allocations are released matters).

Here are a couple of ways `std::unique_ptr{}` could be invalid (but this is not an exhaustive list):

- It was originally created using `nullptr`
- `reset()` or `release()` was called

To check whether `std::unique_ptr{}` is valid, to ensure a null dereference doesn't accidentally occur, the Boolean operator may be used:

```cpp
#include <memory>
#include <iostream>

int main()
{
    auto ptr = std::make_unique<int>(42);
    if (ptr) {
        std::cout << *ptr << '\n';
    }
    ptr.reset();
    if (ptr) {
        std::cout << *ptr << '\n';
    }
}

// > g++ -std=c++17 scratchpad.cpp; ./a.out
// 42
```

As shown in this example, once `reset()` is called on `std::unique_ptr{}`, it becomes invalid (that is, its equal to `nullptr`), and the Boolean operator returns `false`, preventing a `nullptr` dereference.

If `std::unique_ptr{}` is created using the array syntax, the subscript operator may be used to access a specific element in the array, similar to using the subscript operator for a standard C array, or `std::array{}`:

```cpp
#include <memory>
#include <iostream>

int main()
```

```
{
    auto ptr = std::make_unique<int[]>(42);
    std::cout << ptr[0] << '\n';
}

// > g++ -std=c++17 scratchpad.cpp; ./a.out
// 0
```

In the preceding example, an integer array is allocated a size of 42, and the first element in the array is outputted to stdout, which contains the value of 0 since std::make_unique() uses value initialization to zero-initialize all allocations.

 It should be noted that even though the C++ Core Guidelines encourage the use of std::unique_ptr{} instead of manually allocating and deallocating C-style arrays, the guidelines do not encourage the use of the subscript operator to access the array since doing so performs unsafe pointer arithmetic, and could potentially lead to a nullptr dereference. Instead, a newly-allocated array using std::unique_ptr{} should be provided to gsl::span prior to being accessed.

One limitation of C++17 with respect to std::unique_ptr{} is the inability to directly add one to an IO stream such as std::cout. With C++17, the best way to output the address of std::unique_ptr{} is to use the get() function, which returns the address of the pointer. Another way to accomplish this is to create a user-defined overload:

```
#include <memory>
#include <iostream>

template<typename T> std::ostream &
operator<<(std::ostream &os, const std::unique_ptr<T> &ptr)
{
    os << ptr.get();
    return os;
}

int main()
{
    auto ptr = std::make_unique<int>();
    std::cout << ptr << '\n';
    std::cout << ptr.get() << '\n';
}

// > g++ -std=c++17 scratchpad.cpp; ./a.out
// 0x55ed70997e70
```

The std::shared_ptr pointer

In most cases, `std::unique_ptr{}` should be used to allocate dynamic memory. In some use cases, however, `std::unique_ptr{}` is incapable of properly representing pointer ownership. Pointer ownership refers to who owns a pointer, or in other words, who is responsible for allocating, and more importantly, deallocating a pointer. In most cases, a single entity within a program is responsible for this task. There are, however, some use cases where more than one entity must claim responsibility for deallocating a pointer.

The most common scenario where more than one entity must claim ownership over a variable involves threading. Suppose you have two threads:

- Thread #1 creates a pointer (and thus owns it)
- Thread #2 uses the pointer from thread #1

In this example, the second thread owns the pointer just as much as the first thread that created the pointer and provided it in the first place. The following example demonstrates this scenario:

```
#include <thread>
#include <iostream>

class myclass
{
    int m_data{0};

public:

    ~myclass()
    {
        std::cout << "myclass deleted\n";
    }

    void inc()
    { m_data++; }
};

std::thread t1;
std::thread t2;

void
thread2(myclass *ptr)
{
    for (auto i = 0; i < 100000; i++) {
        ptr->inc();
    }
```

```cpp
        std::cout << "thread2: complete\n";
}

void
thread1()
{
    auto ptr = std::make_unique<myclass>();
    t2 = std::thread(thread2, ptr.get());

    for (auto i = 0; i < 10; i++) {
        ptr->inc();
    }

    std::cout << "thread1: complete\n";
}

int main()
{
    t1 = std::thread(thread1);

    t1.join();
    t2.join();
}

// > g++ -std=c++17 -lpthread scratchpad.cpp; ./a.out
// thread1: complete
// myclass deleted
// thread2: complete
```

In this example, the first thread is created, which creates a pointer to `myclass`. It then creates the second thread and passes the newly-created pointer to this second thread. Both threads perform a set of actions on the pointer, and then complete. The problem is that the first thread doesn't have as much work to perform as the second thread, so it completes quickly, releasing the pointer before the second thread has a chance to complete, since in this scenario we have explicitly stated that `thread1` is the owner of the pointer and `thread2` is simply a user of the pointer.

To overcome this issue, C++ provides a second smart pointer, called `std::shared_ptr{}`, that is capable of assigning ownership to more than one entity. The syntax for `std::shared_ptr{}` is almost identical to `std::unique_ptr{}`:

```cpp
#include <memory>
#include <iostream>

int main()
{
    auto ptr = std::make_shared<int>();
```

```
        std::cout << ptr.get() << '\n';
}

// > g++ -std=c++17 scratchpad.cpp; ./a.out
// 0x562e6ba9ce80
```

Internally, `std::shared_ptr{}` maintains the managed object in a separate object that is shared between all copies of the original `std::shared_ptr{}`. This managed object stores a count of the total number of `std::shared_ptr{}` copies. Each time a copy is created, the count inside the managed object increases. When `std::shared_ptr{}` needs access to the pointer itself, it must use its pointer to the managed object to ask for the pointer (that is, `std::shared_ptr{}` doesn't store the pointer itself, but rather stores a pointer to a managed object that stores the pointer). Each time `std::shared_ptr{}` is destroyed, the managed object's count is decreased, and when the count reaches 0, the pointer is finally released back to the heap.

Using this pattern, `std::shared_ptr{}` is capable of providing ownership of a single pointer to multiple entities. The following rewrites the preceding example using `std::shared_ptr{}` instead of `std::unique_ptr{}`:

```
#include <thread>
#include <iostream>

class myclass
{
    int m_data{0};

public:

    ~myclass()
    {
        std::cout << "myclass deleted\n";
    }

    void inc()
    { m_data++; }
};

std::thread t1;
std::thread t2;

void
thread2(const std::shared_ptr<myclass> ptr)
{
    for (auto i = 0; i < 100000; i++) {
        ptr->inc();
```

```
        }

        std::cout << "thread2: complete\n";
    }

    void
    thread1()
    {
        auto ptr = std::make_shared<myclass>();
        t2 = std::thread(thread2, ptr);

        for (auto i = 0; i < 10; i++) {
            ptr->inc();
        }

        std::cout << "thread1: complete\n";
    }

    int main()
    {
        t1 = std::thread(thread1);

        t1.join();
        t2.join();
    }

    // > g++ -std=c++17 -lpthread scratchpad.cpp; ./a.out
    // thread1: complete
    // thread2: complete
    // myclass deleted
```

As shown in this example, `thread2` is given a copy of the original `std::shared_ptr{}`, creating in effect two copies that point to a single managed object. When `thread1` completes, `thread2` still maintains a reference to the managed object and as a result, the pointer remains intact. It's not until the second thread completes that the managed object's reference count reaches 0 and the pointer is released back to the heap.

It should be noted that there are some disadvantages to `std::shared_ptr{}`:

- **Memory footprint**: Since `std::shared_ptr{}` maintains a pointer to a managed object, `std::shared_ptr{}` could result in two mallocs instead of one (some implementations are capable of allocating a single, larger chunk of memory and using it for both the pointer and the managed object). Regardless of the implementation, the amount of memory that is needed by `std::shared_ptr{}` is larger than that of `std::unique_ptr{}`, which is often the same size sd a regular C-style pointer.

- **Performance**: All access to the pointer must first be redirected to the managed object since `std::shared_ptr{}` does not actually have a copy of the pointer itself (just a pointer to the managed object). As a result, additional function calls (that is, pointer dereferences) are required.

- **Memory leaks**: There is a tradeoff between `std::unique_ptr{}` and `std::shared_ptr{}`, and neither provides the perfect solution for managing memory in a way that prevents possible `nullptr` dereferences while at the same time preventing memory leaks. As demonstrated, the use of `std::unique_ptr{}` in some situations could result in a `nullptr` dereference. On the other hand, `std::shared_ptr{}` could result in a memory leak if the number of copies of `std::shared_ptr{}` never reaches 0. Although these problems with smart pointers exist, the use of `new()`/`delete()` manually doesn't address these issues (and almost certainly makes them worse), and in general, if the right smart pointer type is used in the right scenario, these types of issues can be alleviated.

- **Cyclic references**: It is possible to create cyclic references with `std::shared_ptr{}`.

Like `std::unique_ptr{}`, `std::shared_ptr{}` provides a `reset()` function:

```
#include <memory>
#include <iostream>

int main()
{
    auto ptr1 = std::make_shared<int>();
    auto ptr2 = ptr1;
    std::cout << ptr1.get() << '\n';
    std::cout << ptr2.get() << '\n';
    ptr2.reset();
    std::cout << ptr1.get() << '\n';
    std::cout << ptr2.get() << '\n';
}
```

```
// > g++ -std=c++17 scratchpad.cpp; ./a.out
// 0x555b99574e80
// 0x555b99574e80
// 0x555b99574e80
// 0
```

In this example, two copies of `std::shared_ptr{}` are created. We first output the address of these pointers to `stdout`, and as expected, the address is valid, and they are the same (as they both point to the same managed object). Next, we release using the `reset()` function, the second pointer and then output the address of the pointers again. The second time around, the first `std::shared_ptr{}` still points to a valid pointer, while the second points to `nullptr`, since it no longer has a reference to the original managed object. The pointer is eventually released back to the heap when the `main()` function completes.

One issue with the C++17 version of `std::shared_ptr{}` is a lack of an array version, similar to `std::unique_ptr{}`. That is, there is no `std::shared_ptr<type[]>` version of `std::shared_ptr{}`, similar to the `std::unique_ptr<type[]>{}` API. As a result, there is no way to allocate an array using `std::make_shared()`, and there is no subscript operator to access each element in the array. Instead, you must do the following:

```cpp
#include <memory>
#include <iostream>

int main()
{
    auto ptr = std::shared_ptr<int>(new int[42]());
    std::cout << ptr.get()[0] << '\n';
}

// > g++ -std=c++17 scratchpad.cpp; ./a.out
// 0
```

C++ also provides a method for determining how many copies of `std::shared_ptr{}` exist (which essentially just asks the managed object for its reference count):

```cpp
#include <memory>
#include <iostream>

int main()
{
    auto ptr1 = std::make_shared<int>();
    auto ptr2 = ptr1;
    std::cout << ptr1.get() << '\n';
    std::cout << ptr2.get() << '\n';
    std::cout << ptr1.use_count() << '\n';
    ptr2.reset();
```

```
        std::cout << ptr1.get() << '\n';
        std::cout << ptr2.get() << '\n';
        std::cout << ptr1.use_count() << '\n';
}

// > g++ -std=c++17 scratchpad.cpp; ./a.out
// 0x5644edde7e80
// 0x5644edde7e80
// 2
// 0x5644edde7e80
// 0
// 1
```

This example is similar to the preceding `reset()` example, but adds a call to the
`use_count()` function that reports the total number of copies of `std::shared_ptr{}`. As
shown, when two copies of `std::shared_ptr{}` are created, `use_count()` reports 2.
When `reset()` is run, `use_count()` reduces to 1, and eventually when `main()` completes,
this count will reduce to 0 and the pointer will be released to the heap. It should be noted
that this function should be used with caution in multithreaded environments as races can
occur with respect to the reported count.

Similar to `std::unique_ptr{}`, a Boolean operator is provided to `std::shared_ptr{}` to
check whether the pointer is valid. Unlike `std::unique_ptr{}`, the Boolean operator
doesn't determine whether the managed object has been released (as there might be a copy
of `std::shared_ptr{}` lying around somewhere). Instead, the Boolean operator reports
whether or not `std::shared_ptr{}` is maintaining a reference to the managed object.
If `std::shared_ptr{}` is valid, it has a reference to the managed object (and thus access to
the allocated pointer), and the Boolean operator reports `true`. If `std::shared_ptr{}` is
invalid, it no longer maintains a reference to the managed object (and thus doesn't have
access to the allocated pointer), returning `nullptr` when `get()` is called, and the
Boolean operator reports `false`:

```
#include <memory>
#include <iostream>

int main()
{
    auto ptr = std::make_shared<int>();
    if (ptr) {
        std::cout << "before: " << ptr.get() << '\n';
    }
    ptr.reset();
    if (ptr) {
        std::cout << "after: "<< ptr.get() << '\n';
    }
```

```
    }
```

```
// > g++ -std=c++17 scratchpad.cpp; ./a.out
// before: 0x55ac226b5e80
```

As shown in the preceding example, when the `reset()` function is called, the pointer is no longer valid, as the smart pointer's internally-managed object is now pointing to `nullptr`, and thus, the Boolean operator returns `false`. Since there are no other copies of `std::shared_ptr{}` (that is, the managed object's count is 0), the allocated pointer is also released back to the heap.

Like `std::unique_pt{}r`, both the `*` and `->` operators are provided to dereference `std::shared_ptr{}` (but no subscript operator since arrays are not supported):

```cpp
#include <memory>
#include <iostream>

struct mystruct {
    int data;
};

int main()
{
    auto ptr = std::make_shared<mystruct>();
    std::cout << ptr->data << '\n';
}

// > g++ -std=c++17 scratchpad.cpp; ./a.out
// 0
```

Finally, one issue with `std::shared_ptr{}` is that of cyclic references. The following example does the best job of describing the issue:

```cpp
#include <memory>
#include <iostream>

class myclass2;

class myclass1
{
public:

    ~myclass1()
    {
        std::cout << "delete myclass1\n";
    }
```

```
        std::shared_ptr<myclass2> m;
};

class myclass2
{
public:

    ~myclass2()
    {
        std::cout << "delete myclass2\n";
    }

    std::shared_ptr<myclass1> m;
};

int main()
{
    auto ptr1 = std::make_shared<myclass1>();
    auto ptr2 = std::make_shared<myclass2>();
    ptr1->m = ptr2;
    ptr2->m = ptr1;
}

// > g++ -std=c++17 scratchpad.cpp; ./a.out
```

In this example, two classes are created—myclass1 and myclass2. Both myclass1 and myclass2 maintain std::shared_ptr{} references to each other (that is, for whatever reason, both classes claim ownership over the other). When the pointers are destroyed, no memory is released back to the heap because none of the destructors is ever called. To understand why, we need to break down the number of copies that are made, and where they exist.

The original std::shared_ptr{} for ptr1 and ptr2 are both created in the main() function, when means the #1 and #2 managed objects both have a use_count() of 1 upon creation. Next, ptr1 is given a copy of std::shared_ptr{} for ptr2, and vice version, meaning the #1 and #2 managed objects now both have a use_count() of 2. When main() completes, the std::shared_ptr{} for ptr2 in the main() function (not std::shared_ptr{} in ptr1) is destroyed, but since there is still a std::shared_ptr{} copy of ptr2 in ptr1, the pointer itself is not released. Next, ptr1 in main() is destroyed, but since the copy of ptr2 still exists in one of the copies of ptr1, ptr1 itself is not released, and thus, we have created a copy of ptr1 and ptr2 that point to each other, but with no copies of these pointers left in the code itself to release this memory, and thus memory is permanently deleted.

To solve this, `std::shared_ptr{}` provides a version of itself called `std::weak_ptr{}`. It has all the same properties of `std::shared_ptr{}`, but doesn't increment the reference counter of the managed object. Although the `get()` function could be used instead to store a raw pointer, `std::weak_ptr{}` still maintains a connection with the managed object, providing a means to determine whether the managed object has been destroyed, something you cannot do with a raw pointer. To demonstrate this, the preceding example has been converted to use `std::weak_ptr{}` in `myclass1` and `myclass2` instead of `std::shared_ptr{}`:

```cpp
#include <memory>
#include <iostream>

class myclass2;

class myclass1
{
public:

    ~myclass1()
    {
        std::cout << "delete myclass1\n";
    }

    std::weak_ptr<myclass2> m;
};

class myclass2
{
public:

    ~myclass2()
    {
        std::cout << "delete myclass2\n";
    }

    std::weak_ptr<myclass1> m;
};

int main()
{
    auto ptr1 = std::make_shared<myclass1>();
    auto ptr2 = std::make_shared<myclass2>();
    ptr1->m = ptr2;
    ptr2->m = ptr1;
}
```

```
// > g++ -std=c++17 scratchpad.cpp; ./a.out
// delete myclass2
// delete myclass1
```

As shown in this example, even though a cyclic reference still exists, the allocated pointers are released back to the heap when `main()` completes. Finally, it should be noted that it is possible to convert `std::unique_ptr` to `std::shared_ptr` using the following syntax:

```
auto ptr = std::make_unique<int>();
std::shared_ptr<int> shared = std::move(ptr);
```

Since `std::unique_ptr` is being moved, it no longer owns the pointer, and instead `std::shared_ptr` now owns the pointer. Moving from `std::shared_ptr` to `std::unqiue_ptr` is not allowed.

Learning about mapping and permissions

In this section, the reader will learn how to map memory using C++ patterns. You will learn how to map memory (a common system-programming technique), while doing so using C++ patterns.

The basics

`malloc()`/`free()`, `new()`/`delete()`, and `std::unique_ptr{}`/`std::shared_ptr{}` are not the only methods for allocating memory on a POSIX system. C++-style allocators are another, more complicated, method for allocating memory that will be discussed in greater detail in Chapter 9, *A Hands-On Approach to Allocators*. A more direct, POSIX style for allocating memory is to use `mmap()`:

```cpp
#include <iostream>
#include <sys/mman.h>

constexpr auto PROT_RW = PROT_READ | PROT_WRITE;
constexpr auto MAP_ALLOC = MAP_PRIVATE | MAP_ANONYMOUS;

int main()
{
    auto ptr = mmap(0, 0x1000, PROT_RW, MAP_ALLOC, -1, 0);
    std::cout << ptr << '\n';

    munmap(ptr, 0x1000);
}
```

```
// > g++ -std=c++17 scratchpad.cpp; ./a.out
// 0x7feb41ab6000
```

The mmap() function may be used to map memory from different sources into a program. For example, if you want to make device memory into your application, you would use mmap(). If MAP_ANONYMOUS is passed to mmap(), it can be used to allocate memory the same way you would allocate memory using malloc() and free(). In the preceding example, mmap() is used to allocate a 4k page of memory that is marked read/write. The use of MAP_PRIVATE tells mmap() that you do not intend to share this memory with other applications (for example, for interprocess communication). Mapping memory this way compared to malloc()/free() has some advantages and disadvantages.

Advantages:

- **Fragmentation**: Allocating memory using MAP_ANONYMOUS usually maps memory in sizes that are multiples of a page size, or, worst case, a power of two. The is because mmap() is asking the OS kernel for a block memory, and that memory must be mapped into the application, which can only be done in blocks no smaller than a page. As a result, fragmentation of this memory is far less likely that multiple, random memory allocations usually made using malloc().
- **Permissions**: When using mmap(), you can state the permissions you wish to apply to the newly-allocated memory. This is especially useful if you need memory with special permissions, such as read/execute memory.
- **Shared memory**: The memory allocated using mmap() can also be shared by another application instead of being allocated privately for a specific application, as with malloc().

Disadvantages:

- **Performance**: malloc()/free() allocate and deallocate to a block of memory that is managed by the C library inside the application itself. If more memory is needed, the C library will call into the OS, using functions such as brk() or even mmap(), to get more memory from the OS. When free is called, the released memory is provided back to the memory being managed by the C library, and in a lot of cases is never actually provided back to the OS. For this reason, malloc()/free() can quickly allocate memory for the application because no OS-specific calls are being made (unless of course the C library runs out of memory). mmap(), on the other hand, has to call into the OS on every single allocation. For this reason, it does not perform as well as malloc()/free() since an OS call can be expensive.

- **Granularity**: For the same reason that `mmap()` reduces fragmentation, it also reduces granularity. Every single allocation made by `mmap()` is at least a page in size, even if the requested memory is only a byte.

To demonstrate the potential waste of `mmap()`, see the following:

```
#include <iostream>
#include <sys/mman.h>

constexpr auto PROT_RW = PROT_READ | PROT_WRITE;
constexpr auto MAP_ALLOC = MAP_PRIVATE | MAP_ANONYMOUS;

int main()
{
    auto ptr1 = mmap(0, 42, PROT_RW, MAP_ALLOC, -1, 0);
    auto ptr2 = mmap(0, 42, PROT_RW, MAP_ALLOC, -1, 0);

    std::cout << ptr1 << '\n';
    std::cout << ptr2 << '\n';

    munmap(ptr1, 42);
    munmap(ptr2, 42);
}

// > g++ -std=c++17 scratchpad.cpp; ./a.out
// 0x7fc1637ad000
// 0x7fc1637ac000
```

In this example, 42 bytes are allocated twice, but the resulting addresses are a 4k page apart. This is because allocations made by `mmap()` must be at least a page in size, even though the requested amount was only 42 bytes. The reason that `malloc()/free()` does not have this waste is that these functions request large chunks of memory at a time from the OS, and then manage this memory using various different allocation schemes internally within the C library. For more information on how this is done, there is a very good explanation within `newlib` on the topic: `https://sourceware.org/git/?p=newlib-cygwin.git;a=blob;f=newlib/libc/stdlib/malloc.c`.

Permissions

`mmap()` may be used to allocate memory with special parameters. For example, suppose you need to allocate memory that has read/execute permissions instead of the read/write permissions that are typically associated with `malloc()/free()`:

```cpp
#include <iostream>
#include <sys/mman.h>

constexpr auto PROT_RE = PROT_READ | PROT_EXEC;
constexpr auto MAP_ALLOC = MAP_PRIVATE | MAP_ANONYMOUS;

int main()
{
    auto ptr = mmap(0, 0x1000, PROT_RE, MAP_ALLOC, -1, 0);
    std::cout << ptr << '\n';

    munmap(ptr, 0x1000);
}

// > g++ -std=c++17 scratchpad.cpp; ./a.out
// 0x7feb41ab6000
```

As shown, allocating memory with read/execute permissions is the same as allocating memory with read/write permissions substituting `PROT_WRITE` with `PROT_EXEC`.

 On systems that support read/write or read/execute (also known as W^E, which states that write is mutually exclusive with execute), write and execute permissions should not be used together at the same time. Specifically, in the event of malicious use of your program, preventing executable memory from also having write permissions can prevent a number of known cyber attacks.

The problem with allocating memory as read/execute and not read/write/execute is that there is no easy way to place executable code into your newly-allocated buffer as the memory was marked as read/execute only. The same is true if you wish to allocate read-only memory. Once again, since write permissions were never added, there is no way to add data to read-only memory as it doesn't have write permissions.

To make the situation worse, some operating systems prevent applications from allocating read/write/execute memory as they attempt to enforce W^E permissions. To overcome this issue, while still providing a means to set the desired permissions, POSIX provides mprotect(), which allows you to change the permissions of memory that has already been allocated. Although this may be used with memory that is managed by malloc()/free(), it should instead be used with mmap() memory permissions that can only be enforced at the page level on most architectures. malloc()/free() allocate from a large buffer that is shared among all of the program's allocations, while mmap() only allocates memory with page granularity, and therefore is not shared by other allocations.

The following shows an example of how to use mprotect:

```
#include <iostream>
#include <sys/mman.h>

constexpr auto PROT_RW = PROT_READ | PROT_WRITE;
constexpr auto MAP_ALLOC = MAP_PRIVATE | MAP_ANONYMOUS;

int main()
{
    auto ptr = mmap(0, 0x1000, PROT_RW, MAP_ALLOC, -1, 0);
    std::cout << ptr << '\n';

    if (mprotect(ptr, 0x1000, PROT_READ) == -1) {
        std::clog << "ERROR: Failed to change memory permissions\n";
        ::exit(EXIT_FAILURE);
    }

    munmap(ptr, 0x1000);
}

// > g++ -std=c++17 scratchpad.cpp; ./a.out
// 0x7fb05b4b6000
```

In this example, mmap() is used to allocate a buffer the size of a 4k page with read/write permissions. Once the memory is allocated, mprotect() is used to change the permissions of the memory to read-only. Finally, munmap() is used to release the memory back to the operating system.

Smart pointers and mmap()

With respect to C++, the biggest issue with mmap() and munmap() is that they suffer from a lot of the same disadvantages as malloc()/free():

- **Memory leaks**: Since mmap() and munmap() must be executed manually, it's possible the user could forget to call munmap() when the memory is no longer needed, or a complex logic bug could result in munmap() not being called at the right time.
- **Memory mismatch**: It's possible that the users of mmap() could call free() instead of munmap() by accident, resulting in a mismatch that is almost certain to generate instability because memory from mmap() is coming from the OS kernel, while free() is expecting memory from application heap.

To overcome this, mmap() should be wrapped with std::unique_ptr{}:

```cpp
#include <memory>
#include <iostream>

#include <string.h>
#include <sys/mman.h>

constexpr auto PROT_RW = PROT_READ | PROT_WRITE;
constexpr auto MAP_ALLOC = MAP_PRIVATE | MAP_ANONYMOUS;

class mmap_deleter
{
    std::size_t m_size;

public:
    mmap_deleter(std::size_t size) :
        m_size{size}
    { }

    void operator()(int *ptr) const
    {
        munmap(ptr, m_size);
    }
};

template<typename T, typename... Args>
auto mmap_unique(Args&&... args)
{
    if (auto ptr = mmap(0, sizeof(T), PROT_RW, MAP_ALLOC, -1, 0)) {

        auto obj = new (ptr) T(args...);
```

```
        auto del = mmap_deleter(sizeof(T));

        return std::unique_ptr<T, mmap_deleter>(obj, del);
    }

    throw std::bad_alloc();
}

int main()
{
    auto ptr = mmap_unique<int>(42);
    std::cout << *ptr << '\n';
}

// > g++ -std=c++17 scratchpad.cpp; ./a.out
// 42
```

In this example, the main function calls mmap_unique() instead of std::make_unqiue(), as std::make_unique() allocates memory using new()/delete(), and we wish to use mmap()/munmap() instead. The first part of the mmap_unique() function allocates memory using mmap() the same way as our previous examples. In this case, permissions were set to read/write, but they could have also been changed using mprotect() to provide read-only or read/execute if desired. If the call to mmap() fails, std::bad_alloc() is thrown, just like the C++ library.

The next line in this example uses the new() placement operator, as discussed earlier in in the *Placement new* section. The goal of this call is to create an object whose constructor has been called to initialize the T type as required. In the case of this example, this is setting an integer to 42, but if a class were used instead of an integer, the classes constructor would be called with whatever arguments were passed to mmap_unique().

The next step is to create a custom deleter for our std::unqiue_ptr{}. This is done because by default, std::unqiue_ptr{} will call the delete() operator instead of munmap(). The custom deleter takes a single argument that is the size of the original allocation. This is needed because munmap() needs to know the size of the original allocation, unlike delete() and free(), which just take a pointer.

Finally, std::unique_ptr{} is created with the newly-created object and custom deleter. From this point on, all of the memory that was allocated using mmap() can be accessed using the standard std::unique_ptr{} interface, and treated as a normal allocation. When the pointer is no longer needed, and std::unique_ptr{} is out of scope, the pointer will be released back to the OS kernel by calling munmap() as expected.

Shared memory

In addition to allocating memory, `mmap()` may be used to allocate shared memory, typically for interprocess communications. To demonstrate this, we start by defining a shared memory name, `"/shm"`, and our read, write, and execute permissions:

```
#include <memory>
#include <iostream>

#include <fcntl.h>
#include <unistd.h>
#include <string.h>
#include <sys/mman.h>

constexpr auto PROT_RW = PROT_READ | PROT_WRITE;

auto name = "/shm";
```

Next, we must define our custom deleter, which uses `munmap()` instead of `free()`:

```
class mmap_deleter
{
    std::size_t m_size;

public:
    mmap_deleter(std::size_t size) :
        m_size{size}
    { }

    void operator()(int *ptr) const
    {
        munmap(ptr, m_size);
    }
};
```

In this example, we build off of the previous example, but instead of having a single `mmap_unique()` function, we now have a server and a client version. Although typically shared memory would be used for interprocess communication, in this example, we share memory in the same application to keep things simple.

The `main` function creates both a server and a client-shared pointer. The server version creates shared memory using the following:

```
template<typename T, typename... Args>
auto mmap_unique_server(Args&&... args)
{
    if(int fd = shm_open(name, O_CREAT | O_RDWR, 0644); fd != -1) {
        ftruncate(fd, sizeof(T));

        if (auto ptr = mmap(0, sizeof(T), PROT_RW, MAP_SHARED, fd, 0)) {

            auto obj = new (ptr) T(args...);
            auto del = mmap_deleter(sizeof(T));

            return std::unique_ptr<T, mmap_deleter>(obj, del);
        }
    }

    throw std::bad_alloc();
}
```

This function is similar to the `mmap_unique()` function in the previous example, but opens a handle to a shared memory file instead of allocating memory using `MAP_ANONYMOUS`. To open the shared memory file, we use the `POSIX` `shm_open()` function. This function is similar to the `open()` function. The first parameter is the name of the shared memory file. The second parameter defines how the file is opened, while the third parameter provides the mode. `shm_open()` is used to open the shared memory file, and the file descriptor is checked to make sure the allocation succeeded (that is, the file descriptor is not −1).

Next, the file descriptor is truncated. This ensures that the size of the shared memory file is equal to the size of the memory we wish to share. In this case, we wish to share a single T type, so we need to get the size of T. Once the shared memory file has been properly sized, we need to map in the shared memory using `mmap()`. The call to `mmap()` is the same as our previous examples, with the exception that `MAP_SHARED` is used.

Finally, like the previous example, we leverage the `new()` placement operator to create the newly-allocated type in shared memory, we create the custom deleter, and then finally, we return `std::unique_ptr{}` for this shared memory.

To connect to this shared memory (which could be done from another application), we need to use the client version of the `mmap_unique()` function:

```
template<typename T>
auto mmap_unique_client()
{
```

```
if(int fd = shm_open(name, O_RDWR, 0644); fd != -1) {
    ftruncate(fd, sizeof(T));

    if (auto ptr = mmap(0, sizeof(T), PROT_RW, MAP_SHARED, fd, 0)) {

        auto obj = static_cast<T*>(ptr);
        auto del = mmap_deleter(sizeof(T));

        return std::unique_ptr<T, mmap_deleter>(obj, del);
    }
}

throw std::bad_alloc();
}
```

The server and client versions of these functions look similar, but there are differences. First and foremost, the shared memory file is opened without O_CREAT. This is because the server creates the shared memory file, while the client connects to the shared memory file, so there is no need to pass O_CREAT in the client version. Finally, the signature of the client version of this function doesn't take any arguments like the server version. This is because the server version uses the new() placement to initialize the shared memory, which doesn't need to be done a second time. Instead of using the new placement, static_cast() is used to convert void * to the proper type prior to delivering the pointer to the newly created std::unique_ptr{}:

```
int main()
{
    auto ptr1 = mmap_unique_server<int>(42);
    auto ptr2 = mmap_unique_client<int>();
    std::cout << *ptr1 << '\n';
    std::cout << *ptr2 << '\n';
}

// > g++ -std=c++17 scratchpad.cpp -lrt; ./a.out
// 42
// 42
```

The result of this example is that memory is shared between a server and a client, wrapping the shared memory in std::unique_ptr{}. Furthermore, as shown in the example, the memory is properly shared, as can be seen by 42 being printed for both the server and client version of the pointer. Although we use this for an integer type, this type of shared memory can be used with any complex type as needed (although care should be taken when attempting to share classes, especially those that leverage inheritance and contain vTable).

Learning importance of memory fragmentation

No chapter on memory management would be complete without a brief discussion of fragmentation. Memory fragmentation refers to a process in which memory is broken up into chunks, often spread out, almost always resulting in the allocator's inability to allocate memory for an application, ultimately resulting in `std::bad_alloc()` being thrown in C++. When programming systems, fragmentation should always be a concern as it can dramatically impact the stability and reliability of your program, especially on resource-constrained systems, such as embedded and mobile applications. In this section, the reader will get a brief introduction to fragmentation, and how it affects the programs they create.

There are two types of fragmentation—external and internal fragmentation.

External fragmentation

External fragmentation refers to the process by which memory is allocated and deallocated in different sized chunks, ultimately leading to large amounts of unusable, unallocatable memory. To demonstrate this, suppose we have five allocations:

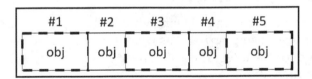

All five allocations succeed, and all of the memory is allocated. Now, let's suppose that the second and fourth allocations are released back to the heap:

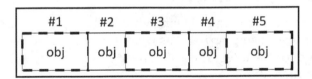

By releasing memory back to the heap, memory is now available for allocation again. The problem is that this memory is spread out due to the original 1, 3, and 5 allocations. Now let's suppose we want to make a final allocation:

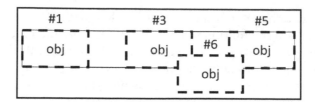

The final allocation fails, even though there is enough free memory for the allocation, because the free memory is spread out – in other words, the free memory is fragmented.

External fragmentation, in the general case, is an extremely difficult problem to solve, and this problem has been studied for years, with operating systems implementing various approaches over time. In Chapter 9, *A Hands-On Approach to Allocators*, we will discuss how C++ allocators can be used to address some external fragmentation issues in your program using various different custom allocator patterns.

Internal fragmentation

Internal fragmentation refers to memory being wasted during an allocation. For example, when we allocate an integer using mmap(), as we did in the preceding examples, mmap() allocates an entire page for the integer, wasting nearly 4k of memory in the process. This is known as internal fragmentation:

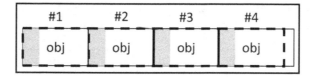

Like external fragmentation, the lost memory from internal fragmentation cannot be used for other allocations. In fact, the view of memory at a high level would look just like that of external fragmentation. The difference is that external fragmentation continuously takes large chunks of free, unallocated memory and breaks it up into smaller and smaller fragmented memory, which at some point becomes too small to be allocated in the future. Internal fragmentation would appear the same, but in some cases, even larger, unusable blocks of memory would appear fragmented throughout all of the memory. This unusable memory is not unusable because it isn't large enough for a given allocation, but instead because the unusable memory has been claimed by a smaller, previous allocation that simply doesn't use all of the memory that it was given.

It should be noted that when solving fragmentation issues, often the solution is to optimize for one type of fragmentation over another, with each choice having its advantages and disadvantages.

Internal over external fragmentation

Allocators used by `malloc()` and `free()` often favor optimizing for internal fragmentation over external fragmentation. The goal is to provide an allocator with as little waste as possible and then leverage various different allocation patterns to reduce the likelihood of external fragmentation as much as possible. These types of allocators are preferred for applications as they minimize the memory requirements of a single application on any given operating system, leaving the additional memory for other applications. Furthermore, if external fragmentation prevents an allocation from occurring, the application always asks the OS for more memory (until the OS runs dry).

External over internal fragmentation

Operating systems tend to optimize for external fragmentation over internal fragmentation. This reason for this is that operating systems generally can only allocate memory at the page granularity, meaning internal fragmentation in a lot of cases is unavoidable. Furthermore, if external fragmentation is allowed to occur over time, it would result in the operating system eventually crashing if given enough time to execute. For this reason, operating systems use allocation patterns such as the buddy allocator pattern, which optimize for external fragmentation, even at the expense of large amounts of internal fragmentation.

Summary

In this chapter, we learned various ways to allocate memory using `new()` and `delete()` and `malloc()` and `free()`, including aligned memory and C-style arrays. We looked at the difference between global memory (memory in the global space), stack memory (or scoped memory), and dynamically-allocated memory (memory that is allocated using `new()` and `delete()`). The safety concerns of `new()` and `delete()` were also discussed, and we demonstrated how C++ smart pointers, including `std::shared_ptr{}` and `std::unique_ptr{}`, may be used to prevent common instability issues in programs, and how they provide C++ Core Guidance support. We concluded this chapter with a quick review of fragmentation and how it can affect system programs.

In the next chapter, we will cover file inputer and output including read and writing to a file, and the filesystem APIs that were added by C++17.

Questions

1. What is the difference between `new()` and `new[]()`?
2. Can `delete()` be safely used to release memory back to heap that was allocated using `new[]()`?
3. What is the difference between global memory and static memory?
4. How does one allocate aligned memory using `new()`?
5. Can `std::make_shared()` be used to allocate an array?
6. When should `std::shared_ptr{}` be used instead of `std::unique_ptr{}`?
7. Can `mmap()` be used to allocate read/execute memory?
8. What is the difference between internal and external fragmentation?

Further reading

- https://www.packtpub.com/application-development/c17-example
- https://www.packtpub.com/application-development/getting-started-c17-programming-video

8
Learning to Program File Input/Output

File **input/output** (**I/O**) is an essential part of most system-level programs. It can be used for debugging, saving program states, handling user-specific data, and even interfacing with physical devices (thanks to POSIX block and character devices).

Prior to C++17, working with file I/O was difficult, as filesystem management had to be handled using non-C++ APIs, which are often unsafe, platform-specific, or even incomplete.

In this chapter, we will provide a hands-on review of how to open, read, and write to files, and work with paths, directories, and the filesystem. We will conclude by providing three different examples that demonstrate how to log to a file, tail an existing file, and benchmark the C++ file input/output APIs.

This chapter will cover the following topics:

- Ways to open a file
- Reading and writing to a file
- File utilities

Technical requirements

In order to compile and execute the examples in this chapter, the reader must have the following:

- A Linux-based system capable of compiling and executing C++17 (for example, Ubuntu 17.10+)
- GCC 7+
- CMake 3.6+
- An internet connection

To download all the code in this chapter, including the examples, and code snippets, see the following link: `https://github.com/PacktPublishing/Hands-On-System-Programming-with-CPP/tree/master/Chapter08`.

Opening a file

There are many ways to open a file. We will discuss some of these in the following sections, and how to accomplish this using the `std::fstream` C++ APIs.

Different ways to open a file

Opening a file in C++ is as simple as providing a `std::fstream` object with the filename and path of the object you wish to open. This is shown as follows:

```
#include <fstream>
#include <iostream>

int main()
{
    if (auto file = std::fstream("test.txt")) {
        std::cout << "success\n";
    }
    else {
        std::cout << "failure\n";
    }
}

// > g++ -std=c++17 scratchpad.cpp; touch test.txt; ./a.out
// success
```

In this example, we open a file named `test.txt`, which we previously created using the POSIX `touch` command. This file is opened with read/write permissions (as that is the default mode).

The file is stored in a variable named `file`, and it is checked to ensure it was properly opened using the bool operator overload that `std::fstream` provides. If this file is successfully opened, we output `success` to `stdout`.

The preceding example leverages the fact that a `std::fstream` object has an overloaded `bool` operator that returns true when the file is successfully opened. Another way to more explicitly perform this action is to use the `is_open()` function, as follows:

```
#include <fstream>
#include <iostream>

int main()
{
    if (auto file = std::fstream("test.txt"); file.is_open()) {
        std::cout << "success\n";
    }
}

// > g++ -std=c++17 scratchpad.cpp; touch test.txt; ./a.out
// success
```

In this preceding example, instead of relying on the `bool` operator overload, we leverage C++17 to check whether the file is open using `is_open()` in the `if` statement. The preceding examples were further simplified by the use of the constructor to initialize the `std::fstream`, instead of explicitly calling `open()` as follows:

```
#include <fstream>
#include <iostream>

int main()
{
    auto file = std::fstream();
    if (file.open("test.txt"); file.is_open()) {
        std::cout << "success\n";
    }
}

// > g++ -std=c++17 scratchpad.cpp; touch test.txt; ./a.out
// success
```

In this example, the `std::fstream` object is created with the default constructor, meaning no file has yet to be opened, allowing us to postpone opening the file until we are ready to do so. We then open the file using the `open()` function, and then, similar to the preceding example, we leverage C++17 to check to see if the file opened prior to outputting `success` to `stdout`.

In all of the preceding examples, there was no need to call `close()` on the file. This is because, like other C++ classes such as `std::unique_ptr` that leverage RAII, `std::fstream` objects close the file automatically for you on destruction.

It is possible, however, to close the file explicitly if so desired, as follows:

```
#include <fstream>
#include <iostream>

int main()
{
    std::cout << std::boolalpha;

    if (auto file = std::fstream("test.txt")) {
        std::cout << file.is_open() << '\n';
        file.close();
        std::cout << file.is_open() << '\n';
    }
}

// > g++ -std=c++17 scratchpad.cpp; touch test.txt; ./a.out
// true
// false
```

In this example, we open a text file and use `is_open()` to check whether the file is open. The first use of `is_open()` returns true, since the file was successfully opened. We then close the file explicitly using `close()`, and then check whether the file is open again using `is_open()`, which now returns false.

Modes for opening a file

Up until now, we have opened the file using the default mode. There are two modes that may be used to open a file:

- `std::ios::in`: Opens the file for reading
- `std::ios::out`: Opens the file for writing

In addition, there are several other modes that may be used in conjunction with these two, to modify how a file is opened:

- `std::ios::binary`: Opens the file for binary use. By default, `std::fstream` is in text mode, which applies specific rules about how a file is formatted using newline characters, and which types of character may be read/written to a file. These rules are usually appropriate for text files, but cause problems when you attempt to read/write binary data to a file. In this case, `std::ios::binary` should be added to your mode specifier.

- `std::ios::app`: When this mode is used with `std::ios::out`, all writes to the file append to the end of the file.
- `std::ios::ate`: When this mode is used with either `std::ios::in` or `std::ios::out`, the file is positioned at the end of the file once it has been successfully opened. That is, reads and writes to the file occur at the end of the file, even right after the file is opened.
- `std::ios::trunc`: When this mode is used with either `std::ios::in` or `std::ios::out`, the contents of the files are deleted prior to opening the file.

To demonstrate these modes, the first example opens a file for reading in binary mode:

```
#include <fstream>
#include <iostream>

int main()
{
    constexpr auto mode = std::ios::in | std::ios::binary;
    if (auto file = std::fstream("test.txt", mode)) {
        std::cout << "success\n";
    }
}

// > g++ -std=c++17 scratchpad.cpp; touch test.txt; ./a.out
// success
```

All of the modes are constant values, and for this reason, in the preceding example, `constexpr` is used to create a new constant called `mode` that represents opening a file in read-only, binary mode. To open a file for read-only in text mode instead of binary mode, simply remove the `std::ios::binary` mode, as follows:

```
#include <fstream>
#include <iostream>

int main()
{
    constexpr auto mode = std::ios::in;
    if (auto file = std::fstream("test.txt", mode)) {
        std::cout << "success\n";
    }
}

// > g++ -std=c++17 scratchpad.cpp; touch test.txt; ./a.out
// success
```

In the preceding example, we open the file in read-only, text mode. The same logic may also be used for write-only, as follows:

```
#include <fstream>
#include <iostream>

int main()
{
    constexpr auto mode = std::ios::out | std::ios::binary;
    if (auto file = std::fstream("test.txt", mode)) {
        std::cout << "success\n";
    }
}

// > g++ -std=c++17 scratchpad.cpp; touch test.txt; ./a.out
// success
```

Here, we open the file in write-only, binary mode. To open a file in write-only, test mode, use the following:

```
#include <fstream>
#include <iostream>

int main()
{
    constexpr auto mode = std::ios::out;
    if (auto file = std::fstream("test.txt", mode)) {
        std::cout << "success\n";
    }
}

// > g++ -std=c++17 scratchpad.cpp; touch test.txt; ./a.out
// success
```

Once again, since `std::ios::binary` has been left out, this code opens the file in write-only, text mode.

To open a file in write-only, binary mode at the end of the file (instead of the beginning of the file, which is the default), use the following:

```
#include <fstream>
#include <iostream>

int main()
{
    constexpr auto mode = std::ios::out | std::ios::binary |
std::ios::ate;
        if (auto file = std::fstream("test.txt", mode)) {
```

```
        std::cout << "success\n";
    }
}

// > g++ -std=c++17 scratchpad.cpp; touch test.txt; ./a.out
// success
```

In this example, we open the file in write-only, binary mode at the end of the file by adding `std::ios::ate` to the mode variable. This moves the output pointer in the file to the end of the file, but allows writing to occur at any place within the file.

To ensure that the file is always appended to the end of the file, open the file using `std::ios::app` instead of `std::ios::ate`, as follows:

```
#include <fstream>
#include <iostream>

int main()
{
    constexpr auto mode = std::ios::out | std::ios::binary |
std::ios::app;
    if (auto file = std::fstream("test.txt", mode)) {
        std::cout << "success\n";
    }
}

// > g++ -std=c++17 scratchpad.cpp; touch test.txt; ./a.out
// success
```

In the preceding example, writes and additions to the file are always appended to the file as the file was opened using `std::ios::app`.

It should be noted that in all of the previous examples that used `std::ios::out`, the file was opened using `std::ios::trunc`. This is due to the fact that truncate mode is the default when using `std::ios::out`, unless `std::ios::ate` or `std::ios::app` is used. The problem with this is that there is no way to open a file for write-only at the beginning of the file without truncating the file.

To overcome this issue, the following may be used:

```cpp
#include <fstream>
#include <iostream>

int main()
{
    constexpr auto mode = std::ios::out | std::ios::binary |
std::ios::ate;
    if (auto file = std::fstream("test.txt", mode); file.seekp(0)) {
        std::cout << "success\n";
    }
}

// > g++ -std=c++17 scratchpad.cpp; touch test.txt; ./a.out
// success
```

In this example, we open the file in write-only, binary mode at the end of the file, and then we use `seekp()` (a function that will be explained later) to move the output position in the file to the beginning of the file.

Although `std::ios::trunc` is the default when `std::ios::out` is used, if `std::ios::in` is also used (that is, read/write mode), you must explicitly add `std::ios::trunc` if you wish to clear the contents of the file prior to opening the file, as follows:

```cpp
#include <fstream>
#include <iostream>

int main()
{
    constexpr auto mode = std::ios::in | std::ios::out |
std::ios::trunc;
    if (auto file = std::fstream("test.txt", mode)) {
        std::cout << "success\n";
    }
}

// > g++ -std=c++17 scratchpad.cpp; touch test.txt; ./a.out
// success
```

Here, the file is opened in read/write mode, and the contents of the file are deleted prior to opening the file.

Reading and writing to a file

The following sections will help you to understand how to read and write to a file using the `std::fstream` C++ APIs.

Reading from a file

C++ provides several different methods for reading a file, including by field, by line, and by number of bytes.

Reading by field

The most type-safe method for reading from a file is by field, the code which is as follows:

```
#include <fstream>
#include <iostream>

int main()
{
    if (auto file = std::fstream("test.txt")) {
        std::string hello, world;
        file >> hello >> world;
        std::cout << hello << " " << world << '\n';
    }
}

// > g++ -std=c++17 scratchpad.cpp; echo "Hello World" > test.txt;
./a.out
// Hello World
```

In this example, we open a file for reading and writing (since that is the default mode). If the file is successfully opened, we read in two strings into two variables—`hello` and `world` respectively. To read the two strings, we use >> `operator()`, which behaves just like `std::cin` as discussed in Chapter 6, *Learning to Program Console Input/Output*.

For a string, the stream reads characters until the first whitespace or newline is discovered. As with `std::cin`, numeric variables can also be read, as follows:

```
#include <fstream>
#include <iostream>

int main()
{
```

```
        if (auto file = std::fstream("test.txt")) {
            int answer;
            file >> answer;
            std::cout << "The answer is: " << answer << '\n';
        }
    }


    // > g++ -std=c++17 scratchpad.cpp; echo "42" > test.txt; ./a.out
    // The answer is: 42
```

In this example, we read in an integer instead of a string, and, just like a string, the stream reads in bytes until a whitespace or newline is discovered, and then interprets the input as a number. Of course, if the field being read is not a number, 0 is read, as follows:

```
    // > g++ -std=c++17 scratchpad.cpp; echo "not_a_number" > test.txt; ./a.out
    // The answer is: 0
```

It should be noted that an error flag is set when this occurs, which we will discuss later in this chapter.

As with other C++ streams, std::fstream can be overloaded to provide support for user-defined types, as follows:

```
    #include <fstream>
    #include <iostream>

    struct myclass
    {
        std::string hello;
        std::string world;
    };

    std::fstream &operator >>(std::fstream &is, myclass &obj)
    {
        is >> obj.hello;
        is >> obj.world;

        return is;
    }

    std::ostream &operator<<(std::ostream &os, const myclass &obj)
    {
        os << obj.hello;
        os << ' ';
        os << obj.world;

        return os;
    }
```

```
int main()
{
    if (auto file = std::fstream("test.txt")) {
        myclass obj;
        file >> obj;
        std::cout << obj << '\n';
    }
}


// > g++ -std=c++17 scratchpad.cpp; echo "Hello World" > test.txt; ./a.out
// Hello World
```

In this example, we create a user-defined type called `myclass`. In the `main()` function, we open a file, and if the file is successfully opened, we create a `myclass{}` object, read the file into the `myclass{}` object, and then output the results of the `myclass{}` object to `stdout`.

To read the file into the `myclass{}` object, we overload `>>` `operator()` for `std::fstream{}` which reads in two strings, and stores the results in the `myclass{}` object. To output the `myclass{}` object to `stdout`, we build upon what we learned in `Chapter 6`, *Learning to Program Console Input/Output*, with respect to user-defined overloads of `std::ostream`, and provide a user-defined overload for our `myclass{}` object.

The result is that `Hello World` is read from the file and output to `stdout`.

Reading bytes

In addition to reading fields from a file, C++ provides support for reading bytes directly from the file. To read a single byte from the stream, use the `get()` function, as follows:

```
#include <fstream>
#include <iostream>

int main()
{
    if (auto file = std::fstream("test.txt")) {
        char c = file.get();
        std::cout << c << '\n';
    }
}

// > g++ -std=c++17 scratchpad.cpp; echo "Hello World" > test.txt;
./a.out
// H
```

Reading more than one byte in C++17 is still an unsafe operation, as there is no ability to read *x* number of bytes directly into a `std::string`. This means that a standard C-style buffer must be used instead, as follows:

```cpp
#include <fstream>
#include <iostream>

int main()
{
    if (auto file = std::fstream("test.txt")) {
        char buf[25] = {};
        file.read(buf, 11);
        std::cout << buf << '\n';
    }
}

// > g++ -std=c++17 scratchpad.cpp; echo "Hello World" > test.txt; ./a.out
// Hello World
```

In the preceding example, we create a standard C-style character buffer called `buf`, and then read 11 bytes from the file into this character buffer. Finally, we output the results to `stdout`.

We need to ensure that the total number of bytes being read does not exceed the total size of the buffer itself—an operation that often leads to a coding error, generating hard-to-debug buffer overflows.

The simple solution to this problem is to use a wrapper around the `read()` function that checks to make sure the requested number of bytes does not exceed the total size of the buffer, as follows:

```cpp
#include <fstream>
#include <iostream>

template<typename T, std::size_t N>
void myread(std::fstream &file, T (&str)[N], std::size_t count)
{
    if (count >= N) {
        throw std::out_of_range("file.read out of bounds");
    }

    file.read(static_cast<char *>(str), count);
}

int main()
{
    if (auto file = std::fstream("test.txt")) {
```

```
            char buf[25] = {};
            myread(file, buf, 11);
            std::cout << buf << '\n';
        }
    }

    // > g++ -std=c++17 scratchpad.cpp; echo "Hello World" > test.txt; ./a.out
    // Hello World
```

In this example, we create a template function called `myread()` that encodes the total size of the buffer into the function itself during compilation. Before a read occurs, the size of the buffer can be checked to ensure a buffer overflow will not occur.

It should be noted that this works well for arrays, but is problematic for dynamically-allocated arrays, as the total size of the buffer must also be passed to our wrapper function, potentially leading to hard-to-debug logic bugs (that is, not providing the proper size of the buffer, swapping the total number of bytes to read with the buffer size, and so on).

To overcome these types of issues, `gsl::span` should be used instead.

When reading bytes instead of fields, it can be helpful to know from where in the file you are currently reading. As you read from a file stream, both a read and a write pointer are maintained internally within the stream. To get the current read position, use the `tellg()` function, as follows:

```
#include <fstream>
#include <iostream>

int main()
{
    if (auto file = std::fstream("test.txt")) {
        std::cout << file.tellg() << '\n';
        char c = file.get();
        std::cout << file.tellg() << '\n';
    }
}

// > g++ -std=c++17 scratchpad.cpp; echo "Hello World" > test.txt;
./a.out
// 0
// 1
```

Here, we open a file as usual and output the current read pointer, which as expected is 0. We then read a single character from the file, and output the read pointer again. This time, the pointer is 1, indicating we have successfully read a single byte.

Another method for reading a single byte is to use the `peek` function, which functions similarly to `get()`, except that the internal read pointer is not incremented, as follows:

```
#include <fstream>
#include <iostream>

int main()
{
    if (auto file = std::fstream("test.txt")) {
        std::cout << file.tellg() << '\n';
        char c = file.peek();
        std::cout << file.tellg() << '\n';
    }
}

// > g++ -std=c++17 scratchpad.cpp; echo "Hello World" > test.txt;
./a.out
// 0
// 0
```

This example is the same as the previous one, except that `peek()` is used instead of `get()`. As shown, the read pointer is `0` both before and after `peek()` is used to read a byte from the buffer, demonstrating that `peek()` doesn't increment the read pointer within the stream.

The reverse is also provided by C++. Instead of reading a byte from the file without moving the read pointer, it is also possible to move the read pointer without reading bytes from the stream using the `ignore()` function, as follows:

```
#include <fstream>
#include <iostream>

int main()
{
    if (auto file = std::fstream("test.txt")) {
        std::cout << file.tellg() << '\n';
        file.ignore(1);
        std::cout << file.tellg() << '\n';
    }
}

// > g++ -std=c++17 scratchpad.cpp; echo "Hello World" > test.txt;
./a.out
// 0
// 1
```

In this example, we move the read pointer in our file stream by a single byte, and use `tellg()` to verify that the read pointer has in fact been moved. The `ignore()` function increments the read pointer relative to the current read pointer.

C++ also provides the `seekg()` function, which sets the read pointer to an absolute position, shown as follows:

```cpp
#include <fstream>
#include <iostream>

int main()
{
    if (auto file = std::fstream("test.txt")) {
        std::string hello, world;

        file >> hello >> world;
        std::cout << hello << " " << world << '\n';

        file.seekg(1);

        file >> hello >> world;
        std::cout << hello << " " << world << '\n';
    }
}

// > g++ -std=c++17 scratchpad.cpp; echo "Hello World" > test.txt;
./a.out
// Hello World
// ello World
```

In the preceding example, the `seekg()` function is used to set the read pointer to 1 byte into the file after reading, effectively rewinding, allowing us to read the file again.

Reading by line

Finally, the last type of file read is by line, meaning that you read each line from the file, one at a time, as follows:

```cpp
#include <fstream>
#include <iostream>

int main()
{
    if (auto file = std::fstream("test.txt")) {
        char buf[25] = {};
        file.getline(buf, 25, '\n');
```

```
        std::cout << buf << '\n';
    }
}


// > g++ -std=c++17 scratchpad.cpp; echo "Hello World" > test.txt;
./a.out
// Hello World
```

In this example, we create a standard C character buffer, read a line from the file, and output the line to `stdout`. Unlike the `read()` function, `getline()` keeps reading until either the size of the buffer is reached (the second argument), or a delimiter is seen.

Since a line is defined differently depending on the OS you're using (although in this case, we will stick to Unix), the `getline()` function takes a delimiter argument, allowing you to define what the end of a line is.

Like the `read()`, function, this operation is unsafe as it requires the user to ensure that the total buffer size given to `getline()` is, in fact, the total size of the buffer—providing a convenient mechanism to introduce hard-to-debug buffer overflows.

Unlike the `read()` function, C++ provides a non-member version of `getline()` that accepts any stream type (including `std::cin`), and `std::string` instead of a standard C-style string, as follows:

```
#include <fstream>
#include <iostream>

int main()
{
    if (auto file = std::fstream("test.txt")) {
        std::string str;
        std::getline(file, str);
        std::cout << str << '\n';
    }
}


// > g++ -std=c++17 scratchpad.cpp; echo "Hello World" > test.txt;
./a.out
// Hello World
```

In the preceding example, instead of calling `file.getline()`, we instead call `std::getline()`, and provide the function with `std::string`, which can dynamically change its size depending on the number of bytes that need to be read—preventing possible buffer overflows.

It should be noted that in order to achieve this, the `std::string` will perform a `new()` / `delete()` automatically for you—which (especially with respect to system programming) might introduce inefficiencies that are unacceptable. In this case, the `file.getline()` version should be used, with a wrapper class, similar to what we did with the `read()` function.

Finally, if changes are made to a file that has already been opened, the following will sync the current stream with these changes:

```
#include <fstream>
#include <iostream>

int main()
{
    if (auto file = std::fstream("test.txt")) {
        file.sync();
    }
}
```

As shown in the preceding code, the `sync()` function may be used to resync an already open file with changes to the file.

Writing to a file

Symmetrically like `std::cin` and file reading, a file writing is also provided that behaves similarly to `std::cout`. Unlike reading, there are only two different modes of file writing—by field and by byte.

Writing by field

To write to a file by field, use `<< operator()`, similar to `std::cout`, as follows:

```
#include <fstream>
#include <iostream>

int main()
{
    if (auto file = std::fstream("test.txt")) {
        std::string hello{"Hello"}, world{"World"};
        file << hello << " " << world << '\n';
    }
}
```

```
// > g++ -std=c++17 scratchpad.cpp; echo "" > test.txt; ./a.out; cat
test.txt
// Hello World
```

In the preceding example, we open a file as usual and then create two `std::string` objects with `hello` and `world` added to the strings respectively. Finally, these strings are written to the file. Note that there is no need to close or flush the file, as this is done for us on destruction of the file stream object.

Like `std::cout`, C++ natively supports standard C character buffers and numeric types, as follows:

```
#include <fstream>
#include <iostream>

int main()
{
    if (auto file = std::fstream("test.txt")) {
        file << "The answer is: " << 42 << '\n';
    }
}

// > g++ -std=c++17 scratchpad.cpp; echo "" > test.txt; ./a.out; cat
test.txt
// The answer is: 42
```

In the preceding example, we write a standard C character buffer and an integer directly to the file. User-defined types are also supported with respect to writing, as follows:

```
#include <fstream>
#include <iostream>

struct myclass
{
    std::string hello{"Hello"};
    std::string world{"World"};
};

std::fstream &operator <<(std::fstream &os, const myclass &obj)
{
    os << obj.hello;
    os << ' ';
    os << obj.world;

    return os;
}
```

```
int main()
{
    if (auto file = std::fstream("test.txt")) {
        file << myclass{} << '\n';
    }
}

// > g++ -std=c++17 scratchpad.cpp; echo "" > test.txt; ./a.out; cat
test.txt
// Hello World
```

In this example, we open a file and write a `myclass{}` object to the file. The `myclass{}` object is a struct that contains two member variables initialized with `Hello` and `World`. A user-defined `<< operator()` overload is then provided that writes to a provided file stream the contents of the `myclass{}` object, resulting in `Hello World` being written to the file.

Writing bytes

In addition to writing by field, writing a stream of bytes is also supported. In the following example, we write a single byte to the file (in addition to a newline) using the `put()` function, which is similar to `get()` but used for writing instead of reading:

```
#include <fstream>
#include <iostream>

int main()
{
    if (auto file = std::fstream("test.txt")) {
        file.put('H');
        file.put('\n');
    }
}

// > g++ -std=c++17 scratchpad.cpp; echo "" > test.txt; ./a.out; cat
test.txt
// H
```

Multiple bytes can also be written using the `write()` function, as follows:

```cpp
#include <fstream>
#include <iostream>

int main()
{
    if (auto file = std::fstream("test.txt")) {
        file.write("Hello World\n", 12);
    }
}

// > g++ -std=c++17 scratchpad.cpp; echo "" > test.txt; ./a.out; cat
test.txt
// Hello World
```

In the preceding example, we write 12 bytes to the file (11 characters for the string `Hello World`, and one additional string for the newline).

Like the `read()` function, the `write()` function is unsafe and should be wrapped to ensure that the total number of bytes written to the file does not exceed the total size of the buffer (otherwise a buffer overflow would occur). To demonstrate how even standard C-style `const` character buffers are unsafe, see the following:

```cpp
#include <fstream>
#include <iostream>

int main()
{
    if (auto file = std::fstream("test.txt")) {
        file.write("Hello World\n", 100);
    }
}

// > g++ -std=c++17 scratchpad.cpp; echo "" > test.txt; ./a.out; cat
test.txt
// Hello World
// ;◆◆◆◆◆D◆◆◆d)◆◆◆◆◆◆◆◆◆$=◆◆◆DR◆◆◆◆d◆◆◆d◆◆◆◆◆[
```

As shown in this example, attempting to write 100 bytes from a standard C `const` character buffer that is only 13 bytes in size (11 for `Hello World`, 1 for the new line, and 1 for the `\0` null termination), results in a buffer overflow. In this case, the buffer overflow results in corrupted bytes being written to the file, which, at best, leaks parts of the program, but could also generate instability, including hard-to-debug segmentation faults.

To overcome this, a wrapper should be used whenever using these types of unsafe functions, as follows:

```cpp
#include <string.h>

#include <fstream>
#include <iostream>

void
mywrite(std::fstream &file, const char *str, std::size_t count)
{
    if (count > strlen(str)) {
        throw std::out_of_range("file.write out of bounds");
    }

    file.write(str, count);
}

int main()
{
    if (auto file = std::fstream("test.txt")) {
        mywrite(file, "Hello World\n", 100);
    }
}

// > g++ -std=c++17 scratchpad.cpp; echo "" > test.txt; ./a.out; cat
test.txt
// terminate called after throwing an instance of 'std::out_of_range'
// what(): file.write out of bounds
// Aborted (core dumped)
```

In the preceding example, we create a wrapper around the `write()` function, similar to the `read()` function wrapper that we created previously. When we attempt to write more bytes than the total size of the standard C `const` character buffer, we generate an exception that can be used to trace the error to our attempt to write 100 bytes.

It should be noted that this wrapper only works with standard C `const` character buffers that are generated by the compiler. It is possible to declare this type of buffer manually where this type of function will fail, as follows:

```cpp
#include <string.h>

#include <fstream>
#include <iostream>

void
mywrite(std::fstream &file, const char *str, std::size_t count)
```

```
    {
        if (count > strlen(str)) {
        std::cerr << count << " " << strlen(str) << '\n';
            throw std::out_of_range("file.write out of bounds");
        }

        file.write(str, count);
    }

    int main()
    {
        if (auto file = std::fstream("test.txt")) {
            const char str1[6] = {'H','e','l','l','o','\n'};
            const char str2[6] = {'#','#','#','#','#','\n'};
            mywrite(file, str1, 12);
            mywrite(file, str2, 6);
        }
    }

    // > g++ -std=c++17 scratchpad.cpp; echo "" > test.txt; ./a.out; cat
    test.txt
    // Hello
    // World
    // World
```

In this example, we create two standard C const character buffers. The first buffer consists of the word Hello with a newline, and the second buffer consists of the word World with a newline. We then write Hello to the file, but instead of writing 6 characters, we write 12. Finally, we write World to the file, and we provide the correct number of bytes, which is 6.

The resulting output is Hello World, with World being written to the file twice. The reason for this is a carefully crafted buffer overflow. The first write to the file writes Hello to the buffer, but provides the write() function with 12 bytes instead of 6. Our wrapper in this case is looking for a null terminator, which does not exist (as we have defined our standard C const character buffers manually, removing the null terminator).

As a result, the mywrite() function doesn't detect the overflow, and write both buffers.

There is no safe way to overcome this type of problem (the read() function has similar issues) without the use of the guideline support library, diligence, and a static analyzer capable of detecting the use of a these types of buffers unsafely being used (which is not a trivial thing for a static analyzer to do). As a result, in general, functions such as read() and write() should be avoided in favor of by-field and by-line alternatives when possible.

Similar to `tellg()`, the write stream also has the ability to get the current write pointer position using the `tellp()` function, as follows:

```
#include <fstream>
#include <iostream>

int main()
{
    if (auto file = std::fstream("test.txt")) {
        std::cout << file.tellp() << '\n';
        file << "Hello";
        std::cout << file.tellp() << '\n';
        file << ' ';
        std::cout << file.tellp() << '\n';
        file << "World";
        std::cout << file.tellp() << '\n';
        file << '\n';
        std::cout << file.tellp() << '\n';
    }
}

// > g++ -std=c++17 scratchpad.cpp; echo "" > test.txt; ./a.out; cat
test.txt
// 0
// 5
// 6
// 11
// 12
// Hello World
```

In the preceding example, `Hello World` is written to the file, and the `tellp()` function is used to output the write pointer position, which results in 0, 5, 6, 11, and 12.

It is also possible to move the write pointer to an absolute position within the file using the `seekp()` function, as follows:

```
#include <fstream>
#include <iostream>

int main()
{
    if (auto file = std::fstream("test.txt")) {
        std::cout << file.tellp() << '\n';
        file << "Hello World\n";
        std::cout << file.tellp() << '\n';
        file.seekp(0);
        std::cout << file.tellp() << '\n';
```

```
            file << "The answer is: " << 42 << '\n';
            std::cout << file.tellp() << '\n';
        }
    }

    // > g++ -std=c++17 scratchpad.cpp; echo "" > test.txt; ./a.out; cat
    test.txt
    // 0
    // 12
    // 0
    // 18
    // The answer is: 42
```

In this example, we write `Hello World` to the file, and then move the write pointer within the stream back to the beginning of the file. We then write `The answer is: 42` to the file. Along the way, we use `tellp()` to output the location of the write pointer, showing how the write pointer moves as we perform these actions.

As a result, the file consists of `The answer is: 42`, instead of `Hello World`, as `Hello World` is overwritten.

Finally, as with the `sync()` function, the writes to a file can be flushed to the filesystem when desired using the following:

```
#include <fstream>
#include <iostream>

int main()
{
    if (auto file = std::fstream("test.txt")) {
        file.flush();
    }
}
```

It should be noted that although you can flush the file manually (for example, if you know a change must hit the filesystem), the file will be closed and flushed to the filesystem automatically when the `std::fstream` object loses scope and is destroyed.

at different types of errors could occur.
nctions for determining the state of the stream, as

true, no errors have occurred, and the stream
ile.

true, the end of the file has been reached. Internal
this function.

true, an internal error has occurred, but the
ample, if a numerical conversion error occurs.

true, an error has occurred, and the stream is no
if the stream fails to open a file.

() should return true, while the other three
follows:

```
.pha;

:ream("test.txt")) {
lello"}, world{"World"};
' << world << '\n';
 " << file.good() << '\n';
 " << file.fail() << '\n';
 " << file.bad() << '\n';
 " << file.eof() << '\n';
```

```
pad.cpp; echo "" > test.txt; ./a.out; cat
```

d is written to a file successfully, resulting

In addition to using the good() function, ! operator() can be used to detect whether an error has occurred, as follows:

```cpp
#include <fstream>
#include <iostream>

int main()
{
    std::cout << std::boolalpha;

    if (auto file = std::fstream("test.txt")) {
        std::string hello{"Hello"}, world{"World"};
        file << hello << " " << world << '\n';
        if (!file) {
            std::cout << "failed\n";
        }
    }
}

// > g++ -std=c++17 scratchpad.cpp; echo "" > test.txt; ./a.out; cat
test.txt
// Hello World
```

Here, Hello World is successfully written to the file, and as a result, the good() function returns true, which means ! operator() returns false, resulting in the failed string never being output to stdout.

Similarly, the bool operator can be used, which returns the same result as good(), as follows:

```cpp
#include <fstream>
#include <iostream>

int main()
{
    std::cout << std::boolalpha;

    if (auto file = std::fstream("test.txt")) {
        std::string hello{"Hello"}, world{"World"};
        file << hello << " " << world << '\n';
        if (file) {
            std::cout << "success\n";
        }
    }
}

// > g++ -std=c++17 scratchpad.cpp; echo "" > test.txt; ./a.out; cat
```

```
    test.txt
    // success
    // Hello World
```

In the preceding code, `Hello World` is successfully written to the file, resulting in the `bool` operator returning `true`; this means that the `good()` function would also return `true`, since they return the same result.

If an error occurs, the error status remains triggered until the stream is closed, or until the `clear()` function is used, telling the stream that you have dealt with the error, as follows:

```
#include <fstream>
#include <iostream>

int main()
{
    std::cout << std::boolalpha;

    if (auto file = std::fstream("test.txt")) {
        int answer;
        std::cout << file.good() << '\n';
        file >> answer;
        std::cout << file.good() << '\n';
        file.clear();
        std::cout << file.good() << '\n';
    }
}

// > g++ -std=c++17 scratchpad.cpp; echo "not_a_number" > test.txt; ./a.out
// true
// false
// true
```

In the preceding example, a string is written to a text file. This test file is opened for reading, and an integer is read. The problem is that the value written to the file is not actually a number, causing the file stream to report an error.

The `clear` function is then used to clear the error, after which the `good()` function continues to report `true`.

Understanding file utilities

All of the C++ APIs described in this chapter thus far were added prior to C++17. Although C++ provided the ability to read and write a file, it didn't provide all of the other file operations that are needed to manage a filesystem, including file paths, directory management, and so on.

This section will focus on the `std::filesystem` additions in C++17 that address most of these shortcomings.

Paths

A path is nothing more than a string that represents a node in a filesystem. On UNIX systems, this is usually a string consisting of a series of directory names, /, and a filename, usually with an extension. The purpose of a path is to represent the name and location of a file, which can then be used to perform an action on the file such as opening the file for reading and writing, changing the file's permissions, or even removing the file from the filesystem.

It should be noted that a path can represent many different types of nodes in a filesystem, including files, directories, links, devices, and so on. A more complete list will be presented later in this chapter. Consider the following example:

```
/home/user/
```

This is a path that refers to a directory named `user`, located in a root directory named `home`. Now consider the following:

```
/home/user/test.txt
```

This refers to a file named `test.txt` in this same directory. The file's stem is `test`, while the file's extension is `.txt`. In addition, the file's root is / (which is the case on most UNIX systems).

On UNIX systems, paths can take on different forms, including the following:

- **Block devices**: The path refers to a POSIX-style block device such as `/dev/sda`
- **Character devices**: The path refers to a POSIX-style character device such as `/dev/random`
- **Directories**: The path refers to a regular directory
- **Fifo**: The path refers to a pipe or other form of IPC

- **Socket**: The path refers to a POSIX socket
- **Symlink**: The path refers to a POSIX symlink
- **Files**: The path refers to a regular file

To determine what type a path is, C++17 provides the following test functions:

```
#include <iostream>
#include <filesystem>

int main()
{
    using namespace std::filesystem;

    std::cout << std::boolalpha;
    std::cout << is_block_file("/dev/sda1") << '\n';
    std::cout << is_character_file("/dev/random") << '\n';
    std::cout << is_directory("/dev") << '\n';
    std::cout << is_empty("/dev") << '\n';
    std::cout << is_fifo("scratchpad.cpp") << '\n';
    std::cout << is_other("scratchpad.cpp") << '\n';
    std::cout << is_regular_file("scratchpad.cpp") << '\n';
    std::cout << is_socket("scratchpad.cpp") << '\n';
    std::cout << is_symlink("scratchpad.cpp") << '\n';
}

// > g++ -std=c++17 scratchpad.cpp -lstdc++fs; ./a.out
// true
// true
// true
// false
// false
// false
// true
// false
// false
```

As shown in the preceding example, `/dev/sda` is a block device, `/dev/random` is a character device, `/dev` is a directory that is not empty, and the `scratchpad.cpp` file that is used to compile all the examples in this chapter is a regular file.

To determine if a path exists, C++17 provides the `exists()` function, as follows:

```
#include <iostream>
#include <filesystem>

int main()
{
```

```
    std::cout << std::boolalpha;
    std::cout << std::filesystem::exists("/dev") << '\n';
    std::cout << std::filesystem::exists("/dev/random") << '\n';
    std::cout << std::filesystem::exists("scratchpad.cpp") << '\n';
}

// > g++ -std=c++17 scratchpad.cpp -lstdc++fs; ./a.out
// true
// true
// true
```

Here the directory /dev exists, and so do the character device /dev/random and the regular file scratchpad.cpp.

Every program that executes must execute from a given directory. To determine this directory, C++17 provides the current_path() function, as follows:

```
#include <iostream>
#include <filesystem>

int main()
{
    std::cout << std::filesystem::current_path() << '\n';
}

// > g++ -std=c++17 scratchpad.cpp -lstdc++fs; ./a.out
// "/home/user/Hands-On-System-Programming-with-CPP/Chapter08"
```

In this example, current_path() is used to get the current directory that a.out is executing from. The path that was provided by current_path() is an absolute path. To turn an absolute path into a relative path, use the relative() function, as follows:

```
#include <iostream>
#include <filesystem>

int main()
{
    auto path = std::filesystem::current_path();
    std::cout << std::filesystem::relative(path) << '\n';
}

// > g++ -std=c++17 scratchpad.cpp -lstdc++fs; ./a.out
// "."
```

As shown in this example, the relative path for the current path is simply (.).

Similarly, to turn a relative path into an absolute path, C++17 provides the `canonical()` function:

```
#include <iostream>
#include <filesystem>

int main()
{
    std::cout << std::filesystem::canonical(".") << '\n';
    std::cout << std::filesystem::canonical("../Chapter08") << '\n';
}

// > g++ -std=c++17 scratchpad.cpp -lstdc++fs; ./a.out
// "/home/user/Hands-On-System-Programming-with-CPP/Chapter08"
// "/home/user/Hands-On-System-Programming-with-CPP/Chapter08"
```

In this example, we use the `canonical()` function to convert a relative path to an absolute path. It should be noted that getting the absolute path of `.` is another way to return the same result of `current_path()`.

Also note that the `canonical()` function returns the absolute path with all references to `../` and `./` resolved, reducing the absolute path to its minimal form. If this type of path is not desired, the `absolute()` function may be used instead, as follows:

```
#include <iostream>
#include <filesystem>

int main()
{
    std::cout << std::filesystem::absolute("../Chapter08") << '\n';
}

// > g++ -std=c++17 scratchpad.cpp -lstdc++fs; ./a.out
// "/home/user/Hands-On-System-Programming-with-CPP/Chapter08/../Chapter08"
```

As shown in this example, the `../` is not removed by the `absolute()` function.

Since there are different ways to represent the same path (that is, relative, canonical, and absolute), C++17 provides the `equivalent()` function, as follows:

```
#include <iostream>
#include <filesystem>

int main()
{
 auto path1 = std::filesystem::path{"."};
 auto path2 = std::filesystem::path{"../Chapter08"};
```

```
    auto path3 = std::filesystem::path{"../Chapter08/../Chapter08"};
    auto path4 = std::filesystem::current_path();
    auto path5 = std::filesystem::current_path() / "../Chapter08/";

    std::cout << std::boolalpha;
    std::cout << std::filesystem::equivalent(path1, path2) << '\n';
    std::cout << std::filesystem::equivalent(path1, path3) << '\n';
    std::cout << std::filesystem::equivalent(path1, path4) << '\n';
    std::cout << std::filesystem::equivalent(path1, path5) << '\n';
}

// > g++ -std=c++17 scratchpad.cpp -lstdc++fs; ./a.out
// true
// true
// true
// true
```

All the paths referenced in this example refer to the same directory, regardless of whether they are relative, canonical, or absolute.

If you wish to determine if two paths are lexically equal (containing the same exact characters), use == operator() instead, as follows:

```
#include <iostream>
#include <filesystem>

int main()
{
    auto path1 = std::filesystem::path{"."};
    auto path2 = std::filesystem::path{"../Chapter08"};
    auto path3 = std::filesystem::path{"../Chapter08/../Chapter08"};
    auto path4 = std::filesystem::current_path();
    auto path5 = std::filesystem::current_path() / "../Chapter08/";

    std::cout << std::boolalpha;
    std::cout << (path1 == path2) << '\n';
    std::cout << (path1 == path3) << '\n';
    std::cout << (path1 == path4) << '\n';
    std::cout << (path1 == path5) << '\n';
}

// > g++ -std=c++17 scratchpad.cpp -lstdc++fs; ./a.out
// false
// false
// false
// false
```

The code here is the same as the preceding code, apart from the use of == operator() instead of the equivalent() function. The previous example returned true for all of the paths since they all refer to the same path, while the preceding example returns false because the same paths are not lexically equal, even though they are technically the same path.

Note the use of / operator() in these examples. C++17 provides different concatenation functions for paths that conveniently provide a clean, readable way of adding to an existing path: /, /=, and +=. / operator() (and the self-modifying version /= operator()) concatenates two paths while adding a / for you, as follows:

```
#include <iostream>
#include <filesystem>

int main()
{
    auto path = std::filesystem::current_path();
    path /= "scratchpad.cpp";

    std::cout << path << '\n';
}

// > g++ -std=c++17 scratchpad.cpp -lstdc++fs; ./a.out
// "/home/user/Hands-On-System-Programming-with-
CPP/Chapter08/scratchpad.cpp"
```

In this example, scratchpad.cpp is added to the path using /= operator(), and a / is added for us. If you wish to add the / yourself, or you do not wish for a / to be added at all, you can use += operator(), as follows:

```
#include <iostream>
#include <filesystem>

int main()
{
    auto path = std::filesystem::current_path();
    path += "/scratchpad.cpp";

    std::cout << path << '\n';
}

// > g++ -std=c++17 scratchpad.cpp -lstdc++fs; ./a.out
// "/home/user/Hands-On-System-Programming-with-
CPP/Chapter08/scratchpad.cpp"
```

The result here is the same as in the previous example, with the difference being that += operator() is used instead of /= operator(), and so the / needs to be added manually.

In addition to concatenation, C++17 provides some additional path modifiers. One such function is remove_filename(), which removes the filename from a path, as follows:

```
#include <iostream>
#include <filesystem>

int main()
{
    auto path = std::filesystem::current_path();
    path /= "scratchpad.cpp";

    std::cout << path << '\n';
    path.remove_filename();
    std::cout << path << '\n';
}

// > g++ -std=c++17 scratchpad.cpp -lstdc++fs; ./a.out
// "/home/user/Hands-On-System-Programming-with-
CPP/Chapter08/scratchpad.cpp"
// "/home/user/Hands-On-System-Programming-with-CPP/Chapter08/"
```

As shown, the remove_filename() function removes the filename from the path.

It is also possible to replace the filename with something else, instead of removing it, as follows:

```
#include <iostream>
#include <filesystem>

int main()
{
    auto path = std::filesystem::current_path();
    path /= "scratchpad.cpp";

    std::cout << path << '\n';
    path.replace_filename("test.cpp");
    std::cout << path << '\n';
}

// > g++ -std=c++17 scratchpad.cpp -lstdc++fs; ./a.out
// "/home/user/Hands-On-System-Programming-with-
CPP/Chapter08/scratchpad.cpp"
// "/home/user/Hands-On-System-Programming-with-CPP/Chapter08/test.cpp"
```

As shown, the filename `scratchpad.cpp` was replaced with `test.cpp`.

As well as replacing the filename, it is also possible to replace the extension, as follows:

```
#include <iostream>
#include <filesystem>

int main()
{
    auto path = std::filesystem::current_path();
    path /= "scratchpad.cpp";

    std::cout << path << '\n';
    path.replace_extension("txt");
    std::cout << path << '\n';
}

// > g++ -std=c++17 scratchpad.cpp -lstdc++fs; ./a.out
// "/home/user/Hands-On-System-Programming-with-
CPP/Chapter08/scratchpad.cpp"
// "/home/user/Hands-On-System-Programming-with-
CPP/Chapter08/scratchpad.txt"
```

As shown, the extension for `scratchpad.cpp` was changed to `.txt`.

Finally, if you need to, it's possible to clear a path using the `clear()` function, as follows:

```
#include <iostream>
#include <filesystem>

int main()
{
    auto path = std::filesystem::current_path();
    path /= "scratchpad.cpp";

    std::cout << path << '\n';
    path.clear();
    std::cout << path << '\n';
}

// > g++ -std=c++17 scratchpad.cpp -lstdc++fs; ./a.out
// "/home/user/Hands-On-System-Programming-with-
CPP/Chapter08/scratchpad.cpp"
// ""
```

As shown in the preceding code, the `clear()` function deletes the contents of the path (as if it were default constructed).

As stated, a path consists of different parts including a root name, directory, stem, and extension. To dissect a path into these different components, C++17 provides some helper functions, as follows:

```cpp
#include <iostream>
#include <filesystem>

int main()
{
    auto path = std::filesystem::current_path();
    path /= "scratchpad.cpp";

    std::cout << std::boolalpha;
    std::cout << path.root_name() << '\n';
    std::cout << path.root_directory() << '\n';
    std::cout << path.root_path() << '\n';
    std::cout << path.relative_path() << '\n';
    std::cout << path.parent_path() << '\n';
    std::cout << path.filename() << '\n';
    std::cout << path.stem() << '\n';
    std::cout << path.extension() << '\n';
}

// > g++ -std=c++17 scratchpad.cpp -lstdc++fs; ./a.out
// ""
// "/"
// "/"
// "home/user/Hands-On-System-Programming-with-
CPP/Chapter08/scratchpad.cpp"
// "/home/user/Hands-On-System-Programming-with-CPP/Chapter08"
// "scratchpad.cpp"
// "scratchpad"
// ".cpp"
```

In this example, we dissect the path of the `scratchpad.cpp` file into its different parts. The parent path is `/home/user/Hands-On-System-Programming-with-CPP/Chapter08`, the filename is `scratchpad.cpp`, the stem is `scratchpad`, and the extension is `.cpp`.

Not all paths contain all the parts that a path could potentially contain. This can occur when a path points to a directory, or when it is ill-formed.

To figure out which parts a path contains, use the following helpers:

```cpp
#include <iostream>
#include <filesystem>

int main()
```

```
{
    auto path = std::filesystem::current_path();
    path /= "scratchpad.cpp";

    std::cout << std::boolalpha;
    std::cout << path.empty() << '\n';
    std::cout << path.has_root_path() << '\n';
    std::cout << path.has_root_name() << '\n';
    std::cout << path.has_root_directory() << '\n';
    std::cout << path.has_relative_path() << '\n';
    std::cout << path.has_parent_path() << '\n';
    std::cout << path.has_filename() << '\n';
    std::cout << path.has_stem() << '\n';
    std::cout << path.has_extension() << '\n';
    std::cout << path.is_absolute() << '\n';
    std::cout << path.is_relative() << '\n';
}

// > g++ -std=c++17 scratchpad.cpp -lstdc++fs; ./a.out
// false
// true
// false
// true
// true
// true
// true
// true
// true
// true
// false
```

As shown here, you can determine whether a path has a root path, root name, root
directory, relative path, parent path, filename, stem, and extension. You can also determine
whether the path is an absolute path or a relative path.

Finally, C++17 provides different mechanisms for managing paths on a filesystem,
depending on the type of path you're using. For example, if you wish to create a directory
or delete a path (regardless of its type), use the `create_directory()` and `remove()`
functions respectively, as follows:

```
#include <iostream>
#include <filesystem>

int main()
{
    auto path = std::filesystem::current_path();
    path /= "test";
```

```
        std::cout << std::boolalpha;
        std::cout << std::filesystem::create_directory(path) << '\n';
        std::cout << std::filesystem::remove(path) << '\n';
}

// > g++ -std=c++17 scratchpad.cpp -lstdc++fs; ./a.out
// true
// true
```

In the preceding example, we use the `create_directory()` function to create a directory, and then we use the `remove()` function to delete it.

We can also rename a path using the `rename()` function, as follows:

```
#include <iostream>
#include <filesystem>

int main()
{
        auto path1 = std::filesystem::current_path();
        auto path2 = std::filesystem::current_path();
        path1 /= "test1";
        path2 /= "test2";

        std::cout << std::boolalpha;
        std::cout << std::filesystem::create_directory(path1) << '\n';
        std::filesystem::rename(path1, path2);
        std::cout << std::filesystem::remove(path1) << '\n';
        std::cout << std::filesystem::remove(path2) << '\n';
}

// > g++ -std=c++17 scratchpad.cpp -lstdc++fs; ./a.out
// true
// false
// true
```

In this example, we create a directory using the `create_directory()` function. We rename the directory using the `rename()` function, and then delete both the old directory path and the new one. As shown, the attempt to delete the directory that has been renamed fails, as that path no longer exists, while attempting to delete the new directory succeeds, as that path does exist.

The `remove()` function will remove any path (assuming the program has the proper permissions), unless the path points to a directory that is not empty, in which case it will fail. To remove a directory that is not empty, use the `remove_all()` function, as follows:

```
#include <fstream>
#include <iostream>
#include <filesystem>

int main()
{
    auto path = std::filesystem::current_path();
    path /= "test";

    std::cout << std::boolalpha;
    std::cout << std::filesystem::create_directory(path) << '\n';

    std::fstream(path / "test1.txt", std::ios::app);
    std::fstream(path / "test2.txt", std::ios::app);
    std::fstream(path / "test3.txt", std::ios::app);

    std::cout << std::filesystem::remove_all(path) << '\n';
}

// > g++ -std=c++17 scratchpad.cpp -lstdc++fs; ./a.out
// true
// 4
```

As shown here, we create a directory and add some files to the directory using `std::fstream`. We then delete the newly created directory using `remove_all()` instead of `remove()`. If we used the `remove()` function, the program would throw an exception, as follows:

```
terminate called after throwing an instance of
'std::filesystem::__cxx11::filesystem_error'
  what(): filesystem error: cannot remove: Directory not empty
[/home/user/Hands-On-System-Programming-with-CPP/Chapter08/test]
Aborted (core dumped)
```

Another common operation to perform on a filesystem is to iterate over all of the files in a directory. To do this, C++17 provides a directory iterator, as follows:

```
#include <fstream>
#include <iostream>
#include <filesystem>

int main()
{
```

```
    auto path = std::filesystem::current_path();
    path /= "test";

    std::cout << std::boolalpha;
    std::cout << std::filesystem::create_directory(path) << '\n';

    std::fstream(path / "test1.txt", std::ios::app);
    std::fstream(path / "test2.txt", std::ios::app);
    std::fstream(path / "test3.txt", std::ios::app);

    for(const auto &p: std::filesystem::directory_iterator(path)) {
        std::cout << p << '\n';
    }

    std::cout << std::filesystem::remove_all(path) << '\n';
}

// > g++ -std=c++17 scratchpad.cpp -lstdc++fs; ./a.out
// true
// "/home/user/Hands-On-System-Programming-with-
CPP/Chapter08/test/test1.txt"
// "/home/user/Hands-On-System-Programming-with-
CPP/Chapter08/test/test3.txt"
// "/home/user/Hands-On-System-Programming-with-
CPP/Chapter08/test/test2.txt"
// 4
```

In the preceding example, we create a directory using the `create_directory()` function, add some files to the directory, and then use a directory iterator to iterate over all the files.

The directory iterator functions like any other iterator in C++, which means, as shown in the preceding example, that we can leverage the ranged for syntax.

Finally, C++17 provides a convenient function for determining the path to the temporary directory, which can be used to create temporary directories as needed for your program, as follows:

```
#include <fstream>
#include <iostream>
#include <filesystem>

int main()
{
    std::cout << std::filesystem::temp_directory_path() << '\n';
}

// > g++ -std=c++17 scratchpad.cpp -lstdc++fs; ./a.out
```

```
// "/tmp"

#endif
```

It should be noted that on POSIX systems, the temporary directory is usually /tmp, as shown here. However, it's still prudent to use the temp_directory_path() instead of hard-coding this path.

Understanding the logger example

In this section, we will extend the debugging example in Chapter 6, *Learning to Program Console Input/Output*, to include a rudimentary logger. The goal of this logger is to redirect additions to the std::clog stream to a log file in addition to the console.

Just like the debugging functions in Chapter 6, *Learning to Program Console Input/Output*, we would like the logging functions to be compiled out if the debugging level is not sufficient, or if debugging has been disabled.

To accomplish this, please see the following code: https://github.com/PacktPublishing/Hands-On-System-Programming-with-CPP/blob/master/Chapter08/example1.cpp.

To start, we will need to create two constant expressions—one for the debug level, and one to enable or disable debugging outright, as follows:

```
#ifdef DEBUG_LEVEL
constexpr auto g_debug_level = DEBUG_LEVEL;
#else
constexpr auto g_debug_level = 0;
#endif

#ifdef NDEBUG
constexpr auto g_ndebug = true;
#else
constexpr auto g_ndebug = false;
#endif
```

Next, we will need to create a global variable, as follows:

```
std::fstream g_log{"log.txt", std::ios::out | std::ios::app};
```

The global variable is the log file stream. This will be used to write additions to the std::clog stream to a log file. Since this is a log file, we open it as write-only, append, meaning we can only write to the log, and all writes must append to the end of the file.

Next, we will need to define the `log` function itself. This function needs to be able to output to both `std::clog` and to our log file stream without executing the debug logic more than once (as this could result in unexpected behavior).

The following implements the `log` function with this goal in mind:

```
template <std::size_t LEVEL>
constexpr void log(void(*func)()) {
    if constexpr (!g_ndebug && (LEVEL <= g_debug_level)) {
        std::stringstream buf;

        auto g_buf = std::clog.rdbuf();
        std::clog.rdbuf(buf.rdbuf());

        func();

        std::clog.rdbuf(g_buf);

        std::clog << "\033[1;32mDEBUG\033[0m: ";
        std::clog << buf.str();

        g_log << "\033[1;32mDEBUG\033[0m: ";
        g_log << buf.str();
    };
}
```

Like the debug functions in Chapter 6, *Learning to Program Console Input/Output*, this `log` function starts by wrapping the business logic of the function in a `constexpr if` statement (a feature new to C++17), providing the compiler with a means to compile out the code if debugging is disabled, or if the provided debug level is greater than the current debug level.

If debugging should take place, the first step is to create a string stream, which behaves just like `std::clog` and the log file stream, but saves the results of any additions to the stream to a `std::string`.

The read buffer for `std::clog` is then saved, and the read buffer of the string stream is provided to `std::clog`. Any additions to the `std::clog` stream will be redirected to our string stream instead of `stderr`.

Next, we execute the user-provided `debug` function, collecting the debug string and storing it in the string stream. Finally, the `read()` buffer for `std::clog` is restored to `stderr`, and we output the string stream to both `std::clog` and the log file stream.

The last step is to create our `protected_main ()` function that logs `Hello World`. Note that, for demonstration, we also add `Hello World` to `std::clog` manually, without the `log` function, to demonstrate that `std::clog` functions as normal and only logs to our log file when the `log` function is used. This is shown with the following code:

```
int
protected_main(int argc, char** argv)
{
    (void) argc;
    (void) argv;

    log<0>([]{
        std::clog << "Hello World\n";
    });

    std::clog << "Hello World\n";

    return EXIT_SUCCESS;
}
```

To compile this code, we leverage the same `CMakeLists.txt` file that we have been using for the other examples: https://github.com/PacktPublishing/Hands-On-System-Programming-with-CPP/blob/master/Chapter08/CMakeLists.txt.

With this code in place, we can compile and execute this code using the following:

```
> git clone
https://github.com/PacktPublishing/Hands-On-System-Programming-with-CPP.git
> cd Hands-On-System-Programming-with-CPP/Chapter08/
> mkdir build
> cd build

> cmake ..
> make
> ./example1
DEBUG: Hello World
Hello World

> cat log.txt
DEBUG: Hello World
```

Notice how both the `debug` statements are output to `stderr` (both the statement in the `log` function, and the statement manually executed without the `log` function). Yet, the log file only has a single statement in it, demonstrating the `log` function is responsible for redirecting additions to `std::clog` to both the log file and `stderr`, while leaving `std::clog` intact for future uses.

Learning about the tail file example

In this example, we will create a simple program to tail a file. The goal of this example is to mimic the behavior of `tail -f -n0`, which outputs new additions to a file. The `-f` argument tells the tail to follow the file and `-n0` tells tail to only output to `stdout` new additions.

The first step is to define the mode we plan to use when opening the file we are tailing, as follows:

```
constexpr auto mode = std::ios::in | std::ios::ate;
```

In this case, we will open the file as read-only, and move the read pointer to the end of the file on open.

The next step is to create a `tail` function that watches for changes to a file and outputs the changes to `stdout`, as follows:

```
[[noreturn]] void
tail(std::fstream &file)
{
    while (true) {
        file.peek();
        while(!file.eof()) {
            auto pos = file.tellg();

            std::string buf;
            std::getline(file, buf, '\n');

            if (file.eof() && !file.good()) {
                file.seekg(pos);
                break;
            }

            std::cout << buf << '\n';
        }

        sleep(1);

        file.clear();
        file.sync();
    }
}
```

This `tail` function starts by telling the compiler that this function does not return, as the function is wrapped in a `while(true)` loop that never ends.

Next, the function checks whether the end of the file has been reached by first peeking the file, and then checking the end-of-file bit using `eof()`. If it has, the program sleeps for a second, clears all status bits, resyncs with the filesystem to see if any new changes have been made, and then loops again.

If the read pointer is not at the end of the file, its current position is read in case its position in the file needs to be restored. The next line in the file is read and stored in a buffer.

It's possible that attempting to read the next line using `getline` will fail (for example, when the last character in a file is not a newline). If this occurs, the contents of the buffer should be ignored (as it is not a complete line), and the read pointer needs to be restored to its original position.

If the next line is successfully read, it is output to `stdout`, and we loop again to see if more lines need to be read.

The last function in this example must parse the arguments provided to our program to get the file name to tail, open the file, and then call the `tail` function with the newly opened file, as follows:

```cpp
int
protected_main(int argc, char **argv)
{
    std::string filename;
    auto args = make_span(argv, argc);

    if (args.size() < 2) {
        std::cin >> filename;
    }
    else {
        filename = ensure_z(args[1]).data();
    }

    if (auto file = std::fstream(filename, mode)) {
        tail(file);
    }

    throw std::runtime_error("failed to open file");
}
```

As with previous examples, we parse the arguments using a `gsl::span` to ensure safety and remain compliant with C++ Core Guidelines. If no arguments are provided to the program, we wait for the user to provide the program with the filename to tail.

If a filename is provided, we open the file and call `tail()`. If the file cannot be opened, we throw an exception.

To compile this code, we leverage the same `CMakeLists.txt` file that we have been using for the other examples: `https://github.com/PacktPublishing/Hands-On-System-Programming-with-CPP/blob/master/Chapter08/CMakeLists.txt`.

With this code in place, we can compile and execute this code using the following:

```
> git clone
https://github.com/PacktPublishing/Hands-On-System-Programming-with-CPP.git
> cd Hands-On-System-Programming-with-CPP/Chapter08/
> mkdir build
> cd build

> cmake ..
> make
> touch test.txt
> ./example2 test.txt
```

From another terminal, we can make changes to the file as follows:

```
> cd Hands-On-System-Programming-with-CPP/Chapter08/build
> echo "Hello World" > test.txt
```

This would result in the example program outputting the following to `stdout`:

```
Hello World
```

To ensure the program is ignoring incomplete lines, we can add an incomplete line to the file, as follows:

```
> echo -n "Hello World" > test.txt
```

This results in no output from the example program.

Comparing C++ versus mmap benchmark

In this example, we will benchmark the difference between reading the contents of a file using `std::fstream` and reading them using `mmap()`.

It should be noted that the `mmap()` function leverages a system call to directly map a file into the program, and we expect `mmap()` to be faster than the C++ APIs highlighted in this chapter. This is because the C++ APIs have to perform an additional memory copy, which is obviously slower.

We will start this example by defining the size of the file we plan to read, as follows:

```
constexpr auto size = 0x1000;
```

Next, we must define a `benchmark` function to record how long it takes to perform an action:

```
template<typename FUNC>
auto benchmark(FUNC func) {
    auto stime = std::chrono::high_resolution_clock::now();
    func();
    auto etime = std::chrono::high_resolution_clock::now();

    return etime - stime;
}
```

In the preceding function, we leverage a high-resolution timer to record how long it takes to execute a user-provided function. It should be noted that this benchmark program is relatively generic, and can be used for a lot of non-trivial functions (as trivial functions are often difficult to benchmark, even with high-resolution timers).

Finally, we need to create a file read, and then we need to read the file using `std::fstream` and `mmap()` as follows:

```
int
protected_main(int argc, char** argv)
{
    (void) argc;
    (void) argv;

    using namespace std::chrono;

    {
        char buf[size] = {};
        if (auto file = std::fstream("test.txt", std::ios::out)) {
            file.write(buf, size);
        }
    }

    {
        char buf[size];
        if (auto file = std::fstream("test.txt", std::ios::in)) {
            auto time = benchmark([&file, &buf]{
                file.read(buf, size);
            });

            std::cout << "c++ time: "
```

```
                                    << duration_cast<microseconds>(time).count()
                                    << '\n';
            }
      }

      {
            void *buf;
            if (int fd = open("test.txt", O_RDONLY); fd != 0) {
                  auto time = benchmark([&fd, &buf]{
                        buf = mmap(NULL, size, PROT_READ, 0, fd, 0);
                  });

                  munmap(buf, size);

                  std::cout << "mmap time: "
                              << duration_cast<microseconds>(time).count()
                              << '\n';
            }
      }

      return EXIT_SUCCESS;
}
```

The first step in the `protected_main()` function is to create the file we plan to read, as follows:

```
char buf[size] = {};
if (auto file = std::fstream("test.txt", std::ios::out)) {
    file.write(buf, size);
}
```

To do this, we open the file we plan to read using write-only, which also opens the file using `std::ios::trunc` by default, erasing the contents of the file for us just in case. Finally, we write `size` number of zeros to the file.

The next step is to read the file using `std::fstream`, as follows:

```
char buf[size];
if (auto file = std::fstream("test.txt", std::ios::in)) {
    auto time = benchmark([&file, &buf]{
        file.read(buf, size);
    });

    std::cout << "c++ time: "
                << duration_cast<microseconds>(time).count()
                << '\n';
}
```

Before we read the file using `std::fstream`, we open the file using read-only, which opens the file at the beginning of the file. Our file read is then encapsulated in our benchmark function. The results of the benchmark are output to `stdout`.

Finally, the last step is to do the same for `mmap()`, as follows:

```
void *buf;
if (int fd = open("test.txt", O_RDONLY); fd != 0) {
    auto time = benchmark([&fd, &buf]{
        buf = mmap(NULL, size, PROT_READ, 0, fd, 0);
    });

    munmap(buf, size);

    std::cout << "mmap time: "
              << duration_cast<microseconds>(time).count()
              << '\n';
}
```

As with `std::fstream`, the file is opened first, and then the use of `mmap()` is encapsulated in our benchmark function.

To compile this code, we leverage the same `CMakeLists.txt` file that we have been using for the other examples: https://github.com/PacktPublishing/Hands-On-System-Programming-with-CPP/blob/master/Chapter08/CMakeLists.txt.

With this code in place, we can compile and execute this code using the following:

```
> git clone
https://github.com/PacktPublishing/Hands-On-System-Programming-with-CPP.git
> cd Hands-On-System-Programming-with-CPP/Chapter08/
> mkdir build
> cd build

> cmake ..
> make
> ./example3
c++ time: 16
mmap time: 3
```

As shown, `mmap()` executes faster than `std::fstream`.

Summary

In this chapter, we learned how to open a file in different ways, depending on how we plan to use the file itself. Once opened, we learned how to read and write to the file using the `std::fstream` C++ APIs.

We learned the difference between fields and bytes, and the advantages and disadvantages of both methods of reading and writing, as well as common unsafe practices. In addition, we learned about support functions that provide the ability to move pointers within the `std::fstream` APIs to manipulate how a file is read and written.

Furthermore, in this chapter, we gave an extensive overview of the new filesystem APIs added to C++17, including paths and their support functions for manipulating files and directories.

We concluded this chapter with three examples. In the first we wrote a logger to redirect the output of `std::clog` to a log file and `stdout`. The second example demonstrated how to rewrite the tail POSIX command using C++.

Finally, in the third example, we wrote some benchmarking code to compare the difference in performance of POSIX, C and C++. In the next chapter, we will cover C++ allocators including how to create stateful allocators such as a memory pool that can be used when system programming to improve memory performance and efficiency when applicable.

Questions

1. What is the name of the function used to see whether a file was successfully opened?
2. What is the default mode for opening a file?
3. What happens if you attempt to read a non-numeric value into a numeric variable from a file?
4. What types of error could occur if you unsafely use the `read()` or `write()` functions?
5. Does `/= operator()` add a / to your path for you automatically?
6. What is the stem of the following path—`/home/user/test.txt`?
7. What is the parent directory of the following path—`/home/user/test.txt`?

Further reading

- https://www.packtpub.com/application-development/c17-example
- https://www.packtpub.com/application-development/getting-started-c17-programming-video

9
A Hands-On Approach to Allocators

In `Chapter 7`, *A Comprehensive Look at Memory Management*, we learned how to allocate and deallocate memory using C++-specific techniques, including the use of `std::unique_ptr` and `std::shared_ptr`. In addition, we learned about fragmentation and how it is capable of wasting large amounts of memory depending on how memory is allocated and then later deallocated. System programmers often have to allocate memory from different pools (sometimes originating from different sources), and handle fragmentation to prevent the system from running out of memory during operation. This is especially true for embedded programmers. Placement `new()` may be used to solve these types of issues, but implementations based on placement new are often hard to create and even harder to maintain. Placement `new()` is also only accessible from user-defined code, providing no control over the allocations that originate from the C++ standard library APIs (such as `std:: list` and `std:: map`).

To solve these types of issues, C++ provides a concept called the **allocator**. C++ allocators define how memory should be allocated and deallocated for a specific type T. In this chapter, you will learn how to create your own allocators while covering the intricate details of the C++ allocator concept. This chapter will end with two different examples; the first example will demonstrate how to create a simple, cache-aligned allocator that is stateless, while the second will provide a functional example of a stateful object allocator that maintains a free pool for fast allocations.

The objectives of this chapter are as follows:

- Introducing the C++ allocators
- Studying an examples of stateless, cache-aligned allocator
- Studying an example of stateful, memory-pool allocator

Technical requirements

In order to compile and execute the examples in this chapter, the reader must have the following:

- A Linux-based system capable of compiling and executing C++17 (for example, Ubuntu 17.10+)
- GCC 7+
- CMake 3.6+
- An internet connection

To download all of the code in this chapter, including the examples and code snippets, please see the following link: `https://github.com/PacktPublishing/Hands-On-System-Programming-with-CPP/tree/master/Chapter09`.

Introducing the C++ allocators

C++ allocators define a template class that allocates memory for a specific type T and are defined by the allocator concept definition. There are two different types of allocators:

- Allocators that are equal
- Allocators that are unequal

An allocator that is equal is an allocator that can allocate memory from one allocator and deallocate memory from another, for example:

```
myallocator<myclass> myalloc1;
myallocator<myclass> myalloc2;

auto ptr = myalloc1.allocate(1);
myalloc2.deallocate(ptr, 1);
```

As shown in the preceding example, we create two instances of `myallocator{}`. We allocate memory from one of the allocators and then deallocate memory from the other allocator. For this to be valid, the allocators must be equal:

```
myalloc1 == myalloc2; // true
```

If this does not hold true, the allocators are considered unequal, which greatly complicates how the allocators can be used. An unequal allocator is usually an allocator that is stateful, meaning it stores a state within itself that prevents an allocator from deallocating memory from another instance of the same allocator (because the state is different).

Learning about the basic allocator

Before we dive into the details of a stateful, unequal allocator, let's review the most basic allocator, which is a stateless, equal allocator. This most basic allocator takes the following form:

```cpp
template<typename T>
class myallocator
{
public:

  using value_type = T;
  using pointer = T *;
  using size_type = std::size_t;

public:

  myallocator() = default;

  template <typename U>
  myallocator(const myallocator<U> &other) noexcept
  { (void) other; }

  pointer allocate(size_type n)
  {
  if (auto ptr = static_cast<pointer>(malloc(sizeof(T) * n))) {
  return ptr;
  }

  throw std::bad_alloc();
  }

  void deallocate(pointer p, size_type n)
  { (void) n; return free(p); }
};

template <typename T1, typename T2>
bool operator==(const myallocator<T1> &, const myallocator<T2> &)
{ return true; }

template <typename T1, typename T2>
bool operator!=(const myallocator<T1> &, const myallocator<T2> &)
{ return false; }
```

To start, all allocators are template classes, as follows:

```cpp
template<typename T>
class myallocator
```

It should be noted that allocators can have any number of template arguments, but at least one is needed to define the type that the allocator will allocate and deallocate. In our example, we use the following aliases:

```
using value_type = T;
using pointer = T *;
using size_type = std::size_t;
```

Technically speaking, the only alias that is required is the following:

```
using value_type = T;
```

Since, however, `T*` and `std::size_t` are required to create a minimal allocator, these aliases might as well be added to provide a more complete implementation. The optional aliases include the following:

```
using value_type = T;
using pointer = T *;
using const_pointer = const T *;
using void_pointer = void *;
using const_void_pointer = const void *;
using size_type = std::size_t;
using difference_type = std::ptrdiff_t;
```

If a custom allocator doesn't provide these, the preceding default values will be provided for you.

As shown, all allocators must provide a default constructor. This is due to the fact that C++ containers will create the allocator on their own, in some cases more than once, and they will use the default constructor to do so, which means the construction of an allocator must be possible without the need of an additional argument.

The `allocate()` function in our example is the following:

```
pointer allocate(size_type n)
{
    if (auto ptr = static_cast<pointer>(malloc(sizeof(T) * n))) {
        return ptr;
    }

    throw std::bad_alloc();
}
```

As with all of the functions being explained in this example, the function signature of the `allocate()` function is defined by the allocator concept, which means that each function in the allocator must take on a specific signature; otherwise, the allocator will not compile correctly when used by existing containers.

In the preceding example, `malloc()` is used to allocate some memory, and if `malloc` doesn't return `nullptr`, the resulting pointer is returned. Since the allocator allocates pointers of the `T*` type, and not `void *`, we must statically cast the result of `malloc()` before returning the pointer. The number of bytes provided to `malloc()` is equal to `sizeof(T) * n`. This is because the n parameter defines the total number of objects the allocator must allocate—because some containers will allocate several objects at once and expect that the objects being allocated are contiguous in memory. Examples of this include `std::deque` and `std::vector`, and it's up to the allocator to ensure these rules hold true in memory. Finally, if `malloc()` returns `nullptr`, indicating the requested memory could not be allocated, we throw `std::bad_alloc()`.

It should be noted that in our example, we use `malloc()` instead of `new()`. Here, `malloc()` should be used instead of `new()` because the container will construct the object being allocated for you. For this reason, we don't want to use `new()`, since it would also construct the object, meaning the object would be constructed twice, which would lead to corruption and undefined behavior. For this reason, `new()` and `delete()` should never be used in an allocator.

The `deallocate` function performs the opposite of the `allocate` function, freeing memory and releasing it back to the operating system:

```
void deallocate(pointer p, size_type n)
{ (void) n; free(p); }
```

In the preceding example, to deallocate memory, we simply need to call `free()`. Note that we are creating an *equal* allocator, which means that `ptr` does not need to originate from the same allocator performing the deallocation. The number of allocations, n, however, must match the original allocation, which in our case may be safely ignored, since we are using `malloc()` and `free()`, which automatically keep track of the size of the original allocation for us. Not all allocators will have this property.

In our simple example, there are two additional requirements to conform to a C++ allocator that are far less obvious in terms of what exactly their purpose is. The first is the use of a copy constructor using a template type of U, as follows:

```
template <typename U>
myallocator(const myallocator<U> &other) noexcept
{ (void) other; }
```

This is because when you use the allocator with a container, you specify the type in the container's definition, for example:

```
std::list<myclass, myallocator<myclass>> mylist;
```

In the preceding example, we create an `std::list` of the `myclass{}` type, with an allocator that allocates and deallocates `myclass{}` objects. The problem is, `std::list` has its own internal data structures that must also be allocated. Specifically, `std::list` implements a linked list, and as a result, `std::list` must be able to allocate and deallocate linked list nodes. In the preceding definition, we defined an allocator that allocates and deallocates `myclass{}` objects, but `std::list` will actually allocate and deallocate nodes and these two types are not the same. To solve this, `std::list` will create a copy of the `myclass{}` allocator using the template version of the copy constructor, providing `std::list` with the ability to create its own node allocator using the allocator that it was originally provided. For this reason, the template version of the copy constructor is required for a fully functional allocator.

The second odd addition to the preceding example is the use of the equality operators, as follows:

```
template <typename T1, typename T2>
bool operator==(const myallocator<T1> &, const myallocator<T2> &)
{ return true; }

template <typename T1, typename T2>
bool operator!=(const myallocator<T1> &, const myallocator<T2> &)
{ return false; }
```

The equality operators define whether the allocator is *equal* or *unequal*. In the preceding example, we have created a stateless allocator, which means that the following is valid:

```
myallocator<int> myalloc1;
myallocator<int> myalloc2;

auto ptr = myalloc1.allocate(1);
myalloc2.deallocate(ptr, 1);
```

If the preceding property holds true, the allocators are equal. Since, in our example, `myalloc1{}` calls `malloc()` when allocating, and `myalloc2{}` calls `free()` when deallocating, we know that they are interchangeable, which means the preceding holds true and our example implements an *equal* allocator. The preceding equality operators simply state this equality formally, providing APIs, such as C++ containers, with a means to create new allocators as needed.

Understanding the allocator's properties and options

The basic allocator we just discussed provides only the required functionality to create and use an allocator with existing C++ data structures (and other user-defined types that leverage object allocation). In addition to the optional aliases we discussed, there are several other options and properties that make up C++ allocators.

Learning the properties

C++ allocators must adhere to a certain set of properties, most of which are either obvious or easily adhered to.

The value pointer type

The first set of properties ensures that the pointer type returned by the allocator is, in fact, a pointer:

```
myallocator<myclass> myalloc;

myclass *ptr = myalloc.allocate(1);
const myclass *cptr = myalloc.allocate(1);

std::cout << (*ptr).data1 << '\n';
std::cout << (*cptr).data2 << '\n';

std::cout << ptr->data1 << '\n';
std::cout << cptr->data2 << '\n';

// 0
// 32644
// 0
// 32644
```

If the pointer returned by the allocator is truly a pointer, it's possible to dereference the pointer to access the memory it points to, as shown in the preceding example. It should also be noted that in this example, we get relatively random values returned when attempting to output the resulting allocated memory to `stdout`. This is because there is no requirement to zero memory from an allocator, as this operation is done for us by the container that uses this memory, which is more performant.

Equality

As stated previously, if an allocator is equal when compared, they return `true`, as shown here:

```cpp
myallocator<myclass> myalloc1;
myallocator<myclass> myalloc2;

std::cout << std::boolalpha;
std::cout << (myalloc1 == myalloc2) << '\n';
std::cout << (myalloc1 != myalloc2) << '\n';

// true
// false
```

If two allocators of the same type return `true`, it means a container that uses this allocator is free to allocate and deallocate memory with different instances of the same allocator freely, which ultimately enables the use of certain optimizations. For example, it's possible for a container to never actually store an internal reference to an allocator, and instead to create an allocator only when memory needs to be allocated. From that point on, the container manages memory internally, and only deallocates memory on destruction, at which time the container will create yet another allocator to perform deallocations, once again assuming the allocators are equal.

As we've covered, allocator equality usually correlates with statefulness. Typically, stateful allocators are not equal, while stateless allocators are equal; but this rule doesn't always hold true, especially when a copy is made of a stateful allocator, which is required by the spec to provide equality (or at least the ability to deallocate previously-allocated memory that was allocated from the copy). We will provide more details on this specific issue when we cover stateful allocators.

One issue with allocators prior to C++17 was that there was no easy way for a container to identify whether an allocator was equal, without first creating two instances of the same allocator at initialization, comparing them, and then setting the internal state based on the result. Due to this limitation in the C++ allocator concept, containers either assumed stateless allocators (which was the case with older versions of C++ libraries), or they assumed all allocators were stateful, removing the possibility of optimizations.

To overcome this, C++17 introduced the following:

```cpp
using is_always_equal = std::true_type;
```

If this is not provided by your allocator, as is the case with the preceding examples, the default value is `std::empty`, telling the container that the old-style comparisons are required to determine equality. If this alias is provided, the container will know how to optimize itself.

Different allocation types

How memory is allocated by a container depends entirely on the type of container, and as a result, an allocator must be able to support different allocation types, such as the following:

- All allocations by an allocator must be contiguous in memory. There is no requirement for one allocation to be contiguous in memory with another allocation, but each individual allocation must be contiguous.
- An allocator must be able to allocate more than one element in a single allocation. This can sometimes be problematic depending on the allocator.

To explore these properties, let's use the following example:

```
template<typename T>
class myallocator
{
public:

    using value_type = T;
    using pointer = T *;
    using size_type = std::size_t;
    using is_always_equal = std::true_type;

public:

    myallocator()
    {
        std::cout << this << " constructor, sizeof(T): "
                  << sizeof(T) << '\n';
    }

    template <typename U>
    myallocator(const myallocator<U> &other) noexcept
    { (void) other; }

    pointer allocate(size_type n)
    {
        if (auto ptr = static_cast<pointer>(malloc(sizeof(T) * n))) {
            std::cout << this << " A [" << n << "]: " << ptr << '\n';
            return ptr;
```

```
        }

        throw std::bad_alloc();
    }

    void deallocate(pointer p, size_type n)
    {
        (void) n;

        std::cout << this << " D [" << n << "]: " << p << '\n';
        free(p);
    }
};

template <typename T1, typename T2>
bool operator==(const myallocator<T1> &, const myallocator<T2> &)
{ return true; }

template <typename T1, typename T2>
bool operator!=(const myallocator<T1> &, const myallocator<T2> &)
{ return false; }
```

The preceding allocator is the same as the first allocator, with the exception that debugging statements were added to the constructors and the allocate and deallocate functions, allowing us to see how a container is allocating memory.

Let's examine a simple example of std::list:

```
std::list<int, myallocator<int>> mylist;
mylist.emplace_back(42);

// 0x7ffe97b0e8e0 constructor, sizeof(T): 24
// 0x7ffe97b0e8e0 A [1]: 0x55c0793e8580
// 0x7ffe97b0e8e0 D [1]: 0x55c0793e8580
```

As we can see, we have a single allocation and deallocation from the allocator. The allocator is allocating memory of 24 bytes even though the type provided was an int, which is of 4 bytes in size. This is because `std::list` allocates linked list nodes, which in this case are 24 bytes. The allocator is located at `0x7ffe97b0e8e0`, and the allocation was located at `0x55c0793e8580`. Also, as shown, the number of elements allocated each time the allocate function was called was one. This is because `std::list` implements a linked list, which does a dynamic allocation for each element added to the list. Although this seems extremely wasteful when a custom allocator is leveraged, this can be quite helpful when performing system programming as it is sometimes easier to work with memory when only one element is being allocated at a time (instead of multiple).

Now let's look at `std::vector`, as follows:

```
std::vector<int, myallocator<int>> myvector;
myvector.emplace_back(42);
myvector.emplace_back(42);
myvector.emplace_back(42);

// 0x7ffe1db8e2d0 constructor, sizeof(T): 4
// 0x7ffe1db8e2d0 A [1]: 0x55bf9dbdd550
// 0x7ffe1db8e2d0 A [2]: 0x55bf9dbebe90
// 0x7ffe1db8e2d0 D [1]: 0x55bf9dbdd550
// 0x7ffe1db8e2d0 A [4]: 0x55bf9dbdd550
// 0x7ffe1db8e2d0 D [2]: 0x55bf9dbebe90
// 0x7ffe1db8e2d0 D [4]: 0x55bf9dbdd550
```

In the preceding example, we create `std::vector` with our customer allocator, and then, unlike the previous example, we add three integers to the vector instead of one. This is because `std::vector` has to maintain contiguous memory regardless of the number of elements in the vector (which is one of the main properties of `std::vector`). As a result, if `std::vector` fills up (that is, runs out of memory), `std::vector` must allocate a completely new, contiguous block of memory for all of the elements in `std::vector`, copy `std::vector` from the old memory to the new memory, and then deallocate the previous block of memory as it is no longer large enough.

To demonstrate how this works, we add three elements to `std::vector`:

- The first element allocates a block of memory that is four bytes in size (`n == 1` and `sizeof(T) == 4`).
- The second time we add data to `std::vector`, the current block of memory is full (as only four bytes were allocated the first time around), so `std::vector` must deallocate this previously-allocated memory, allocate a new block of memory, and then copy the old contents of `std::vector`. This time around, however, the allocation sets `n == 2`, so eight bytes are allocated.
- The third time we add an element, `std::vector` is out of memory again, and the process is repeated but with `n == 4`, which means that 16 bytes are allocated.

As a side note, the first allocation starts at `0x55bf9dbdd550`, which also happens to be the location of the third allocation. This is because `malloc()` is allocating memory that is aligned to 16 bytes, which means that the first allocation, although only 4 bytes in size, actually allocated 16 bytes, which would have been enough for `n == 4` in the first place (that is, the implementation of `std::vector` provided by GCC could use an optimization). Since the first allocation is deallocated the second time memory is added to the `std::vector`, this memory is free to be used for the third time an element is used, as the original allocation is still large enough for the requested amount.

It is obvious looking at how the allocator is used, that unless you actually need contiguous memory, `std::vector` is not a good choice for storing a list, as it is slow. `std::list`, however, takes up a lot of additional memory, as each element is 24 bytes, instead of 4. The next and final container to observe is `std::deque`, which finds a happy medium between `std::vector` and `std::list`:

```
std::deque<int, myallocator<int>> mydeque;
mydeque.emplace_back(42);
mydeque.emplace_back(42);
mydeque.emplace_back(42);

// constructor, sizeof(T): 4
// 0x7ffdea986e67 A [8]: 0x55d6822b0da0
// 0x7ffdea986f30 A [128]: 0x55d6822afaf0
// 0x7ffdea986f30 D [128]: 0x55d6822afaf0
// 0x7ffdea986e67 D [8]: 0x55d6822b0da0
```

`std::deque` creates a linked list of memory blocks that can be used to store more than one element. In other words, `std::deque` is a `std::list` of `std::vectors`. Like `std::list`, memory is not contiguous, but like `std::vector`, each element only consumes four bytes and a dynamic memory allocation is not needed for each element added. As shown, `sizeof(T) == 4` bytes, and during the creation of `std::deque`, a large buffer of memory is allocated to store several elements (`128` elements, to be specific). The second, smaller allocation is used for internal bookkeeping.

To further explore `std::deque`, let's add a lot of elements to `std::deque`:

```
std::deque<int, myallocator<int>> mydeque;

for (auto i = 0; i < 127; i++)
    mydeque.emplace_back(42);

for (auto i = 0; i < 127; i++)
    mydeque.emplace_back(42);

for (auto i = 0; i < 127; i++)
    mydeque.emplace_back(42);

// constructor, sizeof(T): 4
// 0x7ffc5926b1b7 A [8]: 0x560285cc0da0
// 0x7ffc5926b280 A [128]: 0x560285cbfaf0
// 0x7ffc5926b280 A [128]: 0x560285cc1660
// 0x7ffc5926b280 A [128]: 0x560285cc1bc0
// 0x7ffc5926b280 D [128]: 0x560285cbfaf0
// 0x7ffc5926b280 D [128]: 0x560285cc1660
// 0x7ffc5926b280 D [128]: 0x560285cc1bc0
// 0x7ffc5926b1b7 D [8]: 0x560285cc0da0
```

In the preceding example, we add `127` elements three times. This is because each allocation allocates enough for `128` elements, with one of the elements being used for bookkeeping. As shown, `std::deque` allocates three blocks of memory.

Copying equal allocators

Copying containers with allocators that are equal is straightforward—this is because the allocators are interchangeable. To explore this, let's add the following overloads to the previous allocator so that we may observe additional operations taking place:

```
myallocator(myallocator &&other) noexcept
{
    (void) other;
    std::cout << this << " move constructor, sizeof(T): "
```

```
                            << sizeof(T) << '\n';
    }

    myallocator &operator=(myallocator &&other) noexcept
    {
        (void) other;
        std::cout << this << " move assignment, sizeof(T): "
                  << sizeof(T) << '\n';
        return *this;
    }

    myallocator(const myallocator &other) noexcept
    {
        (void) other;
        std::cout << this << " copy constructor, sizeof(T): "
                  << sizeof(T) << '\n';
    }

    myallocator &operator=(const myallocator &other) noexcept
    {
        (void) other;
        std::cout << this << " copy assignment, sizeof(T): "
                  << sizeof(T) << '\n';
        return *this;
    }
```

The preceding code adds a copy constructor, `copy assignment` operator, move constructor, and a `move assignment` operator, all of which have debug statements so that we may see what the container is doing. With the preceding addition, we will be able to see when a copy of an allocator is performed. Now let's use this allocator in a container that is copied:

```
std::list<int, myallocator<int>> mylist1;
std::list<int, myallocator<int>> mylist2;

mylist1.emplace_back(42);
mylist1.emplace_back(42);

std::cout << "----------------------------------------\n";
mylist2 = mylist1;
std::cout << "----------------------------------------\n";

mylist2.emplace_back(42);
mylist2.emplace_back(42);
```

In the preceding example, we create two lists. In the first `std::list`, we add two elements to the list and then we copy the list to the second `std::list`. Finally, we add two more elements to the second `std::list`. The output is as follows:

```
0x7fff866d1e50 constructor, sizeof(T): 24
0x7fff866d1e70 constructor, sizeof(T): 24
0x7fff866d1e50 A [1]: 0x557c430ec550
0x7fff866d1e50 A [1]: 0x557c430fae90
----------------------------------------
0x7fff866d1d40 copy constructor, sizeof(T): 24
0x7fff866d1d40 A [1]: 0x557c430e39a0
0x7fff866d1d40 A [1]: 0x557c430f14a0
----------------------------------------
0x7fff866d1e70 A [1]: 0x557c430f3b30
0x7fff866d1e70 A [1]: 0x557c430ec4d0
0x7fff866d1e70 D [1]: 0x557c430e39a0
0x7fff866d1e70 D [1]: 0x557c430f14a0
0x7fff866d1e70 D [1]: 0x557c430f3b30
0x7fff866d1e70 D [1]: 0x557c430ec4d0
0x7fff866d1e50 D [1]: 0x557c430ec550
0x7fff866d1e50 D [1]: 0x557c430fae90
```

As expected, each list creates the allocator that it plans to use, and the allocators create `std::list` nodes of 24 bytes. We then see the first allocator allocate memory for the two elements that are added to the first list. The second list is still empty just prior to copying the first list and, as a result, the second container creates a third, temporary allocator that it can use solely for copying the lists. Once this is done, we add the final two elements to the second list, and we can see the second list uses its original allocator to perform the allocations.

`std::list` is free to allocate memory from one allocator and deallocate from another, and this is seen in the deallocations, which is why `std::list` creates a temporary allocator during the copy, as it is free to do so. Whether a container should create temporary allocators is not the point (although it is likely a debatable optimization).

Moving equal allocators

Moving a container is similar to copying a container if the allocators are equal. Once again, this is because there are no rules as to what the container has to do, since a container can use its original allocator to handle any memory, and if it needs to, it can create a new allocator, as follows:

```
std::list<int, myallocator<int>> mylist1;
std::list<int, myallocator<int>> mylist2;
```

```
mylist1.emplace_back(42);
mylist1.emplace_back(42);

std::cout << "-------------------------------------------\n";
mylist2 = std::move(mylist1);
std::cout << "-------------------------------------------\n";

mylist2.emplace_back(42);
mylist2.emplace_back(42);
```

In the preceding example, instead of copying the first container, we move it instead. As a result, the first container after the move is no longer valid, and the second container now owns the memory from the first container.

The output of this example is as follows:

```
0x7ffe582e2850 constructor, sizeof(T): 24
0x7ffe582e2870 constructor, sizeof(T): 24
0x7ffe582e2850 A [1]: 0x56229562d550
0x7ffe582e2850 A [1]: 0x56229563be90
-------------------------------------------
-------------------------------------------
0x7ffe582e2870 A [1]: 0x5622956249a0
0x7ffe582e2870 A [1]: 0x5622956324a0
0x7ffe582e2870 D [1]: 0x56229562d550
0x7ffe582e2870 D [1]: 0x56229563be90
0x7ffe582e2870 D [1]: 0x5622956249a0
0x7ffe582e2870 D [1]: 0x5622956324a0
```

Similar to the copy example, the two lists are created and each std::list creates an allocator that manages the std::list nodes of 24 bytes. Two elements are added to the first list, and then the first list is moved into the second list. As a result, memory that belongs to the first list is now owned by the second container and no copies are performed. The second allocations to the second list are performed by its own allocator, as are all deallocations, since allocations from the first allocator can be deallocated using the second allocator.

Exploring some optional properties

C++ allocators provide some additional properties that are above and beyond `is_always_equal`. Specifically, the author of a C++ allocator can optionally define the following:

- `propagate_on_container_copy_assignment`
- `propagate_on_container_move_assignment`
- `propagate_on_container_swap`

The optional properties tell a container how the allocator should be handled during a specific operation (that is, copy, move, and swap). Specifically, when a container is copied, moved, or swapped, the allocator isn't touched and, as we will show, this can result in inefficiencies. The propagate properties tell the container to propagate the operation to the allocator. For example, if `propagate_on_container_copy_assignment` is set to `std::true_type` and a container is being copied, the allocator must also be copied when normally it wouldn't be.

To better explore these properties, let's create our first unequal allocator (that is, two different instances of the same allocator may not be equal). As stated, most allocators that are unequal are stateful. In this example, we will create a stateless, unequal allocator to keep things simple. Our last example in this chapter will create an unequal, stateful allocator.

To start our example, we first need to create a managed object for our allocator class, as follows:

```
class myallocator_object
{
public:

    using size_type = std::size_t;

public:

    void *allocate(size_type size)
    {
        if (auto ptr = malloc(size)) {
            std::cout << this << " A " << ptr << '\n';
            return ptr;
        }

        throw std::bad_alloc();
    }
```

```
        void deallocate(void *ptr)
        {
            std::cout << this << " D " << ptr << '\n';
            free(ptr);
        }
    };
```

Unequal allocators must adhere to the following properties:

- All copies of an allocator must be equal. This means that even if we create an unequal allocator, a copy of an allocator must still be equal. This becomes problematic when the rebind copy constructor is used, as this property still holds true (that is, even though two allocators may not have the same type, they may still have to be equal if one is the copy of another).
- All equal allocators must be able to deallocate each other's memory. Once again, this becomes problematic when the rebind copy constructor is used. Specifically, this means that an allocator managing int objects might have to deallocate memory from an allocator managing std::list nodes.

To support these two rules, most unequal allocators end up being wrappers around a managed object. That is, an object is created that can allocate and deallocate memory and each allocator stores a pointer to this object. In the preceding example, myallocator_object{} is the managed object capable of allocating and deallocating memory. To create this object, all we did was move malloc() and free() from the allocator itself into this myallocator_object{}; the code is the same. The only additional logic that was added to myallocator_object{} is the following:

- The constructor takes a size. This is because we cannot create the managed object as a template class. Specifically, the managed object needs to be able to change the type of memory that it manages (because of the rules outlined). The specific need for this will be covered shortly.
- A rebind() function was added that specifically changes the size of the memory being managed by the managed object. Once again, this allows us to change the size of the allocation being performed by myallocator_object{}.

Next, we need to define the allocator itself, as follows:

```
template<typename T>
class myallocator
{
```

The first part of the allocator is the same as the other allocators, requiring the use of a template class that allocators memory for some T type:

```
public:

    using value_type = T;
    using pointer = T *;
    using size_type = std::size_t;
    using is_always_equal = std::false_type;
```

The next part of our allocator defines our type aliases and optional properties. As shown, all three propagate functions are undefined, which tells any container that uses this allocator that when a copy, move, or swap of the container occurs, the allocator is not copied, moved, or swapped as well (the container should continue using the same allocator it was given at construction).

The next set of functions defines our constructors and operators. Let's start with the default constructor:

```
myallocator() :
    m_object{std::make_shared<myallocator_object>()}
{
    std::cout << this << " constructor, sizeof(T): "
              << sizeof(T) << '\n';
}
```

As with all of the constructors and operators, we output to stdout some debug information so that we can watch what the container is doing with the allocator. As shown, the default constructor allocates `myallocator_object{}` and stores it as `std::shared_ptr`. We leverage `std::shared_ptr`, as each copy of the allocator will have to be equal, and as a result, each copy must share the same managed object (so that memory allocated from one allocator can be deallocated from the copy). Since either allocator could be destroyed at any type, both *own* the managed object and as a result, `std::shared_ptr` is the more appropriate smart pointer.

The next two functions are the move constructor and assignment operator:

```
myallocator(myallocator &&other) noexcept :
    m_object{std::move(other.m_object)}
{
    std::cout << this << " move constructor, sizeof(T): "
              << sizeof(T) << '\n';
}

myallocator &operator=(myallocator &&other) noexcept
{
```

```
            std::cout << this << " move assignment, sizeof(T): "
                      << sizeof(T) << '\n';

    m_object = std::move(other.m_object);
    return *this;
}
```

In both cases, we need to `std::move()` our managed object as a result of a move operation. The same thing applies for copying as well:

```
myallocator(const myallocator &other) noexcept :
    m_object{other.m_object}
{
    std::cout << this << " copy constructor, sizeof(T): "
              << sizeof(T) << '\n';
}

myallocator &operator=(const myallocator &other) noexcept
{
    std::cout << this << " copy assignment, sizeof(T): "
              << sizeof(T) << '\n';

    m_object = other.m_object;
    return *this;
}
```

As shown, if a copy is made of the allocator, we must also copy the managed object. As a result, a copy of the allocator leverages the same managed object, which means that the copy can deallocate memory from the original.

The next function is what makes unequal allocators so difficult:

```
template <typename U>
myallocator(const myallocator<U> &other) noexcept :
    m_object{other.m_object}
{
    std::cout << this << " copy constructor (U), sizeof(T): "
              << sizeof(T) << '\n';
}
```

The preceding function is the rebind copy constructor. The point of this constructor is to create a copy of another allocator of a different type. So for example, `std::list` starts off with `myallocator<int>{}`, but it really needs an allocator of the `myallocator<std::list::node>{}` type, not `myallocator<int>{}`. To overcome this, the preceding function allows a container to do something like the following:

```
myallocator<int> alloc1;
myallocator<std::list::node> alloc2(alloc1);
```

In the preceding example, `alloc2` is a copy of `alloc1`, even though `alloc1` and `alloc2` do not share the same `T` type. The problem is, an `int` is four bytes, while in our examples, `std::list::node` has been 24 bytes, which means that not only does the preceding function have to be able to create a copy of an allocator with a different type that is *equal*, it also has to be able to create a copy that is capable of deallocating memory of a different type (specifically, in this case, `alloc2` has to be able to deallocate ints even though it manages `std::list::node` elements). In our example, this is not a problem since we are using `malloc()` and `free()`, but as we will show in our last example, some stateful allocators, such as a memory pool, do not conform well to this requirement.

The `allocate` and `deallocate` functions are defined as follows:

```
pointer allocate(size_type n)
{
    auto ptr = m_object->allocate(sizeof(T) * n);
    return static_cast<pointer>(ptr);
}

void deallocate(pointer p, size_type n)
{
    (void) n;
    return m_object->deallocate(p);
}
```

Since our managed object just calls `malloc()` and `free()`, we can treat the object's `allocate()` and `deallocate()` functions as `malloc()` and `free()` as well, and as such, the implementation is simple.

Our private logic in the `allocator` class is as follows:

```
std::shared_ptr<myallocator_object> m_object;

template <typename T1, typename T2>
friend bool operator==(const myallocator<T1> &lhs, const myallocator<T2> &rhs);
```

```
template <typename T1, typename T2>
friend bool operator!=(const myallocator<T1> &lhs, const myallocator<T2>
&rhs);
```

As stated, we store a smart pointer to the managed object, which allows us to create copies of the allocator. We also state that our equality functions are friends, and although we place these friend functions in the private portion of the class, we could have placed them anywhere as friend declarations are not affected by public/protected/private declarations.

Finally, the equality functions are as follows:

```
template <typename T1, typename T2>
bool operator==(const myallocator<T1> &lhs, const myallocator<T2> &rhs)
{ return lhs.m_object.get() == rhs.m_object.get(); }

template <typename T1, typename T2>
bool operator!=(const myallocator<T1> &lhs, const myallocator<T2> &rhs)
{ return lhs.m_object.get() != rhs.m_object.get(); }
```

Our *equal* allocator example simply returned true for `operator==` and false for `operator!=`, which stated that the allocators were equal (in addition to the use of `is_always_equal`). In this example, `is_always_equal` is set to `false`, and in our equality operators, we compare the managed objects. Each time a new allocator is created, a new managed object is created, and as a result, the allocators are not equal (that is, they are unequal allocators). The problem is, we cannot simply always return `false` for `operator==` because a copy of an allocator must always be equal to the original per the specification, which is the reason we use `std::shared_ptr`. Each copy of the allocator creates a copy of `std::shared_ptr`, and since we compare the address of the managed object if a copy of the allocator is made, the copy and the original have the same managed object and as a result, return `true` (that is, they are equal). Although `std::shared_ptr` may not be used, most unequal allocators are implemented this way, as it provides a simple way to handle the difference between equal and unequal allocators based on whether or not the allocator has been copied.

Now that we have an allocator, let's test it:

```
std::list<int, myallocator<int>> mylist;
mylist.emplace_back(42);

// 0x7ffce60fbd10 constructor, sizeof(T): 24
// 0x561feb431590 A [1]: 0x561feb43fec0
// 0x561feb431590 D [1]: 0x561feb43fec0
```

As you can see, our allocator is capable of allocating and deallocating memory. The allocator in the preceding example was located at `0x561feb431590`, and the element that was allocated by the `std::list` container was located at `0x561feb43fec0`.

Copying an unequal container that has the propagate property set to `false` is simple, as follows:

```
std::list<int, myallocator<int>> mylist1;
std::list<int, myallocator<int>> mylist2;

mylist1.emplace_back(42);
mylist1.emplace_back(42);

mylist2.emplace_back(42);
mylist2.emplace_back(42);

std::cout << "---------------------------------------\n";
mylist2 = mylist1;
std::cout << "---------------------------------------\n";

mylist2.emplace_back(42);
mylist2.emplace_back(42);
```

As shown in the preceding example, we create two lists and populate both lists with two elements each. Once the lists are populated, we then copy the first container into the second, and we output to `stdout` so that we can see how the container handles this copy. Finally, we add two more elements to the just-copied container.

The output of this example is as follows:

```
// 0x7ffd65a15cb0 constructor, sizeof(T): 24
// 0x7ffd65a15ce0 constructor, sizeof(T): 24
// 0x55c4867c3a80 A [1]: 0x55c4867b9210  <--- add to list #1
// 0x55c4867c3a80 A [1]: 0x55c4867baec0  <--- add to list #1
// 0x55c4867d23c0 A [1]: 0x55c4867c89c0  <--- add to list #2
// 0x55c4867d23c0 A [1]: 0x55c4867cb050  <--- add to list #2
// ---------------------------------------
// ---------------------------------------
// 0x55c4867d23c0 A [1]: 0x55c4867c39f0  <--- add to list #2 after copy
// 0x55c4867d23c0 A [1]: 0x55c4867c3a10  <--- add to list #2 after copy
// 0x55c4867d23c0 D [1]: 0x55c4867c89c0  <--- deallocate list #2
// 0x55c4867d23c0 D [1]: 0x55c4867cb050  <--- deallocate list #2
// 0x55c4867d23c0 D [1]: 0x55c4867c39f0  <--- deallocate list #2
// 0x55c4867d23c0 D [1]: 0x55c4867c3a10  <--- deallocate list #2
// 0x55c4867c3a80 D [1]: 0x55c4867b9210  <--- deallocate list #1
// 0x55c4867c3a80 D [1]: 0x55c4867baec0  <--- deallocate list #1
```

As shown, copying the containers does not involve the allocator. When the copy occurs, list two keeps the two allocations it already has, overwriting the values for the first two elements. Since the propagate properties are `false`, the second container keeps the allocator it was originally given, and uses the allocator to allocate the second two elements after the copy, but also deallocate all of the previously-allocated elements when the list loses scope.

The problem with this approach is the need for the container to loop through each element and perform a manual copy. For integers, this type of copy is fine, but we could have stored large structures in the list and as a result, copying the containers would have resulted in copying each element in the container, which is wasteful and expensive. Since the propagate property is `false`, the container has no choice as it cannot use the allocator from the first list and it cannot use its own allocator to copy the elements allocated in the first list (since the allocators are not equal). Although this is wasteful, as will be shown, this approach may still be the fastest approach.

Moving a list has a similar issue:

```
std::list<int, myallocator<int>> mylist1;
std::list<int, myallocator<int>> mylist2;

mylist1.emplace_back(42);
mylist1.emplace_back(42);

mylist2.emplace_back(42);
mylist2.emplace_back(42);

std::cout << "---------------------------------------\n";
mylist2 = std::move(mylist1);
std::cout << "---------------------------------------\n";

mylist2.emplace_back(42);
mylist2.emplace_back(42);
```

In the preceding example, we do the same thing we did in the previous example. We create two lists, and add two elements to each list just before moving one list to another.

The results of this example are as follows:

```
// 0x7ffd65a15cb0 constructor, sizeof(T): 24
// 0x7ffd65a15ce0 constructor, sizeof(T): 24
// 0x55c4867c3a80 A [1]: 0x55c4867c3a10  <--- add to list #1
// 0x55c4867c3a80 A [1]: 0x55c4867c39f0  <--- add to list #1
// 0x55c4867d23c0 A [1]: 0x55c4867c0170  <--- add to list #2
// 0x55c4867d23c0 A [1]: 0x55c4867c0190  <--- add to list #2
// ---------------------------------------
```

```
// ----------------------------------------
// 0x55c4867d23c0 A [1]: 0x55c4867b9c90  <--- add to list #2 after move
// 0x55c4867d23c0 A [1]: 0x55c4867b9cb0  <--- add to list #2 after move
// 0x55c4867d23c0 D [1]: 0x55c4867c0170  <--- deallocate list #2
// 0x55c4867d23c0 D [1]: 0x55c4867c0190  <--- deallocate list #2
// 0x55c4867d23c0 D [1]: 0x55c4867b9c90  <--- deallocate list #2
// 0x55c4867d23c0 D [1]: 0x55c4867b9cb0  <--- deallocate list #2
// 0x55c4867c3a80 D [1]: 0x55c4867c3a10  <--- deallocate list #1
// 0x55c4867c3a80 D [1]: 0x55c4867c39f0  <--- deallocate list #1
```

In the preceding example, we can see that the same inefficiency exists. Since the propagate property is `false`, the container cannot use the allocator from the first list and instead, must continue to use the allocator that it already has. As a result, the move operation cannot simply move the internal container from one list to another, but instead it must loop through the entire container, executing `std::move()` on each individual element such that the memory associated with each node in the list is still managed by the second list's original allocator.

To overcome these issues, we will add the following to our allocator:

```
using propagate_on_container_copy_assignment = std::true_type;
using propagate_on_container_move_assignment = std::true_type;
using propagate_on_container_swap = std::true_type;
```

These properties tell any container that uses this allocator that if a copy, move, or swap of the container occurs, the same operation should occur with the allocator. For example, if we copy `std::list`, the container must not only *copy* the elements, but it should also copy the allocator.

Let's look at the following copy example:

```
std::list<int, myallocator<int>> mylist1;
std::list<int, myallocator<int>> mylist2;

mylist1.emplace_back(42);
mylist1.emplace_back(42);

mylist2.emplace_back(42);
mylist2.emplace_back(42);

std::cout << "----------------------------------------\n";
mylist2 = mylist1;
std::cout << "----------------------------------------\n";

mylist2.emplace_back(42);
mylist2.emplace_back(42);
```

This copy example is the same as our previous copy example. We create two lists and add two elements to each list. We then copy the first list into the second list and then add two additional elements into the second list before finishing (which ultimately will deallocate the lists).

The results of this example are as follows. It should be noted that this output is a bit more complicated, so we will take this one step at a time:

```
// 0x7ffc766ec580 constructor, sizeof(T): 24
// 0x7ffc766ec5b0 constructor, sizeof(T): 24
// 0x5638419d9720 A [1]: 0x5638419d0b60  <--- add to list #1
// 0x5638419d9720 A [1]: 0x5638419de660  <--- add to list #1
// 0x5638419e8060 A [1]: 0x5638419e0cf0  <--- add to list #2
// 0x5638419e8060 A [1]: 0x5638419d9690  <--- add to list #2
```

In the preceding output, both lists are created and two elements are added to each container. Next, the output will show what happens when we copy the second container into the first:

```
// 0x5638419e8060 D [1]: 0x5638419e0cf0
// 0x5638419e8060 D [1]: 0x5638419d9690
// 0x7ffc766ec5b0 copy assignment, sizeof(T): 24
// 0x7ffc766ec450 copy constructor (U), sizeof(T): 4
// 0x7ffc766ec3f0 copy constructor (U), sizeof(T): 24
// 0x7ffc766ec460 copy constructor, sizeof(T): 24
// 0x5638419d9720 A [1]: 0x5638419e8050
// 0x5638419d9720 A [1]: 0x5638419d9690
```

Since we set the propagate property to `false`, the container now has the option to keep the memory used by the first container (for example, to implement a copy-on-write implementation). This is because the container should create a copy of the allocator and any two copies of an allocator are equal (that is, they can deallocate each other's memory). This implementation of glibc does not do this. Instead, it attempts to create a clean view of memory. The two lists, allocators are not equal, which means that once the copy has taken place, the container will no longer be able to deallocate its own, previously-allocated memory (because it will likely no longer have access to its original allocator). As a result, the container deletes all of the memory it previously allocated as its first step. It then creates a temporary allocator using a rebind copy of the first list's allocator (which oddly seems to be unused), just before creating a direct copy of the first list's allocator and using it to allocator new memory for the elements that will be copied.

Finally, now that the copy is complete, the last two elements can be added to the second list, and each list can be destroyed once they lose scope:

```
// 0x5638419d9720 A [1]: 0x5638419d96b0  <--- add to list #2 after copy
// 0x5638419d9720 A [1]: 0x5638419d5e10  <--- add to list #2 after copy
// 0x5638419d9720 D [1]: 0x5638419e8050  <--- deallocate list #2
// 0x5638419d9720 D [1]: 0x5638419d9690  <--- deallocate list #2
// 0x5638419d9720 D [1]: 0x5638419d96b0  <--- deallocate list #2
// 0x5638419d9720 D [1]: 0x5638419d5e10  <--- deallocate list #2
// 0x5638419d9720 D [1]: 0x5638419d0b60  <--- deallocate list #1
// 0x5638419d9720 D [1]: 0x5638419de660  <--- deallocate list #1
```

As shown, since the allocator was propagated, the same allocator is used to deallocate the elements from both lists. This is because once the copy is complete, both lists are now using the same allocator (as a copy of any two allocators must be equal, and the way that we chose to implement this was to create a copy of the same base allocator object when a copy occurs). It should also be noted that the glibc implementation does not choose to implement a copy-on-write scheme, which means not only that the implementation fails to take advantage of the possible optimizations that the propagate property provides, but the implementation of a copy is actually slower, as the copy not only has to copy each element one at a time, but must also allocate new memory for the copy as well.

Now let's look at a move example:

```
std::list<int, myallocator<int>> mylist1;
std::list<int, myallocator<int>> mylist2;

mylist1.emplace_back(42);
mylist1.emplace_back(42);

mylist2.emplace_back(42);
mylist2.emplace_back(42);

std::cout << "-------------------------------------------\n";
mylist2 = std::move(mylist1);
std::cout << "-------------------------------------------\n";

mylist2.emplace_back(42);
mylist2.emplace_back(42);
```

Like our previous move example, this creates two lists, and adds two elements to each list just before moving the first list into the second. Finally, our example adds two elements to the second list (which is now the first list), before completing and deallocating both lists when they lose scope.

The resulting output of this example is as follows:

```
// 0x7ffc766ec580 constructor, sizeof(T): 24
// 0x7ffc766ec5b0 constructor, sizeof(T): 24
// 0x5638419d9720 A [1]: 0x5638419d96b0  <--- add to list #1
// 0x5638419d9720 A [1]: 0x5638419d9690  <--- add to list #1
// 0x5638419d5e20 A [1]: 0x5638419e8050  <--- add to list #2
// 0x5638419d5e20 A [1]: 0x5638419d5e30  <--- add to list #2
// ------------------------------------
// 0x5638419d5e20 D [1]: 0x5638419e8050  <--- deallocate list #2
// 0x5638419d5e20 D [1]: 0x5638419d5e30  <--- deallocate list #2
// 0x7ffc766ec5b0 move assignment, sizeof(T): 24
// ------------------------------------
// 0x5638419d9720 A [1]: 0x5638419d5e10
// 0x5638419d9720 A [1]: 0x5638419e8050
// 0x5638419d9720 D [1]: 0x5638419d96b0  <--- deallocate list #1
// 0x5638419d9720 D [1]: 0x5638419d9690  <--- deallocate list #1
// 0x5638419d9720 D [1]: 0x5638419d5e10  <--- deallocate list #2
// 0x5638419d9720 D [1]: 0x5638419e8050  <--- deallocate list #2
```

Like the previous examples, you can see the lists being created and the first elements being added to each list. Once the move occurs, the second list deletes the memory associated with its previously-added elements. This is because once the move occurs, the memory associated with the second list is no longer needed (as it is about to be replaced with the memory allocated by the first list). This is possible since the first list's allocator will be moved to the second list (since the propagate property was set to `true`), and as a result, the second list will now own all of the first list's memory.

Finally, the last two elements are added to the list and the lists lose scope and deallocate all of their memory. As shown, this is the most optimal implementation. No additional memory is allocated no element-by-element move is needed. The move operation simply moves the memory and allocator from one container to the other. Also, since no copy of the allocators is made, this is a simple operation for any allocator to support, and as such, this property should always be set to true.

Optional functions

In addition to properties, there are several optional functions that provide containers with additional information about the type of allocator they are provided. One optional function is the following:

```
size_type myallocator::max_size();
```

The `max_size()` function tells the container the max size, "n", that an allocator can allocate. In C++17, this function has been deprecated. The `max_size()` function returns the largest possible allocation that the allocator can perform. Curiously, in C++17, this defaults to `std::numeric_limits<size_type>::max() / sizeof(value_type)`, which in most cases is likely not a valid answer as most systems simply do not have this much available RAM, suggesting this function provides little value in practice. Instead, like other allocation schemes in C++, `std::bad_alloc` will be thrown if and when an allocation fails, indicating to the container that the allocation it attempted to perform is not possible.

Another set of optional functions in C++ is the following:

```
template<typename T, typename... Args>
static void myallocator::construct(T* ptr, Args&&... args);

template<typename T>
static void myallocator::destroy(T* ptr);
```

Just like with the `max_size()` function, the construct and destruct functions were deprecated in C++17. Prior to C++17, these functions could be used to construct and destruct the object associated with the provided by `ptr`. It should be noted that this is why we do not use new and delete when allocating memory in a constructor, but instead use `malloc()` and `free()`. If we were to use `new()` and `delete()`, we would accidentally call the constructor and/or destructor of the object twice, which would lead to undefined behavior.

Studying an example of stateless, cache–aligned allocator

In this example, we will create a stateless, equal allocator designed to allocator cache-aligned memory. The goal of this allocator is to show a C++17 allocator that can be leveraged to increase the efficiency of the objects a container is storing (for example, a linked list), as cache-thrashing is less likely to occur.

To start, we will define the allocator as follows:

```
template<typename T, std::size_t Alignment = 0x40>
class myallocator
{
public:

    using value_type = T;
    using pointer = T *;
```

```
            using size_type = std::size_t;
            using is_always_equal = std::true_type;

            template<typename U> struct rebind {
                using other = myallocator<U, Alignment>;
            };

    public:

            myallocator()
            { }

            template <typename U>
            myallocator(const myallocator<U, Alignment> &other) noexcept
            { (void) other; }

            pointer allocate(size_type n)
            {
                if (auto ptr = aligned_alloc(Alignment, sizeof(T) * n)) {
                    return static_cast<pointer>(ptr);
                }

                throw std::bad_alloc();
            }

            void deallocate(pointer p, size_type n)
            {
                (void) n;
                free(p);
            }
    };
```

The preceding allocator is similar to the other equal allocators that we have created in this chapter. There are a couple of notable differences:

- The template signature of the allocator is different. Instead of just defining the allocator type T, we also added an `Alignment` parameter and set the default value to `0x40` (that is, the allocations will be 64-byte-aligned, which is the typical size of a cache line on Intel CPUs).
- We also provide our own rebind structure. Typically, this structure is provided for us, but since our allocator has more than one template argument, we must provide our own version of the rebind structure. This structure is used by a container, such as `std::list`, to create any allocator the container needs without having to create a copy (instead, it can directly create an allocator during initialization). In our version of this rebind structure, we pass the `Alignment` parameter that is provided by the original allocator.

- The rebind copy constructor must also define the `Alignment` variable. In this case, we force the `Alignment` to be the same if a rebind is going to occur, which will be the case as the rebind structure provides the `Alignment` (which is also the same).

To test our example, let's create the allocator and output the address of an allocation to ensure that the memory is aligned:

```
myallocator<int> myalloc;

auto ptr = myalloc.allocate(1);
std::cout << ptr << '\n';
myalloc.deallocate(ptr, 1);

// 0x561d512b6500
```

As shown, the memory that was allocated is at least 64-byte-aligned. The same thing is true for multiple allocations, as follows:

```
myallocator<int> myalloc;

auto ptr = myalloc.allocate(42);
std::cout << ptr << '\n';
myalloc.deallocate(ptr, 42);

// 0x55dcdcb41500
```

As shown, the memory allocated is also at least 64-byte-aligned. We can also use this allocator with a container:

```
std::vector<int, myallocator<int>> myvector;
myvector.emplace_back(42);

std::cout << myvector.data() << '\n';

// 0x55f875a0f500
```

And once again, the memory is still properly aligned.

Compiling and testing

To compile this code, we leverage the same `CMakeLists.txt` file that we have been using for the other examples: https://github.com/PacktPublishing/Hands-On-System-Programming-with-CPP/blob/master/Chapter09/CMakeLists.txt.

With this code in place, we can compile this code using the following:

```
> git clone
https://github.com/PacktPublishing/Hands-On-System-Programming-with-CPP.git
> cd Hands-On-System-Programming-with-CPP/Chapter09/
> mkdir build
> cd build

> cmake ..
> make
```

To execute the example, run the following command:

```
> ./example6
```

The output should resemble the following:

```
0x55aec04dbd00
0x55aec04e8f40
0x55aec04d5d00
===========================================================================
====
test cases: 3 | 3 passed
assertions: - none -
```

As shown in the preceding snippet, we are able to allocate different types of memory, as well as deallocate this memory and all of the addresses are 64-byte-aligned.

Studying an example of a stateful, memory–pool allocator

In this example, we will create a far more complicated allocator, called a **pool allocator**. The goal of the pool allocator is to quickly allocate memory for a fixed-size type while simultaneously (and more importantly) reducing internal fragmentation of memory (that is, the amount of memory that is wasted by each allocation, even if the allocation size is not a multiple of two or some other optimized allocation size).

Memory-pool allocators are so useful that some implementations of C++ already contain pool allocators. In addition, C++17 technically has support for a pool allocator in something called a **polymorphic allocator** (which is not covered in this book, as no major implementations of C++17 have support for polymorphic allocators at the time of writing), and most operating systems leverage pool allocators within the kernel to reduce internal fragmentation.

The major advantages of a pool allocator are as follows:

- The use of `malloc()` is slow. Sometimes `free()` is slow too, but for some implementations, `free()` is as simple as flipping a bit, in which case it can be implemented incredibly fast.
- Most pool allocators leverage a deque structure, meaning the pool allocator allocates a large *block* of memory and then divides this memory up for allocations. Each *block* of memory is linked using a linked list so that more memory can be added to the pool as needed.

Pool allocators also have an interesting property where the larger the block size, the larger the reduction is on internal fragmentation. The penalty for this optimization is that if the pool is not completely utilized, the amount of memory that is wasted increases as the block size increases, so pool allocators should be tailored to meet the needs of the application.

To start our example, we will first create a `pool` class that manages a list of *blocks* and gives out memory from the blocks. The list of blocks will be stored in a stack that grows forever (that is, in this example, we will attempt to defragment the memory in the blocks, or remove a block from the stack if all memory from the block has been freed). Each time we add a block of memory to the pool, we will divide up the block into chunks of the size of `sizeof(T)`, and add the address of each chunk onto a second stack called the address stack. When memory is allocated, we will pop an address off the address stack, and when memory is deallocated, we will push the address back onto the stack.

The beginning of our pool is as follows:

```
class pool
{
public:

    using size_type = std::size_t;

public:

    explicit pool(size_type size) :
        m_size{size}
    { }
```

The pool will act as our managed object for our unequal allocator, as was the case with our previous unequal allocator example. As a result, the pool is not a template class, as we will need to change the size of the pool if the rebind copy constructor is used (more on that specific topic to come). As shown, in our constructor, we store the size of the pool, but we do not attempt to preload the pool.

To allocate, we pop an address from our address stack and return it. If the address stack is empty, we add more addresses to the address stack by allocating another block of memory, adding it to the stack of blocks, dividing up the memory into chunks, and adding the divided up chunks to the address stack, as follows:

```
void *allocate()
{
    if (m_addrs.empty())
    {
        this->add_addrs();
    }

    auto ptr = m_addrs.top();
    m_addrs.pop();

    return ptr;
}
```

To deallocate memory, we push the address provided to the address stack so that it can be allocated again later on. Using this method, allocating and deallocating memory for a container is as simple as popping and pushing an address to a single stack:

```
void deallocate(void *ptr)
{
    m_addrs.push(ptr);
}
```

We will need to change the size of the pool if the rebind copy constructor is used. This type of copy should only occur when attempting to create an allocator of the int type to an allocator of the std::list::node type, which means that the allocator being copied will not have been used yet, meaning a resize is possible. If the allocator has been used, it would mean that the allocator has already allocated memory of a different size and, as a result, a rebind would be impossible with this implementation. Consider the following code for it:

```
void rebind(size_type size)
{
    if (!m_addrs.empty() || !m_blocks.empty())
    {
        std::cerr << "rebind after alloc unsupported\n";
        abort();
    }

    m_size = size;
}
```

It should be noted that there are other ways to handle this specific issue. For example, a std::list could be created that doesn't attempt to use the rebind copy constructor. An allocator could also be created that is capable of managing more than one pool of memory, each pool being capable of allocating and deallocating memory of a specific type (which, of course, would result in a performance hit).

In our private section, we have the add_addrs() function that was seen in the allocate function. The goal of, this function is to refill the address stack. To do this, the this function allocates another block of memory, divides the memory up, and adds it to the address stack:

```
void add_addrs()
{
    constexpr const auto block_size = 0x1000;
    auto block = std::make_unique<uint8_t[]>(block_size);

    auto v = gsl::span<uint8_t>(
        block.get(), block_size
    );

    auto total_size =
        v.size() % m_size == 0 ? v.size() : v.size() - m_size;

    for (auto i = 0; i < total_size; i += m_size)
    {
        m_addrs.push(&v.at(i));
    }

    m_blocks.push(std::move(block));
}
```

Finally, we have the private member variables, which includes the pool's size, the address stack, and the stack of blocks. Note that we use std::stack for this. std::stack uses std::deque to implement the stack, and although a more efficient stack can be written that doesn't leverage iterators, in testing, std::stack is nearly as performant:

```
size_type m_size;

std::stack<void *> m_addrs{};
std::stack<std::unique_ptr<uint8_t[]>> m_blocks{};
```

The allocator itself is nearly identical to the previous unequal allocator we already defined:

```
template<typename T>
class myallocator
{
public:

    using value_type = T;
    using pointer = T *;
    using size_type = std::size_t;
    using is_always_equal = std::false_type;
    using propagate_on_container_copy_assignment = std::false_type;
    using propagate_on_container_move_assignment = std::true_type;
    using propagate_on_container_swap = std::true_type;
```

One difference is that we define `propagate_on_container_copy_assignment` as `false`, specifically to prevent the allocator from being copied as much as possible. This choice is also backed by the fact that we already determined that glibc doesn't provide a huge benefit turning this property on when leveraging an unequal allocator.

The constructors are the same as previously defined:

```
    myallocator() :
        m_pool{std::make_shared<pool>(sizeof(T))}
    {
        std::cout << this << " constructor, sizeof(T): "
                  << sizeof(T) << '\n';
    }

    template <typename U>
    myallocator(const myallocator<U> &other) noexcept :
        m_pool{other.m_pool}
    {
        std::cout << this << " copy constructor (U), sizeof(T): "
                  << sizeof(T) << '\n';

        m_pool->rebind(sizeof(T));
    }

    myallocator(myallocator &&other) noexcept :
        m_pool{std::move(other.m_pool)}
    {
        std::cout << this << " move constructor, sizeof(T): "
                  << sizeof(T) << '\n';
    }

    myallocator &operator=(myallocator &&other) noexcept
    {
```

```
        std::cout << this << " move assignment, sizeof(T): "
                  << sizeof(T) << '\n';

        m_pool = std::move(other.m_pool);
        return *this;
    }

    myallocator(const myallocator &other) noexcept :
        m_pool{other.m_pool}
    {
        std::cout << this << " copy constructor, sizeof(T): "
                  << sizeof(T) << '\n';
    }

    myallocator &operator=(const myallocator &other) noexcept
    {
        std::cout << this << " copy assignment, sizeof(T): "
                  << sizeof(T) << '\n';

        m_pool = other.m_pool;
        return *this;
    }
```

The `allocate` and `deallocate` functions are the same as previously defined, calling the pool's allocation function. One difference is that our pool is only capable of allocating memory in single chunks (that is, the pool allocator is not capable of allocating more than one address while also preserving continuity). As a result, if n is something other than 1 (that is, the container is not `std::list` or `std::map`), we fall back to a `malloc()`/`free()` implementation, which is typically the default implementation:

```
    pointer allocate(size_type n)
    {
        if (n != 1) {
            return static_cast<pointer>(malloc(sizeof(T) * n));
        }

        return static_cast<pointer>(m_pool->allocate());
    }

    void deallocate(pointer ptr, size_type n)
    {
        if (n != 1) {
            free(ptr);
        }

        m_pool->deallocate(ptr);
    }
```

The rest of the allocator is the same:

```
private:

    std::shared_ptr<pool> m_pool;

    template <typename T1, typename T2>
    friend bool operator==(const myallocator<T1> &lhs, const
myallocator<T2> &rhs);

    template <typename T1, typename T2>
    friend bool operator!=(const myallocator<T1> &lhs, const
myallocator<T2> &rhs);

    template <typename U>
    friend class myallocator;
};

template <typename T1, typename T2>
bool operator==(const myallocator<T1> &lhs, const myallocator<T2> &rhs)
{ return lhs.m_pool.get() == rhs.m_pool.get(); }

template <typename T1, typename T2>
bool operator!=(const myallocator<T1> &lhs, const myallocator<T2> &rhs)
{ return lhs.m_pool.get() != rhs.m_pool.get(); }
```

Finally, before we can test our allocator, we will need to define a benchmarking function, capable of giving us an indication of how long a specific operation takes. This function will be defined in better detail in Chapter 11, *Time Interfaces in Unix*. For now, the most important thing to understand is that this function takes a callback function as an input (in our case, a Lambda), and returns a number. The higher the returned number, the longer the callback function took to execute:

```
template<typename FUNC>
auto benchmark(FUNC func) {
    auto stime = std::chrono::high_resolution_clock::now();
    func();
    auto etime = std::chrono::high_resolution_clock::now();

    return (etime - stime).count();
}
```

The first test we will perform is creating two lists and adding elements to each list, while timing how long it takes to add all of the elements to the list. Since each addition to the list requires an allocation, performing this test will give us a rough comparison on how much better our allocator is at allocating memory compared to the default allocator provided by glibc.

```
constexpr const auto num = 100000;

std::list<int> mylist1;
std::list<int, myallocator<int>> mylist2;

auto time1 = benchmark([&]{
    for (auto i = 0; i < num; i++) {
        mylist1.emplace_back(42);
    }
});

auto time2 = benchmark([&]{
    for (auto i = 0; i < num; i++) {
        mylist2.emplace_back(42);
    }
});

std::cout << "[TEST] add many:\n";
std::cout << " - time1: " << time1 << '\n';
std::cout << " - time2: " << time2 << '\n';
```

As stated, for each list, we add 100000 integers to the list and time how long it takes, giving us the ability to compare the allocators. The results are as follows:

```
0x7ffca71d7a00 constructor, sizeof(T): 24
[TEST] add many:
  - time1: 3921793
  - time2: 1787499
```

As shown, our allocator is 219% faster than the default allocator at allocating memory.

In our next test, we will compare our allocator with the default allocator with respect to deallocating memory. To perform this test, we will do the same thing as before, but instead of timing our allocations, we will time how long it takes to remove elements from each list:

```
constexpr const auto num = 100000;

std::list<int> mylist1;
std::list<int, myallocator<int>> mylist2;

for (auto i = 0; i < num; i++) {
```

```
        mylist1.emplace_back(42);
        mylist2.emplace_back(42);
    }

    auto time1 = benchmark([&]{
        for (auto i - 0; i < num; i++) {
            mylist1.pop_front();
        }
    });

    auto time2 = benchmark([&]{
        for (auto i = 0; i < num; i++) {
            mylist2.pop_front();
        }
    });

    std::cout << "[TEST] remove many:\n";
    std::cout << " - time1: " << time1 << '\n';
    std::cout << " - time2: " << time2 << '\n';
```

The results of the `this` function are as follows:

```
0x7fff14709720 constructor, sizeof(T): 24
[TEST] remove many:
  - time1: 1046463
  - time2: 1285248
```

As shown, our allocator is only 81% as fast as the default allocator. This is likely because the `free()` function is more efficient, which is not a surprise, as pushing to a stack could, in theory, be slower than some implementations of `free()`. Even though our `free()` function is slower, the difference is negligible compared to the improvement in both allocations and fragmentation. It is also important to note that the allocation and deallocation speeds are almost the same with this implementation, which is what we would expect.

To ensure we wrote our allocator correctly, the following will run our test again, but instead of timing how long it takes to add elements to the list, we will add up each value in the list. If our total is as we expect, we will know that allocations and deallocations were performed properly:

```
constexpr const auto num = 100000;

std::list<int, myallocator<int>> mylist;

for (auto i = 0; i < num; i++) {
    mylist.emplace_back(i);
}
```

```
uint64_t total1{};
uint64_t total2{};

for (auto i = 0; i < num; i++) {
    total1 += i;
    total2 += mylist.back();
    mylist.pop_back();
}

std::cout << "[TEST] verify: ";
if (total1 == total2) {
    std::cout << "success\n";
}
else {
    std::cout << "failure\n";
    std::cout << " - total1: " << total1 << '\n';
    std::cout << " - total2: " << total2 << '\n';
}
```

As expected, the output of our test is `success`.

Compiling and testing

To compile this code, we leverage the same `CMakeLists.txt` file that we have been using for the other examples: `https://github.com/PacktPublishing/Hands-On-System-Programming-with-CPP/blob/master/Chapter09/CMakeLists.txt`.

With this code in place, we can compile this code using the following:

```
> git clone
https://github.com/PacktPublishing/Hands-On-System-Programming-with-CPP.git
> cd Hands-On-System-Programming-with-CPP/Chapter09/
> mkdir build
> cd build

> cmake -DCMAKE_BUILD_TYPE=Release ..
> make
```

To execute the example, run the following:

```
> ./example7
```

The output should resemble the following:

```
0x7ffca71d7a00 constructor, sizeof(T): 24
[TEST] add many:
  - time1: 3921793
  - time2: 1787499
0x7fff14709720 constructor, sizeof(T): 24
[TEST] remove many:
  - time1: 1046463
  - time2: 1285248
0x7fff5d8ad040 constructor, sizeof(T): 24
[TEST] verify: success
========================================================================
====
test cases: 5 | 5 passed
assertions: - none -
```

As you can see, the output of our example matches the output we provided before. It should be noted that your results might very based on factors such as the hardware or what is already running on the box.

Summary

In this chapter, we looked at how to create our own allocators, and covered the intricate details of the C++ allocator concept. Topics included the difference between equal and unequal allocators, how container propagation is handled, rebinding, and potential issues with stateful allocators. Finally, we concluded with two different examples. The first example demonstrated how to create a simple, cache-aligned allocator that is stateless, while the second provided a functional example of a stateful object allocator that maintains a free pool for fast allocations.

In the next chapter, we will use several examples to demonstrate how to program POSIX sockets (that is, network programming) using C++.

Questions

1. What does `is_always_equal` mean?
2. What determines whether an allocator is equal or unequal?
3. Can a stateful allocator be equal?
4. Can a stateless allocator be equal?
5. What does `propagate_on_container_copy_assignment` do?
6. What does the rebind copy constructor do for a container?
7. What is the difference between `std::list` and `std::vector` with respect to the n variable passed to the allocate function?

Further reading

- https://www.packtpub.com/application-development/c17-example
- https://www.packtpub.com/application-development/getting-started-c17-programming-video

10
Programming POSIX Sockets Using C++

In this chapter, you will learn how to program POSIX sockets using C++17, including more common C++ paradigms, such as **Resource Aquisition Is Initialization** (**RAII**). To begin with, this chapter will discuss what a socket is, and the difference between UDP and TCP. The POSIX APIs will be explained in detail prior to walking you through five different examples. The first example will step you through programming with POSIX sockets by creating a UDP echo server example. The second example will create this same example using TCP instead of UDP and explain the differences. The third example will expand upon our existing debug logger that has been created in previous chapters, while the fourth and fifth examples will explain how to safely process a packet.

In this chapter, we will cover the following topics:

- POSIX sockets
- Leveraging C++ and RAII with sockets
- TCP vs UDP

Technical requirements

In order to compile and execute the examples in this chapter, the reader must have the following:

- A Linux-based system capable of compiling and executing C++17 (for example, Ubuntu 17.10+)
- GCC 7+
- CMake 3.6+
- An internet connection

To download all of the code in this chapter, including the examples, and code snippets, please see the following link: `https://github.com/PacktPublishing/Hands-On-System-Programming-with-CPP/tree/master/Chapter10`.

Beginning with POSIX sockets

Unfortunately, C++ does not contain a native networking library (something that will hopefully be addressed with C++20). For this reason, POSIX sockets are needed to perform networking with C++. The POSIX sockets API defines an API for sending and receiving network packets using the standard, Unix file-descriptor paradigm. When programming with sockets, both a server and a client must be created. Servers are responsible for binding a specific port to the socket protocol that is being developed by the user of the sockets library. Clients are any other application that is connected to a previously-bound port. Both servers and clients have their own IP addresses.

When programming sockets, besides picking address types, such as IPv4 versus IPv6, typically the programmer must also choose between UDP versus TCP. UDP is a connectionless protocol that provides no assurances that a packet is reliably sent, with the advantage being speed and simplicity. UDP is commonly used for data that does not have to be received 100% of the time, such as your position in a video game. TCP, on the other hand, is a connection-based protocol that ensures all packets are received in the order they are sent and is the typical protocol used for its reliability.

Beginning with APIs

The following sections will explain, in detail, the different socket APIs.

The socket() API

All POSIX socket programming starts with the creation of a socket file descriptor using the `socket()` API, which takes the following form:

```
int socket(int domain, int type, int protocol);
```

The domain defines the address type used when creating the socket. In most cases, this would be `AF_INET` for IPv4 or `AF_INET6` for IPv6. In the case of our examples in this chapter, we will use `AF_INET`. The type field usually takes on `SOCK_STREAM` for a TCP connection or `SOCK_DGRAM` for a UDP connection, both of which will be demonstrated in this chapter. Finally, the protocol field in this API will be set to 0 in all of our examples, telling the API to use the default protocol for whichever socket type is specified.

Upon completion of this API, a socket file descriptor is returned, which will be needed by the remaining POSIX APIs. If this API fails, -1 is returned, and `errno` is set to an appropriate error code. It should be noted that `errno` is not thread-safe and its use should be handled with care. A great way to handle these types of errors is to immediately convert the `errno` into a C++ exception, which can be done using the following:

```
if (m_fd = ::socket(AF_INET, SOCK_STREAM, 0); m_fd == -1) {
    throw std::runtime_error(strerror(errno));
}
```

In the preceding example, an IPv4 TCP socket is created. The resulting file descriptor is saved into a memory variable, `m_fd`. Using C++17 syntax, the file descriptor is checked for validity, and if an error is reported (that is, -1), an exception is thrown. To provide a human-readable version of the error, `errno` is converted into a string using `strerror()`. Not only does this provide a string version of `errno`, it also ensures that the process of recording the error doesn't change `errno` in the process, which can happen if a more complicated approach is used.

Finally, when the socket is no longer needed, it should be closed like any other file descriptor using the POSIX `close()` function. It should be noted that most POSIX operating systems will automatically close sockets that are still open when the application closes.

To prevent possible descriptor leaks, the socket file descriptor may be encapsulated in a class, as follows:

```
class mytcpsocket
{
public:
    explicit mytcpsocket(uint16_t port)
    {
        if (m_fd = ::socket(AF_INET, SOCK_STREAM, 0); m_fd == -1) {
            throw std::runtime_error(strerror(errno));
        }
    }

    ~mytcpsocket()
```

```
    {
        close(m_fd);
    }

    auto descriptor() const
    { return m_fd; }

private:

    int m_fd{};
};
```

In the preceding example, we open an IPv4 TCP socket using the logic in the prior example, ensuring any errors are detected and properly reported. The difference is that we store the file descriptor as a member variable, and when `mytcpsocket{}` loses scope, we automatically ensure the file descriptor is properly released back to the operating system. Any time the file descriptor is needed, the `descriptor()` accessor may be used.

The bind() and connect() APIs

Once a socket file descriptor is created, the socket must be bound, or connected, depending on whether the socket is creating the connection (the server), or is connecting to an existing bound socket (client). When communicating via TCP or UDP, binding a socket dedicates a port for the socket. Ports `0-1024` are reserved for specific services and are often managed by the operating system (requiring special privileges to bind). The remaining ports are user-defined and often may be bound without privileges. Determining which port to use is dependent on the implementation. Some ports are predetermined for a specific application, or the application can ask the operating system for an open port to use, which has the added complication of communicating this newly-allocated port to potential client applications.

The `bind()` API takes the following form:

```
int bind(int socket, const struct sockaddr *address, socklen_t
address_len);
```

The `socket` integer parameter is the socket file descriptor that was previously provided by the `socket()` API. The `address` parameter tells the operating system which port to bind to, and which IP address to accept incoming connections from, usually `INADDR_ANY` which tells the operating system that an incoming connection may be accepted from any IP address. Finally, the `address_len` parameter tells the API what the total size of the address structure is.

The total size (in bytes) is needed for the address structure because different structures are supported depending on the socket type you're using. For example, an IPv6 socket has a larger IP address compared to an IPv4 socket. In this chapter, we will discuss IPv4, which uses the `sockaddr_in{}` structure, which defines the following fields:

- `sin_family`: This is identical to the socket domain, which, in the case of IPv4, is `AF_INET`.
- `sin_port`: This defines the port to bind to, which must be converted into network byte order using `htons()`.
- `sin_address`: This defines the IP address to accept incoming connections from, which must also be converted into network byte order using `htonl()`. Often, this is set to `htonl(INADDR_ANY)`, indicating connections are accepted from any IP address.

Since the address structure is variable in length, the `bind()` API takes a pointer to an opaque structure type and uses the length field to ensure the proper information was provided. It should be noted that this type of API is not encouraged by the C++ Core Guidelines as there is no type-safe way of implementing this API. In fact, in order to use this API, `reinterpret_cast()` is needed to convert a `sockaddr_in{}` to the opaque `sockaddr{}` structure. Although the use of `reinterpret_cast()` is not supported by the C++ Core Guidelines, there is no alternative and therefore if sockets are needed, this rule must be broken.

While servers use `bind()` to dedicate a port for the socket, clients use `connect()` to connect to an already-bound port. The `connect()` API has the following form:

```
int connect(int socket, const struct sockaddr *address, socklen_t
address_len);
```

It should be noted that the parameters for `connect()` are identical to `bind()`. Like `bind()`, you must provide the file descriptor returned by the call to `socket()`, and like `bind()`, you must provide, in the case of IPv4, a pointer to a `sockaddr_in{}` structure as well as the size of the `sockaddr_in{}` structure. When filling out the `sockaddr_in{}` structure, you would use the following:

- `sin_family`: This is identical to the socket domain, which, in the case of IPv4, is `AF_INET`.
- `sin_port`: This defines the port to connect to, which must be converted into network byte order using `htons()`.
- `sin_address`: This defines the IP address to connect to, which must also be converted into network byte order using `htonl()`. For loopback connections, this would be set to `htonl(INADDR_LOOPBACK)`.

Finally, both `bind()` and `connect()` return 0 on success or −1 on failure, setting `errno` in the event of an error.

The listen() and accept() APIs

For TCP servers, two additional APIs exist that provide the server with a means to listen for and accept incoming TCP connections—`listen()` and `accept()`.

The `listen()` API has the following form:

```
int listen(int socket, int backlog);
```

The socket parameter is the file descriptor returned by the `socket()` API, and the backlog parameter limits the total number of outstanding connections that may be made. In the examples in this chapter, we will use a backlog of 0, which tells the API to use an implementation-specific value for the backlog.

If `listen()` succeeds, 0 is returned, otherwise −1 is returned and `errno` is set to the appropriate error code.

Once your application is set up to listen for incoming connections, the `accept()` API may be used to accept a connection once it is ready. The `accept()` API has the following form:

```
int accept(int socket, struct sockaddr *address, socklen_t *address_len);
```

Like the other APIs, the `socket` parameter is the file descriptor returned by the `socket()` API and the address, and the `address_len` parameter returns information about the connection. `nullptr` may also be provided for both the address and `address_len` if the connection information is not needed. Upon successful completion of the `accept()` API, a socket file descriptor for the client connection is returned, which may be used to send and receive data to and from the client.

If accept fails to execute, instead of a valid socket file descriptor being returned, `-1` is returned, and `errno` is set appropriately.

It should be noted that both `listen()` and `accept()` are only needed for TCP connections. With a TCP connection, the server creates two or more socket descriptors; the first one is used to bind to a port and listen for connections, while the second one is the socket file descriptor for the client, which is used to send and receive data. UDP, on the other hand, is a connectionless protocol and thus the same socket that is used to bind to a port is also used to send and receive data with the client.

The send(), recv(), sendto(), and recvfrom() APIs

To send information to a server or client after opening a socket, POSIX provides the `send()` and `sendto()` APIs. The `send()` API has the following form:

```
ssize_t send(int socket, const void *buffer, size_t length, int flags);
```

The first parameter is the socket file descriptor for the server or client you wish to send data to. It should be noted that the socket must be connected to a specific client or server to work (such as communicating back to a server, or to a client opened using TCP). The `buffer` parameter points to the buffer you wish to send, `length` defines the length of the buffer you wish to send, and `flags` provides various different settings for how you wish to send the buffer, which in most cases is just set to 0. It should also be noted that when `flags` is set to 0, there is typically no difference between the `write()` function and the `send()` function, and both may be used.

If a server is attempting to communicate with a client using UDP, the server won't know who or how to send information to the client as the server binds to a specific port, not to a specific client. Likewise, if a client using UDP doesn't connect to a specific server, it will not know who or how to send information to the server. For this reason, POSIX provides `sendto()`, which adds the `sockaddr{}` structure to define who and how you wish to send the buffer. `sendto()` has the following form:

```
ssize_t sendto(int socket, const void *buffer, size_t length, int flags,
const struct sockaddr *dest_addr, socklen_t dest_len);
```

The only difference between `send()` and `sendto()` is that `sendto()` also provides the destination `address` and `len` parameters, which provide the user with a way to define who the buffer is sent to.

To receive data from a client or server, POSIX provides the `recv()` API, which has the following form:

```
ssize_t recv(int socket, void *buffer, size_t length, int flags);
```

The `recv()` API takes the same parameters as the `send()` API, with the difference being that the buffer will be written to (which is why it's not labeled `const`) when data is received, and the length field describes the total size of the buffer and not the total number of bytes received.

Likewise, POSIX provides a `recvfrom()` API, which is similar to the `sendto()` API and has the following form:

```
ssize_t recvfrom(int socket, void *restrict buffer, size_t length, int
flags, struct sockaddr *restrict address, socklen_t *restrict address_len);
```

Both the `send()` and `sendto()` functions return the total number of bytes that were sent, while the `recv()` and `recvfrom()` functions return the total number of bytes received. All of these functions return −1 and set `errno` to an appropriate value in the event of an error.

Studying an example on the UDP echo server

In this example, we will walk you through a simple echo server example using UDP. An echo server (as is the same with our previous chapters) echoes any input to its output. In the case of this UDP example, the server echoes data sent to it from a client back to the client. To keep the example simple, character buffers will be echoed. How to properly process structured packets will be covered in the following examples.

Server

To start, we must define the maximum buffer size we plan to send from the client to the server and back, and we must also define the port we wish to use:

```
#define PORT 22000
#define MAX_SIZE 0x10
```

It should be noted that any port number will do so long as it is above 1024, to prevent the need for privileges. In this example, the following includes are needed for the server:

```
#include <array>
#include <iostream>
#include <stdexcept>

#include <unistd.h>
#include <string.h>

#include <sys/socket.h>
#include <netinet/in.h>
```

The server will be defined using a class to take advantage of RAII, providing a clean method for closing the socket opened by the server when it is no longer needed. We also define three private member variables. The first variable will store the socket file descriptor that the server will use throughout the example. The second variable stores the address information of the server, which will be provided to the `bind()` function, while the third parameter stores the address information of the client, which will be used by the `recvfrom()` and `sendto()` functions:

```
class myserver
{
    int m_fd{};
    struct sockaddr_in m_addr{};
    struct sockaddr_in m_client{};

public:
```

The constructor of the server will open the socket and bind the provided port to the socket, as follows:

```
    explicit myserver(uint16_t port)
    {
        if (m_fd = ::socket(AF_INET, SOCK_DGRAM, 0); m_fd == -1) {
            throw std::runtime_error(strerror(errno));
        }

        m_addr.sin_family = AF_INET;
        m_addr.sin_port = htons(port);
        m_addr.sin_addr.s_addr = htonl(INADDR_ANY);

        if (this->bind() == -1) {
            throw std::runtime_error(strerror(errno));
        }
    }
```

The socket is opened using `AF_INET`, which tells the socket API that IPv4 is desired. Additionally, `SOCK_DGRAM` is provided, which tells the socket API that UDP is desired instead of TCP. The result of the call to `::socket()` is saved into the `m_fd` variable, which stores the servers socket file descriptor. Leveraging C++17, if the resulting file descriptor is -1, an error occurred, and we throw the error, which will be recovered later.

Next, we fill in a `sockaddr_in{}` structure:

- `sin_family` is set to `AF_INET` to match the socket, telling the socket API we wish to use IPv4.
- `sin_port` is set to the port number, and `htons` is used to convert host byte order into network byte order for a short.
- `sin_addr` is set to `INADDR_ANY`, which tells the socket API that the server will accept data from any client. Since UDP is a connectionless protocol, this means we may receive data from any client if desired.

Finally, a call to a member function, called `bind()`, is made and the result is checked for an error. If an error occurs, an exception is thrown.

The bind function is nothing more than a wrapper around the `::bind()` socket API, as follows:

```
int bind()
{
    return ::bind(
        m_fd,
        reinterpret_cast<struct sockaddr *>(&m_addr),
        sizeof(m_addr)
    );
}
```

In the preceding code snippet, we call `bind` with the socket file descriptor that is opened in the constructor of our server class, and we provide the `bind` API with the port and address that was also initialized in the constructor prior to calling this function, which tells the socket to bind to port `22000` and any IP address.

Once the socket has been bound, the server is ready to receive data from a client. Since we bound the socket to any IP address, any client can send us information. We could use the `recv()` POSIX API for this, but the problem with this approach is that once we receive data, we will not know who sent us the information. This is fine if we don't need to send that client any information in return, or we embed the client information in the data received, but in the case of a simple echo server, we need to know who to echo the data to. To solve this problem, we use `recvfrom()` instead of `recv()`, as follows:

```
ssize_t recv(std::array<char, MAX_SIZE> &buf)
{
    socklen_t client_len = sizeof(m_client);

    return ::recvfrom(
        m_fd,
```

```
                buf.data(),
                buf.size(),
                0,
                (struct sockaddr *) &m_client,
                &client_len
        );
    }
```

The first parameter is the socket file descriptor that was created during construction, while the second and third parameters are the buffer and its maximum size. Note that our `recv()` member function takes `std::array` instead of a pointer and a size, as a pointer and a size parameter would not be C++-Core-compliant because doing so provides an opportunity for error in reporting the actual size of the array. The last two parameters are a pointer to a `sockaddr_in{}` structure and its size.

It should be noted that in our example we provide `recvfrom()` with a `sockaddr_in{}` structure, as we know that the client that will be connecting will use an IPv4 address. If this is not the case, the `recvfrom()` function will fail, as we will have provided it with a structure that is too small to provide, say, an IPv6 address if it is used. To overcome this issue, you may use `sockaddr_storage{}` instead of `sockaddr_in{}`. The `sockaddr_storage{}` structure is large enough to store an incoming address type. To determine which address type you received, the `sin_family` field may be used, which is required in all of the structures.

Finally, we return the result of the call to `recvfrom()`, which could either be the number of bytes received, or `-1` in the event of an error.

To send a buffer to a client that connects to the UDP server, we use the `sendto()` API, as follows:

```
    ssize_t send(std::array<char, MAX_SIZE> &buf, ssize_t len)
    {
        if (len >= buf.size()) {
            throw std::out_of_range("len >= buf.size()");
        }

        return ::sendto(
            m_fd,
            buf.data(),
            buf.size(),
            0,
            (struct sockaddr *) &m_client,
            sizeof(m_client)
        );
    }
```

As with the other APIs, the first parameter is the socket file descriptor that was opened in the constructor. The buffer is then provided. The difference between `recvrom()` and `sendto()` in this case is that the number of bytes to send is provided instead of the total size of the buffer. This doesn't break C++ Core Guidance as the total size of the buffer is still attached to the buffer itself, and instead the number of bytes to send is a second value used to determine how far into an array we plan to address. We do, however, need to ensure the length field is not out of range. This could be done using a call to `Expects()`, as follows:

```
Expects(len < buf.size())
```

In the case of this example, we explicitly check for an out-of-range error and throw a more verbose error if this should occur. Either approach would work.

As with the `recvfrom()` call, we provide the `sendto()` API with a pointer to a `sockaddr_in{}` structure, which tells the socket which client to send data to. In this case, since the API does not modify the address structure (and thus the structure cannot change in size), a pointer to the length field is not needed.

The next step is to put all of these together to create the echo server itself, as follows:

```cpp
void echo()
{
    while(true)
    {
        std::array<char, MAX_SIZE> buf{};

        if (auto len = recv(buf); len != 0) {
            send(buf, len);
        }
        else {
            break;
        }
    }
}
```

The echo server is designed to receive a buffer of data from a client, send it back to the same client, and repeat. To start, we create an infinite loop that is capable of echoing data from any client until we are told the client has disconnected. The next step is to define a buffer that will be used to both send and receive data to the client. We then call the `recv()` member function and provide it with the buffer we wish the receive function to fill in with data from the client and check whether the number of bytes returned from the client is greater than 0. If the number of bytes returned from the client is greater than 0, we use the `send` member function to send (or echo) the buffer back to the client. If the number of bytes is 0, we assume the client has disconnected as a result, and we stop the infinite loop, which in turn completes the echo process.

The client-information structure (that is, `m_client`) is provided to both the `recvfrom()` and `sendto()` POSIX APIs. This is done intentionally. The only assumption we are making is that all clients connecting will use IPv4. The `recvfrom()` function will fill in the `m_client` structure for us when data is received from a client, telling us who the client was that sent us the information. We then provide this same structure back to the `sendto()` function to tell the API who to echo the data to.

As stated before, when the server class is destroyed we close the socket, as follows:

```
~myserver()
{
    close(m_fd);
}
```

Finally, we complete the server by instantiating the server in a `protected_main()` function, and then begin echoing:

```
int
protected_main(int argc, char** argv)
{
    (void) argc;
    (void) argv;

    myserver server{PORT};
    server.echo();

    return EXIT_SUCCESS;
}

int
main(int argc, char** argv)
{
    try {
        return protected_main(argc, argv);
```

```
    }
    catch (const std::exception &e) {
        std::cerr << "Caught unhandled exception:\n";
        std::cerr << " - what(): " << e.what() << '\n';
    }
    catch (...) {
        std::cerr << "Caught unknown exception\n";
    }

    return EXIT_FAILURE;
}
```

As shown, the `main` function is protected from possible exceptions, and in the `protected_main()` function, we instantiate the server and call its `echo()` member function, which starts the infinite loop for echoing client data.

The client logic

In this example, the following includes are needed for the client:

```
#include <array>
#include <string>
#include <iostream>
#include <stdexcept>

#include <unistd.h>
#include <string.h>

#include <sys/socket.h>
#include <netinet/in.h>
```

Like the server, the client is created using a class to take advantage of RAII:

```
class myclient
{
    int m_fd{};
    struct sockaddr_in m_addr{};

public:
```

In addition to the class definition, two private member variables are defined. The first, like the server, is the socket file descriptor that will be used by the client. The second defines the address information for the server the client desires to communicate with.

The constructor of the client is similar to the server's, with some minor differences:

```cpp
explicit myclient(uint16_t port)
{
    if (m_fd = ::socket(AF_INET, SOCK_DGRAM, 0); m_fd == -1) {
        throw std::runtime_error(strerror(errno));
    }

    m_addr.sin_family = AF_INET;
    m_addr.sin_port = htons(port);
    m_addr.sin_addr.s_addr = htonl(INADDR_LOOPBACK);

    if (connect() == -1) {
        throw std::runtime_error(strerror(errno));
    }
}
```

Like the server, the client creates a socket file descriptor for IPv4 by using `AF_INET` and the protocol type is set to UDP by using `SOCK_DGRAM`. If the `socket()` API returns an error, an exception is thrown. The `sockaddr_in{}` structure that is set up is different from the server. The server's `sockaddr_in{}` structure defines how the server will bind the socket, while the client `sockaddr_in{}` structure defines what server the client will connect to. In the case of this example, we set the address to `INADDR_LOOPBACK` as the server will be running on the same computer. Finally, the `connect()` member function is called, which connects to the server, and if an error occurs, an exception is thrown.

To connect to the server, the following `connect()` member function is used:

```cpp
int connect()
{
    return ::connect(
        m_fd,
        reinterpret_cast<struct sockaddr *>(&m_addr),
        sizeof(m_addr)
    );
}
```

It should be noted that connecting to a server with UDP is optional as UDP is a connectionless protocol. The `connect` function, in this case, tells the operating system which server you plan to communicate with such that `send()` and `recv()` may be used, instead of `sendto()` and `recvfrom()` on the client side. Like the `bind()` member function for the server, the `connect()` function leverages the `sockaddr_in{}` structure filled in by the constructor.

To send data to the server to be echoed, the following `send()` member variable is used:

```
ssize_t send(const std::string &buf)
{
    return ::send(
        m_fd,
        buf.data(),
        buf.size(),
        0
    );
}
```

Since we plan to send the server a string, we pass the `send()` member function a string reference. The `send()` POSIX API is then given the socket file descriptor created in the constructor, the buffer to send to the server to be echoed, and the total length of the buffer being sent. Since we don't use the `flags` field, the `send()` member function could also be written using the `write()` function, as follows:

```
ssize_t send(const std::string &buf)
{
    return ::write(
        m_fd,
        buf.data(),
        buf.size()
    );
}
```

To receive data from the server after it has been echoed, we use the following `recv()` member function:

```
ssize_t recv(std::array<char, MAX_SIZE> &buf)
{
    return ::recv(
        m_fd,
        buf.data(),
        buf.size() - 1,
        0
    );
}
```

There are many ways to implement the `recv()` member function. Since we know the total size of the string being sent to the server, and we know the server will echo the same-sized string back to us, we could always create a second string the same size as the first (or simply reuse the original string if you trust echo actually is occurring). In the case of this example, we create a receive buffer with a specific maximum size to demonstrate a more likely scenario. As a result, in this example, we can send any size string we wish, but the server has its own, internal maximum buffer size that it can accept. The server will then echo the data back to the client. The client itself has its own maximum-sized receive buffer, which ultimately limits the total number of bytes that may be echoed. Since the client is echoing strings, we must reserve one byte for a trailing '\0' to null terminate any string that is received by the client that fills the entire receive buffer.

To send and receive data to and from the server, we create an `echo` function, as follows:

```
void echo()
{
    while(true) {
        std::string sendbuf{};
        std::array<char, MAX_SIZE> recvbuf{};

        std::cin >> sendbuf;
        if (sendbuf == "exit") {
            send({});
            break;
        }

        send(sendbuf);
        recv(recvbuf);

        std::cout << recvbuf.data() << '\n';
    }
}
```

The `echo` function, like the server, first creates an infinite loop so that it can send multiple strings to the server to be echoed. Inside the infinite loop, two buffers are created. The first is the string that will take in user input. The second defines the receive buffer to be used. Once the buffers are defined, we use `std::cin` to get from the user the string to be sent to the server (which will ultimately be echoed).

If the string is the word `exit`, we send 0 bytes to the server and exit the infinite loop. Since UDP is a connectionless protocol, the server has no way of knowing whether the client has disconnected because no such construct exists. Therefore, without sending a signal to the server to stop (in this case we send 0 bytes), the server would stay in an infinite loop as it has no way of knowing when to stop. In this example, this poses an interesting problem because if the client crashes or is killed (for example, with *Ctrl + C*), the server will never be given the 0 byte signal, and thus remain in an infinite loop. There are many ways to solve this issue (that is, by sending a keep-alive signal), but once you go down the path of trying to solve this problem, you quickly end up with a protocol that is so similar to TCP, you might as well use TCP.

Finally, the user-inputted buffer is sent to the server using the `send()` member function, the server echoes the string, and then the client then receives the string using the `recv()` member function. Once the string is received, the data is output to `stdout` using `std::cout`.

Like the server, when the client class is destroyed, the socket file descriptor is closed, closing the socket:

```
~myclient()
{
    close(m_fd);
}
};
```

Finally, the client is created using the same `protected_main()` function as the server and our previous examples:

```
int
protected_main(int argc, char** argv)
{
    (void) argc;
    (void) argv;

    myclient client{PORT};
    client.echo();

    return EXIT_SUCCESS;
}

int
main(int argc, char** argv)
{
    try {
        return protected_main(argc, argv);
```

```
    }
    catch (const std::exception &e) {
        std::cerr << "Caught unhandled exception:\n";
        std::cerr << " - what(): " << e.what() << '\n';
    }
    catch (...) {
        std::cerr << "Caught unknown exception\n";
    }

    return EXIT_FAILURE;
}
```

In the preceding code, the client is instantiated in the `protected_main()` function, and the echo function is called, which accepts user input, sends the input to the server, and outputs any echoed data to `stdout`.

Compiling and testing

To compile this code, we leverage the same `CMakeLists.txt` file that we have been using for the other examples: https://github.com/PacktPublishing/Hands-On-System-Programming-with-CPP/blob/master/Chapter10/CMakeLists.txt.

With this code in place, we can compile this code using the following:

```
> git clone
https://github.com/PacktPublishing/Hands-On-System-Programming-with-CPP.git
> cd Hands-On-System-Programming-with-CPP/Chapter10/
> mkdir build
> cd build

> cmake ..
> make
```

To execute the server, run the following:

```
> ./example1_server
```

To execute the client, open a new terminal and run the following:

```
> cd Hands-On-System-Programming-with-CPP/Chapter10/build
> ./example1_client
Hello ↵
Hello
World
World ↵
exit ↵
```

As shown in the preceding snippet, when the client is executed, and input is entered, the input is echoed back to the terminal. Once complete and the word `exit` is entered, the client exits. Also the server will exit when the client is complete. To demonstrate the connection issue with UDP, instead of entering `exit`, hit *Ctrl + C* on the client—the client will exit but the server will continue to execute, waiting for more input from the client as it will not know the client has completed. To solve this issue, out next example will create the same echo server but using TCP instead.

Studying an example on the TCP echo server

In this example, we will walk the reader through creating an echo server, but using TCP instead of UDP. Just like with the previous example, an echo server echoes any input to its output. Unlike the UDP example, TCP is a connection-based protocol, and thus some of the specifics of how to establish a connection and send/receive data are different in this example.

Server

To start, we must define the maximum buffer size we plan to send from the client to the server and back, and we must also define the port we wish to use:

```
#define PORT 22000
#define MAX_SIZE 0x10
```

For the server, we will need the following includes:

```
#include <array>
#include <iostream>

#include <unistd.h>
#include <string.h>

#include <sys/socket.h>
#include <netinet/in.h>
```

As with the previous examples, we will create the server using a class to take advantage of RAII:

```
class myserver
{
    int m_fd{};
    int m_client{};
    struct sockaddr_in m_addr{};

public:
```

As with UDP, three member variables will be used. The first member variable, m_fd, stores the socket file descriptor for the socket associated with the server. Unlike UDP, this descriptor will not be used to send/receive data with a client. Instead, m_client represents a second socket file descriptor that will be used to send/receive data with the client. Like with UDP, the sockaddr_in{} structure, m_addr, will be filled in with the server address type, which will be bound.

The constructor for the server is similar to the UDP example:

```
    explicit myserver(uint16_t port)
    {
        if (m_fd = ::socket(AF_INET, SOCK_STREAM, 0); m_fd == -1) {
            throw std::runtime_error(strerror(errno));
        }

        m_addr.sin_family = AF_INET;
        m_addr.sin_port = htons(port);
        m_addr.sin_addr.s_addr = htonl(INADDR_ANY);

        if (this->bind() == -1) {
            throw std::runtime_error(strerror(errno));
        }
    }
```

Like the UDP example, a socket file descriptor for the server is created, but instead of SOCK_DGRAM being used, SOCK_STREAM is used instead. The sockaddr_in{} structure is identical to the UDP example with IPv4 being used (that is, AF_INET), the port, and any IP address being used to signal that connections from any IP address will be accepted.

Like the UDP example, the `sockaddr_in{}` structure is then bound using the following member function:

```
int bind()
{
    return ::bind(
        m_fd,
        reinterpret_cast<struct sockaddr *>(&m_addr),
        sizeof(m_addr)
    );
}
```

The preceding `bind()` function is identical to the `bind()` function used in the UDP example.

Unlike UDP, a second, client-specific socket descriptor is created, and the IP address, port, and address type are all set for that socket type, meaning communicating with the client does not require `sendto()` or `recvfrom()` since we have a specific socket file descriptor that already has this additional information bound to it. For this reason, `send()` and `recv()` may be used instead of `sendto()` and `recvfrom()`.

To receive data from the client, the following member function will be used:

```
ssize_t recv(std::array<char, MAX_SIZE> &buf)
{
    return ::recv(
        m_client,
        buf.data(),
        buf.size(),
        0
    );
}
```

The only difference between the UDP example and this example is the use of `recv()` instead of `recvfrom()`, which omits the additional `sockaddr_in{}` structure. If you recall from the previous UDP example, `m_fd` was used with `recvfrom()` instead of `m_client` with `recv()`. The difference is that `m_client` in the UDP example is a `sockaddr_in{}` structure that defines who to receive data from. With TCP, `m_client` is instead a socket descriptor, and who to receive data from is bound to the descriptor, which is why the additional `sockaddr_in{}` structure is not needed.

The same is also true for the `send()` member function:

```
ssize_t send(std::array<char, MAX_SIZE> &buf, ssize_t len)
{
    if (len >= buf.size()) {
```

```
            throw std::out_of_range("len >= buf.size()");
        }

        return ::send(
            m_client,
            buf.data(),
            len,
            0
        );
    }
```

Unlike in the UDP example, the preceding send() function may use the send() POSIX API instead of sendto(), as the address information about who and how to send data to the client is bound to the descriptor and, as such, the additional sockaddr_in{} information may be omitted. The rest of the send() function is identical to the UDP example.

The echo function is quite a bit different from its UDP counterpart:

```
void echo()
{
    if (::listen(m_fd, 0) == -1) {
        throw std::runtime_error(strerror(errno));
    }

    if (m_client = ::accept(m_fd, nullptr, nullptr); m_client == -1) {
        throw std::runtime_error(strerror(errno));
    }

    while(true)
    {
        std::array<char, MAX_SIZE> buf{};

        if (auto len = recv(buf); len != 0) {
            send(buf, len);
        }
        else {
            break;
        }
    }

    close(m_client);
}
```

Since TCP requires connections, the first step in the `echo` function for the server is to tell the POSIX API that you wish to begin listening for incoming connections. In our example, we tell the API to use the default connection backlog, which is implementation-specific, by setting the backlog to 0. The next step is to wait for an incoming connection from a client using the `accept()` POSIX API. By default, this function is a blocking function. The `accept()` function returns a socket file descriptor with the address information bound to the descriptor and as a result, we pass `nullptr` to the address fields in the `accept()` POSIX API as this information is not needed in our example (but might be needed if you, for example, need to filter certain incoming clients).

The next step is to wait for data to be received by the client and then echo that data back to the client using the `send()` member function. This logic is identical to the UDP example. It should be noted that if we receive 0 bytes from the client, we stop processing data from the client, similar to what was done with UDP. The difference is that, as will be shown, on the client side, we do not need to explicitly send 0 bytes to the server for this condition to occur.

The last step in the `echo` function is to close the client socket file descriptor once the client has finished:

```
~myserver()
{
    close(m_fd);
}
};
```

As with the other examples, we close the server's socket file descriptor when the server class is destroyed. Finally, the server is instantiated in a `protected_main()` function, as follows:

```
int
protected_main(int argc, char** argv)
{
    (void) argc;
    (void) argv;

    myserver server{PORT};
    server.echo();
}

int
main(int argc, char** argv)
{
    try {
        return protected_main(argc, argv);
```

```
    }
    catch (const std::exception &e) {
        std::cerr << "Caught unhandled exception:\n";
        std::cerr << " - what(): " << e.what() << '\n';
    }
    catch (...) {
        std::cerr << "Caught unknown exception\n";
    }

    return EXIT_FAILURE;
}
```

Like the UDP example, the server is instantiated, and the `echo()` function is executed.

The client logic

The client logic is similar to the UDP client logic with a few minor exceptions. The following includes are needed:

```
#include <array>
#include <string>
#include <iostream>

#include <unistd.h>
#include <string.h>

#include <sys/socket.h>
#include <netinet/in.h>
```

Just like with the UDP example, a client class is created to leverage RAII, and the `m_fd` and `m_addr` private member variables are defined to store the socket file descriptor for the client, and the address information for the server the client wishes to connect to:

```
class myclient
{
    int m_fd{};
    struct sockaddr_in m_addr{};

public:
```

Unlike the UDP example, but like the TCP server logic, the constructor creates a socket for IPv4 and TCP using both `AF_INET` and `SOCK_STREAM`, as follows:

```
    explicit myclient(uint16_t port)
    {
        if (m_fd = ::socket(AF_INET, SOCK_STREAM, 0); m_fd == -1) {
```

```
        throw std::runtime_error(strerror(errno));
    }

    m_addr.sin_family = AF_INET;
    m_addr.sin_port = htons(port);
    m_addr.sin_addr.s_addr = htonl(INADDR_LOOPBACK);

    if (connect() == -1) {
        throw std::runtime_error(strerror(errno));
    }
}
```

The rest of the constructor is identical to the UDP example, as are the `connect()`, `send()`, and `recv()` functions:

```
 int connect()
{
    return ::connect(
        m_fd,
        reinterpret_cast<struct sockaddr *>(&m_addr),
        sizeof(m_addr)
    );
}

ssize_t send(const std::string &buf)
{
    return ::send(
        m_fd,
        buf.data(),
        buf.size(),
        0
    );
}

ssize_t recv(std::array<char, MAX_SIZE> &buf)
{
    return ::recv(
        m_fd,
        buf.data(),
        buf.size() - 1,
        0
    );
}
```

As shown in the preceding snippet, the client functions almost exactly the same as a UDP client. The difference between a UDP client and a TCP client, other than the use of SOCK_STREAM, lies in the implementation of the echo function:

```
void echo()
{
    while(true) {
        std::string sendbuf{};
        std::array<char, MAX_SIZE> recvbuf{};

        std::cin >> sendbuf;

        send(sendbuf);
        recv(recvbuf);

        std::cout << recvbuf.data() << '\n';
    }
}
```

Unlike the UDP example, the TCP client does not need to check for the exit string. This is because if the client disconnects (for example, *Ctrl + C* is used to kill the client), 0 bytes are received on the server side, telling the server logic the client has been disconnected. This is possible because TCP is a connection-based protocol, and thus, the operating system is maintaining an open connection, including keep-alive signals between the server and the client so that the user of the API doesn't have to do this explicitly. For this reason, in most cases, this is the desired socket type, as it prevents a lot of common problems with connection status:

```
~myclient()
{
    close(m_fd);
}
};
```

As shown in the preceding code, like all of the other examples, when the client is destroyed, the socket file descriptor is closed, as follows:

```
int
protected_main(int argc, char** argv)
{
    (void) argc;
    (void) argv;

    myclient client{PORT};
    client.echo();
}
```

```
int
main(int argc, char** argv)
{
    try {
        return protected_main(argc, argv);
    }
    catch (const std::exception &e) {
        std::cerr << "Caught unhandled exception:\n";
        std::cerr << " - what(): " << e.what() << '\n';
    }
    catch (...) {
        std::cerr << "Caught unknown exception\n";
    }

    return EXIT_FAILURE;
}
```

Finally, the client is instantiated in a `protected_main()` function, and the `echo` function is called.

Compiling and testing

To compile this code, we leverage the same `CMakeLists.txt` file that we have been using for the other examples: `https://github.com/PacktPublishing/Hands-On-System-Programming-with-CPP/blob/master/Chapter10/CMakeLists.txt`.

With this code in place, we can compile this code using the following:

```
> git clone
https://github.com/PacktPublishing/Hands-On-System-Programming-with-CPP.git
> cd Hands-On-System-Programming-with-CPP/Chapter10/
> mkdir build
> cd build

> cmake ..
> make
```

To execute the server, run the following:

```
> ./example2_server
```

To execute the client, open a new terminal and run the following:

```
> cd Hands-On-System-Programming-with-CPP/Chapter10/build
> ./example2_client
Hello ↵
Hello
World
World ↵
<ctrl+c>
```

As shown in the preceding snippet, when the client is executed, and input is entered, the input is echoed back to the terminal. Once complete, and *Ctrl + C* is entered, the client exits. As you can see, the server will exit when the client is complete. The preceding example demonstrates the ease of use of TCP, and its advantages over UDP. The next example will demonstrate how to use TCP for something more useful.

Exploring an example on TCP Logger

To demonstrate something more useful, the following example implements the same logger that we have been developing throughout this book, but as a remote logging facility.

Server

The same macros and includes are needed for this example as with the previous examples in this chapter. To start the server, we must define the log file:

```
std::fstream g_log{"server_log.txt", std::ios::out | std::ios::app};
```

Since the logger will be executing on the same computer to keep the example simple, we will name the file the server is logging to as `server_log.txt`.

The server is identical to the TCP server in the previous example, with the exception that only a `recv()` member function is needed (that is, there is no need for a `send()` function as the server will only be receiving log data):

```
class myserver
{
    int m_fd{};
    int m_client{};
    struct sockaddr_in m_addr{};

public:
    explicit myserver(uint16_t port)
```

```
{
    if (m_fd = ::socket(AF_INET, SOCK_STREAM, 0); m_fd == -1) {
        throw std::runtime_error(strerror(errno));
    }

    m_addr.sin_family = AF_INET;
    m_addr.sin_port = htons(port);
    m_addr.sin_addr.s_addr = htonl(INADDR_ANY);

    if (this->bind() == -1) {
        throw std::runtime_error(strerror(errno));
    }
}

int bind()
{
    return ::bind(
        m_fd,
        reinterpret_cast<struct sockaddr *>(&m_addr),
        sizeof(m_addr)
    );
}

ssize_t recv(std::array<char, MAX_SIZE> &buf)
{
    return ::recv(
        m_client, buf.data(), buf.size(), 0
    );
}
```

The difference between the previous TCP example and this example is the use of the `log()` function instead of the `echo` function. Both functions are similar in that they listen for an incoming connection and then loop infinitely until data is received by the server:

```
void log()
{
    if (::listen(m_fd, 0) == -1) {
        throw std::runtime_error(strerror(errno));
    }

    if (m_client = ::accept(m_fd, nullptr, nullptr); m_client == -1) {
        throw std::runtime_error(strerror(errno));
    }

    while(true)
    {
        std::array<char, MAX_SIZE> buf{};
```

```
                    if (auto len = recv(buf); len != 0) {
                        g_log.write(buf.data(), len);
                        std::clog.write(buf.data(), len);
                    }
                    else {
                        break;
                    }
                }

            close(m_client);
        }
```

The difference with the `log` function is that when data is received by the client, instead of echoing the data back to the server, the data is output to `stdout` and written to the `server_log.txt` log file.

As shown here, the rest of the server logic is the same as the previous example:

```
        ~myserver()
        {
            close(m_fd);
        }
    };

    int
    protected_main(int argc, char** argv)
    {
        (void) argc;
        (void) argv;

        myserver server{PORT};
        server.log();

        return EXIT_SUCCESS;
    }

    int
    main(int argc, char** argv)
    {
        try {
            return protected_main(argc, argv);
        }
        catch (const std::exception &e) {
            std::cerr << "Caught unhandled exception:\n";
            std::cerr << " - what(): " << e.what() << '\n';
        }
        catch (...) {
            std::cerr << "Caught unknown exception\n";
```

```
    }

    return EXIT_FAILURE;
}
```

The socket file descriptor is closed when the server object is destroyed, the server is instantiated in a `protected_main()` function, and the `log()` function is then executed.

The client logic

The client logic for this example is a combination of the debug examples in previous chapters (which we have been building upon) and the previous TCP example.

We start by defining the debug level and enable macros, as with previous examples:

```
#ifdef DEBUG_LEVEL
constexpr auto g_debug_level = DEBUG_LEVEL;
#else
constexpr auto g_debug_level = 0;
#endif

#ifdef NDEBUG
constexpr auto g_ndebug = true;
#else
constexpr auto g_ndebug = false;
#endif
```

The client class is identical to the client class in the previous TCP example:

```
class myclient
{
    int m_fd{};
    struct sockaddr_in m_addr{};

public:
    explicit myclient(uint16_t port)
    {
        if (m_fd = ::socket(AF_INET, SOCK_STREAM, 0); m_fd == -1) {
            throw std::runtime_error(strerror(errno));
        }

        m_addr.sin_family = AF_INET;
        m_addr.sin_port = htons(port);
        m_addr.sin_addr.s_addr = htonl(INADDR_LOOPBACK);

        if (connect() == -1) {
```

```cpp
            throw std::runtime_error(strerror(errno));
        }
    }

    int connect()
    {
        return ::connect(
            m_fd,
            reinterpret_cast<struct sockaddr *>(&m_addr),
            sizeof(m_addr)
        );
    }

    ssize_t send(const std::string &buf)
    {
        return ::send(
            m_fd,
            buf.data(),
            buf.size(),
            0
        );
    }

    ~myclient()
    {
        close(m_fd);
    }
};
```

The only difference between the client in this example and the client in the previous example is that in this example, there is no need for a `recv()` function (as no data is being received from the server), and there is no need for the `echo()` function (or anything similar) as the client will be used directly to send data to the server as needed.

As with the previous debug example, a log file for the client is needed, and in this example, we will also globally instantiate the client, as follows:

```cpp
myclient g_client{PORT};
std::fstream g_log{"client_log.txt", std::ios::out | std::ios::app};
```

As shown, the client log file will be named `client_log.txt`, to prevent a collision with the server log file as both will be running on the same computer to simplify the example.

The `log` function is identical to the `log` function defined in Chapter 8, *Learning to Program File Input/Output,* with the exception that in addition to logging to `stderr` and the client-side log file, the debug string will also be logged to the server:

```
template <std::size_t LEVEL>
constexpr void log(void(*func)()) {
    if constexpr (!g_ndebug && (LEVEL <= g_debug_level)) {
        std::stringstream buf;

        auto g_buf = std::clog.rdbuf();
        std::clog.rdbuf(buf.rdbuf());

        func();

        std::clog.rdbuf(g_buf);

        std::clog << "\033[1;32mDEBUG\033[0m: ";
        std::clog << buf.str();

        g_log << "\033[1;32mDEBUG\033[0m: ";
        g_log << buf.str();

        g_client.send("\033[1;32mDEBUG\033[0m: ");
        g_client.send(buf.str());
    };
}
```

As shown in preceding code, the `log` function encapsulates any output to `std::clog`, and redirects the resulting string to `stderr`, the log file, and for the purpose of this example, to the client object that sends the string to the server to be logged on the server side.

The remaining portion of the example is identical to the previous examples:

```
int
protected_main(int argc, char** argv)
{
    (void) argc;
    (void) argv;

    log<0>([]{
        std::clog << "Hello World\n";
    });

    std::clog << "Hello World\n";

    return EXIT_SUCCESS;
}
```

```
int
main(int argc, char** argv)
{
    try {
        return protected_main(argc, argv);
    }
    catch (const std::exception &e) {
        std::cerr << "Caught unhandled exception:\n";
        std::cerr << " - what(): " << e.what() << '\n';
    }
    catch (...) {
        std::cerr << "Caught unknown exception\n";
    }

    return EXIT_FAILURE;
}
```

The `protected_main()` function outputs `Hello World\n` to `stderr`, which is redirected to include `stderr`, the log file, and finally sent to the server. Another call to `std::clog` is made to show that only calls to `std:clog` that are encapsulated in the `log()` function are redirected.

Compiling and testing

To compile this code, we leverage the same `CMakeLists.txt` file that we have been using for the other examples: `https://github.com/PacktPublishing/Hands-On-System-Programming-with-CPP/blob/master/Chapter10/CMakeLists.txt`.

With this code in place, we can compile this code using the following:

```
> git clone
https://github.com/PacktPublishing/Hands-On-System-Programming-with-CPP.git
> cd Hands-On-System-Programming-with-CPP/Chapter10/
> mkdir build
> cd build

> cmake ..
> make
```

To execute the server, run the following:

```
> ./example3_server
```

To execute the client, open a new terminal and run the following:

```
> cd Hands-On-System-Programming-with-CPP/Chapter10/build
> ./example3_client
Debug: Hello World
Hello World

> cat client_log.txt
Debug: Hello World

> cat server_log.txt
Debug: Hello World
```

As shown in the preceding snippet, when the client is executed, the client and server side both output DEBUG: Hello World to stderr. In addition, the client outputs Hello World to stderr as the second call to std::clog is not redirected. Finally, both log files contain the redirected DEBUG: Hello World.

In all of the examples so far, the one thing that has been ignored is what happens if more than one client attempts to connect to the server. In the examples in this chapter, only one client is supported. To support additional clients, threading is needed, which will be covered in Chapter 12, *Learning to Program POSIC and C++ Threads* where we will expand upon this example to create a logging server capable of logging the debug output of more than one application. The final two examples in this chapter will demonstrate how to process non-string data packets using TCP.

Trying out an example for processing packets

In this example, we will discuss how to process the following packet from the client to the server:

```
struct packet
{
    uint64_t len;
    char buf[MAX_SIZE];

    uint64_t data1;
    uint64_t data2;
};
```

The packet consists of some fixed-width integer data and a string (fields in a network must always be fixed width, as you might not have control of the type of computer your application is running on and non-fixed width types, such as int and long, might change depending on the computer).

This type of packet is common among many programs, but as will be demonstrated, this type of packet has challenges with respect to safely parsing.

The server is identical to the previous TCP examples, minus the recv_packet() function (and the recv() function processes packets instead of std::arrays):

```cpp
class myserver
{
...

    void recv_packet()
    {
        if (::listen(m_fd, 0) == -1) {
            throw std::runtime_error(strerror(errno));
        }

        if (m_client = ::accept(m_fd, nullptr, nullptr); m_client == -1) {
            throw std::runtime_error(strerror(errno));
        }

        packet p{};

        if (auto len = recv(p); len != 0) {
            auto msg = std::string(p.buf, p.len);

            std::cout << "data1: " << p.data1 << '\n';
            std::cout << "data2: " << p.data2 << '\n';
            std::cout << "msg: \"" << msg << "\"\n";
            std::cout << "len: " << len << '\n';
        }

        close(m_client);
    }

...
};
```

In the `recv_packet()` function, we wait to receive data from the client. Once the packet is received from the client, we parse the packet received. The integer data associated with the packet is read and output to `stdout` without issue. The string data, however, is more problematic. Since we don't know the total size of the string data being received, we must account for the entire buffer to safely process the string, and in a sense, maintain type-safety. Of course, in our example, to reduce the total size of the packet, we could have placed the integer data first in the packet, and then created a variable length packet, but this is both unsafe and hard to control or accomplish in more complicated scenarios. Most attempts to solve this problem (of having to send and receive more data than is actually needed) result in an operation that is variable in length, and thus, unsafe.

The rest of the server is identical to the previous examples:

```
int
protected_main(int argc, char** argv)
{
    (void) argc;
    (void) argv;

    myserver server{PORT};
    server.recv_packet();
}

int
main(int argc, char** argv)
{
    try {
        return protected_main(argc, argv);
    }
    catch (const std::exception &e) {
        std::cerr << "Caught unhandled exception:\n";
        std::cerr << " - what(): " << e.what() << '\n';
    }
    catch (...) {
        std::cerr << "Caught unknown exception\n";
    }

    return EXIT_FAILURE;
}
```

As shown in preceding code, the server is instantiated in a `protected_main()` function and the `recv_packet()` function is called.

The client logic

The bulk of the client is also identical to the previous examples:

```cpp
class myclient
{
...

    void send_packet()
    {
        auto msg = std::string("Hello World");

        packet p = {
            42,
            43,
            msg.size(),
            {}
        };

        memcpy(p.buf, msg.data(), msg.size());

        send(p);
    }

...
};
```

The `send_packet()` function is the only part that's different from the previous examples (minus the fact that the `send()` function sends packets instead of a `std::array()`). In the `send_packet()` function, we create a packet without our `"Hello World"` string. It should be noted that to create this packet, we still require some processing, including a memory copy. Once the packet is created, we send it to the server for processing.

The rest of the client is identical to the previous examples:

```cpp
int
protected_main(int argc, char** argv)
{
    (void) argc;
    (void) argv;

    myclient client{PORT};
    client.send_packet();
}

int
main(int argc, char** argv)
```

```
{
    try {
        return protected_main(argc, argv);
    }
    catch (const std::exception &e) {
        std::cerr << "Caught unhandled exception:\n";
        std::cerr << " - what(): " << e.what() << '\n';
    }
    catch (...) {
        std::cerr << "Caught unknown exception\n";
    }

    return EXIT_FAILURE;
}
```

The client is instantiated in a `proceted_main()` function, and the `send_packet()` function is executed.

Compiling and testing

To compile this code, we leverage the same `CMakeLists.txt` file that we have been using for the other examples: https://github.com/PacktPublishing/Hands-On-System-Programming-with-CPP/blob/master/Chapter10/CMakeLists.txt.

With this code in place, we can compile this code using the following:

```
> git clone
https://github.com/PacktPublishing/Hands-On-System-Programming-with-CPP.git
> cd Hands-On-System-Programming-with-CPP/Chapter10/
> mkdir build
> cd build

> cmake ..
> make
```

To execute the server, run the following:

```
> ./example4_server
```

To execute the client, open a new terminal and run the following:

```
> cd Hands-On-System-Programming-with-CPP/Chapter10/build
> ./example4_client
```

On the server side, the following is output to `stdout`:

```
data1: 42
data2: 43
msg: "Hello World"
len: 280
```

As shown in the preceding snippet, the packet data is sent by the client and received by the server. The total size of the packet received by the server is 280 bytes, even though the total size of the string is far smaller. In the next example, we will demonstrate how marshaling packets can safely reduce the total size of a packet at the expense of some additional processing (although likely negligible depending on your use case).

Processing an example of processing JSON

In this final example, we will demonstrate how packets can be marshaled using JSON to safely reduce the size of a network packet, at the expense of some additional processing. To support this example, the following C++ JSON library will be used: `https://github.com/nlohmann/json`.

To incorporate this JSON library into our example, the following will have to be added to our `CMakeLists.txt`, which downloads this header-only library and installs it into our build folder to be used:

```
list(APPEND JSON_CMAKE_ARGS
    -DBUILD_TESTING=OFF
    -DCMAKE_INSTALL_PREFIX-${CMAKE_BINARY_DIR}
)

ExternalProject_Add(
    json
    GIT_REPOSITORY https://github.com/nlohmann/json.git
    GIT_SHALLOW 1
    CMAKE_ARGS ${JSON_CMAKE_ARGS}
    PREFIX ${CMAKE_BINARY_DIR}/external/json/prefix
    TMP_DIR ${CMAKE_BINARY_DIR}/external/json/tmp
    STAMP_DIR ${CMAKE_BINARY_DIR}/external/json/stamp
    DOWNLOAD_DIR ${CMAKE_BINARY_DIR}/external/json/download
    SOURCE_DIR ${CMAKE_BINARY_DIR}/external/json/src
    BINARY_DIR ${CMAKE_BINARY_DIR}/external/json/build
    UPDATE_DISCONNECTED 1
)
```

Server

The server includes and macros are the same, with the exception that JSON must be added, as follows:

```
#include <nlohmann/json.hpp>
using json = nlohmann::json;
```

The server in this example is identical to the previous examples, with the exception of the `recv_packet()` function:

```
class myserver
{
...

    void recv_packet()
    {
        std::array<char, MAX_SIZE> buf{};

        if (::listen(m_fd, 0) == -1) {
            throw std::runtime_error(strerror(errno));
        }

        if (m_client = ::accept(m_fd, nullptr, nullptr); m_client == -1) {
            throw std::runtime_error(strerror(errno));
        }

        if (auto len = recv(buf); len != 0) {
            auto j = json::parse(buf.data(), buf.data() + len);

            std::cout << "data1: " << j["data1"] << '\n';
            std::cout << "data2: " << j["data2"] << '\n';
            std::cout << "msg: " << j["msg"] << '\n';
            std::cout << "len: " << len << '\n';
        }

        close(m_client);
    }

...
};
```

In the `recv_packet()` function, we need to allocate a buffer with some maximum size; this buffer is not required to be received in full, but rather is a placeholder for our JSON buffer, which could be any size up to our maximum. Parsing the JSON data is simple. The integer data and the string data are safely parsed into their integer and `std::string` types, respectively, all adhering to the C++ Core Guidelines in the process. The code is simple to read and follow, and the packet can be changed in the future without having to change any additional logic.

The rest of the server is identical:

```
int
protected_main(int argc, char** argv)
{
    (void) argc;
    (void) argv;

    myserver server{PORT};
    server.recv_packet();
}

int
main(int argc, char** argv)
{
    try {
        return protected_main(argc, argv);
    }
    catch (const std::exception &e) {
        std::cerr << "Caught unhandled exception:\n";
        std::cerr << " - what(): " << e.what() << '\n';
    }
    catch (...) {
        std::cerr << "Caught unknown exception\n";
    }

    return EXIT_FAILURE;
}
```

The server is instantiated in a `protected_main()` function and the `recv_packet()` function is called.

The client logic

Like the server, the client must also include the JSON header:

```
#include <nlohmann/json.hpp>
using json = nlohmann::json;
```

As with the server, the client is the same as the previous examples, minus the
`send_packet()` function:

```
class myclient
{
...

    void send_packet()
    {
        json j;

        j["data1"] = 42;
        j["data2"] = 43;
        j["msg"] = "Hello World";

        send(j.dump());
    }


...
};
```

The `send_packet()` function is equally simple. A JSON packet is constructed and sent to
the server. The difference is that the packet is marshaled into a JSON string before being
sent (using the `dump()` function). This converts all of the data into a single string with
special syntax to define the start and end of each field in a well-established, well-tested
fashion to prevent unsafe parsing. In addition, as will be shown shortly, the total number of
bytes being sent is dramatically reduced.

The rest of the client is identical:

```
int
protected_main(int argc, char** argv)
{
    (void) argc;
    (void) argv;

    myclient client{PORT};
    client.send_packet();
}
```

```
int
main(int argc, char** argv)
{
    try {
        return protected_main(argc, argv);
    }
    catch (const std::exception &e) {
        std::cerr << "Caught unhandled exception:\n";
        std::cerr << " - what(): " << e.what() << '\n';
    }
    catch (...) {
        std::cerr << "Caught unknown exception\n";
    }

    return EXIT_FAILURE;
}
```

The client is instantiated in a `protected_main()` function, and the `send_packet()` function is called.

Compiling and testing

To compile this code, we leverage the same `CMakeLists.txt` file that we have been using for the other examples: `https://github.com/PacktPublishing/Hands-On-System-Programming-with-CPP/blob/master/Chapter10/CMakeLists.txt`.

With this code in place, we can compile this code using the following:

```
> git clone
https://github.com/PacktPublishing/Hands-On-System-Programming-with-CPP.git
> cd Hands-On-System-Programming-with-CPP/Chapter10/
> mkdir build
> cd build

> cmake ..
> make
```

To execute the server, run the following:

```
> ./example5_server
```

To execute the client, open a new terminal and run the following:

```
> cd Hands-On-System-Programming-with-CPP/Chapter10/build
> ./example5_client
```

On the server side, the following is output to `stdout`:

```
data1: 42
data2: 43
msg: "Hello World"
len: 43
```

As shown in the preceding snippet, the packet data is sent by the client and received by the server. The total size of the packet received by the server is 43 bytes, which is 6.5 times more efficient compared to the previous example. In addition to providing a smaller packet, the logic for creating and parsing the packet is similar, and easier to read and modify in the future. Furthermore, with things such as JSON Schema, packets may even be validated prior to processing, a topic outside the scope of this book.

Summary

In this chapter, we learned how to program POSIX sockets using C++17. Specifically, we learned the common APIs associated with POSIX sockets, and how to use them. We concluded this chapter with five different examples. The first example created a UDP echo server, while the second example created a similar echo server using TCP instead of UDP, outlining the differences between the different approaches. The third example expanded upon our debug example by adding a server component to our debugger. The fourth and fifth examples demonstrated how to process a simple network packet, and the benefits of using marshaling to simplify the process.

In the next chapter, we will discuss the C and C++ time interfaces that can be used to get the wall clock, measure elapsed time and perform benchmarking.

Questions

1. What is the main difference between UDP and TCP?
2. What protocol type does UDP use?
3. What protocol type does TCP use?
4. What address type does `AF_INET` represent?
5. What is the difference between `bind()` and `connect()`?
6. What is the difference between `sendto()` and `send()`?
7. How does a UDP server detect when a UDP client is dropped or crashed?
8. What are the benefits of using packet marshaling?

Further reading

- https://www.packtpub.com/application-development/c17-example
- https://www.packtpub.com/application-development/getting-started-c17-programming-video

Time Interfaces in Unix

In this chapter, the reader will learn how to program the POSIX and C++ time interfaces using C++17. To start, this chapter will cover the UNIX epoch and POSIX `time.h` APIs and how to use them. Next, the C++ Chrono APIs will be briefly explained, how they relate to `time.h`, and some examples will also be provided. Finally, this chapter will conclude with two simple examples of how to use the time interfaces. The first example will demonstrate how to read the system clock and output the results to the console on an interval, and the second example will demonstrate how to benchmark software using the C++ high-resolution timer.

In this chapter, we will cover the following topics:

- Learning about POSIX `time.h` APIs
- The C++ Chrono APIs
- Understanding the read system clock with an example
- An example involving a high-resolution timer

Technical requirements

In order to compile and execute the examples in this chapter, the reader must have the following:

- A Linux-based system capable of compiling and executing C++17 (for example, Ubuntu 17.10+)
- GCC 7+
- CMake 3.6+
- An internet connection

To download all of the code in this chapter, including the examples and code snippets, please see the following link: `https://github.com/PacktPublishing/Hands-On-System-Programming-with-CPP/tree/master/Chapter11`.

Learning about POSIX time.h APIs

We will begin this chapter by discussing POSIX `time.h` APIs, which provide APIs for reading various clocks and performing calculations on these clock times. Although these APIs are specific to standard C, as will be demonstrated in the following section, the C time interfaces are still needed when working with C++, a problem that is being addressed in C++20.

Learning about the types of APIs

The UNIX epoch defines the number of seconds from January 1, 1970. Interfaces described in this chapter leverage the UNIX epoch to define the notion of time. The POSIX `time.h` APIs, for the purpose of this chapter, define three different, opaque types:

- `tm`: An opaque structure that holds a date and time.
- `time_t`: A `typedef` that stores a time that is typically implemented using an integer that stores the number of seconds from the UNIX epoch.
- `clock_t`: A `typedef` that stores the amount of processor time the application has executed.

These APIs provide various functions for creating these types and manipulating them. It should be noted that there are different types of clocks:

- **System clock**: The system clock reads the clock that the operating system is maintaining and stores the date and time that is presented to the user (for example, the clock that is shown on the taskbar). This clock can be changed at any point in time, so using it for timing in an application is usually discouraged as the clock being used might move back/forward in time in unexpected ways.
- **Steady clock**: A steady clock is a clock that ticks as the program executes. The more the program executes, the larger this clock grows. It should be noted that this clock will not match the results of the system clock and typically, only the difference between two of these clocks has any real value.
- **High-resolution clock**: This is the same as a steady clock, with the exception that the result being returned has a much higher resolution. These types of clocks are often used for benchmarking.

The time() API

The `time()` API returns the current system clock and takes on the following form:

```
time_t time(time_t *arg);
```

You can either provide the `time()` function with a previously-defined `time_t variable`, or it will return one for you (if you pass `nullptr` as the argument), as follows:

```
#include <ctime>
#include <iostream>

int main()
{
    auto t = time(nullptr);
    std::cout << "time: " << t << '\n';
}

// > g++ -std=c++17 scratchpad.cpp; ./a.out
// time: 1531603643
```

In the preceding example, we create a variable, called `t`, using the `time()` API to get the current number of seconds from the UNIX epoch. We then output this value to `stdout`. It should be noted that the `time_t` typedef is usually implemented using an integer value, which is why we can output its value directly to `stdout`, as shown in the preceding example.

As stated, you can also provide `time()` with your own, previously-defined, variable, as follows:

```
#include <ctime>
#include <iostream>

int main()
{
    time_t t;
    time(&t);
    std::cout << "time: " << t << '\n';
}

// > g++ -std=c++17 scratchpad.cpp; ./a.out
// time: 1531603652
```

The preceding example is identical to the first example, but instead of storing the return value of `time()`, we pass in our `time_t` variable as an argument to the function. Although this syntax is supported, the former is preferred. `time()` will return −1 in the event of an error, which can be checked and handled as needed.

The ctime() typedef

The `time_t` typedef is implementation-specific, and although it is typically implemented using an integer that stores the number of seconds from the Unix epoch, this is not guaranteed to be the case, meaning the preceding examples would likely not compile. Instead, to output the value of a `time_t` variable in a supported fashion, use the `ctime()` API, which takes on the following form:

```
char* ctime(const time_t* time);
```

The `ctime()` API takes a pointer to a `time_t` variable and outputs a standard C character string. The memory that backs the string that is returned is maintained by the `time.h` API (and therefore does not need to be freed) and, as a result, is not thread-safe. This API may be used as follows:

```
#include <ctime>
#include <iostream>

int main()
{
    auto t = time(nullptr);
    std::cout << "time: " << ctime(&t);
}

// > g++ -std=c++17 scratchpad.cpp; ./a.out
// time: Sat Jul 14 15:27:44 2018
```

As can be seen from the preceding example, instead of the number of seconds from the Unix epoch being returned, a human-readable version of the current time and date is returned. It should also be noted that, in addition to the `ctime()` function not being thread-safe, it also does not provide a mechanism for adjusting its output format. As a result, the use of this function is typically discouraged in place of other `time.h` functions.

The localtime() and gmtime() APIs

The time() API returns a time_t value that stores the number of seconds from the Unix epoch, as stated earlier. This value can further be processed to expose date and time information, providing us with the ability to convert the date and time to either the local time or **Greenwich Mean Time** (**GMT**). To do this, the POSIX API provides both the localtime() and gmtime() functions, as follows:

```
struct tm *localtime( const time_t *time );
struct tm *gmtime( const time_t *time );
```

Both of these functions take a pointer to a time_t variable and return a pointer to a tm opaque structure. It should be noted that the structure the return value points to is managed, like ctime(), by the time.h implementation, and thus is not freed by the user, meaning the results of this function are not thread-safe.

The asctime() function

To output an opaque tm structure to stdout (or, in general, just to convert the structure to a standard C string), the POSIX API provides the asctime() function, which has the following form:

```
char* asctime( const struct tm* time_ptr );
```

The asctime() function takes the same form as ctime(), with the exception that a pointer to a tm structure is provided as the main argument instead of a time_t variable, as follows:

```
#include <ctime>
#include <iostream>

int main()
{
    auto t = time(nullptr);
    std::cout << "time: " << asctime(localtime(&t));
}

// > g++ -std=c++17 scratchpad.cpp; ./a.out
// time: Sat Jul 14 15:28:59 2018
```

As shown in the preceding example, there is no difference in the output between ctime()
and asctime(localtime()). To output the same time in GMT instead of local time, use
the following:

```
#include <ctime>
#include <iostream>

int main()
{
    auto t = time(nullptr);
    std::cout << "time: " << asctime(gmtime(&t));
}

// > g++ -std=c++17 scratchpad.cpp; ./a.out
// time: Sat Jul 14 21:46:12 2018
```

As shown in the preceding example, gmtime() and localtime() execute the same, with
the only difference being a time zone change.

The strftime() function

So far, the output of ctime() and asctime() was predetermined by the POSIX API. That
is, there is no way to control the output format. In addition, these functions return internal
memory, preventing their thread safety. To fix these issues, the POSIX API added the
strftime() function, which is the recommended API for converting an opaque tm
structure to a character string, and takes the following form:

```
size_t strftime(char * str, size_t count, const char *format, const struct
tm *time);
```

The str parameter accepts a preallocated, standard C string, while the count parameter
defines the size of the first parameter. The format parameter accepts a null-terminated,
standard C string that defines the format to which to convert the date and time, while the
final time parameter accepts the opaque tm structure to convert to a string. The format
string that is provided to this function is similar to the format string provided to other
POSIX functions, such as printf(). The next couple of examples will demonstrate some of
these format specifiers.

To demonstrate the `strftime()` function, the following outputs the current date to `stdout`:

```
#include <ctime>
#include <iostream>

int main()
{
    auto t = time(nullptr);

    char buf[256]{};
    strftime(buf, sizeof(buf), "%m/%d/%Y", localtime(&t));

    std::cout << "time: " << buf << '\n';
}

// > g++ -std=c++17 scratchpad.cpp; ./a.out
// time: 07/14/2018
```

As shown in the preceding example, the `time()` API is used to get the current date and time. The `localtime()` function is used to convert the result of `time()` (which is `time_t`) to an opaque `tm` structure that represents the local date and time. The resulting `tm` structure is passed to `strftime()` with a format string of `"%m/%d/%Y"`, which outputs *month/day/year* to the standard C string provided. Finally, this string is output to the `stdout`, resulting in `07/14/2018`.

Likewise, this function may be used to output the current time:

```
#include <ctime>
#include <iostream>

int main()
{
    auto t = time(nullptr);

    char buf[256]{};
    strftime(buf, sizeof buf, "%H:%M", localtime(&t));

    std::cout << "time: " << buf << '\n';
}

// > g++ -std=c++17 scratchpad.cpp; ./a.out
// time: 15:41
```

The preceding example is identical to the previous example, the only difference being that the format specifier is `%H:%M`, which represents `hour:minute`, resulting in `15:41`.

Finally, to output the same string as `ctime()` and `asctime()`, use the following example:

```
#include <ctime>
#include <iostream>

int main()
{
    auto t = time(nullptr);

    char buf[256]{};
    strftime(buf, sizeof buf, "%a %b %d %H:%M:%S %Y", localtime(&t));

    std::cout << "time: " << buf << '\n';
}

// > g++ -std=c++17 scratchpad.cpp; ./a.out
// time: Sat Jul 14 15:44:57 2018
```

The preceding example is identical to the previous two examples, with the exception that the format specifier is `"%a %b %d %H:%M:%S %Y"`, which outputs the same results as `ctime()` and `asctime()`.

The difftime() function

Technically speaking, the `time_t` typedef is considered opaque (although it almost always is a signed 32-bit integer on Unix systems). For this reason, to ascertain the difference between two `time_t` values, the `difftime()` function is provided as follows:

```
double difftime(time_t time_end, time_t time_beg);
```

The `difftime()` function takes two `time_t` values and returns the difference as a double (since a non-POSIX function might support fractional times):

```
#include <ctime>
#include <iostream>

#include <unistd.h>

int main()
{
    auto t1 = time(nullptr);
    sleep(2);
    auto t2 = time(nullptr);

    std::cout << "diff: " << difftime(t2, t1) << '\n';
```

```
        std::cout << "diff: " << t2 - t1 << '\n';
}

// > g++ -std=c++17 scratchpad.cpp; ./a.out
// diff: 2
```

As shown in the preceding example, the difftime() function returns the difference between two times. It should be noted that although the preceding code compiles on most systems, difftime() should be used instead of the second example of directly subtracting two values.

The mktime() function

What if you have two opaque tm structures and you wish to calculate their difference? The problem here is that the difftime() function only takes time_t and not the tm structure. To support the reverse of the localtime() and gmtime() functions, which convert time_t into a tm structure, the mktime() function converts a tm structure back into a time_t value, as follows:

```
time_t mktime(struct tm *time);
```

The mktime() function takes a single parameter, which is the opaque tm structure you wish to convert to a time_t value:

```
#include <ctime>
#include <iostream>

int main()
{
    auto t1 = time(nullptr);
    auto lt = localtime(&t1);
    auto t2 = mktime(lt);

    std::cout << "time: " << ctime(&t2);
}

// > g++ -std=c++17 scratchpad.cpp; ./a.out
// time: Sat Jul 14 16:00:13 2018
```

The preceding example gets the current time and date using the time() API, and converts the results into a tm structure using the localtime() API. The resulting tm structure is then converted back into a time_t value using mktime(), and the resulting is output to stdout using ctime().

The clock() function

Up to this point, `time()` has been used to get the current system date and time. The problem with this type of clock is it returns the value the operating system is managing with respect to the current date and time, which can change at any point and time (for example, the user might be flying between time zones). This can be a problem, for example, if you are using the time APIs to keep track of how long something has executed. In this case, when a time zone change occurs, the application using `time()` might record the amount of time that has passed as being negative.

To overcome this issue, POSIX provides the `clock()` function, as follows:

```
clock_t clock(void);
```

The `clock()` API returns a `clock_t` value, which is similar to a `time_t` value. The difference between `time()` and `clock()` is that `time()` returns the current system time, while `clock()` returns a value that represents the total amount of time that has passed since the start of the application, for example:

```
#include <ctime>
#include <iostream>

int main()
{
    std::cout << "clock: " << clock() << '\n';
}

// > g++ -std=c++17 scratchpad.cpp; ./a.out
// clock: 2002
```

In the preceding example, the result of `clock()` is output to `stdout`. As shown, the value is implementation-specific, and only the difference between two `clock_t` values has any meaning. To convert `clock_t` into seconds, POSIX provides the `CLOCKS_PER_SEC` macro, which provides the necessary conversion, as shown in the following example:

```
#include <ctime>
#include <iostream>

#include <unistd.h>

int main()
{
    auto c1 = clock();
    sleep(2);
    auto c2 = clock();
```

```
        std::cout << "clock: " <<
            static_cast<double>(c2 - c1) / CLOCKS_PER_SEC << '\n';
}

// > g++ -std=c++17 scratchpad.cpp; ./a.out
// clock: 3.2e-05
```

In the preceding example, the clock() API is used to get the first clock value, and then the application sleeps for two seconds. Once the application is executed again by the operating system, the clock value is read again and the difference is converted into milliseconds using CLOCKS_PER_SEC (and then multiplied by 1,000). Notice the value does not equate to 2,000 milliseconds. This is because the application does not record execution while sleeping, and thus, only the execute time of the application is seen by clock().

To better demonstrate the difference in time, the following example demonstrates a one-to-one comparison of clock() and time():

```
#include <ctime>
#include <iostream>

#include <unistd.h>

int main()
{
    auto c1 = clock();

    auto t1 = time(nullptr);
    while(time(nullptr) - t1 <= 2);

    auto c2 = clock();

    std::cout << "clock: " <<
        static_cast<double>(c2 - c1) / CLOCKS_PER_SEC << '\n';
}

// > g++ -std=c++17 scratchpad.cpp; ./a.out
// clock: 2.05336
```

The preceding example is identical to the previous example, with the exception being we spin for two seconds using time() instead of sleeping for two seconds, resulting in the clock() returning two seconds.

Exploring C++ Chrono APIs

C++ includes the Chrono APIs which, mostly, provide C++ wrappers around the POSIX `time.h` APIs. For this reason, some time.h functions are still needed to provide full functionality, including the conversion to standard C strings. It should be noted that although some additions have been made in C++17 (specifically `floor()`, `ceil()`, and `round()`), the Chrono APIs are expected to see a relatively large overhaul with the introduction of C++20, which is outside the scope of this book. For this reason, the C++ Chrono APIs are briefly explained in this section to provide an overview of the current APIs.

The system_clock() API

The `std::chrono::system_clock{}` API is similar to `time()` in that it is capable of getting the system clock. `system_clock{}` is also the only clock that is capable of being converted into `time_t` (as it is likely implemented using `time()`), as shown in the following example:

```cpp
#include <chrono>
#include <iostream>

int main()
{
    auto t = std::chrono::system_clock::now();
    std::cout << "time: " << std::chrono::system_clock::to_time_t(t) <<
'\n';
}

// > g++ -std=c++17 scratchpad.cpp; ./a.out
// time: 1531606644
```

In the preceding example, the current system clock is read using the `system_clock::now()` API, and the result is converted into a `time_t` value using the `system_clock::to_time_t()` API. As with the previous example, the result is the number of seconds from the Unix epoch.

The time_point API

The result of the `system_clock::now()` API is a `time_point{}`. C++ does not provide a function to convert a `time_point{}` to a string (it won't until C++20), and as a result, the POSIX functions discussed in the previous section are still needed to perform this translation, as follows:

```
#include <chrono>
#include <iostream>

template<typename C, typename D>
std::ostream &
operator<<(std::ostream &os, std::chrono::time_point<C,D> &obj)
{
    auto t = std::chrono::system_clock::to_time_t(obj);
    return os << ctime(&t);
}

int main()
{
    auto now = std::chrono::system_clock::now();
    std::cout << "time: " << now;
}

// > g++ -std=c++17 scratchpad.cpp; ./a.out
// time: Sat Jul 14 19:01:55 2018
```

In the preceding example, we first define a user-defined overload for `time_point{}`, which is the result of the `std::chrono::system_clock::now()` API. This user-defined overload converts `time_point{}` into a `time_t` value using the C++ `std::chrono::system_clock::to_time_t()` API, and then converts `time_t` into a standard C string using `ctime()`, and streams the result to `stdout`.

Unlike the POSIX `time.h` APIs, the Chrono libraries provided various functions for incrementing, decrementing, and comparing a `time_point{}` using C++ operator overloads, as follows:

```
#include <chrono>
#include <iostream>

template<typename C, typename D>
std::ostream &
operator<<(std::ostream &os, const std::chrono::time_point<C,D> &obj)
{
    auto t = std::chrono::system_clock::to_time_t(obj);
    return os << ctime(&t);
```

```
}

int main()
{
    using namespace std::chrono;

    auto now = std::chrono::system_clock::now();

    std::cout << "time: " << now;

    now += 1h;
    std::cout << "time: " << now;

    now -= 1h;
    std::cout << "time: " << now;
}

// > g++ -std=c++17 scratchpad.cpp; ./a.out
// time: 1531606644
```

In the preceding example, the user-defined overload for `time_point{}` is provided as with the previous example. The current date and time are read using `std::chrono::system_clock::now()`, and the result is output to `stdout`. Finally, the resulting `time_point{}` is incremented by an hour, and then decremented by an hour (using the hour literal), and the results are also output to `stdout`.

In addition, arithmetic comparisons are supported, as follows:

```
#include <chrono>
#include <iostream>

int main()
{
    auto now1 = std::chrono::system_clock::now();
    auto now2 = std::chrono::system_clock::now();

    std::cout << std::boolalpha;
    std::cout << "compare: " << (now1 < now2) << '\n';
    std::cout << "compare: " << (now1 > now2) << '\n';
    std::cout << "compare: " << (now1 <= now2) << '\n';
    std::cout << "compare: " << (now1 >= now2) << '\n';
    std::cout << "compare: " << (now1 == now2) << '\n';
    std::cout << "compare: " << (now1 != now2) << '\n';
}

// > g++ -std=c++17 scratchpad.cpp; ./a.out
// compare: true
```

```
// compare: false
// compare: true
// compare: false
// compare: false
// compare: true
```

In the preceding example, the system clock is read twice, and the resulting `time_point{}` values are compared using the supported comparison operators. It should be noted that the results of this example could be different depending on the system this code is executed on, as the resolution of the time could be different.

Duration

The `time_point{}` type provides arithmetic to increment, decrement, and perform addition and subtraction. This arithmetic is all done using a C++ Chrono `duration{}`, which defines a range of time. Another way to view `duration{}` is that it would be the resulting abstraction of the POSIX `difftime()` call. In fact, the subtraction of two `time_point{}` types results in a `duration{}`.

In the preceding examples, `time_point{}` was incremented and decremented by an hour using the *h* duration literal for an hour. Like the hour literal, C++ provides the following literals for a duration of time, which may be used for this arithmetic:

- **Hour**: *h*
- **Minute**: *min*
- **Second**: *s*
- **Millisecond**: *ms*
- **Microsecond**: *us*
- **Nanosecond**: *ns*

Durations have a relatively complex template structure, which is outside the scope of this book, for defining their resolution (that is, whether a duration is in seconds, milliseconds, or hours), and can technically take on almost any resolution as a result. Although this functionality exists, C++ provides some predefined helpers for converting from one duration to another, preventing you from needing to know the inner workings of `duration{}`:

- `std::chrono::nanoseconds`
- `std::chrono::microseconds`
- `std::chrono::milliseconds`

- `std::chrono::seconds`
- `std::chrono::minutes`
- `std::chrono::hours`

For example, below we will use these predefined helpers to convert the system clock to seconds and milliseconds:

```cpp
#include <chrono>
#include <iostream>

#include <unistd.h>

int main()
{
    using namespace std::chrono;

    auto now1 = system_clock::now();
    sleep(2);
    auto now2 = system_clock::now();

    std::cout << "time: " <<
        duration_cast<seconds>(now2 - now1).count() << '\n';

    std::cout << "time: " <<
        duration_cast<milliseconds>(now2 - now1).count() << '\n';

    std::cout << "time: " <<
        duration_cast<nanoseconds>(now2 - now1).count() << '\n';
}

// > g++ -std=c++17 scratchpad.cpp; ./a.out
// time: 2
// time: 2001
// time: 2001415132
```

In the preceding example, the system clock is read twice, with a sleep for two seconds separating each read. The resulting `time_point{}` values are then subtracted to create a `duration{}`, and the resulting `duration{}` is converted into seconds, milliseconds, and nanoseconds, with the results being output to `stdout` using the `count()` member function, which simply returns the value of `duration{}`.

Like `time_point{}`, a duration can also be manipulated using arithmetic, as follows:

```cpp
#include <chrono>
#include <iostream>
```

```
int main()
{
    using namespace std::chrono;

    seconds t(42);

    t++;
    std::cout << "time: " << t.count() << '\n';

    t--;
    std::cout << "time: " << t.count() << '\n';

    t += 1s;
    std::cout << "time: " << t.count() << '\n';

    t -= 1s;
    std::cout << "time: " << t.count() << '\n';

    t %= 2s;
    std::cout << "time: " << t.count() << '\n';
}

// > g++ -std=c++17 scratchpad.cpp; ./a.out
// time: 43
// time: 42
// time: 43
// time: 42
// time: 0
```

In the preceding example, two `duration{}` variables are created that represent a second, one with the value of `0` seconds, and the second with a value of `42` seconds. Arithmetic is then performed on the first duration and the results are output to `stdout`.

In addition, comparisons are also supported:

```
#include <chrono>
#include <iostream>

int main()
{
    using namespace std::chrono;

    auto t1 = 0s;
    auto t2 = 42s;

    std::cout << std::boolalpha;
    std::cout << "compare: " << (t1 < t2) << '\n';
    std::cout << "compare: " << (t1 > t2) << '\n';
```

```
            std::cout << "compare: " << (t1 <= t2) << '\n';
            std::cout << "compare: " << (t1 >= t2) << '\n';
            std::cout << "compare: " << (t1 == t2) << '\n';
            std::cout << "compare: " << (t1 != t2) << '\n';
    }

    // > g++ -std=c++17 scratchpad.cpp; ./a.out
    // compare: true
    // compare: false
    // compare: true
    // compare: false
    // compare: false
    // compare: true
```

In the preceding example, two durations are created that represent 0 seconds and 42 seconds respectively, and both durations are compared using the comparison operators.

Most of the modifications to the Chrono library that are taking place will likely occur in C++20 with a large number of APIs being added to address the relatively obvious shortcomings of the existing API. In C++17, however, the floor(), ceil(), round(), and abs() APIs were added to the Chrono APIs, which return the floor, ceil, round, or absolute values of a duration, as shown in the following example (with similar APIs also being added to the time_point{} type):

```
    #include <chrono>
    #include <iostream>

    int main()
    {
        using namespace std::chrono;

        auto s1 = -42001ms;

        std::cout << "floor: " << floor<seconds>(s1).count() << '\n';
        std::cout << "ceil: " << ceil<seconds>(s1).count() << '\n';
        std::cout << "round: " << round<seconds>(s1).count() << '\n';
        std::cout << "abs: " << abs(s1).count() << '\n';
    }

    // > g++ -std=c++17 scratchpad.cpp; ./a.out
    // floor: -43
    // ceil: -42
    // round: -42
    // abs: 42001
```

The steady_clock function

`system_clock{}` is similar to `time()`, while `steady_clock{}` is similar to `clock()`, and performs the same objective—to provide a clock that represents the amount of time the application has executed, regardless of the current system date and time (which might change depending on the user of the system); for example:

```
#include <chrono>
#include <iostream>

#include <unistd.h>

int main()
{
    using namespace std::chrono;

    auto now1 = steady_clock::now();
    sleep(2);
    auto now2 = steady_clock::now();

    std::cout << "time: " <<
        duration_cast<seconds>(now2 - now1).count() << '\n';

    std::cout << "time: " <<
        duration_cast<milliseconds>(now2 - now1).count() << '\n';

    std::cout << "time: " <<
        duration_cast<nanoseconds>(now2 - now1).count() << '\n';
}

// > g++ -std=c++17 scratchpad.cpp; ./a.out
// time: 2
// time: 2001
// time: 2001447628
```

In the preceding example, the `steady_clock::now()` function is read twice, with a sleep separating the two calls. The resulting values are subtracted, converted to seconds, milliseconds, and nanoseconds, and the result is output to `stdout`. It should be noted that unlike `clock()`, the resulting steady clock accounts for the time the application slept.

The high_resolution_clock function

On most systems, high_resolution_clock{} and steady_clock{} are the same. In general, high_resolution_clock{} represents the highest-resolution clock available as a steady clock and, as shown in the following example, the result is the same with stead_clock{}:

```cpp
#include <chrono>
#include <iostream>

#include <unistd.h>

int main()
{
    using namespace std::chrono;

    auto now1 = high_resolution_clock::now();
    sleep(2);
    auto now2 = high_resolution_clock::now();

    std::cout << "time: " <<
        duration_cast<seconds>(now2 - now1).count() << '\n';

    std::cout << "time: " <<
        duration_cast<milliseconds>(now2 - now1).count() << '\n';

    std::cout << "time: " <<
        duration_cast<nanoseconds>(now2 - now1).count() << '\n';
}

// > g++ -std=c++17 scratchpad.cpp; ./a.out
// time: 2
// time: 2000
// time: 2002297281
```

In the preceding example, the high_resolution_clock::now() function is read twice, with a sleep separating the two calls. The resulting values are subtracted, converted into seconds, milliseconds, and nanoseconds, and the result is output to stdout.

Studying an example on the read system clock

In this example, we will bring everything we learned in this chapter into a simple demonstration that reads the system clock at an interval specified by the user. To accomplish this, the following inclusions and namespaces are needed:

```
#include <chrono>
#include <iostream>

#include <gsl/gsl>

#include <unistd.h>

using namespace std::chrono;
```

Like the examples throughout this chapter, a user-defined overload for std::ostream{} is provided to convert time_point{} into a standard C string, and then stream the result to stdout:

```
template<typename C, typename D>
std::ostream &
operator<<(std::ostream &os, std::chrono::time_point<C,D> &obj)
{
    auto t = std::chrono::system_clock::to_time_t(obj);
    return os << ctime(&t);
}
```

In our protected_main() function (which is a pattern used throughout this book), we output the current system time on an interval provided by the user, as follows:

```
int
protected_main(int argc, char **argv)
{
    using namespace std::chrono;
    auto args = gsl::make_span(argv, argc);

    if (args.size() != 2) {
        std::cerr << "wrong number of arguments\n";
        ::exit(1);
    }

    gsl::cstring_span<> arg = gsl::ensure_z(args.at(1));

    while(true) {
        auto now = std::chrono::system_clock::now();
```

```
        std::cout << "time: " << now;

        sleep(std::stoi(arg.data()));
    }
}
```

In the preceding code, we convert the arguments list into `gsl::span{}`, and then make sure we were given an argument. If no argument is provided, we exit the program. The argument is then converted into `cstring_span{}`, and an infinite loop is started. In the loop, the system clock is read and output to `stdout`, and then the program sleeps for the amount of time provided by the user:

```
int
main(int argc, char **argv)
{
    try {
        return protected_main(argc, argv);
    }
    catch (const std::exception &e) {
        std::cerr << "Caught unhandled exception:\n";
        std::cerr << " - what(): " << e.what() << '\n';
    }
    catch (...) {
        std::cerr << "Caught unknown exception\n";
    }

    return EXIT_FAILURE;
}
```

As with all of our examples, the `protected_main()` function is executed by the `main()` function, which catches exceptions should they occur.

Compiling and testing

To compile this code, we leverage the same `CMakeLists.txt` file that we have been using for the other examples: `https://github.com/PacktPublishing/Hands-On-System-Programming-with-CPP/blob/master/Chapter11/CMakeLists.txt`.

With this code in place, we can compile this code using the following:

```
> git clone
https://github.com/PacktPublishing/Hands-On-System-Programming-with-CPP.git
> cd Hands-On-System-Programming-with-CPP/Chapter10/
> mkdir build
> cd build
```

```
> cmake ..
> make
```

To execute the example, run the following:

```
> ./example1 2
time: Sun Jul 15 15:04:41 2018
time: Sun Jul 15 15:04:43 2018
time: Sun Jul 15 15:04:45 2018
time: Sun Jul 15 15:04:47 2018
time: Sun Jul 15 15:04:49 2018
```

As shown in the preceding snippet, the example is run with an interval of two seconds, and the application outputs the system clock to the console every two seconds.

Studying an example on high-resolution timer

In this example, we will create a simple benchmark using `high_resolution_clock{}`. To accomplish this, the following inclusions and namespaces are needed:

```
#include <chrono>
#include <iostream>

#include <gsl/gsl>
```

To create a `benchmark` function, we use the following:

```
template<typename FUNC>
auto benchmark(FUNC func) {
    auto stime = std::chrono::high_resolution_clock::now();
    func();
    auto etime = std::chrono::high_resolution_clock::now();

    return etime - stime;
}
```

This function has been seen before in Chapter 8, *Learning to Program File Input/Output*, The Logger Example. This code leverages functional programming to wrap a function call (likely a lambda) between two calls to the high-resolution clock. The results are then subtracted and returned. As we learned in this chapter, `high_resolution_clock{}` returns a `time_point{}` and their difference creates a `duration{}`.

The `protected_main()` function is implemented as follows:

```
int
protected_main(int argc, char **argv)
{
    using namespace std::chrono;

    auto args = gsl::make_span(argv, argc);

    if (args.size() != 2) {
        std::cerr << "wrong number of arguments\n";
        ::exit(1);
    }

    gsl::cstring_span<> arg = gsl::ensure_z(args.at(1));

    auto d = benchmark([&arg]{
        for (uint64_t i = 0; i < std::stoi(arg.data()); i++);
    });

    std::cout << "time: " <<
        duration_cast<seconds>(d).count() << '\n';

    std::cout << "time: " <<
        duration_cast<milliseconds>(d).count() << '\n';

    std::cout << "time: " <<
        duration_cast<nanoseconds>(d).count() << '\n';
}
```

In the preceding code, we convert the arguments list to a `gsl::span{}`, and then check to make sure we were given an argument. If no argument is provided, we exit the program. The argument is then converted into `cstring_span{}`, and a loop that runs for as long as the user wishes is benchmarked. The result of the `benchmark` is then converted into seconds, milliseconds, and nanoseconds and output to `stdout`:

```
int
main(int argc, char **argv)
{
    try {
        return protected_main(argc, argv);
    }
    catch (const std::exception &e) {
        std::cerr << "Caught unhandled exception:\n";
        std::cerr << " - what(): " << e.what() << '\n';
    }
    catch (...) {
```

```
            std::cerr << "Caught unknown exception\n";
    }

    rcturn EXIT_FAILURE;
}
```

As with all of our examples, the `protected_main()` function is executed by the `main()` function, which catches exceptions should they occur.

Compiling and testing

To compile this code, we leverage the same `CMakeLists.txt` file that we have been using for the other examples: `https://github.com/PacktPublishing/Hands-On-System-Programming-with-CPP/blob/master/Chapter11/CMakeLists.txt`.

With this code in place, we can compile this code using the following:

```
> git clone
https://github.com/PacktPublishing/Hands-On-System-Programming-with-CPP.git
> cd Hands-On-System-Programming-with-CPP/Chapter10/
> mkdir build
> cd build

> cmake ..
> make
```

To execute the example, run the following:

```
> ./example2 1000000
time: 0
time: 167
time: 167455690
```

As shown in the preceding snippet, the example is run with a loop of `1000000` iterations, and the amount of time it takes to execute that loop is output to the console.

Summary

In this chapter, we learned how to use both the POSIX and C++ time interfaces to read the system clock, and a steady clock for more precise timing. This chapter concluded with two examples; the first example demonstrated how to read the system clock and output the results to the console on a user-defined interval, and the second demonstrated how to benchmark software using the C++ high-resolution timer. In the next chapter, we will learn how to program both POSIX and C++ threads with examples that build upon the lessons learned in this chapter.

In the next chapter, we will discuss C++ threads, synchronization primitives such as mutexes, and how to program them.

Questions

1. What is the Unix epoch?
2. What type does `time_t` usually represent?
3. What is the difference between `time()` and `clock()`?
4. Why does `difftime()` return a double?
5. What is a C++ `duration{}`?
6. What is the difference between `steady_clock{}` and `high_resolution_clock{}`?

Further reading

- https://www.packtpub.com/application-development/c17-example
- https://www.packtpub.com/application-development/getting-started-c17-programming-video

12
Learning to Program POSIX and C++ Threads

In this chapter, the reader will learn how to program both POSIX and C++ threads. We will start by discussing how to program with POSIX threads, and then move on to C++ threads, providing a comparison of the APIs for each one.

Then we will present three examples. The first will demonstrate how to use threading to perform a parallel computation. The second will demonstrate how to create your own high-resolution timer using threading in order to perform benchmarking (albeit a timer that is likely not very accurate).

The third and final example will build upon our existing debugging example to provide support for multiple clients.

It should be noted that this chapter assumes the reader already has a basic understanding of threading, thread synchronization, and the challenges associated with race conditions and deadlock. Here, we will only focus on the APIs provided by POSIX and C++ for working with threads.

The chapter will cover the following:

- POSIX threads
- C++ threads
- Parallel computation
- Benchmarking with threads
- Thread logging

Technical requirements

In order to follow the examples in this chapter, the reader must have the following:

- A Linux-based system capable of compiling and executing C++17 (for example, Ubuntu 17.10+)
- GCC 7+
- CMake 3.6+
- An internet connection

To download all the code in this chapter, including the examples and code snippets, go to the following link: https://github.com/PacktPublishing/Hands-On-System-Programming-with-CPP/tree/master/Chapter12.

Understanding POSIX threads

A thread is similar to a process, with the main distinctions being the following:

- Threads are contained within processes
- Threads inherently share a memory space with other threads of the same process, while processes do not share resources unless explicitly told to (using inter-process communication mechanisms)

Like processes, however, threads are scheduled for execution at any time by the operating system. This may mean executing in parallel with other threads, leading to performance optimizations if properly used, but at the expense of introducing threading-specific logic bugs, such as race conditions and deadlock.

The goal of this section is to briefly review POSIX threads. These largely influenced the design of C++ threads, which will be discussed later.

The basics of POSIX threads

The most basic use of a thread is to create it, and then join the thread, which, in effect, waits for the thread to finish its work before returning as follows:

```
#include <iostream>
#include <pthread.h>

void *mythread(void *ptr)
```

```
{
    std::cout << "Hello World\n";
    return nullptr;
}

int main()
{
    pthread_t thread1;
    pthread_t thread2;

    pthread_create(&thread1, nullptr, mythread, nullptr);
    pthread_create(&thread2, nullptr, mythread, nullptr);

    pthread_join(thread1, nullptr);
    pthread_join(thread2, nullptr);
}

// > g++ -std=c++17 scratchpad.cpp -lpthread; ./a.out
// Hello World
// Hello World
```

In the preceding example, a `mythread()` function is created with the signature `(void *)(*)(void *)`, which is required by POSIX threads. In this example, the thread simply outputs to `stdout` and returns.

In the `main()` function, two threads are created using the `pthread_create()` function, which takes the following form:

```
int pthread_create(
    pthread_t *thread,
    const pthread_attr_t *attr,
    void *(*start_routine)(void*),
    void *arg
);
```

In this example, a `pthread_t` type is created and passed to the first argument. The attribute argument is ignored using a `nullptr`, and so is the argument to the thread itself (since it is not used). The only other thing we provide the `pthread_create` with function is the thread itself, which is a function pointer to our `mythread()` function.

To wait for the thread to complete, we use the `pthread_join()` function, which takes the following form:

```
int pthread_join(pthread_t thread, void **value_ptr);
```

The previously-created `pthread` is provided as the first argument to this function, while the return value of the `pthread` is ignored using a `nullptr` (since the thread doesn't return a value).

The result of this example is that `Hello World` is output to `stdout` twice (since two threads are created).

It should be noted that there are several issues with this example, which we will only briefly address in this chapter (as entire books can be written on the topic of parallel computing):

- **Type safety**: Both the argument to the thread and its return value are passed as a `void *`, completely removing any and all forms of type safety with respect to the thread itself. As a result, the `pthread` interface is not C++ Core Guideline compliant, and encourages the creation of hard-to-find logic errors. As will be demonstrated, C++ largely addresses these issues, albeit using an interface , which, at times, might seem difficult to follow.
- **Race conditions**: The preceding example does not attempt to address the possible race conditions of both threads outputting to `stdout` at the same time. As a result, if this example is executed enough times, it is likely that corruption with respect to its output would result.
- **No input/output**: Often, threads operate on globally-defined data without the need for input or output, but it is entirely possible that input and/or output may be needed in a different situation. This example doesn't address how to accomplish this.

Threads are implemented differently depending on the operating system, and cross-platform software needs to take this into account. Some operating systems implement threads as separate processes, while others implement threads as separate, scheduleable tasks within a process.

Either way, the POSIX specification dictates that a thread be identifiable, regardless of the underlying implementation.

To identify a thread, the following may be used:

```
#include <iostream>
#include <pthread.h>

void *mythread(void *ptr)
{
    std::cout << "thread id: "
              << pthread_self() << '\n';
```

```
        return nullptr;
}

main()
{
    pthread_t thread1;
    pthread_t thread2;

    pthread_create(&thread1, nullptr, mythread, nullptr);
    pthread_create(&thread2, nullptr, mythread, nullptr);

    pthread_join(thread1, nullptr);
    pthread_join(thread2, nullptr);
}

// > g++ -std=c++17 scratchpad.cpp -lpthread; ./a.out
// thread id: 140232513570560
// thread id: 140232505177856
```

The preceding example is identical to the first, with the exception that, instead of outputting Hello World to stdout, we use the pthread_self() function to output the thread's identifier. The pthread_self() function takes the following form:

```
pthread_t pthread_self(void);
```

Since the pthread_t type is usually implemented using an integer type, in our preceding example, we can output the value of this type to stdout using std::cout.

To provide support for input and output, the pthread API provides a void * for both the input and the output of the thread function. The following example demonstrates how to do this:

```
#include <iostream>
#include <pthread.h>

void *mythread(void *ptr)
{
    (*reinterpret_cast<int *>(ptr))++;
    return ptr;
}

main()
{
    int in_value = 42;
    void *out_value = nullptr;

    pthread_t thread1;
```

```
        pthread_t thread2;

        pthread_create(&thread1, nullptr, mythread, &in_value);
        pthread_create(&thread2, nullptr, mythread, &in_value);

        pthread_join(thread1, &out_value);
        pthread_join(thread2, &out_value);

        std::cout << "value: "
                  << *reinterpret_cast<int *>(out_value) << '\n';
}

// > g++ -std=c++17 scratchpad.cpp -lpthread; ./a.out
// 44
```

In this example, the thread function assumes the parameter it is passed is a pointer to an integer. It takes the value provided, increments it, and then returns it back to the caller (which, in this case, is the `main()` function).

In the `main()` function, we create both an input and an output value, with the input being initialized to 42. A pointer to the input value is provided during the creation of the thread, and a pointer to the output value is provided while joining the threads.

Finally, the resulting value is output to `stdout`. This is 44, since two threads were created, each of which increments the provided input once.

Since both threads are operating on the same integer, it is possible that a race condition could corrupt the results of these threads if they happen to execute at the same time; a problem that will be addressed later on.

Yielding

One advantage to using threads is that they can execute for a very long time without preventing the execution of your main thread/application. The downside is that threads that execute without an end can end up consuming too much CPU.

For example, consider the following code:

```
#include <iostream>
#include <pthread.h>

void *mythread(void *ptr)
{
    while(true) {
        std::clog << static_cast<char *>(ptr) << '\n';
```

```
            pthread_yield();
    }
}

main()
{
    char name1[9] = "thread 1";
    char name2[9] = "thread 2";

    pthread_t thread1;
    pthread_t thread2;

    pthread_create(&thread1, nullptr, mythread, name1);
    pthread_create(&thread2, nullptr, mythread, name2);

    pthread_join(thread1, nullptr);
    pthread_join(thread2, nullptr);
}

// > g++ -std=c++17 scratchpad.cpp -lpthread; ./a.out
// thread 2
// thread 2
// thread 2
// thread 1
// thread 2
// thread 2
// thread 1
// thread 1
// thread 1
```

In the preceding example, we create a thread that uses a while(true) statement, which executes as fast as possible, forever. Such a thread would execute until the operating system decided to preempt the thread to schedule another thread or process, resulting in the output of the thread occurring in a blocked, almost serial fashion.

In some cases, however, the user might need the thread to perform an action and then release its access to the CPU to allow another thread to perform its task. To accomplish this, we use the pthread_yield() API, which takes the following form:

```
int pthread_yield(void)
```

In the preceding example, the use of the yield function provides each thread with an opportunity to execute, resulting in a better-shuffled output of thread 1 and thread 2.

Although this function is provided, it should be noted that the operating system is excellent at handling threads that must perform a lot of work, and pthread_yield() should only be used when the user explicitly understands how it might provide optimization in their specific use case (since overuse of the pthread_yield() function can actually result in performance degradation).

It should also be noted that pthread_yield() is not available on all Unix systems.

In addition to pthread_yield(), the POSIX API also provides functions to put a thread to sleep if there is nothing to do (resulting in better performance and battery life), as follows:

```
#include <iostream>

#include <unistd.h>
#include <pthread.h>

void *mythread(void *ptr)
{
    while (true) {
        sleep(1);
        std::cout << "hello world\n";
    }
}

main()
{
    pthread_t thread;
    pthread_create(&thread, nullptr, mythread, nullptr);
    pthread_join(thread, nullptr);
}

// > g++ -std=c++17 scratchpad.cpp -lpthread; ./a.out
// hello world
// hello world
// hello world
```

In the preceding example, we create a thread that outputs Hello World once a second by creating a single thread that outputs to stdout, and then uses the sleep() function to put the thread to sleep for a second.

It should be noted that the use of sleep() should be handled with care, as it is possible for the operating system to race the sleep() call by yielding before sleep() is called.

Synchronization

Race conditions are a common problem when using threads, and solving race conditions without introducing deadlock (a thread that can no longer execute due to logic bugs with thread synchronization logic) is a complicated topic deserving of its own book.

The following example attempts to demonstrate the issues with potential race conditions:

```cpp
#include <array>
#include <iostream>
#include <pthread.h>

int count = 0;

void *mythread(void *ptr)
{
    count++;
}

main()
{
    while (true) {
        count = 0;
        for (auto i = 0; i < 1000; i++) {
            std::array<pthread_t, 8> threads;

            for (auto &t : threads) {
                pthread_create(&t, nullptr, mythread, nullptr);
            }

            for (auto &t : threads) {
                pthread_join(t, nullptr);
            }
        }

        std::cout << "count: " << count << '\n';
    }
}

// > g++ -std=c++17 scratchpad.cpp -lpthread; ./a.out
// count: 7992
// count: 7996
// count: 7998
// count: 8000
// count: 8000
```

To produce a race condition, we must execute threads fast enough, and for long enough (especially on modern hardware), that one thread performs an operation on a shared resource when another thread is in the middle of completing its own operation on that same shared resource.

There are many, many ways to do this. In the case of the preceding example, we have a thread that increments a counter, and then we create 8000 of these threads, increasing the chance that a race condition might occur. At some point during execution, two threads read the current value of the counter at the exact same time, incrementing the value and storing the incremented value at the same time. This results in the counter only being incremented once, even though two threads were executing.

As a result, and as can be seen from the output of the example, the count in some cases is less than 8000. In these cases, race conditions occurred, resulting in corruption.

To solve this issue, we must protect the critical region, which, in this case, is the part of the thread that uses the shared resource. The following example demonstrates one way to do this using a mutex (which ensures mutual exclusion to a critical region):

```
#include <array>
#include <iostream>
#include <pthread.h>

int count = 0;
pthread_mutex_t lock = PTHREAD_MUTEX_INITIALIZER;

void *mythread(void *ptr)
{
    pthread_mutex_lock(&lock);
    count++;
    pthread_mutex_unlock(&lock);
}

main()
{
    while (true) {
        count = 0;
        for (auto i = 0; i < 1000; i++) {
            std::array<pthread_t, 8> threads;

            for (auto &t : threads) {
                pthread_create(&t, nullptr, mythread, nullptr);
            }

            for (auto &t : threads) {
                pthread_join(t, nullptr);
```

```
              }
          }

          std::cout << "count: " << count << '\n';
      }
  }

  // > g++ -std=c++17 scratchpad.cpp -lpthread; ./a.out
  // count: 8000
  // count: 8000
  // count: 8000
  // count: 8000
  // count: 8000
```

In the preceding example, we wrap the critical region with a mutex. A mutex leverages atomic operations (operations that are guaranteed by hardware to manipulate a shared resource without corruption) to gain access to a critical region, one thread at a time.

If a thread attempts to gain access to a critical region while another thread is actively using the region, it waits until the thread is complete. Once the thread is complete, all the waiting threads race to get access to the critical region, and the thread that wins gets access while the remaining threads continue to wait. (Each operating system has its own way of implementing this to prevent the possibility of starvation; another topic that is beyond of scope of this book.)

As can be seen from the output of the preceding example, the use of a mutex around the critical region (in this case, the incrementing of the count variable) prevents the possibility of a race condition, resulting in 8000 being output every time.

The problem with mutexes is that each time the mutex is locked, a thread must wait until it is unlocked before it can continue. This is what protects the critical region from other threads, but it results in deadlock if the same thread attempts to lock the same mutex more than once (for example, when using recursion), or if mutexes are locked in the wrong order.

To overcome this problem, the POSIX API provides the ability to turn a mutex into a recursive mutex, as follows:

```
#include <iostream>
#include <pthread.h>

int count = 0;
pthread_mutex_t lock;
pthread_mutexattr_t attr;

void *mythread(void *ptr)
```

```
{
    pthread_mutex_lock(&lock);
    pthread_mutex_lock(&lock);
    pthread_mutex_lock(&lock);
    count++;
    pthread_mutex_unlock(&lock);
    pthread_mutex_unlock(&lock);
    pthread_mutex_unlock(&lock);
}

int main()
{
    pthread_mutexattr_init(&attr);
    pthread_mutexattr_settype(&attr, PTHREAD_MUTEX_RECURSIVE);
    pthread_mutex_init(&lock, &attr);

    pthread_t thread1;
    pthread_t thread2;

    pthread_create(&thread1, nullptr, mythread, nullptr);
    pthread_create(&thread2, nullptr, mythread, nullptr);

    pthread_join(thread1, nullptr);
    pthread_join(thread2, nullptr);

    std::cout << "count: " << count << '\n';
}

// > g++ -std=c++17 scratchpad.cpp -lpthread; ./a.out
// count: 2
```

In the preceding example, we are able to lock the mutex more than once without causing a deadlock by first setting the mutex to recursive mode using a mutex attribute. It should be noted that this additional flexibility typically comes with additional overhead.

The last POSIX API we will discuss in this chapter is the condition variable. As was demonstrated previously, a mutex may be used to synchronize access to critical regions of code. Another form of thread synchronization is to ensure threads execute in the proper order, which is what condition variables allow.

In the following example, threads 1 and 2 may execute at any time:

```
#include <iostream>
#include <pthread.h>

pthread_mutex_t lock = PTHREAD_MUTEX_INITIALIZER;
```

```
void *mythread1(void *ptr)
{
    pthread_mutex_lock(&lock);
    std::cout << "Hello World: 1\n";
    pthread_mutex_unlock(&lock);

    return nullptr;
}

void *mythread2(void *ptr)
{
    pthread_mutex_lock(&lock);
    std::cout << "Hello World: 2\n";
    pthread_mutex_unlock(&lock);

    return nullptr;
}

main()
{
    pthread_t thread1;
    pthread_t thread2;

    pthread_create(&thread2, nullptr, mythread2, nullptr);
    pthread_create(&thread1, nullptr, mythread1, nullptr);

    pthread_join(thread1, nullptr);
    pthread_join(thread2, nullptr);
}

// > g++ -std=c++17 scratchpad.cpp -lpthread; ./a.out
// Hello World: 2
// Hello World: 1
```

In this example, we create two threads, each outputting to stdout in a critical region that is guarded using a mutex. The rest of the example is the same as with previous examples in this chapter. As shown, thread 2 is executed first, and then thread 1 (this is largely due to thread 2 being created first). However, there is still the possibility that thread 1 could have executed first, as there is nothing controlling the order in which threads execute.

To solve this, the POSIX API provides a condition variable that may be used to synchronize the order of threads, as shown here:

```
#include <iostream>
#include <pthread.h>

bool predicate = false;
```

```cpp
pthread_cond_t cond = PTHREAD_COND_INITIALIZER;
pthread_mutex_t lock = PTHREAD_MUTEX_INITIALIZER;

void *mythread1(void *ptr)
{
    pthread_mutex_lock(&lock);
    std::cout << "Hello World: 1\n";
    predicate = true;
    pthread_mutex_unlock(&lock);
    pthread_cond_signal(&cond);

    return nullptr;
}

void *mythread2(void *ptr)
{
    pthread_mutex_lock(&lock);
    while(!predicate) {
        pthread_cond_wait(&cond, &lock);
    }
    std::cout << "Hello World: 2\n";
    pthread_mutex_unlock(&lock);

    return nullptr;
}

main()
{
    pthread_t thread1;
    pthread_t thread2;

    pthread_create(&thread2, nullptr, mythread2, nullptr);
    pthread_create(&thread1, nullptr, mythread1, nullptr);

    pthread_join(thread1, nullptr);
    pthread_join(thread2, nullptr);
}

// > g++ -std=c++17 scratchpad.cpp -lpthread; ./a.out
// Hello World: 1
// Hello World: 2
```

As we can see, `thread 1` executes first, and then `thread 2`, even though `thread 2` was created first. To accomplish this, we use the `pthread_cond_wait()` and `pthread_cond_signal()` functions, as follows:

```
bool predicate = false;
int pthread_cond_wait(pthread_cond_t *cond, pthread_mutex_t *mutex);
int pthread_cond_signal(pthread_cond_t *cond);
```

The `pthread_cond_wait()` function takes a pointer to a condition variable, and a mutex. When it is executed, it unlocks the mutex and waits for a call to `pthread_cond_signal()` to be executed. Once the signal is sent, `pthread_cond_wait()` locks the mutex again and continues execution.

The use of the `predicate` variable, which is also guarded by the mutex, is used to ensure that any spurious wake-ups are handled. Specifically, it is possible for the `pthread_cond_wait()` function to wake up even though the condition variable has not yet been signaled. As a result, you must always pair the `pthread_cond_wait()` function with a `predicate`.

Exploring C++ threads

In the previous section, we learned how POSIX provides support for threads. In this section, we will discuss C++ threads, which are largely inspired by POSIX threads. They provide similar functionality while simplifying the APIs in some ways, and also providing type safety.

The basics of C++ threads

To demonstrate the simplicity of C++ threads, the following example, like the first example in this chapter, creates two threads and then waits for them to finish executing:

```
#include <thread>
#include <iostream>

void mythread()
{
    std::cout << "Hello World\n";
}

main()
{
    std::thread t1{mythread};
```

```
        std::thread t2{mythread};

        t1.join();
        t2.join();
}

// > g++ -std=c++17 scratchpad.cpp -lpthread; ./a.out
// Hello World
// Hello World
```

There are some notable differences compared to the POSIX version of this example:

- The thread function itself may take on a number of different function signatures, and is not limited to `(void *) (*) (void *)`. In this example, the thread function uses the `void(*) ()` signature.
- The constructor of the thread type also creates the thread (no need to define the type, and then explicitly create the thread later).

It should be noted that in Linux, the `pthread` library still needs to be linked to the example. This is because, under the hood, C++ is using `pthread` instances to provide thread support.

Like the POSIX version, C++ also provides the ability to get the thread ID, as follows:

```
#include <thread>
#include <iostream>

void mythread()
{
    std::cout << "thread id: "
              << std::this_thread::get_id() << '\n';
}

main()
{
    std::thread t1{mythread};
    std::thread t2{mythread};

    std::cout << "thread1 id: " << t1.get_id() << '\n';
    std::cout << "thread2 id: " << t2.get_id() << '\n';

    t1.join();
    t2.join();
}

// > g++ -std=c++17 scratchpad.cpp -lpthread; ./a.out
// thread1 id: 139960486229760
// thread2 id: 139960477837056
```

```
// thread id: 139960477837056
// thread id: 139960486229760
```

In the preceding example, we use both the `this_thread` namespace and the thread itself to get the ID, demonstrating that there are two different ways to query a thread's ID (depending on the point of view of the caller).

The input and output of C++ threads is a good example of how C++ threading, in some ways, is more complicated than POSIX threading. As was stated, the biggest issue with POSIX threads with respect to input and output is a clear lack of type safety.

To solve this, C++ provides a concept called C++ futures, which, by itself, probably deserves its own chapter. We will describe them here briefly, to give the reader some general knowledge of how they work.

In the following example, we create a `mythread()` function that has the signature `int(*)(int)`, which takes a value, adds one, and returns the result (very similar to the preceding POSIX example of input and output):

```cpp
#include <thread>
#include <future>
#include <iostream>

int mythread(int value)
{
    return ++value;
}

int main()
{
    std::packaged_task<int(int)> task1(mythread);
    std::packaged_task<int(int)> task2(mythread);

    auto f1 = task1.get_future();
    auto f2 = task2.get_future();

    std::thread t1(std::move(task1), 42);
    std::thread t2(std::move(task2), 42);

    t1.join();
    t2.join();

    std::cout << "value1: " << f1.get() << '\n';
    std::cout << "value2: " << f2.get() << '\n';
}

// > g++ -std=c++17 scratchpad.cpp -lpthread; ./a.out
```

```
// Hello World
// Hello World
```

With C++ futures, we need to first tell C++ the signature type of our thread to ensure type safety. To accomplish this in our example (there are many ways to leverage the future's APIs, this is simply one of them), we create a `std::packaged_task{}` and provide it with our thread function signature.

This does a couple of things. First, it tells the APIs which thread to call, and, in addition, it sets storage aside for the result of the thread that can be retrieved later using `std::future{}`. Once `std::packaged_task{}` is created, we get the `std::future{}` from `packaged_task{}` using the `get_future()` function.

Finally, we start the thread by creating a thread object and passing it the `std::packaged_task{}` object created previously.

We can provide the thread with its initial input in the constructor of the thread, which takes all of the arguments of the thread as additional, template-based arguments. To retrieve the result of the thread, we use `get()` from the future, which is valid once the thread has completed and been joined (hence the name *future*).

Although futures are, in some ways, more complicated than simply passing a `void *` around, the interface is elegant, allowing for threads to take on any desired signature type while also providing type safety. (No `reinterpret_casts()` were needed to provide this example, ensuring Core Guideline Compliance and reducing the likelihood of hard-to-find logic bugs.)

Yielding

Similar to POSIX threads, C++ threads provide the ability to yield a thread, relinquishing the CPU so that other threads that need to perform their tasks may do so. This is expressed as follows:

```
#include <thread>
#include <iostream>

void mythread(const char *str)
{
    while(true) {
        std::clog << str << '\n';
        std::this_thread::yield();
    }
}
```

```
main()
{
    std::thread t1{mythread, "thread 1"};
    std::thread t2{mythread, "thread 2"};

    t1.join();
    t2.join();
}

// > g++ -std=c++17 scratchpad.cpp -lpthread; ./a.out
// thread 2
// thread 2
// thread 1
// thread 1
// thread 1
// thread 1
// thread 1
// thread 2
// thread 1
```

In the preceding example, we leverage the `yield()` function provided by the `this_thread` namespace, which yields the calling thread. As a result, it is better capable of shuffling the output of the thread between the two threads, as previously demonstrated.

In addition to yielding, a thread might need to stop its execution for a given amount of time. Similar to `sleep()` in POSIX, C++ provides the ability to sleep the currently executing thread. The difference with C++ is that a more granular API is provided, allowing the user to easily decide which type of granularity they prefer (including nanosecond and second resolutions), as follows:

```cpp
#include <thread>
#include <chrono>
#include <iostream>

using namespace std::chrono_literals;

void mythread()
{
    while (true) {
        std::this_thread::sleep_for(1s);
        std::cout << "hello world\n";
    }
}

main()
{
    std::thread t{mythread};
```

```
        t.join();
}

// > g++ -std=c++17 scratchpad.cpp -lpthread; ./a.out
// hello world
// hello world
// hello world
```

In the preceding example, we create a thread that outputs Hello World to stdout. Just prior to outputting to stdout, the thread sleeps for a second by calling the sleep_for() provided by the this_thread namespace, and using the second literal to define 1 second, resulting in Hello World being output to stdout each second.

Synchronization

Another notable difference between POSIX threads and C++ threads is the simplicity of thread synchronization. Like the POSIX APIs, C++ provides the ability to create a mutex, as follows:

```cpp
#include <mutex>
#include <thread>
#include <iostream>

int count = 0;
std::mutex mutex;

void mythread()
{
    mutex.lock();
    count++;
    mutex.unlock();
}

main()
{
    std::thread t1{mythread};
    std::thread t2{mythread};

    t1.join();
    t2.join();

    std::cout << "count: " << count << '\n';
}

// > g++ -std=c++17 scratchpad.cpp -lpthread; ./a.out
```

```
// count: 2
```

In the preceding example, we create a thread that increments a shared counter, which is surrounded by a C++ `std::mutex{}`, in effect creating a guarded critical region. We then create two threads, wait for them to complete, and then output the result to `stdout`, which ends up being 2 as we executed two threads.

The problem with POSIX threads and the preceding C++ example is seen when a thread has to leave a critical region in more than one place, as follows:

```
void mythread()
{
    mutex.lock();

    if (count == 1) {
        mutex.unlock();
        return;
    }

    count++;
    mutex.unlock();
}
```

In the preceding example, the critical region is exited in more than one place, and, as a result, the mutex must be unlocked in multiple places to prevent deadlock. Although this seems a simple example, an uncountable number of deadlock bugs have resulted from simply forgetting to unlock a mutex before returning from a critical region.

To prevent this problem, C++ provides `std::lock_guard{}`, which provides a simple mechanism for unlocking a mutex using **Resource Acquisition Is Initialization (RAII)** as follows:

```
#include <mutex>
#include <thread>
#include <iostream>

int count = 0;
std::mutex mutex;

void mythread()
{
    std::lock_guard lock(mutex);

    if (count == 1) {
        return;
    }
}
```

```
        count++;
    }

main()
{
    std::thread t1{mythread};
    std::thread t2{mythread};

    t1.join();
    t2.join();

    std::cout << "count: " << count << '\n';
}

// > g++ -std=c++17 scratchpad.cpp -lpthread; ./a.out
// count: 1
```

In the preceding example, we create an RAII-based lock guard in the thread instead of manually locking and unlocking the mutex. As a result, in this example, the entire thread is in the critical region as the mutex is locked when the guard is created and unlocked when the lock goes out of scope (that is, when the thread returns).

As demonstrated in the preceding example, it's impossible to accidentally forget to unlock the mutex, as unlocking the mutex is handled for us by the lock guard.

In some cases, the user might wish the thread to perform other useful work while waiting to gain access to a critical region. To accomplish this, `std::mutex{}` provides `try_lock()` as an alternative to `lock()`, which returns `false` if the lock could not be acquired:

```
#include <mutex>
#include <thread>
#include <iostream>

int count = 0;
std::mutex mutex;

void mythread()
{
    while(!mutex.try_lock());
    count++;
    mutex.unlock();
}

main()
{
    std::thread t1{mythread};
```

```
    std::thread t2{mythread};

    t1.join();
    t2.join();

    std::cout << "count: " << count << '\n';
}

// > g++ -std=c++17 scratchpad.cpp -lpthread; ./a.out
// count: 2
```

In the preceding example, we continue to try to lock the mutex in an endless `while` loop. We could, however, perform some additional work if `try_lock()` returns `false`, or we could sleep for a given amount of time before trying again, thereby reducing stress on the operating system and battery.

If you wish to use `try_lock` with a lock guard to prevent the need to manually unlock the mutex, you may do so using the following:

```
#include <mutex>
#include <thread>
#include <chrono>
#include <iostream>

int count = 0;
std::mutex mutex;

using namespace std::chrono_literals;

void mythread()
{
    std::unique_lock lock(mutex, std::defer_lock);

    while(!lock.try_lock()) {
        std::this_thread::sleep_for(1s);
    }

    count++;
}

main()
{
    std::thread t1{mythread};
    std::thread t2{mythread};

    t1.join();
    t2.join();
```

```
        std::cout << "count: " << count << '\n';
}

// > g++ -std=c++17 scratchpad.cpp -lpthread; ./a.out
// count: 2
```

In this example, we introduce two new features of C++ threads. The first is
`std::unique_lock{}`, which is similar to `std::lock_guard{}`.

`std::lock_guard{}` is a simple RAII wrapper around a mutex,
while `std::unique_lock` provides similar facilities to `std::unique_ptr{}`, in that the
resulting lock is movable (not copyable), and provides additional APIs above and beyond a
simple RAII wrapper.

As a side note, with respect to all of these lock guards, don't forget to define the guard's
variable, otherwise the lock will be locked and unlocked immediately, resulting in hard-to-
find bugs.

One of the additional APIs provided by `std::unique_lock` is the ability to defer locking
the mutex (that is, not locking on the construction of the lock itself). This provides the user
with the ability to better control when locking occurs, using one of the many lock functions,
such as `lock()`, `try_lock()`, `try_lock_for()`, and `try_lock_until()`.

In our preceding example, we try to lock the critical region, and, if that fails, we sleep for a
second before trying again. Other modifiers include the `std::adopt_lock{}` and
`std::try_lock{}` modifiers, which either assume the mutex is already locked, or that the
constructor tries to lock without blocking.

In addition to regular mutexes, C++ also provides, like POSIX, a recursive mutex, as shown
in the following code:

```
#include <mutex>
#include <thread>
#include <iostream>

int count = 0;
std::recursive_mutex mutex;

void mythread()
{
    std::lock_guard lock1(mutex);
    std::lock_guard lock2(mutex);
    count++;
}

main()
```

```
{
    std::thread t1{mythread};
    std::thread t2{mythread};

    t1.join();
    t2.join();

    std::cout << "count: " << count << '\n';
}

// > g++ -std=c++17 scratchpad.cpp -lpthread; ./a.out
// count: 2
```

In this example, we are capable of creating two lock guards on the same recursive lock without creating deadlock (as destructors are executed in reverse order to construction, ensuring the locks are unlocked in the proper order).

Another common problem with mutexes relates to locking more than one mutex at the same time; that is to say, if more than one critical region exists and a particular operation must operate on both critical regions at the same time. To accomplish this, C++17 added `std::scoped_lock{}`, which is similar to `std::lock_guard{}`, but accepts more than one lock, as follows:

```
#include <mutex>
#include <thread>
#include <iostream>

int count = 0;
std::mutex mutex1;
std::mutex mutex2;

void mythread()
{
    std::scoped_lock lock(mutex1, mutex2);
    count++;
}

main()
{
    std::thread t1{mythread};
    std::thread t2{mythread};

    t1.join();
    t2.join();

    std::cout << "count: " << count << '\n';
}
```

```
// > g++ -std=c++17 scratchpad.cpp -lpthread; ./a.out
// count: 2
```

In this example, more than one mutex is locked and unlocked using the
`std::scoped_lock{}` class.

`std::unique_lock{}` is similar to `std::unique_ptr{}` in that it guards a resource and
prevents copying. Similar to `std::shared_ptr{}` the mutex APIs also provide
`std::shared_lock{}`, which provides the ability for more than one thread to gain access
to the same mutex. The following code demonstrates this:

```cpp
#include <shared_mutex>
#include <thread>
#include <iostream>

int count = 0;
std::shared_mutex mutex;

void mythread1()
{
    while(true) {
        std::unique_lock lock(mutex);
        count++;
    }
}

void mythread2()
{
    while(true) {
        std::shared_lock lock(mutex);
        std::cout << "count: " << count << '\n';
    }
}

main()
{
    std::thread t1{mythread1};
    std::thread t2{mythread2};
    std::thread t3{mythread2};

    t1.join();
    t2.join();
    t3.join();
}

// > g++ -std=c++17 scratchpad.cpp -lpthread; ./a.out
// count: 999
```

```
// count: 1000
// count: 1000
// count: 1000
// count: 1000
// count: 1000
// count: count: 1000
// count: 1000
```

In the preceding example, we have two threads—a producer and a consumer. The producer (`mythread1`) increments a counter, while the consumer (`mythread2`) outputs the count to `stdout`. In the `main()` function we create three threads—one producer and two consumers.

We could implement this scenario using a regular `std::mutex`; however, such an implementation would be suboptimal as both consumers are not modifying the counter, meaning multiple consumers could safely execute simultaneously without corrupting the results if they happen to collide (as no modifications are being made).

If a regular `std::muted` is used, however, the consumers would have to wait on each other, which would also be suboptimal (obviously ignoring the fact that `stdout` is also a shared resource that should be treated as its own critical region to prevent corruption of `stdout` itself).

In order to solve this problem, we leverage `std::shared_mutex` instead of a regular `std::mutex`. In the producer, we lock the mutex using `std::unique_lock{}`, which ensures exclusive access to the critical region. In the consumer, however, we leverage `std::shared_lock{}`, which only waits on previous locks using `std::unique_lock{}`. If the mutex was acquired using `std::shared_lock{}`, the thread continues execution without waiting, sharing access to the critical region.

Finally, prior to C++17 with the addition of `std::scoped_lock{}`, the only way to lock more than one mutex was to use the `std::lock()` (and friends) functions, as follows:

```cpp
#include <mutex>
#include <thread>
#include <iostream>

int count = 0;
std::mutex mutex1;
std::mutex mutex2;

void mythread()
{
    std::unique_lock lock1(mutex1, std::defer_lock);
    std::unique_lock lock2(mutex2, std::defer_lock);
```

```
    std::lock(lock1, lock2);

    count++;
}

main()
{
    std::thread t1{mythread};
    std::thread t2{mythread};

    t1.join();
    t2.join();

    std::cout << "count: " << count << '\n';
}

// > g++ -std=c++17 scratchpad.cpp -lpthread; ./a.out
// count: 2
```

As with POSIX, C++ also provides the ability to control the order in which threads execute, using condition variables. In the following example, we create two threads and synchronize the order of their execution using a condition variable, similar to the condition variable example for POSIX:

```
#include <mutex>
#include <condition_variable>
#include <thread>
#include <iostream>

std::mutex mutex;
std::condition_variable cond;

void mythread1()
{
    std::cout << "Hello World: 1\n";
    cond.notify_one();
}

void mythread2()
{
    std::unique_lock lock(mutex);
    cond.wait(lock);
    std::cout << "Hello World: 2\n";
}

main()
{
    std::thread t2{mythread2};
```

```
    std::thread t1{mythread1};

    t1.join();
    t2.join();
}

// > g++ -std=c++17 scratchpad.cpp -lpthread; ./a.out
// Hello World: 1
// Hello World: 2
```

As shown in the preceding example, although the second thread is created first, it executes last. This is accomplished by creating a C++ condition variable. In the second thread, we protect the critical region using `std::unique_lock{}`, and then we wait for the first thread to signal that it has completed by making a call to `notify_one()`.

Once the first thread has completed and notified the second thread, the second thread finishes its execution.

This same approach also works for more than one thread in broadcast mode using C++ threads, as follows:

```
#include <mutex>
#include <condition_variable>
#include <thread>
#include <iostream>

std::mutex mutex;
std::condition_variable cond;

void mythread1()
{
    std::cout << "Hello World: 1\n";
    cond.notify_all();
}

void mythread2()
{
    std::unique_lock lock(mutex);
    cond.wait(lock);
    std::cout << "Hello World: 2\n";
    cond.notify_one();
}

main()
{
    std::thread t2{mythread2};
    std::thread t3{mythread2};
```

```
        std::thread t1{mythread1};

        t1.join();
        t2.join();
        t3.join();
    }

    // > g++ -std=c++17 scratchpad.cpp -lpthread;  ./a.out
    // Hello World: 1
    // Hello World: 2
    // Hello World: 2
```

In this example, the first thread completes its work and then signals to all the remaining threads to complete. The second thread protects the critical region with a mutex, and waits for a signal from the first thread.

The problem is that once the first thread executes and signals that it is done, the remaining threads will attempt to execute, but only one thread can acquire the critical region, resulting in the third thread waiting for the critical region to be unlocked and being notified. For this reason, when the second thread is complete, it must notify the condition variable again to unlock the remaining thread, allowing all three to complete.

To overcome this, we will combine everything learned in this section, as follows:

```cpp
#include <shared_mutex>
#include <condition_variable>
#include <thread>
#include <iostream>

std::shared_mutex mutex;
std::condition_variable_any cond;

void mythread1()
{
    std::unique_lock lock(mutex);
    std::cout << "Hello World: 1\n";

    cond.notify_all();
}

void mythread2()
{
    std::shared_lock lock(mutex);
    cond.wait(lock);

    std::cout << "Hello World: 2\n";
}
```

```
main()
{
    std::thread t2{mythread2};
    std::thread t3{mythread2};
    std::thread t1{mythread1};

    t1.join();
    t2.join();
    t3.join();
}

// > g++ -std=c++17 scratchpad.cpp -lpthread; ./a.out
// Hello World: 1
// Hello World: 2
// Hello World: 2
```

This example is identical to the previous example, with one simple change. Instead of `std::mutex{}`, we make use of `std::shared_mutex{}`, and `std::shared_lock{}` is used to lock the mutex.

In order to be able to use a shared mutex in place of a regular mutex, `std::condition_variable_any{}` must be used instead of `std::condition_variable{}`. By using `std::shared_mutex{}` instead of `std::mutex{}`, when the first thread signals that it has completed, the remaining threads are free to complete their work and process the critical region simultaneously.

Finally, C++ provides a convenient mechanism for calling a function once if more than one thread is needed, but allowing only one to execute initialization logic (a feature that POSIX also provides but is not covered in this book), as follows:

```
#include <mutex>
#include <thread>
#include <iostream>

std::once_flag flag;

void mythread()
{
    std::call_once(flag, [] {
        std::cout << "Hello World\n";
    });
}

main()
{
    std::thread t1{mythread};
    std::thread t2{mythread};
```

```
        t1.join();
        t2.join();
}

// > g++ -std=c++17 scratchpad.cpp -lpthread; ./a.out
// Hello World
```

In this example, more than one thread is created, but `Hello World` is only executed once using the `std::call_once{}` wrapper. It should be noted that although this seems simple, `std::call_once{}` ensures that the flag that holds the state as to whether or not the wrapped logic has yet to be executed is flipped atomically, thereby preventing the possibility of race conditions, however unlikely they might be.

Studying an example on parallel computation

In this example, we will demonstrate how to perform a parallel computation task that will calculate prime numbers, using threading. In this example, the following inclusion files and namespaces are required:

```
#include <list>
#include <mutex>
#include <thread>
#include <iostream>
#include <algorithm>

#include <gsl/gsl>
using namespace gsl;

using namespace std::string_literals;
```

Calculating prime values is an expensive operation for large numbers, but thankfully, they can be calculated in parallel. It should be noted that in our example, we don't attempt to optimize our search algorithm, as our goal here is to provide a readable example of threading. There are many methods, some simple, for improving the performance of the code in this example.

To store the prime numbers that our program finds, we will define the following class:

```
class primes
{
    std::list<int> m_primes;
    mutable std::mutex m_mutex;
```

```
public:

    void add(int prime)
    {
        std::unique_lock lock(m_mutex);
        m_primes.push_back(prime);
    }

    void print()
    {
        std::unique_lock lock(m_mutex);
        m_primes.sort();

        for (const auto prime : m_primes) {
            std::cout << prime << ' ';
        }

        std::cout << '\n';
    }
};

primes g_primes;
```

This class provides a place for us to store each prime number using the add() function. Once all the primes that we plan to search for are found, we provide a print() function that is capable of printing the identified prime numbers in sorted order.

The thread that we will use to check whether a number is a prime number is as follows:

```
void check_prime(int num)
{
    for (auto i = 2; i < num; i++) {
        if (num % i == 0) {
            return;
        }
    }

    g_primes.add(num);
}
```

In this thread, we loop through every possible multiple of the number provided, and check to see whether the modulus is 0. If it is 0, the number is not a prime. If no multiple is found, the number is a prime and it is added to our list.

Finally, in our `protected_main()` function, we search for a set of primes. We start by first converting all of our arguments so that they may be processed:

```
int
protected_main(int argc, char** argv)
{
    auto args = make_span(argv, argc);

    if (args.size() != 4) {
        std::cerr << "wrong number of arguments\n";
        ::exit(1);
    }
```

We are expecting three arguments. The first argument will provide the highest possible number we wish to check to see whether it is a prime number; the second argument is the total number of threads we wish to create to search for prime numbers, and the third will determine whether we want to print the results.

The next task is to get the highest possible prime number to search for, as well as to get the total number of threads to create. Consider the following code:

```
int max_prime = std::stoi(args.at(1));
int max_threads = std::stoi(args.at(2));

if (max_prime < 3) {
    std::cerr << "max_prime must be 2 or more\n";
    ::exit(1);
}

if (max_threads < 1) {
    std::cerr << "max_threads must be 1 or more\n";
    ::exit(1);
}
```

Once we know how many primes to search for, and how many threads to create, we search for our prime numbers as follows:

```
for (auto i = 2; i < max_prime; i += max_threads) {

    std::list<std::thread> threads;
    for (auto t = 0; t < max_threads; t++) {
        threads.push_back(std::thread{check_prime, i + t});
    }

    for (auto &thread : threads) {
        thread.join();
    }
```

```
    }
```

In this code, we search for all the primes up to the number provided by the user, incrementing by the total number of threads provided by the user. We then create a list of threads, providing each thread with the number it should look for prime from.

Once all the threads are created, we wait for the threads to finish. It should be noted that there are many ways to further optimize this logic, including preventing the recreation of threads, thus preventing the overuse of `malloc()`, but this example provides a simple mechanism to demonstrate the point of this example.

The last thing we do in the `protected_main()` function is check to see whether the user wants to see the results, and to print them if so:

```cpp
if (args.at(3) == "print"s) {
    g_primes.print();
}

return EXIT_SUCCESS;
}
```

Finally, we execute the `protected_main()` function using our `main()`, and catch any exceptions that might arise as follows:

```cpp
int
main(int argc, char** argv)
{
    try {
        return protected_main(argc, argv);
    }
    catch (const std::exception &e) {
        std::cerr << "Caught unhandled exception:\n";
        std::cerr << " - what(): " << e.what() << '\n';
    }
    catch (...) {
        std::cerr << "Caught unknown exception\n";
    }

    return EXIT_FAILURE;
}
```

Compiling and testing

To compile this code, we leverage the same CMakeLists.txt file that we have been using for the other examples—find it at the following link: https://github.com/PacktPublishing/Hands-On-System-Programming-with-CPP/blob/master/Chapter12/CMakeLists.txt.

With this code in place, we can compile this code using the following:

```
> git clone
https://github.com/PacktPublishing/Hands-On-System-Programming-with-CPP.git
> cd Hands-On-System-Programming-with-CPP/Chapter12/
> mkdir build
> cd build

> cmake ..
> make
```

To execute the example, run the following:

```
> time ./example1 20 4 print
2 3 5 7 11 13 17 19
```

As shown in this snippet, the prime numbers up to 20 are identified. To demonstrate the effectiveness of threading, execute the following:

```
> time ./example1 50000 4 no
real 0m2.180s
user 0m0.908s
sys 0m3.280s

> time ./example1 50000 2 no
real 0m2.900s
user 0m1.073s
sys 0m3.230s

> time ./example1 50000 1 no
real 0m4.546s
user 0m0.910s
sys 0m3.615s
```

As can be seen, as the total number of threads decreases, the total amount of time the application takes to find the prime numbers increases.

Studying an example on benchmarking with threads

In previous chapters, we discussed how to benchmark software using various different mechanisms. In this chapter, we will explore creating our own high-resolution timer using a thread, instead of using the high-resolution timer provided by the C++ chrono APIs.

To accomplish this, we will create a thread with the sole job of counting as fast as possible. It should be noted that although this will provide a high-resolution timer that is extremely sensitive, it has a lot of disadvantages compared to computer architectures such as Intel. These provide hardware instructions with higher resolution than is possible here, while being less susceptible to CPU frequency scaling.

In this example, the following inclusion and namespaces are needed:

```
#include <thread>
#include <mutex>
#include <condition_variable>
#include <iostream>

#include <gsl/gsl>
using namespace gsl;
```

We will store the high-resolution timer in a count variable, as follows:

```
int count = 0;
bool enable_counter = true;

std::mutex mutex;
std::condition_variable cond;
```

The enable_counter Boolean will be used to turn the timer off, while the mutex and condition variable will be used to turn the timer on at the correct time.

Our high-resolution timer will consist of the following:

```
void tick()
{
    cond.notify_one();

    while (enable_counter) {
        count++;
    }
}
```

The timer will notify the condition variable that it is running once it is started, and will continue to count until the `enable_counter` flag is set to `false`. To time an operation, we will use the following:

```
template<typename FUNC>
auto timer(FUNC func) {
    std::thread timer{tick};

    std::unique_lock lock(mutex);
    cond.wait(lock);

    func();

    enable_counter = false;
    timer.join();

    return count;
}
```

This logic creates the timer thread, and then waits for it to start using the condition variable. Once the timer is started, it will execute the function under test and then disable the timer and wait for the thread to complete, returning the resulting total number of ticks.

In our `protected_main()` function, we ask the user for the total number of times to loop in a `for` loop, and then time how long it takes to execute the `for` loop, outputting the results to `stdout` when we are done, as follows:

```
int
protected_main(int argc, char** argv)
{
    auto args = make_span(argv, argc);

    if (args.size() != 2) {
        std::cerr << "wrong number of arguments\n";
        ::exit(1);
    }

    auto ticks = timer([&] {
        for (auto i = 0; i < std::stoi(args.at(1)); i++) {
        }
    });

    std::cout << "ticks: " << ticks << '\n';

    return EXIT_SUCCESS;
}
```

Finally, we execute the `protected_main()` function using our `main()`, and catch any exceptions that might arise, as follows:

```
int
main(int argc, char** argv)
{
    try {
        return protected_main(argc, argv);
    }
    catch (const std::exception &e) {
        std::cerr << "Caught unhandled exception:\n";
        std::cerr << " - what(): " << e.what() << '\n';
    }
    catch (...) {
        std::cerr << "Caught unknown exception\n";
    }

    return EXIT_FAILURE;
}
```

Compiling and testing

To compile this code, we leverage the same `CMakeLists.txt` file that we have been using for the other examples: https://github.com/PacktPublishing/Hands-On-System-Programming-with-CPP/blob/master/Chapter12/CMakeLists.txt.

With this code in place, we can compile this code using the following:

```
> git clone
https://github.com/PacktPublishing/Hands-On-System-Programming-with-CPP.git
> cd Hands-On-System-Programming-with-CPP/Chapter12/
> mkdir build
> cd build

> cmake ..
> make
```

To execute the code, run the following:

```
> ./example2 1000000
ticks: 103749316
```

As shown in this snippet, the example is run with a loop of `1000000` iterations, and the number of ticks it took to execute the loop is output to the console.

Studying an example on thread logging

The final example in this chapter will build upon our existing debugger example to add support for multiple clients. In Chapter 10, *Programming POSIX Sockets Using C++*, we added support for networking to the example debugger, providing the ability to offload our debugging logs to a server in addition to the local system.

The problem with this is that the server could only accept one connection before closing, as it didn't have the logic for handling more than one client. In this example, we will fix that issue.

To start, we will need to define our port and max debug string length, as follows:

```
#define PORT 22000
#define MAX_SIZE 0x1000
```

The server will require the following include statements:

```
#include <array>
#include <unordered_map>

#include <sstream>
#include <fstream>
#include <iostream>

#include <mutex>
#include <thread>

#include <unistd.h>
#include <string.h>

#include <sys/socket.h>
#include <netinet/in.h>
```

As with our previous example, the log file will be defined as global, and a mutex will be added to synchronize access to the log:

```
std::mutex log_mutex;
std::fstream g_log{"server_log.txt", std::ios::out | std::ios::app};
```

Instead of the recv() function being defined in the server, we will define it globally to provide easy access to our client threads (each client will spawn a new thread):

```
ssize_t
recv(int handle, std::array<char, MAX_SIZE> &buf)
{
    return ::recv(
```

```
            handle,
            buf.data(),
            buf.size(),
            0
        );
    }
```

As with the `recv()` function, the `log()` function will also be moved out of the server and will create our client threads. Each time a connection is made by a client, the server will spawn a new thread (the `log()` function), which is implemented as follows:

```
void
log(int handle)
{
    while(true)
    {
        std::array<char, MAX_SIZE> buf{};

        if (auto len = recv(handle, buf); len != 0) {

            std::unique_lock lock(log_mutex);

            g_log.write(buf.data(), len);
            std::clog.write(buf.data(), len);

            g_log.flush();
        }
        else {
            break;
        }
    }

    close(handle);
}
```

The only difference with using the `log()` function, compared to the example in Chapter 10, *Programming POSIX Sockets Using C++*, is the addition of `std::unique_lock{}` to guard access to the log (in the event that more than one client attempts to write to the log at the same time). The handle is passed to the log function instead of the handle being a member of the server, and we flush the log file after each write to ensure all the writes are actually written to disk, as we will close the server application by killing it.

Finally, the server is modified to accept incoming connections and spawn threads as a result. The server starts with the same logic in the previous example:

```
class myserver
{
```

```
        int m_fd{};
        struct sockaddr_in m_addr{};

    public:

        myserver(uint16_t port)
        {
            if (m_fd = ::socket(AF_INET, SOCK_STREAM, 0); m_fd == -1) {
                throw std::runtime_error(strerror(errno));
            }

            m_addr.sin_family = AF_INET;
            m_addr.sin_port = htons(port);
            m_addr.sin_addr.s_addr = htonl(INADDR_ANY);

            if (bind() == -1) {
                throw std::runtime_error(strerror(errno));
            }
        }

        int bind()
        {
            return ::bind(
                m_fd,
                reinterpret_cast<struct sockaddr *>(&m_addr),
                sizeof(m_addr)
            );
        }
```

The server's constructor creates a socket, and binds the socket to the ports identified. The major difference with the server is in the use of the `listen()` function, which used to be the `log()` function. Consider the following code for it:

```
        void listen()
        {
            if (::listen(m_fd, 0) == -1) {
                throw std::runtime_error(strerror(errno));
            }

            while (true) {
                if (int c = ::accept(m_fd, nullptr, nullptr); c != -1) {

                    std::thread t{log, c};
                    t.detach();

                    continue;
                }
```

```
                throw std::runtime_error(strerror(errno));
        }
    }
```

The `listen()` function listens on the socket for new connections. When a connection is made, it creates a thread using the `log()` function and provides the `log` function with the handle of the new client.

There is no need to ensure the server and or clients are closed properly, as TCP will handle this for us, eliminating the need to track each client thread once created (that is, there is no need to `join()` the thread when it is complete). For this reason, we use the `detach()` function, which tells C++ that a `join()` will not take place, and the thread should continue to execute even after the thread object is destroyed.

Finally, we loop, waiting for more clients to connect.

The remaining logic for the server is the same. We create the server in the `protected_main()` function and execute the `protected_main()` function in our `main()` function, attempting to catch any exceptions that might occur. The following code shows this:

```
int
protected_main(int argc, char** argv)
{
    (void) argc;
    (void) argv;

    myserver server{PORT};
    server.listen();
}

int
main(int argc, char** argv)
{
    try {
        return protected_main(argc, argv);
    }
    catch (const std::exception &e) {
        std::cerr << "Caught unhandled exception:\n";
        std::cerr << " - what(): " << e.what() << '\n';
    }
    catch (...) {
        std::cerr << "Caught unknown exception\n";
    }

    return EXIT_FAILURE;
```

```
    }
```

Finally, the client logic for this example is identical to the client logic found in Chapter 10, *Programming POSIX Sockets using C++*.

Compiling and testing

To compile this code, we leverage the same CMakeLists.txt file that we have been using for the other examples—https://github.com/PacktPublishing/Hands-On-System-Programming-with-CPP/blob/master/Chapter11/CMakeLists.txt.

With this in place, we can compile the code using the following:

```
> git clone
https://github.com/PacktPublishing/Hands-On-System-Programming-with-CPP.git
> cd Hands-On-System-Programming-with-CPP/Chapter12/
> mkdir build
> cd build

> cmake ..
> make
```

To execute the server, run the following:

```
> ./example3_server
```

To execute the client, open a new Terminal and run the following:

```
> cd Hands-On-System-Programming-with-CPP/Chapter12/build
> ./example3_client
Debug: Hello World
Hello World

> ./example3_client
Debug: Hello World
Hello World

> cat client_log.txt
Debug: Hello World
Debug: Hello World

> cat server_log.txt
Debug: Hello World
Debug: Hello World
```

As shown in this snippet, when the client is executed, the client and server side both output `DEBUG: Hello World` to `stderr`. In addition, the client outputs `Hello World` to `stderr` as the second call to `std::clog` is not redirected.

Both log files contain the redirected `DEBUG: Hello World`. Finally, we can execute the client more than once, resulting in the server logging the output from both clients instead of just one.

Summary

In this chapter, we discussed how to program threads using both POSIX and C++ APIs. We then discussed three examples. The first example demonstrated how to use threading to perform a parallel computation, while the second demonstrated how to create your own high-resolution timer using threading to perform benchmarking.

Finally, the third example built upon our existing debugging example to provide support for multiple clients. The next, and final, chapter will discuss the error handling features provided by C and C++, including C style error handling and exceptions.

Questions

1. How do you get the ID of a thread using POSIX? What about when using C++?
2. What is the main issue with POSIX thread input and output?
3. What is a race condition?
4. What is deadlock?
5. What is `std::future{}` in C++, and what problem is it trying to solve?
6. What is the main reason for using `std::call_once()`?
7. What is the difference between `std::shared_mutex` and `std::mutex`?
8. What is the purpose of a recursive mutex?

Further reading

- `https://www.packtpub.com/application-development/c17-example`
- `https://www.packtpub.com/application-development/getting-started-c17-programming-video`

13
Error – Handling with Exceptions

In this final chapter, we will learn how to perform error handling while system programming. Specifically, three different methods will be presented. The first method will demonstrate how to use POSIX-style error handling, while the second method will demonstrate how to use the standard C-style set jump exceptions. The third method will demonstrate how to use C++ exceptions, and the pros and cons of each approach will be discussed. Finally, this chapter will conclude with an example that demonstrates how C++ exceptions outperform POSIX-style error handling.

In this chapter, we will cover the following topics:

- POSIX-style error handling
- Exception support in C++
- An example with Exception Benchmark

Technical requirements

In order to compile and execute the examples in this chapter, the reader must have the following:

- A Linux-based system capable of compiling and executing C++17 (for example, Ubuntu 17.10+)
- GCC 7+
- CMake 3.6+
- An internet connection

To download all of the code in this chapter, including the examples, and code snippets, please see the following link: `https://github.com/PacktPublishing/Hands-On-System-Programming-with-CPP/tree/master/Chapter13`.

Error handling POSIX-style

POSIX-style error handling provides the most basic form of error handling possible, capable of being leveraged on almost any system, in almost any program. Written with standard C in mind, POSIX-style error handling takes the following form:

```
if (foo() != 0) {
    std::cout << errno << '\n';
}
```

Generally, each function called either returns 0 on `success` or −1 on failure, and stores the error code into a global (non-thread safe) implementation-defined macro, called `errno`. The reason 0 is used for `success` is that on most CPUs, comparing a variable to 0 is faster than comparing a variable to any other value, and the `success` case is the expected case. The following example demonstrates how this pattern is used:

```
#include <cstring>
#include <iostream>

int myfunc(int val)
{
    if (val == 42) {
        errno = EINVAL;
        return -1;
    }

    return 0;
}

int main()
{
    if (myfunc(1) == 0) {
        std::cout << "success\n";
    }
    else {
        std::cout << "failure: " << strerror(errno) << '\n';
    }

    if (myfunc(42) == 0) {
        std::cout << "success\n";
```

```
    }
    else {
        std::cout << "failure: " << strerror(errno) << '\n';
    }
}

// > g++ -std=c++17 scratchpad.cpp; ./a.out
// success
// failure: Invalid argument
```

In this example, we create a function called `myfunc()`, which takes an integer and returns an integer. The function accepts any value as its parameter as *valid* except for 42. If 42 is provided as the input function, the function returns −1 and sets `errno` to `EINVAL`, which states that the function was provided an invalid argument.

In the `main` function, we call `myfunc()`, both with a valid input, and an invalid input and test, to see whether an error has occurred, resulting in `success` for the valid input and `failure: Invalid argument` for the invalid input. It should be noted that we leverage the `strerror()` function, which converts POSIX-defined error codes into their string equivalent. It should also be noted that this simple example will be leveraged throughout this chapter as we build and improve upon it.

The first issue that arises from this simple example is that the output of the function is leverage for error handling, but what if the function needs to output a value other than an error code? There are two ways to handle this. The first way to handle this is to constrain valid output of the function (that is, not all outputs are considered valid). This is generally how POSIX handles this problem. The following example demonstrates this:

```cpp
#include <cstring>
#include <iostream>

int myfunc(int val)
{
    if (val == 42) {
        errno = EINVAL;
        return 0;
    }

    return 42;
}

int main()
{
    if (auto handle = myfunc(1); handle != 0) {
        std::cout << "success: " << handle << '\n';
    }
```

```
        else {
            std::cout << "failure: " << strerror(errno) << '\n';
        }

        if (auto handle = myfunc(42); handle != 0) {
            std::cout << "success: " << handle << '\n';
        }
        else {
            std::cout << "failure: " << strerror(errno) << '\n';
        }
    }

// > g++ -std=c++17 scratchpad.cpp; ./a.out
// success: 42
// failure: Invalid argument
```

In the preceding example, we create a `myfunc()` function that returns a `handle` given valid input, and 0 given invalid input. This is similar to a lot of POSIX functions that return file handles. In this case, the notion of `success` is reversed, and, in addition, a handle may never take on a value of 0, as this is used to represent an error. Another possible method for providing error handling while also providing function output is to return more than one value, as follows:

```
#include <utility>
#include <cstring>
#include <iostream>

std::pair<int, bool>
myfunc(int val)
{
    if (val == 42) {
        errno = EINVAL;
        return {0, false};
    }

    return {42, true};
}

int main()
{
    if (auto [handle, success] = myfunc(1); success) {
        std::cout << "success: " << handle << '\n';
    }
    else {
        std::cout << "failure: " << strerror(errno) << '\n';
    }
```

```
    if (auto [handle, success] = myfunc(42); success) {
        std::cout << "success: " << handle << '\n';
    }
    else {
        std::cout << "failure: " << strerror(errno) << '\n';
    }
}

// > g++ -std=c++17 scratchpad.cpp; ./a.out
// success: 42
// failure: Invalid argument
```

In the preceding example, we return `std::pair{}` (which is really just a struct with two values). The first value in the pair is our handle, while the second value in our pair determines whether the handle is valid. Using this mechanism, 0 could be a valid handle as we have a way to tell the user of this function whether it is valid. Another way to do this is to provide the function with an argument that acts as an *output* and not as an *input,* a practice that is discouraged by the C++ Core Guidelines. This is depicted by means of the following code:

```
#include <cstring>
#include <iostream>

int myfunc(int val, int &error)
{
    if (val == 42) {
        error = EINVAL;
        return 0;
    }

    return 42;
}

int main()
{
    int error = 0;

    if (auto handle = myfunc(1, error); error == 0) {
        std::cout << "success: " << handle << '\n';
    }
    else {
        std::cout << "failure: " << strerror(error) << '\n';
    }

    if (auto handle = myfunc(42, error); error == 0) {
        std::cout << "success: " << handle << '\n';
    }
```

```
        else {
            std::cout << "failure: " << strerror(error) << '\n';
        }
    }

    // > g++ -std=c++17 scratchpad.cpp; ./a.out
    // success: 42
    // failure: Invalid argument
```

In this example, `myfunc()` takes two arguments, with the second argument accepting an integer intended to store an error. If the error integer remains at 0, no error has occurred. If, however, the error integer is set, an error has occurred, which we detect and output the failure as a result. Although this method is discouraged by the C++ Core Guidelines (mainly because there are better ways to perform error handling in C++), this method has the added benefit that the error integer is thread-safe, unlike the use of `errno`, which is not thread-safe.

Besides the verbosity of POSIX-style error handling and a tendency for error values to be ignored, the biggest issue with POSIX-style error handling is the numerous branch statements that must be executed continuously in the unlikely event that an error might occur. The following example demonstrates this:

```cpp
#include <cstring>
#include <iostream>

int myfunc(int val)
{
    if (val == 42) {
        errno = EINVAL;
        return -1;
    }

    return 0;
}

int nested1(int val)
{
    if (auto ret = myfunc(val); ret != 0) {
        std::cout << "nested1 failure: " << strerror(errno) << '\n';
        return ret;
    }
    else {
        std::cout << "nested1 success\n";
    }

    return 0;
}
```

```cpp
int nested2(int val)
{
    if (auto ret = nested1(val); ret != 0) {
        std::cout << "nested2 failure: " << strerror(errno) << '\n';
        return ret;
    }
    else {
        std::cout << "nested2 success\n";
    }

    return 0;
}

int main()
{
    if (nested2(1) == 0) {
        std::cout << "nested2(1) complete\n";
    }
    else {
        std::cout << "nested2(1) failure: " << strerror(errno) << '\n';
    }

    if (nested2(42) == 0) {
        std::cout << "nested2(42) complete\n";
    }
    else {
        std::cout << "nested2(42) complete: " << strerror(errno) << '\n';
    }
}

// > g++ -std=c++17 scratchpad.cpp; ./a.out
// nested1 success
// nested2 success
// nested2(1) complete
// nested1 failure: Invalid argument
// nested2 failure: Invalid argument
// nested2(42) failure: Invalid argument
```

In this example, we create the same my func() function that returns an error if the input provided is 42. We then call this function from a function that is called by another function (that is, we are making nested calls to our myfunc(), a practice that is highly likely to occur while system programming). Since myfunc() might return an error, and our nested functions are unable to handle the error, they must also return an error code, which, in turn, must also be checked. The bulk of the code in this example provides nothing more than error handling logic, designed to forward the results of an error to the next function in the hope that the next function is capable of handling the error.

This nested error forwarding may be referred to as `stack unwinding`. Each time we call a function that could return an error, we check whether an error has occurred and we return the result to the next function in the stack. This process of unwinding the call stack is repeated until we get to a function in the call stack that is capable of handling the error. In our case, this is the `main()` function.

The problem with POSIX-style error handling is that stack unwinding must be performed manually, and thus, this code is executed continuously in the `success` case, resulting in poor-performing, verbose code, as demonstrated by the preceding example, which checks a simple integer value in only three nested calls.

Finally, it should be noted that POSIX-style error handling does support **Resource Acquisition Is Initialization** (**RAII**), meaning objects defined in the scope of a function are destroyed properly the function exits in both the `success` case and the error case, as demonstrated in the following example:

```cpp
#include <cstring>
#include <iostream>

class myclass
{
public:
    ~myclass()
    {
        std::cout << "destructor called\n";
    }
};

int myfunc(int val)
{
    myclass c{};

    if (val == 42) {
        errno = EINVAL;
        return -1;
    }

    return 0;
}

int main()
{
    if (myfunc(1) == 0) {
        std::cout << "success\n";
    }
    else {
```

```
        std::cout << "failure: " << strerror(errno) << '\n';
    }

    if (myfunc(42) -- 0) {
        std::cout << "success\n";
    }
    else {
        std::cout << "failure: " << strerror(errno) << '\n';
    }
}

// > g++ -std=c++17 scratchpad.cpp; ./a.out
// destructor called
// success
// destructor called
// failure: Invalid argument
```

In the preceding example, we create a simple class that outputs a string to stdout on destruction and creates an instance of this class in our myfunc() function. When myfunc() is called, both on success and failure, the destructor of the class is called properly on exit. In our next error handling mechanism, called set jump, we will demonstrate how a lot of the issues with POSIX-style error handling are addressed while also demonstrating that the key limitation with set jump is a lack of RAII support, possibly resulting in undefined behavior.

Learning about set jump exceptions

Set jump exceptions may be viewed as C-style exceptions. Like C++-style exceptions, set jump exceptions provide the user with the ability to set a place in the code to return to in the event of an error, and a method for generating the exception that performs the jump. The following code example demonstrates this:

```
#include <cstring>
#include <csetjmp>

#include <iostream>

std::jmp_buf jb;

void myfunc(int val)
{
    if (val == 42) {
        errno = EINVAL;    // Invalid argument
        std::longjmp(jb, -42);
```

```
    }
}

int main()
{
    if (setjmp(jb) == -42) {
        std::cout << "failure: " << strerror(errno) << '\n';
        std::exit(EXIT_FAILURE);
    }

    myfunc(1);
    std::cout << "success\n";

    myfunc(42);
    std::cout << "success\n";
}

// > g++ -std=c++17 scratchpad.cpp; ./a.out
// success
// failure: Invalid argument
```

In this example, we create our `myfunc()` function, but instead of returning an error code, we execute a long jump, which acts like a *goto*, jumping to the last place in the call stack that a call to `setjmp()` was made. In our `main` function, we first call `setjmp()` to place our return point, and then we make calls to our `myfunc()` function with both a valid input and an invalid input.

Immediately, we have addressed several issues with POSIX-style error handling. As can be seen in the preceding example, the code is far less complicated, removing the need to check for error conditions. In addition, `myfunc()` returns a void, as no error code needs to be returned, meaning there is no longer a need to constrain the output of a function to support an error case, as can be seen in the following example:

```
#include <cstring>
#include <csetjmp>

#include <iostream>

std::jmp_buf jb;

int myfunc(int val)
{
    if (val == 42) {
        errno = EINVAL;
        std::longjmp(jb, -1);
    }
```

```
        return 42;
}

int main()
{
    if (setjmp(jb) == -1) {
        std::cout << "failure: " << strerror(errno) << '\n';
        std::exit(EXIT_FAILURE);
    }

    auto handle1 = myfunc(1);
    std::cout << "success: " << handle1 << '\n';

    auto handle2 = myfunc(42);
    std::cout << "success: " << handle2 << '\n';
}

// > g++ -std=c++17 scratchpad.cpp; ./a.out
// success: 42
// failure: Invalid argument
```

In this example, `myfunc()` returns a *handle*, and the error case is handled using a set jump exception. As a result, `myfunc()` may return any value, and the user of the function knows whether a handle is valid based on whether a long jump was called.

Since a return value of `myfunc()` is no longer needed, we also no longer need to check the return value of `myfunc()`, meaning our nested example is greatly simplified, as follows:

```
#include <cstring>
#include <csetjmp>

#include <iostream>

std::jmp_buf jb;

void myfunc(int val)
{
    if (val == 42) {
        errno = EINVAL;
        std::longjmp(jb, -1);
    }
}

void nested1(int val)
{
    myfunc(val);
    std::cout << "nested1 success\n";
```

```
    }

void nested2(int val)
{
    nested1(val);
    std::cout << "nested2 success\n";
}

int main()
{
    if (setjmp(jb) == -1) {
        std::cout << "failure: " << strerror(errno) << '\n';
        exit(EXIT_FAILURE);
    }

    nested2(1);
    std::cout << "nested2(1) complete\n";

    nested2(42);
    std::cout << "nested2(42) complete\n";
}

// > g++ -std=c++17 scratchpad.cpp; ./a.out
// nested1 success
// nested2 success
// nested2(1) complete
// failure: Invalid argument
```

As can be seen, the only error logic in this example exists in `myfunc()` checking to ensure the input is valid. The remaining error logic has been removed. Not only does this result in code that is easier to read and maintain, but the resulting code also performs better, as we are no longer executing branch statements, but manually unwinding the call stack by hand.

Another benefit of using set jump exceptions is that it is possible to create thread-safe error handling. In our previous example, we set `errno` in the event of an error, which is then read when we reach the code that is capable of handling the error. With set jump, `errno` is no longer needed as we can return the error code in the long jump itself, using the following approach:

```
#include <cstring>
#include <csetjmp>

#include <iostream>

void myfunc(int val, jmp_buf &jb)
{
    if (val == 42) {
```

```cpp
        std::longjmp(jb, EINVAL);
    }
}

int main()
{
    std::jmp_buf jb;

    if (auto ret = setjmp(jb); ret > 0) {
        std::cout << "failure: " << strerror(ret) << '\n';
        std::exit(EXIT_FAILURE);
    }

    myfunc(1, jb);
    std::cout << "success\n";

    myfunc(42, jb);
    std::cout << "success\n";
}

// > g++ -std=c++17 scratchpad.cpp; ./a.out
// success
// failure: Invalid argument
```

In the preceding example, instead of setting `errno` and returning -1 in our long jump, we return the error code in our long jump, and, using the C++17 syntax, store the value from the long jump in our call to set jump and make sure this value is greater than 0. The first time set jump is called, it returns 0 as no error has occurred yet, meaning the branch is not taken. If, however, set jump is called a second time (when our long jump is called), the value that is placed in the call to our long jump is returned instead, resulting in the branch being taken and an error reported in a thread-safe manner.

Note that the only modification we need to make to our example is that we must pass the jump buffer of every function, which is highly inconvenient, especially in the case of nested function calls. In our previous examples, the jump buffer was stored globally, which is not thread-safe, but is more convenient, and results in cleaner code.

In addition to an awkward mechanism for providing thread safety, the main disadvantage to using set jump for error handling is a lack of support for RAII, meaning objects created in the scope of a function may not have their destructors called on exit (a problem that is actually implementation-specific). The reason destructors are not called is that the function never technically exits. set jump/long jump stores the instruction pointer and non-volatile registers in the jump buffer on a call to set jump.

When a long jump is performed, the application overwrites the instruction pointer and CPU registers with the values stored in the jump buffer and then continues execution as if the code after the call to `setjump()` was never executed. For this reason, the destructors of an object are never executed, as demonstrated in the following example:

```cpp
#include <cstring>
#include <csetjmp>

#include <iostream>

jmp_buf jb;

class myclass
{
public:
    ~myclass()
    {
        std::cout << "destructor called\n";
    }
};

void myfunc(int val)
{
    myclass c{};

    if (val == 42) {
        errno = EINVAL;
        std::longjmp(jb, -1);
    }
}

int main()
{
    if (setjmp(jb) == -1) {
        std::cout << "failure: " << strerror(errno) << '\n';
        exit(EXIT_FAILURE);
    }

    myfunc(1);
    std::cout << "success\n";

    myfunc(42);
    std::cout << "success\n";
}

// > g++ -std=c++17 scratchpad.cpp; ./a.out
// destructor called
```

```
// success
// failure: Invalid argument
```

In this example, we create a simple class that outputs a string to stdout when the class is destroyed. We then create an instance of this class in myfunc(). In the success case, the destructor is called as myfunc() exits, resulting in the destructor being called. In the failure case, however, myfunc() never exits, resulting in the destructor not being called.

In the next section, we will talk about C++ exceptions that build upon set jump exceptions to not only provide support for RAII, but also provide the ability to return complex data types in the event of an error.

Understanding exception support in C++

C++ exceptions provide a mechanism for reporting errors in a thread-safe manner, without the need to manually unwind the call stack, while also providing support for RAII and complex data types. To better understand this, refer to the following example:

```
#include <cstring>
#include <iostream>

void myfunc(int val)
{
    if (val == 42) {
        throw EINVAL;
    }
}

int main()
{
    try {
        myfunc(1);
        std::cout << "success\n";

        myfunc(42);
        std::cout << "success\n";
    }
    catch(int ret) {
        std::cout << "failure: " << strerror(ret) << '\n';
    }
}

// > g++ -std=c++17 scratchpad.cpp; ./a.out
// success
// failure: Invalid argument
```

In the preceding example, our `myfunc()` function has been greatly simplified compared to its POSIX-style equivalent. Just like our previous examples, if the input provided to the function is `42`, the error is returned (in this case, it is actually thrown). If the input provided is not `42`, the function returns successfully.

Like set jump, calls to `myfunc()` no longer need to check the return value of the function as no return value is provided. To handle the error case, we wrap our call to `myfunc()` in a `try...catch` block. If any of the code in the `try{}` block results in an exception being thrown, the `catch[]` block will be executed. As with most C++, the `catch` block is type-safe, meaning you must state what type of return data you plan to receive in the event of an exception being thrown. In this case, we throw `EINVAL`, which is an integer, so we catch an integer and output the result to `stdout`.

Similar to set jump, `myfunc()` no longer needs to return an error code, which means it is free to output any value it wants (meaning the output is not constrained), as shown in the next example:

```cpp
#include <cstring>
#include <iostream>

int myfunc(int val)
{
    if (val == 42) {
        throw EINVAL;
    }

    return 42;
}

int main()
{
    try {
        auto handle1 = myfunc(1);
        std::cout << "success: " << handle1 << '\n';

        auto handle2 = myfunc(42);
        std::cout << "success: " << handle2 << '\n';
    }
    catch(int ret) {
        std::cout << "failure: " << strerror(ret) << '\n';
    }
}

// > g++ -std=c++17 scratchpad.cpp; ./a.out
// success: 42
// failure: Invalid argument
```

In the preceding example, `myfunc()` returns a handle, which may take on any value, since the user of this function will know whether the handle is valid if an exception has been thrown.

Similar to set jump, our nested case is greatly simplified compared to our POSIX-style error handling example, as we no longer need to manually unwind the call stack:

```cpp
#include <cstring>
#include <iostream>
void myfunc(int val)
{
    if (val == 42) {
        throw EINVAL;
    }
}

void nested1(int val)
{
    myfunc(val);
    std::cout << "nested1 success\n";
}

void nested2(int val)
{
    nested1(val);
    std::cout << "nested2 success\n";
}

main()
{
    try {
        nested2(1);
        std::cout << "nested2(1) complete\n";

        nested2(42);
        std::cout << "nested2(42) complete\n";
    }
    catch(int ret) {
        std::cout << "failure: " << strerror(ret) << '\n';
    }
}

// > g++ -std=c++17 scratchpad.cpp; ./a.out
// nested1 success
// nested2 success
// nested2(1) complete
// failure: Invalid argument
```

The preceding example is similar to our set jump example, the main difference being that we throw an exception instead of performing a long jump, and we catch the exception using the `try...catch` block.

Unlike set jump, C++ exceptions support RAII, meaning objected defined within the scope of a function are properly destroyed as the function exits:

```cpp
#include <cstring>
#include <iostream>

class myclass
{
public:
    ~myclass()
    {
        std::cout << "destructor called\n";
    }
};

void myfunc(int val)
{
    myclass c{};

    if (val == 42) {
        throw EINVAL;
    }
}

main()
{
    try {
        myfunc(1);
        std::cout << "success\n";

        myfunc(42);
        std::cout << "success\n";
    }
    catch(int ret) {
        std::cout << "failure: " << strerror(ret) << '\n';
    }
}

// > g++ -std=c++17 scratchpad.cpp; ./a.out
// destructor called
// success
// destructor called
// failure: Invalid argument
```

As can be seen in the preceding example, the destructor is called in both the success case and the failure case. To accomplish this, C++ includes a stack unwinder, which is capable of automatically unwinding the stack, similar to how we manually unwound the call stack using POSIX-style error handling, but automatically and without the need to execute branch statements through the code, resulting in optimal performance (as if error checking was not taking place). This is called **zero-overhead exception handling**.

The details of how the unwinder automatically unwinds the call stack without incurring any performance overhead, while still supporting RAII in a thread-safe manner, is outside the scope of this book, since this process is extremely complicated. However, a brief explanation follows.

When C++ exceptions are enabled and your code is compiled, a set of stack-unwinding instructions are also compiled for each function and placed the executable in a place where the C++ exception unwinder can find them. The compiler then compiles the code as if error handling is not taking place, and the code executes as such. If an exception is thrown, a thread-safe object is created that wraps the data being thrown and is stored. From there, the execution of the function is reversed using the call stack-unwinding instructions that were previously saved in the executable, eventually resulting in the function that threw the exception being exited to its caller. Before the function exits, all destructors are executed, and this process is continued for each function that was called in the call stack until a catch{} block is encountered that is capable of handling the data that was thrown.

Here are some key points to keep in mind:

- The unwind instructions are stored in a table in the executable. Each time a function's execution needs to be reversed (from a register point of view), the unwinder must look up these instructions for the next function in the table. This operation is slow (although some optimizations have been added, including the use of a hash table). For this reason, exceptions should never be used for control flow as they are slow and inefficient in the error case, while extremely efficient in the success case. C++ exceptions should only be used for error handling.
- The more functions you have in a program, or the larger the functions are (that is, the more the function touches the CPUs registers), the more information that must be stored in the unwind instructions table, resulting in a larger program. If C++ exceptions are never used in your program, this information is still compiled and stored in the application. For this reason, exceptions should be disabled if they are not used.

In addition to being thread-safe, performant, and capable of supporting RAII, C++ exceptions all support complex data types. The typical data type that is used by C++ includes strings, as follows:

```cpp
#include <cstring>
#include <iostream>

void myfunc(int val)
{
    if (val == 42) {
        throw std::runtime_error("invalid val");
    }
}

int main()
{
    try {
        myfunc(1);
        std::cout << "success\n";

        myfunc(42);
        std::cout << "success\n";
    }
    catch(const std::runtime_error &e) {
        std::cout << "failure: " << e.what() << '\n';
    }
}

// > g++ -std=c++17 scratchpad.cpp; ./a.out
// success
// failure: invalid val
```

In the preceding example, we throw a `std::runtime_error{}` exception. This exception is one of many, provided by C++, that inherits `std::exception`, which supports the ability to store a string in addition to the exception type itself. In the preceding example, we store `invalid val`. The preceding code is capable of not only detecting the provided string but also the fact that `std::runtime_exception{}` was thrown.

In some cases, you might not know what type of exception is being thrown. This is usually the case when an exception that doesn't inherit `std::exception` is thrown, such as raw strings and integers. To catch any exception, use the following:

```cpp
#include <cstring>
#include <iostream>

void myfunc(int val)
{
```

```
        if (val == 42) {
            throw -1;
        }
    }

main()
{
    try {
        myfunc(1);
        std::cout << "success\n";

        myfunc(42);
        std::cout << "success\n";
    }
    catch(...) {
        std::cout << "failure\n";
    }
}

// > g++ -std=c++17 scratchpad.cpp; ./a.out
// success
// failure
```

In the preceding example, we throw an integer and we catch it using the . . . syntax, which states that we wish to catch all exceptions. It's always good practice to have this type of catch statement at least somewhere in your code to ensure that all exceptions are being caught. In all of our examples throughout this book, we have included this catch statement for that very reason. The major disadvantage to this type of catch{} block is that we must use std::current_exception() to get the exception, for example:

```
#include <cstring>
#include <iostream>
#include <stdexcept>

void myfunc1(int val)
{
    if (val == 42) {
        throw std::runtime_error("runtime_error");
    }
}

void myfunc2(int val)
{
    try {
        myfunc1(val);
    }
    catch(...) {
```

```
            auto e = std::current_exception();
            std::rethrow_exception(e);
        }
    }

    int main()
    {
        try {
            myfunc2(42);
        }
        catch(const std::exception& e) {
            std::cout << "caught: " << e.what() << '\n';
        }
    }

    // > g++ -std=c++17 scratchpad.cpp; ./a.out
    // caught: runtime_error
```

In the preceding example, we throw `std::runtime_error()` from `myfunc1()`. In
`myfunc2()`, we catch the exception using the . . . syntax, stating that we wish to catch all
exceptions. To get the exception, we must use `std::current_exception()`, which
returns `std::exception_ptr{}`. `std::exception_ptr{}` is an implementation-specific
pointer type that can be re-thrown using `std::rethrow_exception()`. Using this
function, we can then catch the exception using the preceding standard method and output
the message within. It should be noted that if you wish to catch an exception,
`std::current_exception()` is not the recommended way, as you would need to re-
throw the exception to get the `what()` from it since `std::exception_ptr` does not
provide an interface for getting `what()`. It should also be noted that
`std::current_exception()` will not help if an exception was thrown that is not a
subclass of `std::exception{}`.

Finally, it's possible to replace `subclass std::exception` with your own, custom data.
To do this, refer to the following example:

```
    #include <cstring>
    #include <iostream>
    #include <stdexcept>

    class myexception : public std::exception
    {
        int m_error{0};

    public:

        myexception(int error) noexcept :
            m_error{error}
```

```
      { }

      const char *
      what() const noexcept
      {
        return "error";
      }

      int error() const noexcept
      {
          return m_error;
      }
};

void myfunc(int val)
{
    if (val == 42) {
        throw myexception(42);
    }
}

int main()
{
    try {
        myfunc(1);
        std::cout << "success\n";

        myfunc(42);
        std::cout << "success\n";
    }
    catch(const myexception &e) {
        std::cout << "failure: " << std::to_string(e.error()) << '\n';
    }
}

// > g++ -std=c++17 scratchpad.cpp; ./a.out
// success
// failure: 42
```

In the preceding example, we subclass `std::exception` to create our own exception that is capable of storing an error number. As with all subclasses of `std::exception{}`, the `what()` function should be overloaded to provide a message that uniquely identifies your custom exception. In our case, we also provide a function to retrieve the error code that was stored when the exception was created and thrown.

Another common task is to create a custom string for your exception. This, however, can lead to a common mistake, which is to return a constructed string in the what() function:

```
const char *
what() const noexcept
{
    return ("error: " + std::to_string(m_error)).c_str();
}
```

The preceding code produced undefined behavior, and a hard-to-find bug. In the preceding code, we store an error code just like we did in the previous example, but instead of returning it, we return the error code in a string in the what() function. To do this, we leverage the std::to_string() function to convert our error code into a std::string. We then prepend error:, and return the resulting standard C string.

The problem with the preceding example is that a pointer to the standard C string is returned and then std::string{} is destroyed when the what() function exits. The code that attempts to use the string returned by this function will end up reading deleted memory. The reason this is hard to find is that in some cases, this code will execute as expected, only because the contents of memory likely didn't change fast enough. Given enough time, however, this code will likely lead to corruption.

Instead, to create a string that outputs the same message, put the resulting error code in the constructor of an existing exception:

```
#include <cstring>
#include <iostream>

class myexception : public std::runtime_error
{
public:
    myexception(int error) noexcept :
        std::runtime_error("error: " + std::to_string(42))
    { }
};

void myfunc(int val)
{
    if (val == 42) {
        throw myexception(42);
    }
}

int main()
{
    try {
```

```
        myfunc(1);
        std::cout << "success\n";

        myfunc(42);
        std::cout << "success\n";
    }
    catch(const std::exception &e) {
        std::cout << "failure: " << e.what() << '\n';
    }
}

// > g++ -std=c++17 scratchpad.cpp; ./a.out
// success
// failure: error: 42
```

In the preceding example, we subclass `std::runtime_error{}` instead of `std::exception` directly, and create our `what()` message during the construction of the exception. This way, when `what()` is called, the exception information is available without corruption.

We will end this chapter with a note about the only real addition to C++17 with respect to exception support. Throwing an exception while an exception is already thrown is generally discouraged. To accomplish this, you must throw an exception from the destructor of a class that has been marked as `except()`, and that is destroyed during stack-unwinding. Prior to C++17, a destructor could detect whether this was about to happen by leveraging the `std::uncaught_exception()` function, which would return true if an exception was in the process of being thrown. To support throwing an exception while an exception is already being thrown, C++17 changed this function to return an integer that represents the total number of exceptions currently being thrown:

```
#include <cstring>
#include <iostream>

class myclass
{
public:
    ~myclass()
    {
        std::cout << "uncaught_exceptions: "
                  << std::uncaught_exceptions() << '\n';
    }
};

void myfunc(int val)
{
    myclass c{};
```

```
        if (val == 42) {
            throw EINVAL;
        }
    }

    int main()
    {
        try {
            myfunc(1);
            std::cout << "success\n";

            myfunc(42);
            std::cout << "success\n";
        }
        catch(int ret) {
            std::cout << "failure: " << strerror(ret) << '\n';
        }
    }

    // > g++ -std=c++17 scratchpad.cpp; ./a.out
    // uncaught_exceptions: 0
    // success
    // uncaught_exceptions: 1
    // failure: Invalid argument
```

In the preceding example, we create a class that outputs to stdout, the total number of exceptions currently being thrown. This class is then instantiated in myfunc(). In the success case, no exceptions are in the process of being thrown when the class is destroyed. In the error case, one exception is reported as being thrown when the class is destroyed.

Studying an example on exception benchmark

In this final example, we will demonstrate that C++ exceptions outperform POSIX-style exceptions (a claim that is largely dependent on the hardware you're executing on, as compiler optimizations and aggressive branch prediction can improve the performance of POSIX-style error handling).

POSIX-style error handling requires the user to check the result of a function each time it is executed. When function nesting occurs (which will almost certainly happen), this issue is exacerbated even further. In this example, we will take this case to the extreme, creating a recursive function that checks the results of itself thousands of times, while executing the test hundreds of thousands of times. Each test will be benchmarked and the results will be compared.

There are a lot of factors that could change the results of this test, including branch prediction, optimizations, and the operating system. The goal of this test is to take the example so far to the extreme that most of these issues are washed out in the noise, and any performance-related issues with any approach are easily identifiable.

To start, we will need the following includes:

```
#include <csetjmp>

#include <chrono>
#include <iostream>
```

We will also need the following globally-defined jump buffer, as we will be comparing C++ exceptions to set jump and POSIX-style error handling:

```
jmp_buf jb;
```

We will also use the same benchmark code we have used in previous chapters:

```
template<typename FUNC>
auto benchmark(FUNC func) {
    auto stime = std::chrono::high_resolution_clock::now();
    func();
    auto etime = std::chrono::high_resolution_clock::now();

    return (etime - stime).count();
}
```

Our first recursive function will return an error using POSIX-style error handling:

```
int myfunc1(int val)
{
    if (val >= 0x10000000) {
        return -1;
    }

    if (val < 0x1000) {
        if (auto ret = myfunc1(val + 1); ret == -1) {
            return ret;
        }
```

```
    }

    return 0;
}
```

As shown, the return value of the function is compared as expected. The second function will return an error using set jump:

```cpp
void myfunc2(int val)
{
    if (val >= 0x10000000) {
        std::longjmp(jb, -1);
    }

    if (val < 0x1000) {
        myfunc2(val + 1);
    }
}
```

As expected, this function is less complicated, since no return value needs to be returned or compared. Finally, the third function will return an error using C++ exceptions:

```cpp
void myfunc3(int val)
{
    if (val >= 0x10000000) {
        throw -1;
    }

    if (val < 0x1000) {
        myfunc3(val + 1);
    }
}
```

As expected, this function is almost identical to set jump, with the use of C++ exceptions being the only difference. Since we are not testing RAII, we would expect C++ exceptions to be as fast to execute as set jump, since both do not need to perform a comparison.

Finally in our protected `main` function, we will execute each function the same way we have in our previous examples, to demonstrate that each function executes as expected:

```cpp
void test_func1()
{
    if (auto ret = myfunc1(0); ret == 0) {
        std::cout << "myfunc1: success\n";
    }
    else {
        std::cout << "myfunc1: failure\n";
    }
```

```
    if (auto ret = myfunc1(bad); ret == 0) {
        std::cout << "myfunc1: success\n";
    }
    else {
        std::cout << "myfunc1: failure\n";
    }

    uint64_t total = 0;
    for (auto i = 0; i < num_iterations; i++) {
        total += benchmark([&] {
            myfunc1(0);
        });
    }

    std::cout << "time1: " << total << '\n';
}
```

The first test function tests the C-style error handling logic to ensure that the function returns both success and failure as expected. We then execute the success case several times and time how long it takes to execute, outputting the results to stdout:

```
void test_func2()
{
    if (setjmp(jb) == -1) {
        std::cout << "myfunc2: failure\n";

        uint64_t total = 0;
        for (auto i = 0; i < num_iterations; i++) {
            total += benchmark([&] {
                myfunc2(0);
            });
        }

        std::cout << "time2: " << total << '\n';
        return;
    }

    myfunc2(0);
    std::cout << "myfunc2: success\n";

    myfunc2(bad);
    std::cout << "myfunc2: success\n";
}
```

As shown, we also ensure that the second, C-style exceptions example also returns success and failure as expected. Then, we execute the success case several times to see how long it takes to execute:

```cpp
void test_func3()
{
    try {
        myfunc3(0);
        std::cout << "myfunc3: success\n";

        myfunc3(bad);
        std::cout << "myfunc3: success\n";
    }
    catch(...) {
        std::cout << "myfunc3: failure\n";
    }

    uint64_t total = 0;
    for (auto i = 0; i < num_iterations; i++) {
        total += benchmark([&] {
            myfunc3(0);
        });
    }

    std::cout << "time3: " << total << '\n';
}
```

We do the same thing with our C++ exceptions example. We complete our `protected_main()` function by executing each test, as follows:

```cpp
int
protected_main(int argc, char** argv)
{
    (void) argc;
    (void) argv;

    test_func1();
    test_func2();
    test_func3();

    return EXIT_SUCCESS;
}
```

The results of the benchmark are output to `stdout`:

```
int
main(int argc, char **argv)
{
    try {
        return protected_main(argc, argv);
    }
    catch (const std::exception &e) {
        std::cerr << "Caught unhandled exception:\n";
        std::cerr << " - what(): " << e.what() << '\n';
    }
    catch (...) {
        std::cerr << "Caught unknown exception\n";
    }

    return EXIT_FAILURE;
}
```

As with all of our examples, the `protected_main()` function is executed by the `main()` function, which catches exceptions should they occur.

Compiling and testing

To compile this code, we leverage the same `CMakeLists.txt` file that we have been using for the other examples: `https://github.com/PacktPublishing/Hands-On-System-Programming-with-CPP/blob/master/Chapter13/CMakeLists.txt`.

With this in place, we can compile this code using the following:

```
> git clone
https://github.com/PacktPublishing/Hands-On-System-Programming-with-CPP.git
> cd Hands-On-System-Programming-with-CPP/Chapter13/
> mkdir build
> cd build

> cmake ..
> make
```

To execute the example, run the following code:

```
> ./example1
myfunc1: success
myfunc1: failure
time1: 1750637978
myfunc2: success
```

```
myfunc2: failure
time2: 1609691756
myfunc3: success
myfunc3: failure
time3: 1593301696
```

As shown in the preceding code snippet, C++ exceptions outperformed POSIX-style error handling, and set jump exceptions were comparable.

Summary

In this chapter, we learned three different methods for performing error handling when system programming. The first method was POSIX-style error handling, which involves returning an error code from every function executed and the results of each function being checked to detect an error. The second method involved the use of standard C-style exceptions (that is, set jump), demonstrating how this form of exception-handling solves a lot of issues with POSIX-style error handling, but introduces issues with RAII support and thread safety. The third example discussed the use of C++ exceptions for error handling, and how this form of error handling solves most of the issues discussed in this chapter, with the only disadvantage being an increase in the size of the resulting executable. Finally, this chapter concluded with an example that demonstrated how C++ exceptions outperform POSIX-style error handling.

Questions

1. Why do C++ exceptions outperform POSIX-style error handling?
2. How does a function return an output with POSIX-style error handling?
3. Why doesn't set jump support RAII?
4. How do you catch any exception using a `catch{}` block?
5. Why do C++ exceptions increase the size of an executable?
6. Why should C++ exceptions not be used for control flow?

Further reading

- https://www.packtpub.com/application-development/c17-example
- https://www.packtpub.com/application-development/getting-started-c17-programming-video

Assessments

Chapter 1

1. The act of making system calls to accomplish tasks provided by the operating system is called **system programming**.
2. By calling an operating system's interrupt handlers.
3. Special instructions were added to the CPU to support system calls without the need to call an interrupt handler, which saves more of the CPU state prior to execution.
4. No. Most implementations of `malloc()`/`free()` ask for a large amount of memory from the operating system and then divide up that memory during the program's execution. A system call is only needed when this memory runs out and `malloc()`/`free()` must ask for more.
5. Speculative execution.
6. Type safety is the extent to which a programming language helps to prevent errors due to the differences between types. Strongly typed languages prevent these types of error more than weakly typed languages.
7. C++ templates provide a user with the ability to define your code without having to define type information ahead of time.

Chapter 2

1. Yes. Most of the C standard is also part of the POSIX standard. POSIX generally goes above and beyond to provide additional facilities specific to POSIX operating systems. Examples of C and POSIX functions include `read()` and `write()`.
2. `_start()` is the entry point to an application and is usually provided by the C runtime facilities. `main()` is a function provided by the user and is usually the first function to execute in the user's code, which is eventually called by the C runtime facilities once the application is fully initialized.
3. Executing global constructors and destructors, and initializing C++ exceptions.
4. Before.

5. C++ name mangling embeds the entire signature of a function into the function's symbol. This is not only needed to provide support for function overloading in C++, but also ensures that the linker doesn't accidentally dynamically link two functions with the same name that have different signatures (which can happen in C).

6. C symbols are not mangled. C++ are.

7. A pointer can point to any memory, including a `nullptr`. A reference cannot.

Chapter 3

1. This depends on the CPU architecture. On some CPUs, a short `int` is 16 bits wide, while an `int` is 32 bits wide. This is not the case on all CPUs.

2. This depends on the CPU architecture. On most CPUs, an `int` is 32 bits wide, but this is not always the case.

3. No.

4. An `int32_t` will always be 32 bits wide. On some CPUs, an `int` could be 16, 32, or 64 bits wide.

5. Yes. These are called **exact-width** types and will always be the desired width.

6. Ensures that structures are not automatically padded by the compiler for optimizations.

7. No.

Chapter 4

1. Structured binding provides the ability to retrieve the result of a structure by manually providing individual variables, for example, `auto [first, second] = std::pair{1, 2}`

2. You can now list nested namespace on the same line

3. You no longer need to provide an error message

4. Provides you with the ability to define a variable inside an `if` statement

5. Resource acquisition is initialization

6. To acquire and initialize a resource on construction and release the resource on destruction

7. States who owns a pointer (that is, the entity responsible for deleting the pointer)

8. `Expects()` defines a functions input expectations and `Ensures()` defines a function's output

Chapter 5

1. `rax`.
2. `rdi`.
3. subtracts.
4. A segment is a group of sections.
5. The information needed to handle exceptions.
6. `Fork()` creates a new process, while `exec()` overwrites an existing process with a new program. Both are needed to launch a new program.
7. second.
8. The process ID of the process that completed.

Chapter 6

1. `std::cin` is type-aware.
2. Capable of handling user-defined types providing cleaner, type-safe IO.
3. Format specifiers are often more flexible than `#include <iomanip>`.
4. Use `std::endl` if a flush must occur.
5. `std::cerr` will flush after each write, while `std::clog` will not. Use `std::cerr` when handling errors to ensure that all debugging information is successfully flushed prior to a catastrophic issue.
6. `std::internal`.
7. By using both `std::oct` and `std::uppercase`.
8. By leveraging a `gsl::span`.
9. By leveraging the `rdbuf()` member function.

Chapter 7

1. `new()` allocates a single object, while `new()` allocates an array of objects.
2. No.
3. Global memory is visible to the entire program, while static memory (defined globally) is only visible to the source file in which it is defined.
4. By leveraging an alias with the `alignas()` function, such as `using aligned_int alignas(0x1000) = int;`.

5. Not in C++17 and below

6. `std::shared_ptr` should only be used if more than one object must own the memory (that is, the memory needs to be able to be released by more than one object in any order and at any time).

7. Yes (depending on the operating system and permissions).

8. If you allocate 4 bytes and use 3, you have created internal fragmentation (wasted memory). If you allocate memory in such a way that the allocator no longer has contiguous blocks of memory to give out (even if it has a lot of free memory), you have created external fragmentation.

Chapter 8

1. `is_open()`

2. `std::ios_base::in | std::ios_base::out`

3. 0 is read and a flag is set

4. Buffer overflow errors

5. Yes

6. test

7. `/home/user`

Chapter 9

1. This means that two instances of the same allocator are always equal, which in turn means that both allocators can allocate and deallocate each other's memory.

2. If two instances of the same allocator can allocate and deallocate each other's memory.

3. Yes.

4. Yes.

5. When a container is copied, its allocator is also copied.

6. It provides the container with the ability to create a copy of the allocator it was provided for a different type.

7. For `std::list, n ==1`; for `std::vector, n` can be any number.

Chapter 10

1. UDP is connectionless.
2. `SOCK_DGRAM`
3. `SOCK_STREAM`
4. IPV4.
5. `Bind()` allocates a port, while `connect()` connects to a previously allocated port.
6. `sendto()` takes the address as a parameter and is usually used by UDP, while `send()` is usually used by TCP.
7. It doesn't.
8. Type safety.

Chapter 11

1. Thursday, 1 January 1970
2. The number of seconds since the UNIX epoch began.
3. `clock()` is relative to the execution of the program.
4. Non-POSIX operating systems might support fractional time.
5. A wrapper around `difftime()`.
6. A steady clock provides the actual time, while a high resolution timer provides a number that only provides a value when used with `duration{}`.

Chapter 12

1. `pthread_self()`
2. They are not type safe.
3. When two threads race to read/write the same resource.
4. When a thread waits on a synchronization primitive (for example, a mutex) that will never be released.
5. A C++ future provides a type-safe mechanism for returning the result of a thread.
6. To ensure that a function is only executed once, regardless of the number of threads that call it.

7. `std::shared_mutex` provides the ability to support multiple readers.

8. Allows a single thread to lock the same mutex more than once without entering deadlock.

Chapter 13

1. C++ exceptions do not need to check the return result of every function call.

2. POSIX-style functions must reserve a part of a function's output to convey an error. For example, if a function must return a file handle, `0` is returned in the event of an error, which means that a file handle cannot have the value `0`.

3. Set jump does not unwind the stack, which means destructors are skipped.

4. `catch(...)`

5. Instructions on how to unwind a stack must be stored for every function. This is the tradeoff for increased performance.

6. They are slow.

Other Books You May Enjoy

If you enjoyed this book, you may be interested in these other books by Packt:

C++ Data Structures and Algorithms
Wisnu Anggoro

ISBN: 9781788835213

- Know how to use arrays and lists to get better results in complex scenarios
- Build enhanced applications by using hashtables, dictionaries, and sets
- Implement searching algorithms such as linear search, binary search, jump search, exponential search, and more
- Have a positive impact on the efficiency of applications with tree traversal
- Explore the design used in sorting algorithms like Heap sort, Quick sort, Merge sort and Radix sort
- Implement various common algorithms in string data types
- Find out how to design an algorithm for a specific task using the common algorithm paradigms

C++ Reactive Programming
Praseed Pai

ISBN: 9781788629775

- Understand language-level concurrency in C++
- Explore advanced C++ programming for the FRP
- Uncover the RxCpp library and its programming model
- Mix the FP and OOP constructs in C++ 17 to write well-structured programs
- Master reactive microservices in C++
- Create custom operators for RxCpp
- Learn advanced stream processing and error handling

Leave a review - let other readers know what you think

Please share your thoughts on this book with others by leaving a review on the site that you bought it from. If you purchased the book from Amazon, please leave us an honest review on this book's Amazon page. This is vital so that other potential readers can see and use your unbiased opinion to make purchasing decisions, we can understand what our customers think about our products, and our authors can see your feedback on the title that they have worked with Packt to create. It will only take a few minutes of your time, but is valuable to other potential customers, our authors, and Packt. Thank you!

Index

CPSIA information can be obtained
at www.ICGtesting.com
Printed in the USA
LVHW061003020419
612655LV00008B/175/P

9 781789 137880